The Complete Works of

COUNT TOLSTÓY

Volume XIII.

MY CONFESSION
CRITIQUE
OF DOGMATIC
THEOLOGY

BY

COUNT LEV N. (TOLSTÓY)

Tolstoi

TRANSLATED FROM THE ORIGINAL RUSSIAN AND
EDITED BY

LEO WIENER

*Assistant Professor of Slavic Languages at
Harvard University*

LONDON
J. M. DENT & CO.
29 & 30 BEDFORD STREET, W.C.

2560

Colonial Press : Electrotyped and Printed by
C. H. Simonds & Co., Boston, Mass., U. S. A.

CONTENTS

LIST OF ILLUSTRATIONS

———◆———

MY CONFESSION

Introduction to the Critique of Dogmatic Theology and Investigation of the Christian
Teaching

1879 – 1882

MY CONFESSION

Introduction to the Critique of Dogmatic Theology and Investigation of the Christian
Teaching

I.

I was baptized and educated in the Orthodox Christian
faith. I was taught it from childhood and through the
whole time of my boyhood and youth. But when I, at
eighteen years of age, left the second year's course of the
university, I no longer believed any of the things I had
been taught.

To judge from certain recollections, I had never believed
in earnest; I had only had confidence in what I was
taught and what the grown persons confessed in my
presence; but this confidence was very brittle.

I remember when I was but eleven years old, a boy,
now long dead, Volódinka M——, who attended the
gymnasium, came to our house one Sunday and communicated to us as the latest bit of news a discovery which
had been made at the gymnasium. This discovery was
that there was no God, and that everything which we
were taught was a mere fabrication (that was in the year
1838). I remember how my elder brothers were interested
in that news and how they called me to a council, and
all of us were very much excited about it and received

3

that information as something exceedingly interesting and quite probable.

I also remember how, when my eldest brother, Dmítri, who was a student at the university, suddenly with a passion which was characteristic of his nature abandoned himself to faith and began to attend all the services, to fast, and to lead a pure and moral life, all of us, even the grown persons, never stopped making him a butt of ridicule, and for some reason called him Noah. I remember how Músin-Púshkin, who at that time was the Curator of the Kazán University and who invited us to come to a dance at his house, tried in jest to persuade my brother, who declined to come, by telling him that even David had danced before the ark. At that time I sympathized with the jests of my elders and deduced the conclusion from it that the Catechism ought to be taught, that church ought to be attended, but that all that ought not to be taken too seriously. I also remember that I was very young when I read Voltaire, and that his ridicule not only did not provoke me, but even amused me very much.

My defection from faith took place in the same manner as it has taken place and still takes place in people of our cultivated class. In the majority of cases it happens like this, I think: people live as everybody else lives, and everybody else lives on the basis of principles that not only have nothing in common with the religious teaching, but generally run counter to it; the religious teaching does not enter into life, and in one's relation with other people one never has occasion to come across it, and in one's own life one never has occasion to refer to it; this religious teaching is professed somewhere there, far away from life and independently of it. If you come in contact with it, it is with its external phenomenon, which is not connected with life.

From a man's life, from his acts, it is impossible now,

as it was then, to find out whether he is a believer or not. If there is a difference between one who openly professes Orthodoxy and one who denies it, it is not in favour of the first. The open recognition and profession of Orthodoxy has generally been met with in dull, cruel, and self-important people, while intelligence, honesty, straightforwardness, good-heartedness, and morality are generally met with in people who profess to be unbelievers.

In the schools the pupils are taught the Catechism and are sent to church; officials have to show certificates of having received their communion. But a man of our circle, who is no longer studying and is not holding a government position, may nowadays pass dozens of years, — and formerly that was even more the case, — without thinking once that he is living among Christians and himself is professing the Christian Orthodox faith.

Thus, now as then, the religious teaching, which is accepted through confidence and is supported through external pressure, slowly melts under the influence of knowledge and the experiences of life, which are contrary to the religious teaching, and a man frequently goes on imagining that the religious teaching with which he has been imbued in childhood is in full force in him, whereas there is not even a trace left of it.

S——, an intelligent and truthful man, told me how he came to stop believing. When he was twenty-six years old he once at a night's rest during the chase followed his old habit, acquired in his childhood, and stood up to pray. His elder brother, who took part in the chase, was lying on the hay and looking at him. When S—— got through and was about to lie down, he said to him: "So you are still doing these things?"

That was all that was said. And S—— that very day quit praying and attending church. Thirty years have passed since he stopped praying, receiving the com-

munion, and going to church. Not that he knew the
convictions of his brother and had joined them, not that
he had decided on anything in his mind, but only because
the sentence which his brother had uttered was like the
pressure exerted with a finger against a wall which was
ready to fall of its own weight; the sentence was merely
an indication that where he thought there was faith there
had long been a vacant spot, and that, therefore, the words
which he spoke and the signs of the cross and the obeisances which he made during his praying were quite
meaningless actions. Since he had come to recognize
their meaninglessness, he could not keep them up any
longer.

Thus it has always been with an enormous majority of
people. I am speaking of people of our degree of culture,
of people who are true to themselves, and not of those
who use the very subject of faith as a means for obtaining
any temporary ends. (These people are most confirmed
unbelievers, for, if the faith is to them a means for obtaining any social advantages, it is no longer faith.) The
people of our degree of education are in that condition
when the light of knowledge and of life has melted the
artificial structure, and they have either noticed it and
have cleared the place, or have not yet noticed it.

The religious teaching which was imparted to me in
my childhood disappeared in me just as in others, with
this difference only that, since I began to read philosophical works at fifteen years of age, my apostasy very early
became conscious. With my sixteenth year I quit praying and through my own initiative stopped attending
church and preparing myself for communion. I did not
believe in what I had been told in my childhood, but
I believed in something. I should never have been able
to say what it was I believed in. I believed in God, or,
more correctly, I did not deny God, but what kind of a
God, I should have been at a loss to say. Nor did I deny

Christ and his teaching, but what his teaching consisted in, I should also have been at a loss to say.

Now, as I recall that time, I see clearly that my faith, that something which, outside the animal instincts, moved my life, my only, real faith at that time was a belief in perfection. But what that perfection consisted in, or what its aims were, I should have been unable to say. I tried to perfect myself mentally, — I studied everything that I could and that life brought me in contact with ; I tried to perfect my will and formed rules which I tried to follow ; I perfected myself physically, prompting my strength and agility with all kinds of exercises, and practising endurance and patience in all kinds of privations. All that I regarded as perfection. At first it was, of course, moral perfection, but soon it was changed to perfection in general, that is, to a desire to be better, not before myself or before God, but before other people. And soon that tendency to be better before people gave place to a desire to be stronger than other people, that is, more famous, more influential, richer than others.

II.

SOME day I will tell the history of my life, — it is both touching and instructive, — for those ten years of my youth. I think many, very many, have experienced the same. I wished with all my heart to be good; but I was young, I had passions, and I was alone, completely alone, when I was trying to find the good. Every time I endeavoured to give utterance to what formed my most intimate wishes, namely, that I wished to be morally good, I met with contempt and ridicule; and the moment I surrendered myself to the abominable passions, I was praised and encouraged.

Ambition, lust of power, selfishness, voluptuousness, pride, anger, revenge, — all that was respected. By abandoning myself to these passions I became like a grown person, and I felt that people were satisfied with me. A good aunt of mine, a pure soul, with whom I was living, kept telling me that there was nothing she wished so much for me as that I should have a liaison with a married woman: "*Rien ne forme un jeune homme, comme une liaison avec une femme comme il faut;*" there was another piece of luck she wished for me, and that was that I should be an adjutant, preferably an adjutant to the emperor; and the greatest piece of luck, that I might marry a very rich girl so that, in consequence of this marriage, I might have a very large number of slaves.

I cannot recall those years without dread, loathing, and anguish of heart. I killed people in war and challenged to duels to kill; I lost money at cards, wasting the labour

8

of the peasants ; I punished them, fornicated, and cheated. Lying, stealing, acts of lust of every description, drunkenness, violence, murder — There was not a crime which I did not commit, and for all that I was praised, and my contemporaries have regarded me as a comparatively moral man.

Thus I lived for ten years.

At that time I began to write through vanity, avarice, and pride. In my writings I did the same as in life. In order to have glory and money, for which I wrote, I had to conceal what was good and speak what was bad. And so I did. How often I managed to conceal in my writings, under the aspect of indifference and even light ridicule, those strivings of mine after the good, which formed the meaning of my life. I was successful in that, and I was praised.

When I was twenty-six years old, I arrived in St. Petersburg after the war, and there came in contact with authors. I was received like one of their own, and was flattered. Before I had time to look around, the conventional literary views of life, which these persons whom I met held, were appropriated by me and completely wiped out all my former attempts to become better. These views furnished the looseness of my morals with a theory which justified it.

The view of life which these people, my literary fellows, held, consisted in stating that life was all the time developing, and that in this development the chief part was taken by us, the men of ideas, and that among these men of ideas the greatest influence was exerted by us, artists and poets. Our calling was to teach people. In order that the natural question, " What do I know, and what shall I teach ? " might not present itself to one, this theory explained that it was not necessary to know that, and that an artist and poet taught unconsciously. I was considered a marvellous artist and poet, and so it was quite natural for me to make this theory my own. I, the artist and poet, wrote and taught, myself not knowing what. For this I was paid, and I had excellent food, quarters, women, society; I had fame. Consequently, what I taught was very good.

Faith in the meaning of poetry and in progress in life was a creed, and I was one of its priests. It was very agreeable and profitable to be its priest, and I lived for a long time in that belief, never doubting its truth. But in the second and, especially, in the third year of that life I began to have my doubts about the infallibility of that faith, and started to investigate it. What gave me the first impulse to these misgivings was the fact, which I noticed, that all those priests were not at one among themselves. Some said: " We are the best and most useful teachers; we teach what is necessary, but the others teach incorrectly." And others said: " No, we are the real ones, but you teach incorrectly." And they disputed, quarrelled, scolded, cheated, and deceived each other. Besides, there were many people among us who did not trouble themselves to find out who was right and who wrong, but who simply attained their selfish ends by means of that activity of ours. All that made me doubt the truth of our faith.

Besides, having lost faith in the truth of my literary creed, I began to observe the priests more closely, and I convinced myself that nearly all the priests of that faith, the authors, were immoral people and, for the most part, bad people, insignificant as to their character, who stood much lower than those men whom I used to meet in my former riotous and military life; but they were self-confident and self-satisfied, as only such men can be who either are great saints or who do not know what sanctity is. I got sick of those people, and I got sick of myself, and I understood that that faith was a deception.

But what is strange is that, although I soon comprehended all that lying faith and renounced it, I did not renounce the rank which I was given by those men, — that of artist, poet, teacher. I naïvely imagined that I was a poet, an artist, and that I could teach others, not knowing myself what I was teaching. That was what I did.

From my association with these people I carried away a new vice, — a morbidly developed pride and an insane conviction that I was called to teach people, myself not knowing what.

Now that I think of that time, of my mental state, and of the mental state of those men (however, there are thousands of such even nowadays), I feel pity, and terror, and amusement; there arises precisely the feeling that one experiences in a madhouse.

We were all convinced at that time that we must talk and talk, and write, and print, as fast as possible, and that that was necessary for the good of humanity. And thousands of us, denying and cursing one another, printed and wrote, teaching others. And, without noticing that we knew nothing, that to the simplest question of life, — what is good, and what bad, — we did not know what answer to give, we all spoke together, without listening to our neighbours, and now and then encouraged and praised each other, so that we, too, might be encouraged and praised, and now and then were irritated toward one another, precisely as in a madhouse.

Thousands of workmen day and night worked with all their strength, setting type and printing millions of words, and the post-office spread them all over Russia, and we proceeded to teach, and did not have time enough to teach everything, and kept growing angry because little attention was paid to us.

It is all very strange, but now it is easy to understand. Our real, intimate calculation was that we wanted to get as much money and praise as possible. In order to obtain this end we had nothing to do but write books and newspaper articles. And that we did. But, in order to do such a useless piece of work and be confident that we were very important people, we needed a consideration which would justify our activity, and so we concocted the following : everything which exists is reasonable. Everything which exists develops; everything is developed by means of culture; culture is measured by the dissemination of books and newspapers. We are paid and respected for writing books and newspapers, consequently we are most useful and good men. This reflection would have been very nice, if all of us had been of one mind; but, since for every idea, expressed by one man, there always appeared another idea, diametrically opposed to the first, as expressed by another, that ought to have made us reflect. But we did not observe that; we received money, and the men belonging to our party praised us, consequently we every one of us considered ourselves in the right.

Now it is clear to me that there was no difference between that and a madhouse; but at that time I only dimly suspected that, and, like all insane persons, called everybody insane but myself.

III.

THUS I lived, abandoning myself to that insanity for six years longer, until my marriage. During that time I went abroad. My life in Europe and my associations with prominent men and scholars in Europe confirmed me even more in that faith of perfection in general, in which I was living, because I found the same faith in others. This faith assumed with me that customary form which it has with the majority of cultured people of our time. This faith was expressed by the word "progress." At that time I thought that that word expressed something. I did not yet understand then that, tormented, like any live man, by the questions as to how to live in the best manner possible, I, by saying that I ought to do so in conformity with progress, was giving the same kind of an answer that a man might give, who, being borne in a bark by the waves and by the wind, to the one important question of whither to keep his course, should not reply to the question, but should say: "We are being borne somewhere."

At that time I did not notice it. Only now and then, not my reason, but my feeling, revolted against that common superstition of our time, with which people veil from themselves the comprehension of life. Thus, during my stay in Paris, the sight of a capital punishment showed me the frailty of my superstition of progress. When I saw the head severed from the body, and both falling separately with a thud into a box, I understood, not with my reason, but with my whole being, that no

13

theories of the reasonableness of everything existing and of progress could justify that deed, and that if all men on earth, beginning with the creation, had some theory which made this necessary, — I knew that it was not necessary, that it was bad, and that, therefore, not what people said and did, and not progress, but I with my heart was the judge of what was good and necessary. Another occasion which made me conscious of the insufficiency for life of the superstition of progress was the death of my brother. An intelligent, good, serious man, he grew sick when he was young, suffered for more than a year, and died an agonizing death, without comprehending what he had lived for, and still less why he should die. No theories could give any answers either to me or to him, during his slow and painful death. But those were only rare cases of doubt; in reality I continued to live professing the faith of progress. "Everything develops, and I, too, am developing; why I am developing with the rest, will appear later." That is the way I ought to have then formulated my faith.

When I returned from abroad, I settled in the country and hit upon busying myself with the peasant schools. That occupation was particularly to my liking, because in it there was not that apparent lie which had appalled me in the activity of my literary teachership. Here also I worked in the name of progress, but this time I assumed a critical attitude toward progress. I said to myself that progress in some of its manifestations took place irregularly, and that it was necessary to treat the primitive men, the peasant children, in a free way, by letting them choose the path of progress which they wished. In reality, I was still gyrating around one and the same insoluble problem, which was that I should teach not knowing what. In the higher spheres of my literary activity I saw that it was not possible to teach not knowing what to teach, because I observed that everybody was teaching in his own way, and that by disputing among themselves the men tried to conceal their ignorance; but here, with the peasant children, I thought that the difficulty might be obviated by leaving it to the children to learn what they pleased. Now it is ludicrous for me to think how I temporized in order to gratify my desire to teach, although in the depth of my soul I knew full well that I could not teach what was necessary, because I did not myself know what was necessary. After a year passed in occupations with the school, I went abroad again, in order to learn there how, without knowing anything myself, I might teach others.

I thought that I learned that abroad, and, armed with all that wisdom, I returned to Russia in the year of the liberation of the serfs and, accepting the position of a rural judge, I began to teach the uneducated masses in the schools and the educated people in the periodical which I published. Things apparently went well, but I felt that I was mentally not quite well and that it would not last long. I might have arrived even then at that despair at which I arrived fifteen years later, if I had not had another side of life, which I had not yet explored and which promised me salvation, — my domestic life.

For a year I acted as a rural judge and busied myself with my schools and my periodical, and I was so worn out, especially because I became so much involved, and my struggle in my capacity as rural judge was so oppressive to me, and my activity in the schools was so pale, and I grew so tired of wagging my tongue in my periodical, which still consisted in the same thing, — in the desire to teach others and conceal the fact that I did not know what to teach, — that I grew sick, mentally rather than physically, and gave up everything and went to live with the Bashkirs of the steppe, — to breathe the air, drink kumys, and live an animal life.

When I came back, I got married. The new conditions of my happy family life completely drew me away from all search for the general meaning of life. All my life during that time was centred in my family, my wife, my children, and, therefore, in cares for the increase of the means of existence. The striving after perfection, which before had given way to the striving after perfection in general, after progress, now gave way simply to the striving after making it as comfortable as possible for me and my family.

Thus another fifteen years passed.

Although I regarded authorship as a waste of time, I continued to write during those fifteen years. I had tasted of the seduction of authorship, of the seduction of enormous monetary remunerations and applauses for my insignificant labour, and so I submitted to it, as being a means for improving my material condition and for stifling in my soul all questions about the meaning of my life and life in general.

In my writings I advocated, what to me was the only truth, that it was necessary to live in such a way as to derive the greatest comfort for oneself and one's family.

Thus I proceeded to live, but five years ago something very strange began to happen with me : I was overcome by minutes at first of perplexity and then of an arrest of life, as though I did not know how to live or what to do, and I lost myself and was dejected. But that passed, and I continued to live as before. Then those minutes of perplexity were repeated oftener and oftener, and always in one and the same form. These arrests of life found their expression in ever the same questions : " Why ? Well, and then ? "

At first I thought that those were simply aimless, inappropriate questions. It seemed to me that that was all well known and that if I ever wanted to busy myself with their solution, it would not cost me much labour, —

that now I had no time to attend to them, but that if I wanted to I should find the proper answers. But the questions began to repeat themselves oftener and oftener, answers were demanded more and more persistently, and, like dots that fall on the same spot, these questions, without any answers, thickened into one black blotch.

There happened what happens with any person who falls ill with a mortal internal disease. At first there appear insignificant symptoms of indisposition, to which the patient pays no attention ; then these symptoms are repeated more and more frequently and blend into one temporally indivisible suffering. The suffering keeps growing, and before the patient has had time to look around, he becomes conscious that what he took for an indisposition is the most significant thing in the world to him, — is death.

The same happened with me. I understood that it was not a passing indisposition, but something very important, and that, if the questions were going to repeat themselves, it would be necessary to find an answer for them. And I tried to answer them. The questions seemed to be so foolish, simple, and childish. But the moment I touched them and tried to solve them, I became convinced, in the first place, that they were not childish and foolish, but very important and profound questions in life, and, in the second, that, no matter how much I might try, I should not be able to answer them. Before attending to my Samára estate, to my son's education, or to the writing of a book, I ought to know why I should do that. So long as I did not know why, I could not do anything, I could not live. Amidst my thoughts of farming, which interested me very much during that time, there would suddenly pass through my head a question like this : " All right, you are going to have six thousand desyatínas of land in the Government of Samára, and three hundred horses, — and then ? " And I completely lost my senses and did not know what to think farther. Or, when I thought of the education of my children, I said to myself: "Why?" Or, reflecting on the manner in which the masses might obtain their welfare, I suddenly said to myself: "What is that to me?" Or, thinking of the fame which my works would get me, I said to myself: "All right, you will be more famous than Gógol, Púshkin, Shakespeare, Molière, and all the writers in the world, — what of it?" And I was absolutely unable to make any reply. The questions were not waiting, and I had to answer them at once; if I did not answer them, I could not live.

I felt that what I was standing on had given way, that I had no foundation to stand on, that that which I lived by no longer existed, and that I had nothing to live by.

IV.

My life came to a standstill.   I could breathe, eat, drink,
and sleep, and could not help breathing, eating, drinking,
and sleeping ; but there was no life, because there were
no desires the gratification of which I might find reasonable.   If I wished for anything, I knew in advance that,
whether I gratified my desire or not, nothing would come
of it.   If a fairy had come and had offered to carry out
my wish, I should not have known what to say.   If in
moments of intoxication I had, not wishes, but habits of
former desires, I knew in sober moments that that was a
deception, that there was nothing to wish for.   I could
not even wish to find out the truth, because I guessed
what it consisted in.   The truth was that life was meaningless.   It was as though I had just been living and
walking along, and had come to an abyss, where I saw
clearly that there was nothing ahead but perdition.   And
it was impossible to stop and go back, and impossible to
shut my eyes, in order that I might not see that there
was nothing ahead but suffering and imminent death, —
complete annihilation.

What happened to me was that I, a healthy, happy
man, felt that I could not go on living, — an insurmount-
able force drew me on to find release from life.   I cannot
say that I *wanted* to kill myself.

The force which drew me away from life was stronger,
fuller, more general than wishing.   It was a force like
the former striving after life, only in an inverse sense.   I
tended with all my strength away from life.   The thought
19

of suicide came as naturally to me as had come before the ideas of improving life. That thought was so seductive that I had to use cunning against myself, lest I should rashly execute it. I did not want to be in a hurry, because I wanted to use every effort to disentangle myself: if I should not succeed in disentangling myself, there would always be time for that. And at such times I, a happy man, hid a rope from myself so that I should not hang myself on a cross-beam between two safes in my room, where I was by myself in the evening, while taking off my clothes, and did not go out hunting with a gun, in order not to be tempted by an easy way of doing away with myself. I did not know myself what it was I wanted: I was afraid of life, strove to get away from it, and, at the same time, expected something from it.

All that happened with me when I was on every side surrounded by what is considered to be complete happiness. I had a good, loving, and beloved wife, good children, and a large estate, which grew and increased without any labour on my part. I was respected by my neighbours and friends, more than ever before, was praised by strangers, and, without any self-deception, could consider my name famous. With all that, I was not deranged or mentally unsound, — on the contrary, I was in full command of my mental and physical powers, such as I had rarely met with in people of my age: physically I could work in a field, mowing, without falling behind a peasant; mentally I could work from eight to ten hours in succession, without experiencing any consequences from the strain. And while in such condition I arrived at the conclusion that I could not live, and, fearing death, I had to use cunning against myself, in order that I might not take my life.

This mental condition expressed itself to me in this form: my life is a stupid, mean trick played on me by somebody. Although I did not recognize that "somebody " as having created me, the form of the conception that some one had played a mean, stupid trick on me by bringing me into the world was the most natural one that presented itself to me.

Involuntarily I imagined that there, somewhere, there was somebody who was now having fun as he looked down upon me and saw me, who had lived for thirty or forty years, learning, developing, growing in body and mind, now that I had become strengthened in mind and had reached that summit of life from which it lay all before me, standing as a complete fool on that summit and seeing clearly that there was nothing in life and never would be. And that was fun to him —

But whether there was or was not that somebody who made fun of me, did not make it easier for me. I could not ascribe any sensible meaning to a single act, or to my whole life. I was only surprised that I had not understood that from the start. All that had long ago been known to everybody. Sooner or later there would come diseases and death (they had come already) to my dear ones and to me, and there would be nothing left but stench and worms. All my affairs, no matter what they might be, would sooner or later be forgotten, and I myself should not exist. So why should I worry about all these things ? How could a man fail to see that and live, — that was surprising ! A person could live only so long as he was drunk ; but the moment he sobered up, he could not help seeing that all that was only a deception, and a stupid deception at that ! Really, there was nothing funny and ingenious about it, but only something cruel and stupid.

Long ago has been told the Eastern story about the traveller who in the steppe is overtaken by an infuriated beast. Trying to save himself from the animal, the traveller jumps into a waterless well, but at its bottom he sees a dragon who opens his jaws in order to swallow him.   And the unfortunate man does not dare climb out, lest he perish from the infuriated beast, and does not dare jump down to the bottom of the well, lest he be devoured by the dragon, and so clutches the twig of a wild bush growing in a cleft of the well and holds on to it.   His hands grow weak and he feels that soon he shall have to surrender to the peril which awaits him at either side ; but he still holds on and sees two mice, one white, the other black, in even measure making a circle around the main trunk of the bush to which he is clinging, and nibbling at it on all sides.   Now, at any moment, the bush will break and tear off, and he will fall into the dragon's jaws. The traveller sees that and knows that he will inevitably perish ; but while he is still clinging, he sees some drops of honey hanging on the leaves of the bush, and so reaches out for them with his tongue and licks the leaves. Just so I hold on to the branch of life, knowing that the dragon of death is waiting inevitably for me, ready to tear me to pieces, and I cannot understand why I have fallen on such suffering.   And I try to lick that honey which used to give me pleasure ; but now it no longer gives me joy, and the white and the black mouse day and night nibble at the branch to which I am holding on.   I clearly see the dragon, and the honey is no longer sweet to me. I see only the inevitable dragon and the mice, and am unable to turn my glance away from them.   That is not a fable, but a veritable, indisputable, comprehensible truth.

The former deception of the pleasures of life, which stifled the terror of the dragon, no longer deceives me. No matter how much one should say to me, " You cannot understand the meaning of life, do not think, live ! " I am unable to do so, because I have been doing it too long before.   Now I cannot help seeing day and night, which run and lead me up to death.   I see that alone, because that alone is the truth.   Everything else is a lie.

The two drops of honey that have longest turned my

eyes away from the cruel truth, the love of family and of authorship, which I have called an art, are no longer sweet to me.

"My family — " I said to myself, " but my family, my wife and children, they are also human beings. They are in precisely the same condition that I am in: they must either live in the lie or see the terrible truth. Why should they live? Why should I love them, why guard, raise, and watch them? Is it for the same despair which is in me, or for dulness of perception? Since I love them, I cannot conceal the truth from them, — every step in cognition leads them up to this truth. And the truth is death."

"Art, poetry?" For a long time, under the influence of the success of human praise, I tried to persuade myself that that was a thing which could be done, even though death should come and destroy everything, my deeds, as well as my memory of them; but soon I came to see that that, too, was a deception. It was clear to me that art was an adornment of life, a decoy of life. But life lost all its attractiveness for me. How, then, could I entrap others? So long as I did not live my own life, and a strange life bore me on its waves; so long as I believed that life had some sense, although I was not able to express it, — the reflections of life of every description in poetry and in the arts afforded me pleasure, and I was delighted to look at life through this little mirror of art; but when I began to look for the meaning of life, when I experienced the necessity of living myself, that little mirror became either useless, superfluous, and ridiculous, or painful to me. I could no longer console myself with what I saw in the mirror, namely, that my situation was stupid and desperate. It was all right for me to rejoice so long as I believed in the depth of my soul that life had some sense. At that time the play of lights — of the comical, the tragical, the touching, the beautiful, the terrible in life — afforded me amusement. But when I knew that life was meaningless and terrible, the play in the little mirror could no longer amuse me. No sweetness of honey could be sweet to me, when I saw the dragon and the mice that were nibbling down my support.

That was not all. If I had simply comprehended that life had no meaning, I might have known that calmly, — I might have known that that was my fate. But I could not be soothed by that. If I had been like a man living in a forest from which he knew there was no way out, I might have lived; but I was like a man who had lost his way in the forest, who was overcome by terror because he had lost his way, who kept tossing about in his desire to come out on the road, knowing that every step got him only more entangled, and who could not help tossing.

That was terrible. And, in order to free myself from that terror, I wanted to kill myself. I experienced terror before what was awaiting me, — I knew that that terror was more terrible than the situation itself, but I could not patiently wait for the end. No matter how convincing the reflection was that it was the same whether a vessel in the heart should break or something should burst, and all should be ended, I could not wait patiently for the end. The terror of the darkness was too great, and I wanted as quickly as possible to free myself from it by means of a noose or a bullet. It was this feeling that more than anything else drew me on toward suicide.

V.

" BUT, perhaps, I overlooked something, or did not understand something right ? " I said to myself several times.
" It is impossible that this condition of despair should be
characteristic of men ! " And I tried to find an explanation for these questions in all those branches of knowledge which men had acquired. I searched painfully and
for a long time, and I searched not from idle curiosity, not
in a limp manner, but painfully and stubbornly, day and
night, — I searched as a perishing man searches for his
salvation, — and I found nothing.

I searched in all the branches of knowledge, and not
only failed to find anything, but even convinced myself
that all those who, like myself, had been searching in the
sciences, had failed just as much. They had not only not
found anything, but had also clearly recognized the fact
that that which had brought me to despair, — the meaninglessness of life, — was the only incontestable knowledge
which was accessible to man.

I searched everywhere, and, thanks to a life passed in
study, and also because through my connections with the
learned world I had access to the most learned of men in
every imaginable branch of knowledge, who did not refuse
to disclose to me their knowledge, not only in books, but
also in conversations, I learned everything which science
replies to the question of life.

For a long time I could not believe that science had no
answer to give to the questions of life, except what it gave.
For a long time it seemed to me, as I looked at the im-

portance and seriousness of tone which science assumed, when it enunciated its principles which had nothing in common with the questions of human life, that there was something in it which I did not understand. For a long time I was intimidated by science, and it seemed to me that the inapplicability of the answers to my questions was not the fault of science, but of my own ignorance; but the matter was for me not a joke, a trifle, but an affair of my whole life, and I was against my will led to the conviction that my questions were the only legitimate questions, which served as a foundation of all knowledge, and that not I with my questions was to blame, but science, if it had the presumption to answer these questions.

My question, the one which led me, at fifty years, up to suicide, was the simplest kind of a question, and one which is lying in the soul of every man, from the silliest child to the wisest old man, — that question without which life is impossible, as I have experienced it, in fact. The question is: " What will come of what I am doing to-day and shall do to-morrow? What will come of my whole life ? "

Differently expressed, the question would stand like this: " Why live, wish for anything, why do anything ? " The question may be expressed still differently : " Is there in my life a meaning which would not be destroyed by my inevitable, imminent death ? "

To this one, differently expressed, question I searched for an answer in human knowledge. I found that in relation to this question all human knowledge seemed to be divided into two opposite hemispheres, at the opposite ends of which there were two poles: one, a negative, the other, a positive pole; but that at neither pole was there an answer to the questions of life.

One series of the sciences does not seem to recognize the question, but clearly and definitely answers its own, independently put questions: that is the series of the experimental sciences, and at their extreme point stands mathematics; the other series of knowledge recognizes the question, but gives no answer to it: that is the series of the speculative sciences, and at their extreme point stands metaphysics.

Ever since my early youth I had been interested in the speculative sciences, but later mathematics and the natural sciences attracted me, and so long as I did not clearly put my question, so long as the question did not of itself rise in me, insisting on an answer, I was satisfied with those fictitious answers which sciences give to the question.

In the sphere of the experimental sciences, I said to myself: "Everything develops, is differentiated, moves in the direction of complexity and perfection, and there are laws which govern this progress. You are a part of the whole. Having, in so far as it is possible, learned the whole, and having learned the law of evolution, you will learn your place in this whole, and all about yourself." I am ashamed to confess it, there was a time when I seemed to be satisfied with that. That was the time when I myself was growing more complex and was developing. My muscles grew and became stronger, my memory was being enriched, my ability to think and comprehend was increasing, I grew and developed, and, feeling within me that growth, it was natural for me to think that that was the law of the whole world, in which I should find a solution also to the questions of my life. But the time came when my growth stopped, — I felt that I was not developing, but drying up, that my muscles were growing weaker and my teeth falling out, — and I saw that that law not only explained nothing to me, but that there never was and never could have been such a law, and that I took for a law what I found within me at a certain period of life. I was more severe toward the definition of that law; and it became clear to me that there could be no law of endless development; it became clear to me that saying that in endless space and time everything was developing, perfecting itself, becoming more complex, differentiating, was tantamount to saying nothing. All those are words without any meaning, for in the infinite there is nothing complex, nor simple, nor in front, nor behind, nor better, nor worse.

The main thing was that my personal question, "What am I with my desires?" remained entirely unanswered. And I understood that those sciences were very interesting, very attractive, but that the definiteness and clearness of those sciences were in inverse proportion to their applicability to the questions of life: the less applicable they are to the questions of life, the more definite and clear they are; the more they attempt to give answers to the questions of life, the more they become dim and unattractive. If you turn to that branch of those sciences which attempts to give answers to the questions of life, — to physiology, psychology, biology, sociology, — you come across an appalling scantiness of ideas, the greatest obscurity, an unjustified pretence at solving irrelevant questions, and constant contradictions of one thinker with others and even with himself. If you turn to the branch of knowledge which does not busy itself with the solution of the problems of life, but answers only its special, scientific questions, you are delighted at the power of the human mind, but know in advance that there will be no answers there to the questions of life. These sciences directly ignore the question of life. They say: "We have no answers to what you are and why you live, and we do not busy ourselves with that; but if you want to know the laws of light, of chemical combinations, the laws of the development of organisms, if you want to know the laws of the bodies, their forms, and the relation of numbers and quantities, if you want to know the laws of your mind, we shall give you clear, definite, incontrovertible answers to all that."

In general the relation of the experimental sciences to the question of life may be expressed thus: Question, "Why do I live?" Answer, "In the endlessly large space, in an endlessly long time, infinitely small particles are modified in infinite complexity, and when you understand the laws of these modifications, you will know why you live upon earth."

In the sphere of the speculative sciences I said to myself: "All humanity lives and develops on the basis of spiritual principles, ideals, which guide it. These ideals are expressed in the religions, in the sciences, in the arts, in the forms of political life. These ideals are all the time getting higher and higher, and humanity is moving toward a higher good. I am a part of humanity, and so my calling consists in coöperating in the consciousness and materialization of the ideals of humanity." During the period of my mental insipidity I was satisfied with that; but as soon as the question of life arose clearly within me, all that theory immediately went to pieces. Not to speak of that unscrupulous inexactness with which the sciences of this kind give out the deductions which are based on the study of a small part of humanity as general deductions; not to speak of the mutual contradictions of the different partisans of this conception as to what constitutes the ideals of humanity, — the strangeness, not to say stupidity, of this conception consists in this, that, in order to answer the question, which presents itself to every man, "What am I?" or, "Why do I live?" or, "What shall I do?" a man must first solve the problem, "What is the life of all humanity?" which is not familiar to him, and of which he knows only one tiny part at a tiny period of time. In order to understand what he is, a man must first know what all this mysterious humanity is, which consists of just such men as he himself is, who do not understand themselves.

I must confess, there was a time when I believed all

that. That was the time when I had my favourite ideals, which justified my lusts, and I tried to discover a theory which would allow me to look upon my lusts as a law of humanity. But as soon as the question of life arose in my soul in all its clearness, that answer at once was scattered to the winds, and I understood that, as in the experimental sciences there were real sciences and half-sciences, which attempted to give answers to questions which are not in their domain, so also in this sphere there was a whole series of wide-spread sciences which tried to answer to irrelevant questions. The half-sciences of this sphere, jurisprudence and the social sciences, try to solve the problems of man by apparently solving, each in its own way, the question of the life of all humanity.

But just as in the sphere of the experimental sciences a man who asks in all sincerity how to live cannot be satisfied with the answer, "Study in infinite space the modifications, infinite in time and complexity, of the infinite particles, and then you will understand all life," just so a sincere man cannot be satisfied with the answer, "Study the life of all humanity, whose beginning and end we cannot know, and then you will understand your own life." Just as in the experimental half-sciences, these half-sciences are the more filled with inexactness, obscurities, silliness, and contradictions, the farther they depart from the problems themselves. The problem of experimental science is a causal consecutiveness of material phenomena. Experimental science need only introduce the question of final cause, and nonsense is the result. The problem of speculative science is the consciousness of the causeless essence of life. It needs only introduce the investigation of causal phenomena, such as the social and historical phenomena, and the result is nonsense.

Experimental science gives positive knowledge and manifests the greatness of the human mind only when it does not introduce the final cause into its investigation.

And, on the other hand, speculative science is a science and manifests the greatness of the human mind only when it entirely sets aside the questions of the consecutiveness of causal phenomena and considers man only in relation to the final cause. Such in this sphere is the science which forms the pole of the sphere, metaphysics or philosophy. This science clearly puts the question: "What am I, and what is the whole world? and why am I, and why is the whole world?" And ever since it has been, it has answered in the same way. Whether the philosopher says that the idea, the substance, the spirit, or the will are the essence of life, which is within me and in everything existing, he keeps repeating that this essence exists and that I am that essence; but why it is, he does not know and does not answer, if he is an exact thinker. I ask, why should this essence be? What will result from the fact that it is and that it will be? And philosophy does not answer that, — it asks itself that question; and if it is a sincere philosophy, its whole labour will consist merely in clearly putting that question. And if it sticks firmly to its problem, it cannot do otherwise than answer to the question, "What am I, and what is the whole world?" by saying, "Everything and nothing;" and to the question, "Why?" by saying, "I do not know why."

Twist the speculative answers of philosophy as I may, I shall never get anything resembling an answer, not because, as in the clear, experimental sphere, the answer does not refer to my question, but because, though the whole mental labour is directed to my question, there is no answer, but instead of the answer there is received the same question, only in a complicated form.

VI.

In my search after the question of life I experienced the same feeling which a man who has lost his way in the forest may experience.

He comes to a clearing, climbs a tree, and clearly sees an unlimited space before him; at the same time he sees that there are no houses there, and that there can be none; he goes back to the forest, into the darkness, and he sees darkness, and again there are no houses.

Thus I blundered in this forest of human knowledge, between the clearings of the mathematical and experimental sciences, which disclosed to me clear horizons, but such in the direction of which there could be no house, and between the darkness of the speculative sciences, where I sunk into a deeper darkness, the farther I proceeded, and I convinced myself at last that there was no way out and could not be.

By abandoning myself to the bright side of knowledge I saw that I only turned my eyes away from the question. No matter how enticing and clear the horizons were that were disclosed to me, no matter how enticing it was to bury myself in the infinitude of this knowledge, I comprehended that these sciences were the more clear, the less I needed them, the less they answered my question.

"Well, I know," I said to myself, "all which science wants so persistently to know, but there is no answer to the question about the meaning of my life." But in the speculative sphere I saw that, in spite of the fact that the aim of the knowledge was directed straight to the answer of my question, or because of that fact, there could be no other answer than what I was giving to myself : " What is the meaning of my life ? " — " None." Or, " What will come of my life ? " — " Nothing." Or, " Why does everything which exists exist, and why do I exist ? " — " Because it exists."

Putting the question to the one side of human knowledge, I received an endless quantity of exact answers about what I did not ask : about the chemical composition of the stars, about the movement of the sun toward the constellation of Hercules, about the origin of species and of man, about the forms of infinitely small, imponderable particles of ether ; but the answer in this sphere of knowledge to my question what the meaning of my life was, was always : " You are what you call your life ; you are a temporal, accidental conglomeration of particles. The interrelation, the change of these particles, produces in you that which you call life. This congeries will last for some time ; then the interaction of these particles will cease, and that which you call life and all your questions will come to an end. You are an accidentally cohering globule of something. The globule is fermenting. This fermentation the globule calls its life. The globule falls to pieces, and all fermentation and all questions will come to an end." Thus the clear side of knowledge answers, and it cannot say anything else, if only it strictly follows its principles.

With such an answer it appears that the answer is not a reply to the question. I want to know the meaning of my life, but the fact that it is a particle of the infinite not only gives it no meaning, but even destroys every possible meaning.

Those obscure transactions, which this side of the experimental, exact science has with speculation, when it says that the meaning of life consists in evolution and the coöperation with this evolution, because of their obscurity and inexactness cannot be regarded as answers.

The other side of knowledge, the speculative, so long as it sticks strictly to its fundamental principles in giving a direct answer to the question, everywhere and at all times has answered one and the same : " The world is something infinite and incomprehensible.   Human life is an incomprehensible part of this incomprehensible *all*."   Again I exclude all those transactions between the speculative and the experimental sciences, which form the whole ballast of the half-sciences, the so-called science of jurisprudence and the political and historical sciences.   Into these sciences are just as irregularly introduced the concepts of evolution and perfection, but with this difference, that there it is the evolution of everything, while here it is the evolution of the life of man.   The irregularity is one and the same : evolution, perfection in the infinite, can have neither aim nor direction, and answers nothing in respect to my question.

Where speculative science is exact, namely, in real philosophy, — not in the one which Schopenhauer calls the professorial philosophy, which serves only for distributing all existing phenomena according to new philosophical rubrics and calling them by new names, — where the philosopher does not let out of sight the essential question, the answer is always one and the same, — the answer given by Socrates, Schopenhauer, Solomon, Buddha.

" We shall approach truth in proportion as we remove ourselves from life," says Socrates, preparing himself for death.   " What are we, who love truth, striving after in life ?   To free ourselves from the body and from all evil which results from the life of the body.   If that is so, why should we not rejoice when death comes to us ? The wise man is seeking his death all the time, and therefore death is not terrible to him."

And this is what Schopenhauer says :

" Having learned the internal essence of the world as will, and in all the phenomena, from the unconscious striving of the dark forces of Nature to the full consciousness of the activity of man, having learned only the objectivity of this will, we shall by no means escape the consequence that with the free negation, the self-destruction of the will, there will disappear all those phenomena, that constant striving and tendency without aim or rest on all the stages of objectivity, in which and through which the world exists ; there will disappear the diversity of consecutive forms, and with the form will disappear all its phenomena with their general forms, space and time, and, finally, its last fundamental form, subject and object. When there is no will, there is no concept, no world. Before us nothing only is left. But what opposes this transition to nothingness, our nature, is that very will to exist (*Wille zum Leben*), which forms ourselves as well as the world. That we are so afraid of nothingness, or, what is the same, that we desire to live, signifies that we ourselves are nothing but that desire to live and that we know nothing else. Therefore, what will be left after the complete annihilation of the will for us who are still full of that will is naturally nothing ; and, on the other hand, for those in whom the will has turned away and renounced itself, this our so real world, with all its suns and milky ways, is nothing."

" Vanity of vanities," says Solomon, " vanity of vanities ; all is vanity. What profit hath a man of all his labour which he taketh under the sun ? One generation passeth away, and another generation cometh : but the earth abideth for ever. The thing that hath been, it is that which shall be ; and that which is done is that which shall be done : and there is no new thing under the sun. Is there any thing whereof it may be said, See, this is new ? it hath been already of old time, which was before us. There is no remembrance of former things ; neither shall there be any remembrance of things that are to come with those that shall come after. I the Preacher was king over Israel in Jerusalem. And I gave my heart to seek and search out by wisdom concerning all things that are done under heaven: this sore travail hath God given to the sons of man to be exercised therewith. I have seen all the works that are done under the sun; and behold, all is vanity and vexation of spirit. I communed with mine own heart, saying, Lo, I am come to great estate, and have gotten more wisdom than all they that have been before me in Jerusalem: yea, my heart had great experience of wisdom and knowledge. And I gave my heart to know wisdom, and to know madness and folly: I perceived that this also is vexation of spirit. For in much wisdom is much grief: and he that increaseth knowledge increaseth sorrow.

" I said in mine heart, Go to now, I will prove thee with mirth; therefore enjoy pleasure: and behold, this also is vanity. I said of laughter, It is mad: and of mirth, What doeth it? I sought in mine heart to give myself unto wine, yet acquainting mine heart with wisdom; and to lay hold on folly, till I might see what was that good for the sons of men, which they should do under the heaven all the days of their life. I made me great works; I builded me houses; I planted me vineyards: I made me gardens and orchards, and I planted trees in them of all kind of fruits: I made me pools of water, to water therewith the wood that bringeth forth trees: I got me servants and maidens, and had servants born in my house; also I had great possessions of great and small cattle above all that were in Jerusalem before me; I gathered me also silver and gold, and the peculiar treasure of kings, and of the provinces: I gat me men-singers and women-singers, and the delights of the sons of men, as musical instruments, and that of all sorts. So I was great, and increased more than all that were before me in Jerusalem: also my wisdom remained with me. And whatsoever mine eyes desired I kept not from them, I withheld not my heart from any joy. Then I looked on all the works that my hands had wrought, and on the labour that I had laboured to do: and behold, all was vanity and vexation of spirit, and there was no profit under the sun. And I turned myself to behold wisdom, and madness, and folly. And I myself perceived also that one event happeneth to them all. Then said I in my heart, As it happeneth to the fool, so it happeneth even to me; and why was I then more wise? Then I said in my heart, that this also is vanity. For there is no remembrance of the wise more than of the fool for ever; seeing that which now is in the days to come shall all be forgotten. And how dieth the wise man? as the fool. Therefore I hated life; because the work that is wrought under the sun is grievous unto me: for all is vanity and vexation of spirit. Yea, I hated all my labour which I had taken under the sun: because I should leave it unto the man that shall be after me.

" For what hath man of all his labour, and of the vexation of his heart, wherein he hath laboured under the sun? For all his days are sorrows, and his travail grief; yea, his heart taketh not rest in the night. This is also vanity. There is nothing better for a man, than that he should eat and drink, and that he should make his soul enjoy good in his labour.

" All things come alike to all: there is one event to the righteous and to the wicked; to the good, and to the clean, and to the unclean; to him that sacrificeth, and to him that sacrificeth not: as is the good, so is the sinner; and he that sweareth, as he that feareth an oath. This is an evil among all things that are done under the sun, that there is one event unto all: yea, also the heart of the sons of men is full of evil, and madness is in their heart while they live, and after that they go to the dead.

For to him that is joined to all the living there is hope:
for a living dog is better than a dead lion. For the living
know that they shall die: but the dead know not any
thing, neither have they any more a reward; for the
memory of them is forgotten. Also their love, and their
hatred, and their envy, is now perished, neither have
they any more a portion for ever in any thing that is
done under the sun."

And this is what the Indian wisdom says:

Sakya-Muni, a young, happy prince, from whom have
been concealed diseases, old age, and death, drives out for
pleasure, when he sees a terrible, toothless, slavering old
man. The prince, from whom old age has heretofore
been concealed, is surprised, and he asks the charioteer
what that is, and why that man has come to such a
wretched, loathsome state? And when he learns that
that is the common fate of all men, that he, the youthful
prince, has inevitably the same in store, he cannot proceed in his pleasure drive, but gives order to be driven
home, in order to consider that. Evidently he finds some
consolation, for he again drives out cheerful and happy.
But this time he meets a sick man. He sees an ema-
ciated, livid, shivering man, with blurred eyes. The
prince, from whom diseases have been concealed, stops
and asks what that is. And when he learns that that is
sickness, to which all men are subject, and that he himself, a healthy and happy prince, may be as sick as that
on the morrow, he again has no courage to amuse himself,
orders himself driven home, and again looks for consolation, which he evidently finds, for he has himself driven
out a third time; but this third time he sees again a new
spectacle, — he sees that something is carried by. "What
is that?" — A dead man. "What does a dead man mean?"
asks the prince. He is told that to become dead means
to become what that man is. The prince goes up to the
corpse, and takes off the shroud and looks at him.

"What will be done with him?" asks the prince. He is told that he will be buried in the ground. "Why?" — Because he will certainly never be alive again, and there will be only stench and worms. "And is this the fate of all men? And will the same happen to me? Shall I be buried, and will a stench rise from me, and will worms eat me?" — Yes. "Back! I do not wish to go out for pleasure, and will never be driven out again."

And Sakya-Muni could not find any consolation in life, and he decided that life was the greatest evil, and used all the forces of his soul to free himself from it and to free others, and to do this in such a way that even after death it might not return in some manner, — to annihilate life with its root. Thus speaks the whole Indian wisdom.

So these are the direct answers which human wisdom gives when it answers the question of life.

"The life of the body is an evil and a lie, and so the destruction of this life of the body is a good, and we must wish it," says Socrates.

"Life is that which ought not to be, — an evil, — and the transition into nothingness is the only good of life," says Schopenhauer.

"Everything in the world, foolishness, and wisdom, and riches, and poverty, and merriment, and grief, everything is vanity and nonsense. Man will die, and nothing will be left. And that is foolish," says Solomon.

"It is impossible to live with the consciousness of inevitable suffering, debility, old age, and death, — it is necessary to free oneself from life, from every possibility of life," says Buddha.

And what these powerful minds have said, millions of millions of people have said, thought, and felt like them, and so think and feel I.

Thus, my wandering among the sciences not only did not take me out of my despair, but even increased it. One science gave no reply to the question of life, another

gave me a direct answer and only confirmed my despair
and showed me that what I had arrived at was not the
fruit of my aberration, of a morbid condition of my mind;
on the contrary, it only confirmed me in my belief that
my thoughts were correct and that I agreed with the
deductions of the most powerful minds of humanity.

There is no cause for self-deception. Everything is
vanity. Happy is he who is not born, — death is better
than life : it is necessary to free oneself from it.

VII.

HAVING found no elucidation in science, I began to look for it in life, hoping to find it in the men who surrounded me. I began to observe the people such as I, to see how they lived about me and what attitude they assumed to the question that had brought me to the point of despair.

This is what I found in people who were in the same position as myself through their education and manner of life.

I found that for people of my circle there were four ways out from the terrible condition in which we all are.

The first way out is through ignorance. It consists in not knowing, not understanding that life is evil and meaningless. People of this category — mostly women or very young or very dull persons — have not yet come to understand that question of life which presented itself to Schopenhauer, Solomon, and Buddha. They see neither the dragon that awaits them, nor the mice that are nibbling at the roots of the bushes to which they are holding on, and continue to lick the honey. But they lick the honey only till a certain time: something will direct their attention to the dragon and the mice, and there will be an end to their licking. From them I can learn nothing, — it is impossible to stop knowing what you know.

The second way out is through Epicureanism. It consists in this, that, knowing the hopelessness of life, one

41

should in the meantime enjoy such good as there is, without looking either at the dragon or the mice, but licking
the honey in the best manner possible, especially if there
is a lot of it in one spot. Solomon expresses this way out
like this :

" Go thy way, eat thy bread with joy, and drink thy
wine. Live joyfully with the wife whom thou lovest
all the days of the life of thy vanity, which he hath given
thee under the sun, all the days of thy vanity : for that
is thy portion in this life, and in thy labour which thou
takest under the sun. Whatsoever thy hand findeth to do,
do it with thy might ; for there is no work, nor device,
nor knowledge, nor wisdom, in the grave, whither thou
goest."

Thus the majority of the people of our circle support
the possibility of life in themselves. The conditions in
which they are give them more good than evil, and their
moral dulness makes it possible for them to forget that
the advantage of their situation is a casual one ; that not
everybody can have a thousand wives and palaces, like
Solomon ; that to every man with a thousand wives there
are a thousand men without wives, and for every palace
there are a thousand people who built it in the sweat of
their brows ; and that the accident which has made me a
Solomon to-day, will to-morrow make me a slave of Solomon. The dulness of the imagination of these people
makes it possible for them to forget that which gave
no rest to Buddha, — the inevitableness of sickness, old
age, and death, which sooner or later will destroy all those
pleasures.

Thus think and feel the majority of men of our time
and our manner of life. The fact that some of these people assert that the dulness of their comprehension and
imagination is philosophy, which they call positive, in my
opinion does not take them out of the category of those
who, in order not to see the question, lick the honey.

Such people I could not imitate: as I did not possess their dulness of comprehension, I could not artificially reproduce it in myself.　Just like any live man, I could not tear my eyes away from the mice and the dragon, having once seen them.

The third way out is through force and energy.　It consists in this, that, having comprehended that life is evil and meaningless, one should set out to destroy it. Thus now and then act strong, consistent people.　Having comprehended all the stupidity of the joke which has been played upon them, and seeing that the good of the dead is better than that of the living, and that it is better not to be at all, they go and carry this out and at once put an end to that stupid joke, so long as there are means for it : a noose about the neck, the water, a knife to pierce the heart with, railway trains.　The number of people of our circle who do so is growing larger and larger.　These people commit the act generally at the best period of life, when the mental powers are in full bloom and few habits have been acquired that lower human reason.

I saw that that was the worthiest way out, and I wanted to act in that way.

The fourth way out is through weakness.　It consists in this, that, comprehending the evil and the meaningless-ness of life, one continues to drag it out, knowing in advance that nothing can come of it.　People of this calibre know that death is better than life, but, not hav-ing the strength to act reasonably, to make an end to the deception, and to kill themselves, they seem to be waiting for something.　This is the way of weakness, for if I know that which is better, which is in my power, why not abandon myself to that which is better ?　I belonged to that category.

Thus people of my calibre have four ways of saving themselves from the terrible contradiction.　No matter how much I strained my mental attention, I saw no other way out but those four. The one way out was not to understand that life was meaningless, vanity, and an evil, and that it was better not to live. I could not help knowing it and, having once learned it, I could not shut my eyes to it. The second way out was to make use of life such as it is, without thinking of the future. I could not do that either. Like Sakya-Muni, I could not go out hunting, when I knew that there was old age, suffering, death. My imagination was too vivid. Besides, I could not enjoy the accident of the moment, which for a twinkling threw enjoyment in my path. The third way out was, having come to see that life was an evil and a foolishness, to make an end of it and kill myself. I comprehended that, but for some reason did not kill myself. The fourth way out was to live in the condition of Solomon, of Schopenhauer, — to know that life was a stupid joke played on me, and yet to live, wash and dress myself, dine, speak, and even write books. That was repulsive and painful for me, but still I persisted in that situation.

Now I see that if I did not kill myself, the cause of it was a dim consciousness of the incorrectness of my ideas. No matter how convincing and incontestable seemed to me the train of my thoughts and of the thoughts of the wise men who had brought us to recognize the meaninglessness of life, there was left in me an obscure doubt of the correctness of my judgment.

It was like this: I, my reason, have discovered that life is unreasonable. If there is no higher reason (there is none, and nothing can prove it), reason is the creator of life for me. If there were no reason, there would be no life for me. How then does this reason negate life, since it is itself the creator of life? Life is everything. Reason is the fruit of life, and this reason denies life itself. I felt that something was wrong there.

Life is a meaningless evil, — that was incontestable, I said to myself. But I have lived, still live, and all humanity has lived. How is that? Why does it live, since it can refuse to live? Is it possible Schopenhauer and I alone are so wise as to have comprehended the meaninglessness and evil of life?

The discussion of the vanity of life is not so cunning, and it has been brought forward long ago, even by the simplest kind of men, and yet they have lived and still live. Why do they continue living and never think of doubting the reasonableness of life?

My knowledge, confirmed by the wisdom of the sages, has disclosed to me that everything in the world, — everything organic and inorganic, — everything is constructed with surprising cleverness, only my own condition is stupid. And those fools, the enormous masses of people, know nothing about how everything organic and inorganic is constructed in the world, and yet live, and they think that their life is sensibly arranged!

And it occurred to me that there might be something I did not know, for ignorance acts in precisely that manner. Ignorance always says the same. When it does not know a thing, it says that what it does not know is stupid. In reality it turns out that there is a human entity which has lived as though understanding the meaning of its life, for, if it did not understand it, it could not live, and I say that the whole life is meaningless, and that I cannot live.

Nobody prevents our denying life by committing suicide. If so, kill yourself and stop discussing! You do not like life, very well, then kill yourself! If you live and cannot understand the meaning of life, make an end to it, and do not whirl about in this life, going into discussions about not understanding life. If you have come to a gay company, where all are very happy and know what they are doing, while you feel lonesome and disgusted, go away!

Indeed, what are we, who are convinced of the necessity of suicide and who do not have the courage to commit it, if not the weakest, most inconsistent, and, to speak simply, the most foolish kind of men who carry about their foolishness as a fool carries around his painted wallet?

Our wisdom, however incontestable it may be, has not given us the knowledge of the meaning of our life; but all humanity which is carrying on life — the millions — does not doubt the meaning of life.

Indeed, ever since those most ancient, ancient times since when life has existed, of which I know anything, there have lived men who knew the reflection on the vanity of life, which has shown me the meaninglessness of life, and yet they lived, ascribing some kind of a meaning to it.

Ever since any life began with men, they had that meaning of life, and they have carried on the life that has reached me. Everything which is in me and about me, — everything carnal and non-carnal, — all that is the fruit of their knowledge of life. All the tools of thought, with which I judge this life and condemn it, — all that was done by them, and not by me. I was born, educated, and grew up, thanks to them. They mined the iron, taught how to cut down the forest, domesticated cows and horses, taught how to sow, how to live together, and arranged our life; they taught me to think and to speak. And I, their product, nurtured and fed by them, taught by them, thinking their thoughts, and speaking their words, — I have proved to them that they are meaningless! "There is something wrong there," I said to myself. "I must have made a mistake somewhere." But where the mistake was, I was unable to discover.

VIII.

ALL these doubts, which now I am able to express more or less coherently, I could not express then. Then I only felt that, no matter how logically inevitable and how confirmed by the greatest thinkers were my deductions about the vanity of life, there was something wrong in them. Whether it was in the reflection itself, in the way the question was put, I did not know, — I felt that the mental proof was complete, but that that was not enough. All these deductions did not convince me sufficiently to make me do that which resulted from my reflections, which was, that I should commit suicide. I should be telling an untruth if I said that I arrived through reason at what I did arrive at, and did not kill myself. Reason was at work, but there was also something else at work, which I cannot call otherwise than the consciousness of life. There was also at work that force which compelled me to direct my attention to this rather than to that, and this force brought me out of my desperate situation and directed my reason to something entirely different. This force made me observe that I, with a hundred people like me, did not constitute all humanity and that I did not yet know the life of humanity.

Surveying the narrow circle of my equals, I saw only people who did not understand the question, those who understood the question but stifled it in the intoxication of life, those who had understood life and had made an end of it, and those who understood, but in their weakness waited for the end of their desperate life. I saw no others. It seemed to me that the narrow circle of learned, rich, leisured people, to which I belonged, formed all humanity, and that those billions of men who had lived and were living then were just a kind of animals, and not men.

No matter how strange, how incredibly incomprehensible it now seems to me that I, discussing life, should have been able to overlook all those who surrounded me on all sides, the life of humanity, that I should have been able to err in such a ridiculous manner as to think that my life, and the life of a Solomon and a Schopenhauer, was the real, the normal life, while the life of billions was a circumstance that did not deserve consideration, — no matter how strange that all appears to me now, it was nevertheless so. In the aberration of my pride of mind, it seemed to me so incontestable that Solomon, Schopenhauer, and I had put the question so correctly and so truly that there could be nothing else, — it seemed so incontestable to me that all those billions belonged to those who had not yet reached the whole depth of the question, — that in looking for the meaning of life I never thought: "What meaning have all those billions, who have lived in the world, ascribed to their life?"

I lived for a long time in this madness, which, not in words, but in deeds, is particularly characteristic of us, the most liberal and learned of men. But, thanks either to my strange, physical love for the real working class, which made me understand it and see that it is not so stupid as we suppose, or to the sincerity of my conviction, which was that I could know nothing and that the best that I could do was to hang myself, — I felt that if I wanted to live and understand the meaning of life, I ought naturally to look for it, not among those who had lost the meaning of life and wanted to kill themselves, but among those billions departed and living men who had been carrying their own lives and ours upon their shoulders. And I looked around at the enormous masses of deceased and living men, — not learned and wealthy, but simple men, — and I saw something quite different. I saw that all these billions of men that lived or had lived, all, with rare exceptions, did not fit into my subdivisions, and that I could not recognize them as not understanding the question, because they themselves put it and answered it with surprising clearness. Nor could I recognize them as Epicureans, because their lives were composed rather of privations and suffering than of enjoyment. Still less could I recognize them as senselessly living out their meaningless lives, because every act of theirs and death itself was explained by them. They regarded it as the greatest evil to kill themselves. It appeared, then, that all humanity was in possession of a knowledge of the meaning of life, which I did not recognize and which I contemned. It turned out that rational knowledge did not give any meaning to life, excluded life, while the meaning which by billions of people, by all humanity, was ascribed to life was based on some despised, false knowledge.

The rational knowledge in the person of the learned and the wise denied the meaning of life, but the enormous masses of men, all humanity, recognized this meaning in an irrational knowledge. This irrational knowledge was faith, the same that I could not help but reject. That was God as one and three, the creation in six days, devils and angels, and all that which I could not accept so long as I had not lost my senses.

My situation was a terrible one. I knew that I should not find anything on the path of rational knowledge but the negation of life, and there, in faith, nothing but the negation of reason, which was still more impossible than the negation of life. From the rational knowledge it followed that life was an evil and men knew it, — it depended on men whether they should cease living, and yet they lived and continued to live, and I myself lived, though I had known long ago that life was meaningless and an evil. From faith it followed that, in order to understand life, I must renounce reason, for which alone a meaning was needed.

IX.

THERE resulted a contradiction, from which there were two ways out: either what I called rational was not so rational as I had thought; or that which to me appeared irrational was not so irrational as I had thought. And I began to verify the train of thoughts of my rational knowledge.

In verifying the train of thoughts of my rational knowledge, I found that it was quite correct. The deduction that life was nothing was inevitable; but I saw a mistake. The mistake was that I had not reasoned in conformity with the question put by me. The question was, "Why should I live?" that is, "What real, indestructible essence will come from my phantasmal, destructible life? What meaning has my finite existence in this infinite world?" And in order to answer this question, I studied life.

The solutions of all possible questions of life apparently could not satisfy me, because my question, no matter how simple it appeared in the beginning, included the necessity of explaining the finite through the infinite, and vice versa.

I asked, "What is the extra-temporal, extra-causal, extra-spatial meaning of life?" But I gave an answer to the question, "What is the temporal, causal, spatial meaning of my life?" The result was that after a long labour of mind I answered, "None."

In my reflections I constantly equated, nor could I do otherwise, the finite with the finite, the infinite with the

infinite, and so from that resulted precisely what had to
result : force was force, matter was matter, will was will,
infinity was infinity, nothing was nothing, — and nothing
else could come from it.

There happened something like what at times takes
place in mathematics : you think you are solving an
equation, when you have only an identity. The reasoning is correct, but you receive as a result the answer :
$a = a$, or $x = x$, or $0 = 0$. The same happened with my
reflection in respect to the question about the meaning of
my life. The answers given by all science to that question are only identities.

Indeed, the strictly scientific knowledge, that knowledge which, as Descartes did, begins with a full doubt in
everything, rejects all knowledge which has been taken
on trust, and builds everything anew on the laws of reason and experience, cannot give any other answer to
the question of life than what I received, — an indefinite
answer. It only seemed to me at first that science gave
me a positive answer, — Schopenhauer's answer : " Life
has no meaning, it is an evil." But when I analyzed the
matter, I saw that the answer was not a positive one, but
that it was only my feeling which expressed it as such.
The answer, strictly expressed, as it is expressed by the
Brahmins, by Solomon, and by Schopenhauer, is only
an indefinite answer, or an identity, $0 = 0$, life is nothing.
Thus the philosophical knowledge does not negate anything, but only answers that the question cannot be
solved by it, that for philosophy the solution remains
insoluble.

When I saw that, I understood that it was not right
for me to look for an answer to my question in rational
knowledge, and that the answer given by rational knowledge was only an indication that the answer might be got
if the question were differently put, but only when into
the discussion of the question should be introduced the

question of the relation of the finite to the infinite. I also understood that, no matter how irrational and monstrous the answers might be that faith gave, they had this advantage that they introduced into each answer the relation of the finite to the infinite, without which there could be no answer.

No matter how I may put the question, "How must I live?" the answer is, "According to God's law." "What real result will there be from my life?" — "Eternal torment or eternal bliss." "What is the meaning which is not destroyed by death?" — "The union with infinite God, paradise."

Thus, outside the rational knowledge, which had to me appeared as the only one, I was inevitably led to recognize that all living humanity had a certain other irrational knowledge, faith, which made it possible to live.

All the irrationality of faith remained the same for me, but I could not help recognizing that it alone gave to humanity answers to the questions of life, and, in consequence of them, the possibility of living.

The rational knowledge brought me to the recognition that life was meaningless, — my life stopped, and I wanted to destroy myself. When I looked around at people, at all humanity, I saw that people lived and asserted that they knew the meaning of life. I looked back at myself: I lived so long as I knew the meaning of life. As to other people, so even to me, did faith give the meaning of life and the possibility of living.

Looking again at the people of other countries, contemporaries of mine and those passed away, I saw again the same. Where life had been, there faith, ever since humanity had existed, had given the possibility of living, and the chief features of faith were everywhere one and the same.

No matter what answers faith may give, its every answer gives to the finite existence of man the sense of the infinite, — a sense which is not destroyed by suffering, privation, and death. Consequently in faith alone could we find the meaning and possibility of life. What, then, was faith? I understood that faith was not merely an evidence of things not seen, and so forth, not revelation (that is only the description of one of the symptoms of faith), not the relation of man to man (faith has to be defined, and then God, and not first God, and faith through him), not merely an agreement with what a man was told, as faith was generally understood, — that faith was the knowledge of the meaning of human life, in consequence of which man did not destroy himself, but lived. Faith is the power of life. If a man lives he believes in something. If he did not believe that he ought to live for some purpose, he would not live. If he does not see and understand the phantasm of the finite, he believes in that finite; if he understands the phantasm of the finite, he must believe in the infinite. Without faith one cannot live.

I recalled the whole course of my internal work, and I was frightened. Now it was clear to me that, in order that a man might live, he either must not see the infinite, or must have such an explanation of the meaning of life that the finite is equated to the infinite. I had such an explanation, but it was useless to me so long as I believed in the finite and tried to verify it by reason. Before the light of reason all the former explanation was scattered to the winds; but there came a time when I stopped believing in the finite. Then I began on a rational basis to build from what I knew an explanation which would give me the meaning of life; but nothing came of it. With the best minds of humanity I arrived at the result that $O = O$, and I was very much surprised when I received such a solution, whereas nothing else could have come from it.

What had I been doing when I had been looking for

an answer in the experimental sciences? I wanted to find out why I lived, and for this I studied everything which was outside of me. It is clear that I could have learned many things, but certainly nothing which I needed.

What had I been doing when I searched for an answer in the philosophical sciences? I had studied the thoughts of those beings who had been in the same condition that I was in, and who had no answer to the question of why I lived. It is clear that I could not have learned anything but what I already knew, that it was impossible to know anything.

What am I? A part of the infinite. In these few words lies the whole problem.

Is it possible humanity has begun only yesterday to put this question? And has no one before me put this question, which is so simple that it is on the tip of the tongue of every intelligent child?

This question has been put ever since men have existed; and ever since men have existed, it has been clear that for the solution of this question it is equally insufficient to equate the infinite to the infinite and the finite to the finite, and ever since men have existed the relations of the finite to the infinite have been found and expressed.

All these concepts, with which we equate the finite to the infinite and receive a meaning of life and a concept of God, freedom, goodness, we subject to logical investigation. And these concepts do not stand the critique of reason.

If it were not so terrible it would be ridiculous, with what pride and self-contentment we, like children, take a watch to pieces, pull out the spring, make a toy from it, and then wonder why the watch has stopped going.

What is necessary and precious is a solution of the contradiction of the finite and the infinite and an answer to the question of life, such as would make life possible.

And this one solution, which we find everywhere, at all times, and with all the nations, — a solution brought down from a time in which the life of humanity is lost for us, a solution which is so difficult that we can do nothing like it, we frivolously destroy in order to put once more the question which is inherent in every man, and for which we have no answer.

The conception of an infinite God, of the divineness of the soul, of the connection of human affairs with God, of the unity, the essence of the soul, of the human conception of moral good and evil, are concepts that have been worked out in the remote infinitude of human thought, concepts without which there would be no life and no I, and yet I, rejecting all that labour of all humanity, want to do everything anew and in my own way.

I did not think so at that time, but the germs of the thoughts were already within me. I saw, in the first place, that my position, with that of Schopenhauer and Solomon, in spite of our wisdom, was stupid: we understood life to be an evil, and yet we lived. It is stupid, because, if life is stupid, — and I am so fond of what is rational, — life ought to be destroyed, and there would not be any one to deny it. In the second place, I saw that all our reflections whirled about in a magic circle, like a wheel that does not catch in the cog. No matter how much and how well we might reflect upon the matter, we could not get an answer to the question, except that O was always equal to O, and so our path was evidently faulty. In the third place, I began to understand that in the answers which faith gave there was preserved the profoundest wisdom of humanity, and that I had no right to refute them on the basis of reason, and that these main answers were the only ones that gave an answer to the question of life.

X.

I UNDERSTOOD that, but that did not make it easier for me.

I was prepared now to accept any faith, so long as it did not demand from me a direct denial of reason, which would have been a lie. And so I studied Buddhism and Mohammedanism from books, and, more still, Christianity both from books and from living men who were about me.

Naturally I first of all turned to believing men of my own circle, to learned men, to Orthodox theologians, to old monks, to theologians of the new shade, and even to so-called new Christians, who professed salvation through faith in redemption. I clung to these believers and questioned them about their beliefs, and tried to find out in what they saw the meaning of life.

Although I made all possible concessions and avoided all kinds of disputes, I was unable to accept the faiths of those men, — I saw that what they gave out as faith was not an explanation, but an obfuscation of the meaning of life, and that they themselves affirmed their faith, not in order to answer that question of life which had brought me to faith, but for some other aims which were foreign to me.

I remember the agonizing feeling of terror lest I return to my former despair after hope, which I experienced many, many a time in my relations with these people.

The more they went into details in order to expound to me their doctrines, the more clearly did I see their error and the loss of my hope of finding in their faith the explanation of the meaning of life.

It was not that in the exposition of their doctrine they mixed in with the Christian truths, which had always been near to me, many unnecessary and irrational things, — it was not that which repelled me; what repelled me was that the lives of these people were precisely what my own life was, with this difference only, that theirs did not correspond to those principles which they expounded in their doctrines. I saw clearly that they were deceiving themselves, and that, like myself, they had no other meaning of life than to live so long as life was possible, and to take everything that the hand could hold. I saw that because, if they possessed that meaning by which the terror of privations, suffering, and death is abolished, they would not be afraid of them. But they, the believers of our circle, just like myself, lived in plenty and abundance, tried to increase and preserve their possessions, were afraid of privations, suffering, and death, and, like myself and all of us unbelievers, lived gratifying their desires, and lived just as badly, if not worse, than the unbelievers.

No reflections could convince me of the truthfulness of their faith. Only such actions as would have shown me that they had such a meaning of life that poverty, sickness, death, so terrible to me, were not terrible to them, could have convinced me. But such actions I did not perceive among these varied believers of our circle. On the contrary, I saw such actions among the people of our circle who were the greatest unbelievers, but never among the so-called believers.

I saw that the faith of these men was not the faith I was in search of, and that their faith was not a faith, but one of the Epicurean solaces of life. I saw that this faith was, perhaps, good enough, if not as a consolation, as a certain distraction for a repentant Solomon on his death-bed, but it was not good for the enormous majority of humanity, which is called not to live in solace, enjoying the labours of others, but to create life.

In order that all humanity may be able to live, in order that they may continue living, giving a meaning to life, they, those billions, must have another, a real knowledge of faith, for not the fact that I, with Solomon and Schopenhauer, did not kill myself convinced me of the existence of faith, but that these billions had lived and had borne us, me and Solomon, on the waves of life.

Then I began to cultivate the acquaintance of the believers from among the poor, the simple and unlettered folk, of pilgrims, monks, dissenters, peasants. The doctrine of these people from among the masses was also the Christian doctrine that the quasi-believers of our circle professed. With the Christian truths were also mixed in very many superstitions, but there was this difference: the superstitions of our circle were quite unnecessary to them, had no connection with their lives, were only a kind of an Epicurean amusement, while the superstitions of the believers from among the labouring classes were to such an extent blended with their life that it would have been impossible to imagine it without these superstitions, — it was a necessary condition of that life. I began to examine closely the lives and beliefs of these people, and the more I examined them, the more did I become convinced that they had the real faith, that their faith was necessary for them, and that it alone gave them a meaning and possibility of life. In contradistinction to what I saw in our circle, where life without faith was possible, and where hardly one in a thousand professed to be a believer, among them there was hardly one in a thousand who was not a believer. In contradistinction to what I saw in our circle, where all life passed in idleness, amusements, and tedium of life, I saw that the whole life of these people was passed in hard work, and that they were satisfied with life.   In contradistinction to the people of our circle, who struggled and murmured against fate because of their privations and their suffering, these people accepted diseases and sorrows without any perplexity or opposition, but with the calm and firm conviction that it was all for good.   In contradistinction to the fact that the more intelligent we are, the less do we understand the meaning of life and the more do we see a kind of a bad joke in our suffering and death, these people live, suffer, and approach death, and suffer in peace and more often in joy.   In contradistinction to the fact that a calm death, a death without terror or despair, is the greatest exception in our circle, a restless, insubmissive, joyless death is one of the greatest exceptions among the masses.   And of such people, who are deprived of everything which for Solomon and for me constitutes the only good of life, and who withal experience the greatest happiness, there is an enormous number.   I cast a broader glance about me.   I examined the life of past and present vast masses of men, and I saw people who in like manner had understood the meaning of life, who had known how to live and die, not two, not three, not ten, but hundreds, thousands, millions.   All of them, infinitely diversified as to habits, intellect, culture, situation, all equally and quite contrary to my ignorance knew the meaning of life and of death, worked calmly, bore privations and suffering, lived and died, seeing in that not vanity, but good.

I began to love those people.   The more I penetrated into their life, the life of the men now living, and the life of men departed, of whom I had read and heard, the more did I love them, and the easier it became for me to live.   Thus I lived for about two years, and within me took place a transformation, which had long been working within me, and the germ of which had always been in me.   What happened with me was that the life of our circle, — of the rich and the learned, — not only disgusted me, but even lost all its meaning. All our acts, reflections, sciences, arts, — all that appeared to me in a new light. I saw that all that was mere pampering of the appetites, and that no meaning could be found in it; but the life of all the working masses, of all humanity, which created life, presented itself to me in its real significance. I saw that that was life itself and that the meaning given to this life was truth, and I accepted it.

XI.

When I considered that this belief repelled me and seemed meaningless when it was professed by people who lived contrary to this belief, and that it attracted me and appeared rational when I saw that men lived by it, — I understood why I had rejected that belief and had found it meaningless, while now I accepted it and found it full of meaning. I saw that I had erred and how I had erred. I had erred not so much because I had reasoned incorrectly as because I had lived badly. I saw that the truth had been veiled from me not so much by the aberration of my mind as by my life itself in those exclusive conditions of Epicureanism, of the gratification of the appetites, in which I had passed it. I saw that the question of what my life was, and the answer to it, that it was an evil, were quite correct. What was incorrect was that the answer, which had reference to me only, had been transferred by me to life in general. I asked myself what my life was, and received as an answer: "An evil and an absurdity." And indeed, my life — that life of pampered appetites and whims — was meaningless and evil, and so the answer, "Life is evil and meaningless," had reference only to my life, and not to human life in general. I comprehended the truth, which I later found in the gospel, that men had come to love the darkness more than the light because their deeds were bad, for those who did bad deeds hated the light and did not go to it, lest their deeds be disclosed. I saw that in order to comprehend the meaning of life it was necessary, first of all, that life should not be meaningless and evil, and then only was reason needed for the understanding of it. I comprehended why I had so long walked around such a manifest truth, and that if I were to think and speak of the life of humanity, I ought to think and speak of the life of humanity, and not of the life of a few parasites of life. This truth had always been a truth, just as two times two was four, but I had not recognized it because, if I recognized that two times two was four, I should have had to recognize that I was not good, whereas it was more important and obligatory for me to feel myself good than to feel that two times two was four. I came to love good people and to hate myself, and I recognized the truth. Now everything became clear to me.

What would happen if a hangman, who passes all his life in torturing and chopping off heads, or a desperate drunkard, or an insane man, who has passed all his life in a dark room which he has defiled, and who imagines that he will perish if he leaves that room, — if any of them should ask himself what life is, naturally he could get no other answer to this question than that life is the greatest evil, and the answer of the insane man would be quite correct, but for him alone. What if I was just such a madman? What if all of us, rich men of leisure, were such madmen? And I comprehended that we were indeed such madmen, — I certainly was.

Indeed, a bird lives for the purpose of flying, collecting its food, building its nest, and when I see the bird doing that, I rejoice at its joy. A goat, a hare, a wolf exists in such a way that they have to feed, multiply, and rear their young ones, and when they do so, I have the firm conviction that they are happy, and that their life is rational. What, then, ought man to do? He must procure his sustenance like the animals, but with this difference, that he will perish if he procures it by himself,

— he must procure it not for himself, but for everybody. When he does so, I have the firm consciousness that he is happy and that his life is rational. What had I been doing during my thirty years of conscious life? Not only had I procured no sustenance for everybody, but not even for myself. I had lived as a parasite and, upon asking myself why I lived, I had received the answer: "For no reason." If the meaning of life consisted in sustaining it, how could I, who for thirty years had busied myself not with sustaining life, but with ruining it in myself and in others, have received any other answer than that my life was an absurdity and an evil? It really was an absurdity and an evil.

The life of the world goes on by somebody's will, — somebody is doing some kind of work with the life of this world and with our lives. In order to have the hope of understanding the meaning of this will, it is first of all necessary to fulfil it, to do that which is wanted of us. If I am not going to do what is wanted of me, I shall never be able to understand what is wanted of me, and much less, what is wanted of all of us and of the whole world.

If a naked, starving beggar is picked up on a cross-road, is brought under the roof of a beautiful building, is given to eat and drink, and is made to move a certain stick up and down, it is evident that before the beggar is to discuss why he has been taken up, why he should move that stick, whether the arrangement of the whole building is sensible, he must first move the stick. When he does so, he will comprehend that the stick moves a pump, that the pump raises the water, and that the water flows down the garden beds. Then he will be taken out of the covered well and will be put to do some other work, and he will garner the fruit and will enter into the joy of his master, and, passing from the lower to the higher work, comprehending more and more the arrangement of the whole building, and taking part in it, will never think of asking why he is there, and certainly will not rebuke the master.

Even thus the Master is not rebuked by those who do his will, — simple, working, illiterate people, — those whom we have regarded as beasts ; but we, the wiseacres, eat the Master's food and do not do any of the things that the Master wants us to do, but instead of doing them we sit down in a circle and discuss : " Why should we move the stick ?   That is stupid."   And we thought it out. We reasoned it out that the Master was stupid, or did not exist, and we were wise, only we felt that we were not good for anything and ought to free ourselves from our lives.

XII.

THE recognition of the error of the rational knowledge helped me to free myself from the seduction of idle speculation. The conviction that the knowledge of the truth could be found only through life incited me to doubt the correctness of my life; but what saved me was that I managed to tear myself away from exclusiveness and to see the real life of the working people and to understand that that alone was the real life. I saw that if I wanted to comprehend life and its meaning, I must live, not the life of a parasite, but the real life, and accept the meaning which real humanity has given to it and, blending with that life, verify it.

At that same time the following happened with me: during all the period of that year, when I asked myself nearly every minute whether I had not better make an end of myself by means of the noose or the bullet, my heart, side by side with the train of thoughts and of observations, of which I have spoken, was tormented by an agonizing feeling. This feeling I cannot name otherwise than the search after God.

I say that this search after God was not a reflection, but a feeling, because this search did not result from the train of my thoughts, — it was even diametrically opposed to it, — but from the heart. It was a feeling of terror, of orphanhood, of loneliness amidst everything foreign, and of a hope for somebody's succour.

Although I was fully convinced of the impossibility of

proving the existence of God (for Kant had proved it to me, and I fully comprehended his statement that it was not possible to prove it), I nevertheless tried to find God, hoped to find him, and, following my old habit, turned with prayers to him whom I was looking for and could not find. Now I tried to verify in my mind the proofs of Kant and of Schopenhauer about the impossibility of proving the existence of God, and now I refuted them. Cause, I said to myself, is not such a category of reasoning as space and time. If I am, there is a cause for it, and a first cause. And this first cause of all is what is called God. I stopped at this thought and tried with my whole being to recognize the presence of this cause. The moment I recognized that there was a force in the power of which I was, I felt the possibility of living. But I asked myself: "What is this cause, this force? How am I to think of it? In what relation shall I stand to that which I call God?" and nothing but familiar answers occurred to me: "He is the creator, the provider." These answers did not satisfy me, and I felt that what was necessary for life was being lost in me. I was horrified and began to pray to him whom I was searching after to help me, and the more I prayed, the more evident it became to me that he did not hear me and that there was nobody to turn to. With despair in my heart because there was no God, I said: "O Lord, have mercy on me! Save me! O Lord my God, teach me!" And nobody had mercy on me, and I felt that my life was stopping.

Again and again I arrived from various sides at the same recognition that I could not have appeared in the world without any cause or reason or meaning, that I could not be such a callow bird that has tumbled out of its nest, as I felt myself to be. Let me, fallen bird, lie on my back and pipe in the high grass, — I am piping because I know that my mother carried me in her womb, hatched and warmed me, fed and loved me. Where is she, that mother of mine? If I have been abandoned, who has done it? I cannot conceal from myself that some one bore me loving me. Who is that some one? Again God. He knows and sees my searching, my despair, my struggle. "He is," I said to myself. I needed but for a moment to recognize that, when life immediately rose in me, and I felt the possibility and joy of existence. But again I passed over from the recognition of the existence of God to the search after the relation to him, and again there presented himself to me that God, our creator in three persons, who sent his Son the Redeemer. Again that God, who was separate from the world, from me, melted like a piece of ice, melted under my very eyes, and again nothing was left, and again the source of life ran dry; I fell into despair and felt that there was nothing left for me to do but kill myself. What was worst of all, I felt that I could not do even that.

Not twice, or three times, but dozens, hundreds of times I arrived at these states, now of joy and animation, and now again of despair and the consciousness of the impossibility of life.

I remember, it was early in spring, I was by myself in the forest, listening to the sounds of the woods. I listened and thought all the time of one and the same thing that had formed the subject of my thoughts for the last three years. I was again searching after God.

"All right, there is no God," I said to myself, "there is not such a being as would be, not my concept, but reality, just like my whole life, — there is no such being. And nothing, no miracles, can prove him to me, because the miracles would be my concept, and an irrational one at that.

"But my idea about God, about the one I am searching after?" I asked myself. "Where did that idea come from?" And with this thought the joyous waves of life again rose in me. Everything about me revived, received a meaning ; but my joy did not last long, — the mind continued its work.

" The concept of God is not God," I said to myself. " A concept is what takes place within me ; the concept of God is what I can evoke or can not evoke in myself. It is not that which I am searching after. I am trying to find that without which life could not be." And again everything began to die around me and within me, and I wanted again to kill myself.

Then I looked at myself, at what was going on within me, and I recalled those deaths and revivals which had taken place within me hundreds of times. I remembered that I lived only when I believed in God. As it had been before, so it was even now : I needed only to know about God, and I lived ; I needed to forget and not believe in him, and I died.

What, then, are these revivals and deaths ? Certainly I do not live when I lose my faith in the existence of God ; I should have killed myself long ago, if I had not had the dim hope of finding him. " So what else am I looking for ? " a voice called out within me. " Here he is. He is that without which one cannot live. To know God and live is one and the same thing. God is life."

" Live searching after God, and then there will be no life without God." And stronger than ever all was lighted up within me and about me, and that light no longer abandoned me.

Thus I was saved from suicide. When and how this transformation took place in me I could not say. Just as imperceptibly and by degrees as my force of life had waned, and I had arrived at the impossibility of living, at the arrest of life, at the necessity of suicide, just so by degrees and imperceptibly did that force of life return to me. Strange to say, the force of life which returned to me was not a new, but the same old force which had drawn me on in the first period of my life.

I returned in everything to the most remote, the child-ish and the youthful. I returned to the belief in that will which had produced me and which wanted something of me; I returned to this, that the chief and only purpose of my life was to be better, that is, to live more in accord with that will; I returned to this, that the expression of this will I could find in that which all humanity had worked out for its guidance in the vanishing past, that is, I returned to the faith in God, in moral perfection, and in the tradition which had handed down the meaning of life. There was only this difference, that formerly it had been assumed unconsciously, while now I knew that I could not live without it.

This is what seemed to have happened with me: I do not remember when I was put in a boat, was pushed off from some unknown shore, had pointed out to me the direction toward another shore, had a pair of oars given into my inexperienced hands, and was left alone. I plied my oars as well as I could, and moved on; but the farther I rowed toward the middle, the swifter did the current become which bore me away from my goal, and the more frequently did I come across oarsmen like myself, who were carried away by the current. There were lonely oarsmen, who continued to row; there were large boats, immense ships, full of people; some struggled against the current, others submitted to it. The farther I rowed, the more did I look down the current, whither all those boats were carried, and forget the direction which had been pointed out to me. In the middle of the current, in the crush of the boats and ships which bore me down, I lost my direction completely and threw down the oars. On every side of me sailing vessels and rowboats were borne down the current with merriment and rejoicing, and the people in them assured me and each other that there could not even be any other direction, and I believed them and went down the stream with them. I was carried far away, so far away, that I heard the noise of the rapids where I should be wrecked, and saw boats that had already been wrecked there. I regained my senses. For a long time I could not understand what had happened with me. I saw before me nothing but ruin toward which I was rushing and of which I was afraid; nowhere did I see any salvation, and I did not know what to do; but, on looking back, I saw an endless number of boats that without cessation stubbornly crossed the current, and I thought of the shore, the oars, and the direction, and began to make my way back, up the current and toward the shore.

That shore was God, the direction was tradition, the oars were the freedom given me to row toward the shore, — to unite myself with God. Thus the force of life was renewed in me, and I began to live once more.

XIII.

I RENOUNCED the life of our circle, having come to recognize that that was not life, but only a likeness of life, that the conditions of superabundance in which we lived deprived us of the possibility of understanding life, and that, in order that I might understand life, I had to understand not the life of the exceptions, not of us, the parasites of life, but the life of the simple working classes, of those who produced life, and the meaning which they ascribed to it. The simple working classes about me were the Russian masses, and I turned to them and to the meaning which they ascribed to life. This meaning, if it can be expressed, was like this:

Every man has come into this world by the will of God. God has so created man that every man may either ruin his soul or save it. The problem of each man in life is to save his soul; in order to save his soul, he must live according to God's command, and to live according to God's command, he must renounce all the solaces of life, must work, be humble, suffer, and be merciful. The masses draw this meaning from the whole doctrine, transmitted to them by past and present pastors and by tradition, which lives among the masses.

This meaning was clear to me and near to my heart. But with this meaning of the popular faith, our non-dissenting masses, among whom I lived, inseparably connect much which repelled me and seemed inexplicable to me: the sacraments, the church service, the fasts, the worshipping of relics and images. The masses cannot separate

72

one from the other, nor could I. No matter how strange seemed to me much of what entered into the faith of the masses, I accepted everything, attended services, stood up in the morning and in the evening to pray, fasted, prepared myself for the communion, and at first my reason did not revolt against all that. What formerly had seemed impossible to me, now did not provoke any opposition in me.

My relations toward the faith now and then were quite different. Formerly life itself had appeared to me full of meaning, and faith had appeared to me as an arbitrary assertion of certain entirely unnecessary and irrational principles which were not connected with life. I had asked myself then what meaning these principles had, and, on convincing myself that they had none, I had rejected them. But now, on the contrary, I knew firmly that my life had no meaning and could have none, and the principles of faith not only did not appear to me as unnecessary, but I had been brought by incontestable experience to the conviction that only those principles of faith gave a meaning to life. Formerly I used to look upon them as upon an entirely useless, confused mass of writing, but now, though I did not understand them, I knew that there was a meaning in them, and I said to myself that I must learn to understand them.

I made the following reflection: I said to myself that the knowledge of faith flowed, like all humanity with its reason, from a mysterious beginning. This beginning is God, the beginning of the human body and of man's reason. Just as my body has devolved to me from God, thus my reason and my comprehension of life have reached me, and so all those stages of the development of the comprehension of life cannot be false. Everything which people believe sincerely must be the truth; it may be differently expressed, but it cannot be a lie, and so, if it presents itself to me as a lie, it means only that I do

not understand it.   Besides, I said to myself : the essence
of every faith consists in giving to life a meaning which
is not destroyed by death.   Naturally, in order that faith
may answer the question of a king dying in luxury, of an
old slave worn out by work, of an unthinking child, of a
wise old man, of a half-witted old woman, of a happy
young woman, of a youth swayed by passions, of all men
under all the most varied conditions of life and education,
— naturally, if there is one answer which replies to the
eternal question of life, " Why do I live, and what will
become of my life ? " — this question, though one in its
essence, must be endlessly diversified in its manifestations,
and, the more this answer is one, the more sincere and
profound it is, the stranger and the more contorted it
must, naturally, appear in its attempts at expression,
according to the education and position of each individual.
But these reflections, which for me justified the strangeness
of the ritualistic side of faith, were none the less insufficient to permit me in what for me was the only business
of life, in faith, to commit acts of which I was doubtful.
I wanted with all the forces of my soul to be able to
become one with the masses, by executing the ritualistic
side of their faith ; but I was unable to do so.   I felt
that I should be lying to myself and making light of what
for me was holy, if I did it.   But here I was aided by the
new Russian theological works.

These theologians show that the fundamental dogma of
faith is the infallible church.   From the recognition of this
dogma follows, as its necessary consequence, the truth of
everything professed by the church.   The church as a
collection of believers united in love and, therefore, in
possession of the true knowledge, became the foundation
of my faith.   I said to myself that divine truth could not
be accessible to one person, — that it was revealed only
to a totality of men united in love.   In order to attain
truth, we must not divide ; and in order not to divide, we

must love and make peace with what we disagree with. Truth will be revealed to love, and so, if you do not submit to the ritual of the church, you impair love; and if you impair love, you are deprived of the possibility of discovering the truth. At that time I did not see the sophism which was contained in that reflection. I did not see that the union in love could give the greatest love, but by no means divine truth as it is expressed in definite words in the Nicene Symbol; nor did I at all see that love could in any way make a certain expression of truth obligatory for union. At that time I did not see the mistakes of that reasoning and, thanks to it, I found it possible to receive and execute all the rites of the Orthodox Church, without understanding the greater part of them. I tried then with all the powers of my soul to avoid all reflections and contradictions, and tried to explain, as reasonably as possible, those church rules with which I came in contact.

In executing the rites of the church, I humbled reason and submitted myself to that tradition which all humanity had. I allied myself with my ancestors, with my beloved parents and grandparents. They and all those before them had believed and had procreated me. I allied myself also with millions of people from the masses, whom I respected. Besides, these acts had nothing bad in themselves (bad I called a pampering of the appetites). In getting up early for church service, I knew that I was doing well, if for no other reason, because in humbling the pride of my reason, and in allying myself with my ancestors and contemporaries, in the name of finding the meaning of life, I sacrificed my bodily rest. The same happened while I was preparing myself for communion, while I was saying the daily prayers and making the obeisances, while I was observing all the fasts. No matter how insignificant these sacrifices were, they were brought in the name of what was good. I prepared myself for communion, fasted, observed the proper prayers at home and at church. While listening to divine service, I tried to grasp every word of it and gave it a meaning every time I could. At mass the most important words for me were: " Let us love each other in unity of thought !" The following words, " In singleness of thought we profess the Father and the Son and the Holy Ghost," I omitted, because I could not understand them.

XIV.

It was so necessary for me at that time to believe in order to exist that I unconsciously concealed from myself the contradictions and obscurities of the doctrine. But there was a limit to these attempts to elucidate the rites. If the responsory became clearer and clearer to me in its main words; if I managed to explain to myself in some way the words, "And having mentioned our Lady the Most Holy Mother of God and all the saints, we shall give ourselves, and one another, and our lives to Christ the God;" if I explained the frequent repetitions of the prayers for the Tsar and his relatives by assuming that they were more than others subject to temptation and so needed more praying for, — the prayers about vanquishing the enemy and foe, even though I explained them on the ground that an enemy was an evil, — these prayers and many others, like the Cherubical prayers and the whole sacrament of the offertory or "To the chosen leader," and so forth, almost two-thirds of the service, either had no explanation at all, or I felt that, finding explanations for them, I was lying and thus entirely destroyed my relation to God, and was losing every possibility of faith.

The same I experienced in celebrating the chief holidays. To remember the Sabbath, that is, devote one day to communion with God, was comprehensible to me. But this chief holiday was a celebration of the event of the resurrection, the reality of which I could not imagine or comprehend. And by this name of resurrection the day which is celebrated each week is called in Russian, and on those days took place the sacrament of the eucharist, which was absolutely incomprehensible to me. All the other twelve holidays, except Christmas, were in commemoration of miracles, which I tried not to think of in order not to deny : Ascension Day, Pentecost, Epiphany, the feast of the Intercession of the Holy Virgin, and so forth. In celebrating these holidays and feeling that an importance was ascribed to what to me formed and were the opposite of important, I tried either to discover explanations which would soothe me, or I shut my eyes, in order not to see what was offensive to me.

This happened very strongly with me in the most usual sacraments which are regarded as most important, at christening and at communion. Here I came in contact, not with incomprehensible, but absolutely comprehensible actions : the actions seemed offensive to me, and I was placed in a dilemma, either to lie, or reject them.

I shall never forget the agonizing feeling which I experienced on the day when I went to communion for the first time after many years. The services, the confession, the rules, — all that was comprehensible to me and produced in me a pleasurable consciousness of having the meaning of life revealed to me. The communion itself I explained to myself as an action performed in commemoration of Christ and signifying the purification from sin and the full acceptance of the teaching of Christ. If this explanation was artificial, I did not perceive its artificiality. It was so pleasurable for me to humble and abase myself before the spiritual father, a simple, timid priest, and to turn out all the dirt of my soul to him, while repenting all my vices ; so pleasurable to blend in thought with the humility of the Fathers who had written the prayers of the rules ; so pleasurable to become one with all believers, past and present, that I did not feel the artificiality of my explanation. But when I approached the

Royal Doors, and the priest made me repeat that I believed that what I was going to swallow was the real body and blood, I was cut to the quick; that was not merely a false note, it was a cruel demand made by one who apparently had never known what faith was.

It is only now that I permit myself to say that it was a cruel demand; at that time I did not even think of it, — then it merely pained me inexpressibly. I was no longer in that condition in which I had been in my youth, thinking that everything in life was clear; I had arrived at faith because outside of faith I had found nothing, absolutely nothing, but certain perdition, and so it was not possible to reject that faith, and I submitted to it. I found in my soul a feeling which helped me to bear it. That was the feeling of self-abasement and humility. I humbled myself and swallowed this blood and body without any blasphemous feeling, with the desire to believe, but the blow had been given to me. Knowing in advance what was awaiting me, I could not go there a second time.

I continued to do the rites of the church and still believed that in the faith which I was following there was the truth, and in me took place what now is clear to me, but then seemed strange to me.

When I listened to the conversation of an illiterate peasant, of a pilgrim, about God, about faith, about life, about salvation, the knowledge of the faith was revealed to me. When I came in contact with the masses and heard their opinions about life and about faith, I understood the truth more and more. The same was true during the reading of the menaions and of the prologues, for they became my favourite reading. Leaving out the miracles, upon which I looked as upon fables expressing an idea, this reading disclosed the meaning of life to me. There I found the lives of Macarius the Great, of Prince Ioasaph (the history of Buddha), there were the words of

John Chrysostom, the stories of the traveller in the well, of the monk who had found the gold, of Peter the Martyr; there was the history of the martyrs, all of whom proclaimed one and the same, that death did not exclude life; there was the history of those who were illiterate and foolish and ignorant of the doctrine of the church, and yet had been saved.

But I needed only to come in contact with learned believers, or to take their books, and a doubt of myself, dissatisfaction, a madness of quarrelling, arose in me, and I felt that the more I entered into their speeches, the more did I depart from the truth and walk toward the precipice.

XV.

How often had I envied the peasants their illiteracy and ignorance! From those statements of the faith from which for me resulted apparent absurdities, there resulted nothing false to them; they could accept them and could believe the truth, that truth in which I myself believed. For me, unfortunate man, alone it was evident that the truth was bound up with the lie with thin threads, and that I could not accept it in such a form.

Thus I lived for three years, and at first, when I, like a catechumen, approached truth by degrees, guided only by feeling on my path toward the light, these conflicts did not startle me so much. Whenever I did not understand a thing, I said to myself, "I am guilty, I am bad." But the more I began to be permeated by the truths which I studied, the more did they become a basis of life, the more oppressive and striking did the conflicts grow, and the sharper did the line stand out between what I did not understand, because I could not understand it, and that which could not be understood otherwise than by lying to myself.

In spite of these doubts and sufferings, I still clung to Orthodoxy. But there appeared questions of life, which it became necessary to solve, and here the solution of these questions by the church — contrary to the very foundations of the faith in which I believed — made me definitely renounce all communion with Orthodoxy. These questions were, in the first place, the relation of the Orthodox Church to the other churches, to Catholi-

cism and to the so-called dissenters.   During that time I,
on account of my interest in religion, came in contact
with believers of different creeds, with Catholics, Protestants, Old Ceremonialists, Milkers, and so forth, and
among them I found a large number of morally elevated
men and sincere believers.   I wanted to be a brother to
these people.   What happened ?   The tenet which promised to me that it would unite all in one faith and love,
the same tenet, in the person of its best representatives,
told me that all these people were living in the lie, that
what gave them the strength of life was the temptation of
the devil, and that we alone were in possession of the
only possible truth.   I saw that the Orthodox people regarded all those who did not profess the same faith with
them as heretics, precisely as the Catholics regarded Orthodoxy as a heresy ; I saw that toward all who did not
profess faith with external symbols and words, as Orthodoxy did, Orthodoxy, though trying to conceal it, assumed
a hostile attitude, which could not be otherwise, for, in the
first place, the assertion that you are living in a lie, while
I have the truth, is the most cruel of words which one
man can say to another, and, in the second place, because
a man who loves his children and brothers cannot help
assuming a hostile attitude toward people who wish to
convert his children and brothers to a false faith.   This
hostility increases in proportion as the knowledge of the
doctrine increases.   And I, who had assumed the truth to
be in the union of love, was involuntarily startled to find
that that religious teaching destroyed precisely that which
it ought to build up.

The offence is so manifest to us educated people, who
have lived in countries where several religions are professed,
and who have seen that contemptuous, self-confident, imperturbable negative attitude which a Catholic assumes
toward an Orthodox or a Protestant and an Orthodox
toward a Catholic or a Protestant, and a Protestant to-

ward both the others, and the same relation among the Old Ceremonialists, Pashkovians, Shakers, and members of all religions, that the very manifestedness of the offence at first seems perplexing. You say to yourself : " It cannot be so simple and yet that people should not see that when two statements mutually negate each other, neither the one nor the other can have the one truth which faith must have. There must be something wrong in it. There must be some explanation." I was sure there was, and I tried to find that explanation, and read everything I could in regard to this matter and took counsel with everybody I could. I received no explanation except the one which makes the Súmski hussars think that the first regiment in the world is that of the Súmski hussars, while the yellow hussars think that the first regiment in the world is that of the yellow hussars. The clerical persons of all different creeds, their best representatives, told me nothing but that they believed that they had the truth, while the others were in error, and that all they could do was to pray for the others. I went to see archimandrites, bishops, hermits, ascetics, and asked them, and not one of them made even an attempt at explaining that offensive state of affairs. Only one of them explained everything to me, but he explained it in such a way that I did not ask others after that.

I have said that for every unbeliever who turns toward religion (all our young generation is subject to making this search), this appears as the first question : Why is the truth not in Lutheranism, not in Catholicism, but in Orthodoxy ? He is taught in the gymnasium, and he cannot help knowing — what the peasants do not know — that a Protestant or Catholic professes in the same way the one truth of his own religion. Historical proofs, which by each religion are bent in its favour, are insufficient. Is it not possible, I said, to look at the teaching from a more elevated point, so that from the height of the teaching all differences may disappear, as they disappear for the true believer ? Can we not proceed on the path on which we have started with the Old Ceremonialists ? They assert that the cross, the hallelujah, and the procession around the altar as we practise them are wrong. We say : " You believe in the Nicene Symbol and the seven sacraments as we do, so let us stick to that, and in everything else do as you please." We have united with them by putting the essential in faith above the unessential. Now why can we not say to the Catholics, " You believe in this and that, which is the chief thing, but in relation to *Filioque* and the Pope do as you please " ? Can we not say the same to the Protestants, by agreeing with them on the chief points ? My interlocutor agreed with me, but he said that such concessions would produce a disaffection toward the spiritual power because of its departing from the ancestral faith, whereas it was the business of the spiritual power to preserve in all its purity the Græco-Russian Orthodox faith as transmitted to it from antiquity.

I understood it all. I was looking for faith, for the power of life, and they were looking for the best means of performing before people certain human obligations, and, in performing these human works, they performed them in a human manner. Let them say as much as they please about their compassion for their erring brothers, about praying for them before the throne of the Highest, — for the performance of human acts force is needed, and that has always been applied and always will be applied. If two creeds consider themselves right, they will preach their teachings, and if a lying doctrine is preached to the inexperienced sons of the church which is in the truth, the church cannot help burning the books and removing the man who is seducing her sons. What is to be done with that sectarian who, in the opinion of Orthodoxy, of religion, is burning with a false fire and in the most important matter of life, in religion, is seducing the sons of the church ? What else can be done with him but have his head chopped off or him imprisoned ? In the time of Alexis Mikháylovich they burned him at the stake, that is, they applied the greatest punishment of that time ; in our day they also apply the greatest punishment, by putting him in solitary confinement. I turned my attention to what was being done in the name of religion, and I was frightened and almost entirely renounced Orthodoxy.

The second relation of the church to vital questions was its relation to war and capital punishment.

Just then Russia had a war on its hands and Russians began to kill their brothers in the name of Christian love. It was impossible not to think of it. It was impossible not to see that murder was an evil which was contrary to the first foundations of any religion. And yet they prayed in the churches for the success of our arms, and the teachers of religion acknowledged this murder as a business which resulted from faith. And not only were there these murders in the war, but during all the disturbances, which followed after the war, I saw the orders of the church, her teachers, monks, and hermits, approve the murder of erring, helpless youths. I turned my attention to what was done by men who professed Christianity, and I was horrified.

XVI.

I STOPPED doubting: I was completely convinced that in that knowledge of faith which I had accepted not everything was true. Formerly I should have said that the whole doctrine was wrong, but now I could not say so. The whole nation had the knowledge of the truth, — so much was certain, — or else it could not live. Besides, this knowledge of the truth was now accessible to me, and I had lived with it and had felt all its truth; but in this knowledge there was also a lie. Of that I could have no doubt. Everything which before that had repelled me now stood vividly up before me. Although I saw that in the masses there was less of that alloy of the lie which repelled me than in the representatives of the church, — I nevertheless saw that in the beliefs of the masses the lie was mixed in with the truth.

Whence had come the lie, and whence the truth? Both the lie and the truth are to be found in tradition, in the so-called Holy Tradition and Scripture. The lie and the truth have been transmitted by what is called the church. Willy-nilly I was led to the study, the investigation, of this Scripture and Tradition, — an investigation of which heretofore I had been so much afraid.

I turned to the study of that theology which at one time I had rejected with such contempt, as something useless. At that time it had appeared to me as a series of useless absurdities; at that time I was on all sides surrounded by phenomena of life which had seemed clear to me and filled with meaning; now I should have been glad to reject what would not go into my head, but there was no way out. On this doctrine is reared, — or with it, at least, is insolubly connected, — that one knowledge of the meaning of life which has been revealed to me. However strange this may be for my old, settled head, this is the one hope of salvation. I must carefully, attentively analyze it, in order that I may understand it, — not as I understand a statement of science, — that I am not looking for, nor can I look for it, knowing the peculiarity of the knowledge of faith. I am not going to look for an explanation of everything. I know that the explanation of everything must, like the beginning of everything, be lost in infinity. But I want to understand in such a way as to be brought to what is inevitably inexplicable; I want everything which is inexplicable to be such, not because the demands of my reason are incorrect (they are correct, and outside of them I cannot understand anything), but because I see the limitations of my mind. I want to comprehend in such a way that every inexplicable statement may present itself to me as a necessity of my reason and not as an obligation to believe.

That in the teaching there is truth, there can be no doubt for me; but it is equally certain to me that it also contains the lie, and I must find the truth and the lie and separate one from the other. And to this I proceed. What I have found in this teaching that is false, what truth I have found in it, and to what conclusions I have been drawn, forms the following parts of a work which, if it deserves it and anybody needs it, will no doubt be printed somewhere at some future time.

1879.

THIS was written by me three years ago. Those parts will be printed.

Now, the other day as I looked over and returned to that train of thought and to those feelings which were in me when I passed through all that, I had a dream. This dream expressed to me in concise form what I had lived through and described, and so I think that for those who have understood me the description of this dream will refresh and collect into one all that has been at such a length told in these pages. Here is the dream.

I see that I am lying on my bed. I feel neither well nor ill: I am lying on my back. But I begin to think whether it is right for me to lie down; my legs somehow do not feel comfortable: either I have not enough space to stretch them or the bed is not even,— in any case I feel uncomfortable; I move my legs and at the same time begin to consider how and on what I am lying, which has never occurred to me before. I examine my bed, and I see that I am lying on plaited rope strips that are attached to the side pieces of the bed. My feet are lying on one such strip, my thighs on another,— my legs are just uncomfortable. For some reason I know that these strips may be moved, and with the motion of my legs I push away the extreme strip under my feet, thinking that it will be more comfortable that way. But I have pushed it away too far, and I try to fetch it back with a motion of my legs, when the strip under my thighs slips away, too, and my legs hang down. I move my whole body in order to get myself in a good position, quite sure that I will fix myself right; but with this motion other strips slip away and change their positions under me, and I see that the matter is only getting worse: the whole lower part of my body slips and hangs down, but my feet do not reach the ground. I hold on only with the upper part of my back, and I feel not only uncomfortable, but for some reason also nauseated. It is only then that I ask myself what before has not entered my head. I ask myself: " Where am I, and on what am I lying ? " I look around and first of all glance beneath me, where my body hangs down, and whither, I feel, I must drop at once. I look down and do not believe my eyes. I am not only on a height, which is like the top of a very high tower or mountain, but on a height such as I could never have imagined.

I cannot make out whether I see anything down below, in that bottomless pit, over which I am hanging, and whither I am being drawn. My heart is compressed, and I experience terror. It is terrible to look there. If I look down, I feel that I shall at once slip from my last strip, and perish. I do not look. But not to look is even worse, for I think of what will happen to me if I slip down from the last strip. I feel that terror makes me lose my last hold, and slowly my back slips lower and lower. Another moment and I shall fall off. Just then the thought occurs to me that it cannot be the truth. It is a dream. Awaken ! I try to awaken, but I cannot. What shall I do, what shall I do ? I ask myself, and look up. Above there is also an abyss. I look into this abyss of the heaven, and try to forget the abyss below me, and indeed I am successful. The infinity below repels and frightens me; the infinity above me attracts and confirms. I am still hanging over the pit on the last strips which have not yet slipped out from under me; I know that I am hanging, but I look only up, and my terror disappears. As frequently happens in a dream, a voice says to me:

"Observe! It is it!"

And I look farther and farther into the infinity above me, and I feel that I am calming down; I remember everything which has happened, and I recall how it has all happened, — how I moved my legs, how I hung down, how I became frightened, and how I saved myself from terror by looking up. And I ask myself: "Well, am I now still hanging in the same way? I do not so much look around as feel with my whole body the point of support on which I am suspended. I see that I no longer hang or fall, but am firmly held. I ask myself how I am held; I feel around and look about me, and I see that beneath me, under the middle of my body, there is one strip, and that, looking up, I lie on it in the most stable equilibrium, and that it is that strip alone that has been holding me up all the while.

As happens in a dream, I now see the mechanism by means of which I am held, and I find it very natural, comprehensible, and incontestable, although in waking this mechanism has no meaning whatever. In my sleep I even wonder how it was that I could not understand it before. It turns out that at my head there is a pillar, and the stability of this pillar is subject to no doubt, although this slender pillar has nothing to stand on. Then there is a loop which is ingeniously and yet simply attached to the pillar, and if you lie with the middle of your body in this loop and look up, there cannot even be a question about falling. All that was clear to me, and I was happy and calm. It was as though some one were saying to me: "Remember! Do not forget!"

And I awoke.

1882.

CRITIQUE OF DOGMATIC THEOLOGY

1881–1882

CRITIQUE OF DOGMATIC THEOLOGY

PREFACE

I WAS inevitably led to the investigation of the doctrine of the faith of the Orthodox Church. In the communion with the Orthodox Church I had found salvation from despair. I was firmly convinced that in this doctrine lay the only truth, but many, very many, manifestations of this doctrine, which were contrary to those fundamental concepts which I had about God and his law, compelled me to turn to the study of the doctrine itself.

I did not then assume that the doctrine was false, — I was afraid of supposing that, — for one untruth in that doctrine destroyed the whole doctrine, and then I should lose the main support which I had found in the church as the carrier of truth, as the source of that knowledge of the meaning of life which I was trying to find in faith. So I began to study the books which expounded the Orthodox doctrine. In all those works the doctrine, in spite of the diversity of details and some difference in consecutiveness, is one and the same ; so, too, the connection between the parts and the fundamental principle is one and the same.

I read and studied those books, and here is the feeling

which I have carried away from that study. If I had not been led by life to the inevitable necessity of faith; if I had not seen that this faith formed the foundation of the life of all men ; if this feeling, shattered by life, had not been strengthened anew in my heart; if the foundation of my faith had been only confidence ; if there were within me only the faith of which theology speaks (taught to believe), I, after reading these books, not only would have turned an atheist, but should have become a most malignant enemy of every faith, because I found in these doctrines not only nonsense, but the conscious lie of men who had chosen the faith as a means for obtaining certain ends.

The reading of these books has cost me a terrible labour, not so much on account of the effort which I was making in order to understand the connection between the expressions, the one which the people who wrote them saw, as on account of the inner struggle which I had to carry on all the time with myself, in order, as I read these books, to abstain from indignation.

I used up a great deal of paper, analyzing word after word, at first the Symbol of Faith, then Filarét's Catechism, then the Epistle of the Eastern Patriarchs, then Makári's Introduction to Theology, and then his Dogmatic Theology. A serious, scientific tone, such as these books, particularly the new ones, like Makári's Theology, are written in, was impossible during the analysis of these books. It was impossible to condemn or reject the ideas expressed, because it was impossible to catch a single clearly expressed idea. The moment I got ready to take hold of an idea, in order to pass ·judgment upon it, it slipped away from me, because it was purposely expressed obscurely, and I involuntarily returned to the analysis of the expression of the idea itself, — when it appeared that there was no definite idea ; the words had not the meaning which they generally have in language, but a special one, the definition of which was not tangible. The definition or elucidation of a thought, if there was any, was always in a reverse sense; to define or clear up a difficult word use was made of a word or series of words entirely incomprehensible. For a long time I wavered in doubt, did not permit myself to deny what I did not understand, and with all the forces of mind and soul tried to understand that teaching in the same way as those understood it who said that they believed in it, and demanded that others, too, should believe in it. This was the more difficult for me, the more detailed and quasi-scientific the exposition was.

When I read the Symbol of Faith in church Slavic, in its word-for-word translation from the obscure Greek text, I managed somehow to combine my conceptions of faith, but when I read the Epistle of the Eastern Patriarchs, who express those dogmas more in detail, I was unable to combine my conceptions of faith, and was almost unable to make out what was meant by the words which I read. With the reading of the Catechism this disagreement and lack of comprehension increased. When I read the Theology, at first Damascene's and then Makári's, my lack of comprehension and my disagreement reached its farthest limits. But at last I began to understand the external connection which united those words, and that train of thoughts which had guided the writer, and the reason why I could not agree with them.

I worked over it for a long time and finally reached a point when I knew the Theology like a good seminarist, and I am able, following the trend of the thoughts which have guided the authors, to explain the foundation of everything, the connection between the separate dogmas, and the meaning in this connection of every dogma, and, above all, I am able to explain why such and not another connection, strange as it is, was chosen. When I attained to that, I was shocked. I saw that all that doctrine was an artificial code (composed from the mere external, most inexact terms) of the expressions of the beliefs of a great variety of men, discordant among themselves and mutually contradictory. I saw that harmonization was of no use to anybody, that nobody could ever believe all that doctrine, and never did, and that, therefore, there must be some external purpose in the impossible combination of these various doctrines into one and in promulgating them as truth. I even comprehended that purpose. I also understood why this doctrine was sure to produce atheists in the seminaries, where it is taught, and I understood the strange feeling which I experienced while reading those books. I had read the so-called blasphemous works of Voltaire and Hume, but never had I experienced such an undoubted conviction of the full faithlessness of a man as what I experienced in reference to the composers of the Catechisms and the Theologies. When you read in these works the quotations from the apostles and the so-called fathers of the church, of which the Theology is composed, you see that those are expressions of believing men, you hear the voice of their heart, in spite of the awkwardness, crudity, and at times falseness of their expressions; but when you read the words of the compiler, it becomes clear to you that the compiler did not care at all for the sincere meaning of the expression quoted by him, — he does not even try to comprehend it. All he needs is a casual word, in order to attach by means of it an idea of the apostle to an expression of Moses or of a new father of the church. All he wants is to form such a code as will make it appear that everything which is written in the so-called Holy Scriptures and in the fathers of the church was written only in order to prove the Symbol of Faith. And so I came at last to see that all that doctrine, the one in which, I then thought, the faith of the masses was expressed, was not only a lie, but also a deception, which had taken form through the ages and had a definite, base purpose.

Here is that doctrine. I expound it according to the Symbol of Faith, the Epistle of the Eastern Patriarchs, Filarét's Catechism, and, mainly, Makári's Dogmatic Theology, a book which the church regards as the best dogmatic theology.

FIRST PART OF THE DOGMATIC THEOLOGY

I.

THE Introduction consists of the exposition of (1) the aim, (2) the subject, (3) the origin of the Orthodox Christian dogmas, (4) the division of the dogmas, (5) the character of the plan and method, (6) a sketch of the history of the science of dogmatic theology.

Though the Introduction does not speak of the subject, it cannot be omitted, because it defines in advance what will be expounded in the whole book and how it will be expounded.

"1.   The Orthodox dogmatic theology, taken in the sense of a science, has to expound the Christian dogmas in a systematic order with the greatest fulness, clearness, and thoroughness possible, and, of course, only in the spirit of the Orthodox Church.

"2.   Under the name of Christian dogmas are understood the revealed truths which are transmitted to men by the church as incontestable and invariable rules of the saving faith."

Farther on it explains that revealed truths are called the truths which are found in tradition and in the Scriptures.   Tradition and the Scriptures are recognized as truths because the church recognizes them as such, and the church is recognized as a truth because it recognizes these, Tradition and the Scriptures.

"3.   From the conception given about the Christian

dogmas it appears that they have all a divine origin. Consequently, no one has the right either to multiply or diminish their number, or to change and transform them in any manner whatsoever: as many as were revealed by God in the beginning, so many must there remain of them for all time, as long as Christianity shall exist."

Revealed in the very beginning. It does not say what is meant by "revealed in the very beginning." In the beginning of the world, or in the beginning of Christianity? In either case, when was that beginning? It says that the dogmas did not appear one after another, but all at once, in the beginning, but when that beginning was, it does not say, neither here, nor anywhere else in the whole book. It goes on:

" But, although they remain invariable in their revelation, both as to their number and their essence, the dogmas of the church have none the less to be disclosed, and are disclosed, in the church to the believers. Ever since men have begun to make these dogmas, which were handed down through revelation, their own, and to draw them into the circle of their ideas, these sacred truths began inevitably to be modified in the concepts of various entities (the same happens with any truth when it becomes the possession of man), — inevitably there had to appear, and did appear, various opinions, various misconceptions in regard to the dogmas, even various mutilations of the dogmas, or heresies, intentional and unintentional. In order to guard the believers against all that, to show them what and how they should believe on the basis of the revelation, the church has from the very beginning offered to them, by tradition from the holy apostles themselves, short models of faith, or symbols."

The dogmas are invariable in number and essence, and were revealed in the beginning, and, at the same time, they have to be disclosed. That is incomprehensible, and still more incomprehensible is this, that before it said simply " in the beginning," and we assumed, with the Theology, that it was from the beginning of everything ; but now the beginning is referred to the beginning of Christianity. Besides, these words give us the very meaning which the author has denied in the beginning. There it said, in the beginning everything was revealed, and here it says that the dogmas are disclosed by the church, and toward the end it says that the church *has* from the very beginning (of something) *offered*, not the church *offered* from the beginning, by tradition from the holy apostles, short models of faith, or symbols, that is, there appears an internal contradiction. It is evident that by the word " dogma " two mutually excluding ideas are understood. According to the definition of the Theology, a dogma is a truth as taught by the church. According to this definition dogmas may be disclosed, as the author, indeed, says they are, that is, they may appear, be modified, become more complicated, as has happened in reality. But the author, having evidently given an inexact definition to the word " dogma," by saying that it is a teaching of the truth, instead of saying a teaching of that which is regarded as the truth, or even by saying simply that the dogma is a truth of faith, has given to the dogma still another meaning which excludes the first, and so has been drawn into a contradiction. But the author needs this contradiction. He wants to understand by dogma the truth in itself, the absolute truth, and a truth as expressed by certain words. This contradiction is necessary in order that, teaching what the church regards as truth, it shall be possible to assert that what it teaches is the absolute truth. This false reasoning is important not only because it inevitably leads to contradiction and excludes all possibility of a rational exposition, but also because it involuntarily rouses suspicion in regard to the consequent exposition. According to the definition of the church, a dogma is a revealed divine truth, taught by the church for the sake of the saving faith. I am a man of God. In revealing this truth, God has revealed it to me, too. I am in search of the saving faith, and what I say to myself, billions of people have said. Then, teach it to me! The truths are revealed by God (revealed to me as much as to you), so how can I help believing these truths and accepting them? This is all I want, and they are divine. So teach them to me! Don't be afraid that I will reject them. But the church seems to be afraid that I may reject what is necessary for my salvation and wants to compel me in advance to assert that all the dogmas which it may teach me are truths. There can be no doubt that what God has revealed to men who are in search of him is truth. Give me these truths! But here, instead of the truths, I receive a bit of intentionally incorrect reasoning, the purpose of which is to assure me in advance that everything which I am going to be told is the truth. Instead of vanquishing me in favour of the truth, this reasoning has the opposite effect upon me. It is evident to me that the reasoning is irregular, and that they want to assure themselves in advance of my confidence in what they are going to tell me. But how do I know that what I am to be taught as a truth is not a lie? I know that in the Dogmatic Theology, and in the Catechism, and in the Epistle of the Eastern Patriarchs, and even in the Symbol of Faith there is, among the number of dogmas, one about the holy, infallible church, which is guided by the Holy Ghost, and which is the keeper of the dogmas. If the dogmas cannot be expounded in themselves, but only by leaning on the dogma of the church, they ought to begin with the dogma of the church. If everything is based upon it, they ought to say so and begin with it, and not place, beginning with the 1st article, as is done here, the dogma of the church at the foundation of everything, without mentioning it except in passing, as something well known, and not as is done in Filarét's Catechism, Chapter III., where it says that God's revelation is preserved in the church by means of tradition. The church is composed of all who are united by faith in tradition, and it is they who are united by tradition that keep the tradition.

Tradition is always preserved by those who believe in the tradition. That is always so. But is it right, — is it not a lie? And that care with which, without saying anything about the dogmas, they want to catch in advance my agreement to every dogma, compels me to be on guard. I do not say that I do not believe in the holiness and infallibility of the church. At the time when I began this investigation I fully believed in it, in it alone (it seemed to me that I believed). But it is necessary to know what is to be understood by the church and in any case, if everything is to be based on the dogma of the church, to begin with it, as Khomyakóv has done. But if they do not begin with the dogma of the church, but with the dogma of God, as is the case in the Symbol of Faith, in the Epistle of the Eastern Patriarchs, in the Catechism, and in all Dogmatic Theologies, they ought to expound the most essential dogmas, the truths revealed by God to men.

I am a man, — God has me, too, in view. I am searching after salvation, how then could I refuse to receive that one thing which I am searching after with all the powers of my soul! I cannot help accepting it, I certainly will accept it. If my union with the church will strengthen it, so much the better. Tell me the truths as you know them! Tell them to me at least as they are told in the Symbol of Faith which we have all learned by heart! If you are afraid that in the dimness and feebleness of my mind, in the corruption of my heart, I shall not understand them, help me (you know these divine truths, — you, the church, are teaching us), help my feeble understanding, but do not forget that, no matter what you may say, you will be talking to the understanding. You will be speaking the divine truths as expressed in words, but the words must again be comprehended only through reason. Elucidate these truths to my understanding ; show me the futility of my objections ; soften my obdurate heart with the irresistible sympathy and striving after the good and the true, which I shall find in you ; and do not catch me with words, with an intentional deception, which impairs the sacredness of the subject of which you speak. I am touched by the prayer of the three hermits, of which the popular legend speaks ; they prayed to God : " There are three of you, three of us, have mercy on us ! " I know that their conception of God is wrong, but I am attracted to them and want to imitate them, just as one feels like laughing, looking at those who laugh, and like yawning, looking at those who yawn, because I feel with all my heart that they are searching after God and do not see the falseness of their expression ; but sophisms, intentional deception, in order to catch in their trap those who are not cautious or firm in reason, repels me.

Indeed, what is before us is the exposition of revealed truths about God, about man, about salvation. The men know that and, instead of expounding what they know, they make a series of false deductions, by which they want to convince us that everything which they are going to say about God, about man, about salvation, will be expressed in such a way that it cannot be expressed in any other way, and that it is impossible not to believe everything they are going to tell me.

Maybe you are going to expound to me a revealed truth, but the method which you use in making the exposition is the same that is applied in the exposition of an intentional lie. Let us zealously look at the truths themselves, — what they consist in, and how they are expressed.

II.

In the Symbol of Faith, in the Epistle of the Eastern Patriarchs, in Filarét's Catechism, in the Dogmatic Theology, the first dogma is the dogma about God. The general title of the first part is: "Of God in himself, and of his general relation to the world and to man (θεολογία ἁπλῆ, that is, simple theology)." That is the title of the first part. The second part will be: "About God the Saviour and about his special relation to the human race (θεολογία οἰκονομική, theology of house-management)."

If I know anything about God, if I have had any conception about him, these two titles of the two parts destroy all my knowledge of God. I cannot connect my conception about God with a conception about a God for whom there exist two different relations to man, — one, general, — the other, special. The concept "special" attached to God destroys my conception about God. If God is the God whom I have comprehended, he can have no special relation to man. But, perhaps, I do not understand the words right, or my conceptions are incorrect. Farther on I read about God: "Division I. Of God in himself." Now I am waiting for the expression of the truth about God, revealed by God to men for their salvation and known to the church. But, before getting an exposition of this revealed truth, I meet with Art. 9, which speaks of the degree of our cognition of God according to the doctrine of the church. This article, like the Introduction, does not speak of the subject itself, but in the same way prepares me to understand what is going to be expounded:

"The Orthodox Church begins all its doctrine about God in the Symbol of Faith with the words, 'I believe,' and the first dogma which it wishes to impart consists in the following: God is incomprehensible to the human intellect; men can know him only in part, — as much as he has been pleased to reveal himself for their faith and piety. An irrefutable truth." (p. 66.)

To those who are not used to this kind of an exposition I must explain (for I myself did not comprehend it for a long time) that by irrefutable truth is to be understood, not that God is incomprehensible, but that he is comprehensible, but comprehensible only in part. In that does the truth lie. This truth, it goes on to say:

"Is clearly expounded in Holy Scripture and is disclosed in detail in the writings of the holy fathers and teachers of the church, on the basis even of common sense. The Holy Books preach on the one hand that (a) God dwelleth in the light which no man can approach unto; whom no man hath seen nor can see (3 Tim. vi. 16); that (b) not only for men, but also for all his creatures his being is unknown, his judgments unsearchable, and his ways past finding out (Rom. xi. 33–34; John i. 18; 1 John iv. 12; Sirach xvii. 3–4), and that (c) God alone knows God: for what man knoweth the things of a man, save the spirit of man which is in him? even so the things of God knoweth no man, but the spirit of God (1 Cor. ii. 11), and no man knoweth the Son, but the Father, neither knoweth any man the Father, save the Son (Matt. xi. 27)." (p. 67.)

On the other hand the Holy Books announce to us that the Invisible and Incomprehensible One was pleased to appear to men, and that God is inaccessible to reason, but that his existence is comprehensible. Here are the truths:

"(a) For the invisible things of him from the creation of the world are clearly seen, being understood by the things that are made, even his eternal power and Godhead (Rom. i. 20; Psalm xix. 1–4; Wis. of Sol. xiii. 1–5), and still more (b), in the supernatural revelation, when he at sundry times and in divers manners spake in time past unto the fathers by the prophets, hath in these last days spoken unto us by his Son (Heb. i. 1–2; Wis. of Sol. ix. 16–19), and when this only-begotten Son of God, appearing on earth in the flesh (1. Tim. iii. 16), gave us light and understanding that we might know the true God (1 John v. 20), and then preached his teaching through the apostles, having sent down upon them the spirit of truth, which searcheth all things, yea, the deep things of God (John xiv. 16–18, 1 Cor. ii. 10). Finally the Holy Books assert that although thus the Son of God, being in the bosom of the Father, hath declared to us God, no man hath seen him (John i. 18)." (p. 68.)

I beg the reader to observe the inexactness of the text. The actual text (John i. 18) runs like this: No man hath seen God at any time; the only-begotten Son, which is in the bosom of the Father, he hath declared him, but nowhere does it say, " being in the bosom of the Father hath declared to us God."

" For now we see the Invisible One as with a glass in divining, and now we know the Incomprehensible One only in part (1 Cor. xiii. 12)."

I beg the reader to observe the incorrectness of this text, too. In the text cited it does not say: " Now we know the Incomprehensible One only in part." It does not say " in part," nor is there a word said about the " Incomprehensible One," and even nothing is said about knowing God, but about love and human knowledge in general. Look at the whole chapter! All this chapter speaks only of human knowledge, which is imperfect, and, evidently, there is no purpose even there of speaking about the knowledge of God.

" Now we walk by faith, not by sight (2 Cor. v. 7)." (p. 68.)

For we walk by faith, not by sight, that is, we live. Here again nothing is said about the knowledge of God in part, but about living by faith.   All these texts are adduced in order to prove that God is incomprehensible and comprehensible only in part.   Again we find here an intentional mixing up of ideas.   The author purposely mixes up two ideas : the comprehensibility of the existence of God and the comprehensibility of God himself. When we speak of the beginning of everything, of God, we evidently recognize and comprehend his existence. But when we speak of God's essence, we obviously cannot comprehend that.   Why then prove that he is comprehensible in part ?   If nothing in the world is completely comprehensible to us, then it is evident that God, the beginning of all beginnings, is absolutely incomprehensible.   Why prove it ? and why prove it in such a strange manner, by adducing incorrect words from John, which prove that no man has ever seen God, and inexact words from Paul, which refer to something quite different, to the proof of the comprehensibility of God in part ?

These strange texts and the strange proofs arise from this, that the word " comprehensibility " is used here and elsewhere in a double sense : in its natural sense of understanding and in the sense of knowledge taken on trust. If the author had understood comprehensibility as comprehensibility, he would not have tried to prove that we comprehend God in part, but would have admitted at once that we cannot comprehend him ; but he understands here by the word " comprehensibility " knowledge taken on faith, purposely mixing up this conception with the conception of the recognition of the existence of God. And so it turns out with him that we can comprehend God in part.   When he adduces the text about our comprehending God through his creations, he has in mind the recognition of God's existence ; but when he quotes the text that " God spoke to the fathers through

the prophets" and then "through the Son," he has in
mind the knowledge which is taken on faith, as we shall
see later on.   For the same reason he quotes Paul's text,
that " we walk by faith," as a proof of comprehensibility,
by which he means the knowledge taken on faith.   By
comprehensibility the author does not understand a more
or less firm conviction of the existence of God, but a
greater or lesser quantity of knowledge about God, though
entirely incomprehensible, taken on faith.   Farther on
he says:

" The holy fathers and the teachers of the church
have disclosed this truth in detail, especially in reference
to the heretical opinions which have arisen in regard to it."

The heretical opinions consist, in the author's opinion,
in this, that God is entirely comprehensible and absolutely
incomprehensible; but the truth, in the author's opinion,
consists in this, that God is incomprehensible, and at the
same time comprehensible in part.   Although the word
" in part " is not at all used in what the author is talking
about, and has not even external authority; although the
word, in the sense in which it is used here, is not even
used in Holy Scripture, the author insists that God is
comprehensible in part, meaning by it that he is known
in part.   How can something comprehensible be known
fully or in part ?   There is an exposition of two opinions
of what is supposed to be extreme heresy: of those who
maintained that God was absolutely comprehensible, and
of others who maintained that God was absolutely incomprehensible, and both opinions are rejected and an argument
is adduced in favour of comprehensibility and incomprehensibility.   In reality, it is clear that neither opinion,
about the absolute comprehensibility and the absolute
incomprehensibility, has ever been expressed, or ever could
be expressed.   In all these seeming arguments pro and
con we find this expressed, that God, by the very fact
that he is mentioned, that he is thought and spoken of,

is recognized as existing.   But, at the same time, since
the conception of God cannot be anything but a conception of the beginning of everything conceived by reason,
it is evident that God, as the beginning of everything,
cannot be comprehended by reason.   Only by following
along the path of rational thinking can God be found
at the extreme limit of reason, but the moment this
conception is reached, reason ceases to comprehend.   It
is this that is expressed in all the passages which are
quoted from Holy Scripture and from the holy fathers,
seemingly for and against the comprehensibility of God.

From the profound, sincere statements of the apostles
and the fathers of the church, which prove only the
incomprehensibility of God, is deduced, in a mere external
manner, the comprehensibility of God.   It is the dialectic
problem of the Theology to prove that God cannot be
comprehended altogether, but that he can be comprehended
" in part."   Not only is the reasoning purposely twisted,
but in these pages I for the first time came across a direct
mutilation, not only of the meaning, but also of the words
of Holy Scripture.   The real text of John i. 18: " No
man hath seen God at any time; the only begotten Son,
which is in the bosom of the Father, he hath declared
him," is rendered by different words.   From the famous
13th chapter of 1 Corinthians, which treats on love, one
verse is quoted in a mutilated form in order to prove the
thesis.

Then follow quotations from the holy fathers: " The
Divinity will be limited if it is comprehended by reason,
for conception is a form of limitation," says one of those
whom the Theology counts among the advocates of incomprehensibility.

" What I call incomprehensible is not that God exists,
but what he is.   Do not use our sincerity as a cause for
atheism," says Gregory the Divine, whom the Theology
counts among the advocates of comprehensibility.

From all this the author concludes that God can be comprehended " in part," meaning by the word " comprehend " to receive the knowledge of him on faith, and proceeds to the exposition of the dogmas which will be a revelation of how God is to be comprehended in part. Like the Introduction, this Art. 9 does not expound the subject at all, but prepares us for the exposition of what follows.   The purpose of this article consists apparently in preparing the reader to renounce his conception of God as God, as incomprehensible by his essence of the beginning of everything, and in preventing his daring to deny that information about God which will be imparted to him as truths based on tradition.   This article concludes with a quotation from St. John Damascene, which expresses the idea of the whole:

" The Deity is unspeakable and incomprehensible, for no man knoweth the Father, but the Son, and no man knoweth the Son, but the Father (Matt. xi. 27).   Even so the Spirit of God knoweth the things of God, just as the spirit of man knoweth the things of a man (1 Cor. ii. 11). Outside of the first blessed being no one has known God, unless God has revealed himself to him, — no one, not only of men, but even of the primordial forces, of the Cherubim and the Seraphim.   However, God has not left us in complete ignorance of himself, for the knowledge of God's existence God himself has implanted in the nature of each.   And creation itself, its keeping and management, proclaim the Deity (Wis. of Sol. xiii. 5).   Besides, at first through the law and the prophets, then through his only-begotten Son, our Lord and God and Saviour Jesus Christ, God has communicated to us the knowledge of himself, in so far as we are able to comprehend him." (p. 73.)

In this conclusion, which expresses the idea of the whole, the internal contradiction is very startling.   In the first part it says that nobody can comprehend God, nobody knows his ways and purposes, and here, in the second part, it says: " Still, God has not left us in ignorance, but through the prophets, his Son, and the apostles has let us know about himself, in so far as we are able to comprehend him." But we have just said that we cannot comprehend God, and here we suddenly assert that we know that he did not wish to leave us in ignorance, that we know the means which he has used for the purpose of attaining his end, that we know the real prophets and the real Son and the real apostles, whom he has sent to instruct us. It turns out that after we have recognized his incomprehensibility, we have suddenly discovered all the details of his purposes, his means. We judge of him as of a master who wants to inform his labourers of something. One or the other: either he is incomprehensible, and then we cannot know his purposes and actions, or he is entirely comprehensible, if we know his prophets and know that these prophets are not false, but real. And so it turns out:

" For this reason everything transmitted to us by the law, the prophets, the apostles, and the evangelists we accept, acknowledge, and respect, and we search after nothing else. Thus God, being omniscient and solicitous of the advantage of all men, has revealed everything which is useful for us to know, and has kept from us what we cannot grasp. Let us be satisfied with this and hold on to it, without removing the eternal landmarks or transgressing the divine Tradition (Prov. xxii. 28)." (p. 74.)

If so, we involuntarily ask ourselves: Why were these prophets and apostles true, and not those who are regarded as false? It turns out that God is incomprehensible and we are absolutely unable to know him, but that he has transmitted the knowledge of himself to men, not to all men, but to the prophets and the apostles, and this knowledge is kept in holy Tradition, and this alone we are to believe, because it alone, the church, is true, that is, those who believe in the Tradition, who observe the Tradition.

In the Introduction we had the same. After long discussions about what a dogma was, the whole business was brought down to this, that a dogma was a truth, because it was taught by the church, and the church were the men who were united by the faith in these dogmas.

We have the same thing here: God may be comprehended in part, a little bit, and how to know him "a little bit" the church alone knows, and everything which it will tell will be a sacred truth.

In the question of the dogma we had a double definition of the dogma, as an absolute truth and as a teaching, and so the contradiction consisted in this, that the dogma was now one unchangeable truth, revealed from the very beginning, and now a teaching of the church, which was evolved by degrees.

Here, in the question of comprehensibility, by which is understood knowledge on trust, as taught by the church, the author contradicts himself. To the word "comprehensibility" a double meaning is ascribed: the meaning of comprehensibility and of knowledge taken on trust. Neither St. John Damascene, nor Filarét, nor Makári can help seeing that for the greater comprehensibility we must have a greater clearness, and the affirmation that what I am told, I am told through people who by the church are called prophets, in no way can add any comprehensibility to the mind, and that we can only comprehend "in part" what is comprehensible, and so they substitute for the concept of comprehensibility the concept of knowledge, and then they say that this knowledge has been transmitted by the prophets, and the question of comprehensibility is entirely set aside; thus, if the knowledge transmitted through the prophets makes God more incomprehensible than he has been to me before, this knowledge is still true. But, in addition to this double definition, we have here also a contradiction between the expressions of the church Tradition itself.

Texts are quoted, and of these some deny the comprehensibility of God, and the others recognize it.   It was
necessary either to reject one or the other, or to harmonize
them.   Theology does neither the one, nor the other, nor
the third, but simply enunciates that everything which is
to follow on the attributes of the divisions of God according to his essence and his persons is the truth, because
thus teaches the infallible church, that is, the Tradition.
Thus, as in the first case, in discussing the Introduction,
all the reasoning appears unnecessary, and all is brought
down to this, that whatever is going to be expounded is
the truth, because the church teaches it; even thus all
the reasoning is unnecessary now, because the foundation
of the whole doctrine is the infallible church.

But here, in addition to this repeated method, for the
first time appears the teaching of the church itself, the
code of that doctrine, and in it we find an absence of
unity, — it contradicts itself.

In the Introduction, the foundation of everything was
assumed to be the church, that is, the tradition of the
men who were united through the tradition, but there I
did not yet know how this tradition was expressed.   Here
appears the Tradition itself, that is, extracts from Holy
Scripture, and these extracts contradict each other and
are connected by nothing but words.

As I said in the beginning, I believed that the church
was the carrier of truth.   After having worked through
the seventy-three pages of the Introduction and the exposition of how the church teaches about the dogmas and the
incomprehensibility of God, I, to my sorrow, convinced
myself that the exposition of the subject was inexact, and
that into the exposition were accidentally or intentionally
introduced irregular discussions about (1) the dogma being
an absolute truth and at the same time the instruction in
that which the church regards as truth, (2) that the announcement through the prophets, the apostles, and Jesus

Christ of what God is is the same as the comprehensibility of God. In the discussions of either point there is not only obscurity, but even unscrupulousness. No matter what subject I may wish to expound, no matter how convinced I may be of my incontestable knowledge of the whole truth in expounding the subject, I cannot act otherwise than say, " I am going to expound this and that, and this I consider the truth, and for this reason," but I will not say that everything which I am going to say is an incontestable truth. And no matter what subject I may be expounding, I cannot do otherwise than say, " The subject which I am going to expound is not fully comprehensible." My whole exposition will consist in making it more comprehensible, and the greater comprehensibility of the subject will be a sign of the correctness of my exposition. But if I say, " The subject which I am going to expound is comprehensible only in part and its comprehensibility is given to me by a certain tradition, and everything which this tradition says, even when it makes the subject more incomprehensible still, and only what this tradition says, is the truth," then it is evident that nobody will believe me.

But maybe the method of this Introduction was irregular, and the exposition of the revealed truths may still be regular. We shall listen to this revelation.

III.

" 10. THE essence of everything which it has pleased God to reveal to us about himself, outside his relation to other creatures, the Orthodox Church expresses in brief in the following words of Athanasius's Symbol: ‘This is the Catholic creed: let us worship the one God in the Trinity, and the Trinity in the One, neither blending the hypostases, nor separating the substance.’" (p. 74.)

The fundamental truth which it has pleased God to reveal about himself to the church through the prophets and the apostles, and which the church reveals to us, is that God is one and three, three and one. The expression of this truth is such that I not merely cannot understand it, but indubitably understand that it cannot be understood. Man understands through reason. In the human mind there are no laws more definite than those which refer to numbers. And so the first thing which it has pleased God to reveal about himself to men is expressed in numbers: I myself $= 3$, and $3 = 1$, and $1 = 3$.

It is impossible that God should so answer the people whom he has himself created and to whom he has given reason in order to understand him; it is impossible for him to answer thus. A decent man, speaking to another, is not going to use to him strange, incomprehensible words. Where is there a man, however feeble in intellect, who to a child's question would not be able to reply in such a way that the child might understand him? How then will God, revealing himself to me, speak in such a way that I cannot understand him? Have not I, without

115

having any faith, given myself an explanation of life, just as every unbeliever has such an explanation? No matter how poor such an explanation may be, every explanation is at least an explanation. But this is not an explanation: it is merely a connection of words without any meaning and giving no idea of anything. I tried to find the meaning of life through rational knowledge, and found that life had no meaning. Then it seemed to me that faith gave that meaning and so I turned to the keeper of faith, to the church. And here, with its very first statement, the church affirms that there is no sense in the very concept of God. But, maybe, it only seems to me that it is senseless, because I do not understand the whole significance of it. Certainly that is not the invention of one person; it is that which billions have believed in. One and trine: what does that mean? I read farther:

"Chapter I. Of God, one in substance." (p. 74.) It is necessary, in the first place, to show that God is one in substance, and, in the second place, to disclose the idea of the very substance of God. Then there follows the doctrine about the unity of God in fourteen pages, divided into articles. ("The Doctrine of the Church, and a Short History of the Dogma about the Unity of God.")

There are proofs of the unity of God from Holy Scripture and from reason. The moral application of the dogma. An exposition of the proofs and explanations of the unity of God.

God is for me and for every believer, above all, the beginning of all beginnings, the cause of all causes, a being out of time and space, the extreme limit of reason. No matter how I may express this idea, I cannot say that God is one, for to that concept I cannot apply the conception of number, which results from time and space, and so I can say just as little that there are seventeen Gods, as that there is one. God is the beginning of everything, God is God. That is the way I formerly comprehended God (and I am sure not I alone). But now I am taught that God is one. My perplexity before the expression that God is one and three is not only not cleared away, but my conception of God is almost lost when I read the fourteen pages which prove the unity of God. From the very first words, instead of elucidating that terrible statement about the unity and trinity of God, which has crushed out my idea of God, I am carried into the sphere of discussion about those Christian and pagan doctrines which have denied the unity of God.

It says there: " As opponents of the Christian doctrine about the unity of God have appeared (*a*) first of all, naturally, the pagans and polytheists who were to be converted to Christianity ; (*b*) then, beginning with the second century, the Christian heretics, known under the general name of Gnostics, of whom some, under the influence of Eastern philosophy and theosophy, recognized the one supreme God, but at the same time admitted a multitude of lower gods, or æons, who emanated from him and created the existing world ; and others, also carried away by the philosophy which, among other things, endeavoured to solve the origin of evil in the world, assumed the existence of two hostile, coeval principles, the principle of good and the principle of evil, as the prime causes of all good and evil in the world ; (*c*) a little later, with the end of the third, and still more beginning with the middle of the fourth, century, the new Christian heretics, the Manicheans, who, with the same idea, assumed two gods, a good and an evil god, to the first of whom they subordinated the eternal kingdom of light, and to the second the eternal kingdom of darkness ; (*d*) from the end of the sixth century, a small sect of tritheists, who, not understanding the Christian doctrine of the three persons in the one Divinity, assumed three distinct gods, who were as distinct as, for example, three persons or entities of the human race, although they all had the same substance, and as distinct as are the entities of any kind or class of beings; (e) finally, beginning with the seventh and up to the twelfth century, the Diacletians, whom many regarded as a branch of the Manichean sect, and who, indeed, like the Manicheans, worshipped two gods, the god of good and the god of evil." (pp. 76 and 77.)

I am told that God is one and trine, and I am told this is a divine, revealed truth. I cannot understand it, and I look for an explanation. What use is there in telling me how incorrectly the pagans believed in assuming two or three gods? It is clear to me that they did not have the same conception about God which I have, — so what is the use of talking to me about them? I want to have the dogma explained to me, so why talk to me about these pagans and Christians who believed in two and in three gods? I am not a bitheist nor a tritheist. The refutal of these bitheists and tritheists does not clear up my question; and yet it is on this conception of the heretics that the whole exposition of the dogma about the unity of God is based, and not by accident. As before, when, in the question about the comprehensibility and incomprehensibility of God, the exposition of the church doctrine about it was connected with and even based on the refutal of the false doctrines, so even here, the doctrine is not expounded directly on the basis of traditions, reason, or mutual connection, but only on the basis of the contradictions of the other teachings, called heresies. In the doctrine about the Trinity, the divinity of the Son, the substance of the Son, there is everywhere one and the same method: it does not say there that the church teaches so and so for this or that reason, but it always says that some have taught that God is entirely comprehensible, others, that God is entirely incomprehensible, but that neither is correct, for the truth is so and so.

In the doctrine about the Son it does not say that the Son is this or that, but some have taught that he is entirely God, and others, that he is entirely man, and so we teach that he is so and so.

In the doctrine about the church and grace, about the creation, about the redemption, there is everywhere one and the same method. Never does the doctrine result from itself, but always from a dispute, where it is proved that neither one opinion nor the other is correct, but both taken together.

Here, in the exposition of the dogma about the unity of God, this method is particularly striking, because the impossibility of polytheism, or rather arithmotheism, is so indubitable to us and to all men who believe in God that the disclosure of the dogma about this, where it says that God is trine, acts directly contrary to the aim which the author has in view. That low sphere of disputing with the polytheists, to which the author descends, and those false methods, which he uses in doing so, almost destroy the concept of God, which every believer in him has.

The author says that God is one, not in the sense in which any pagan god, taken separately from all the other gods, might be.

" But he is one in the sense of there being no other God, neither equal to him, nor higher, nor lower ; but he alone is the only God." (p. 77.)

Farther on the words of some father of the church are adduced : " When we say that the Eastern churches believe in one God the Father, the Almighty, the one Lord, we must understand here that he is called one not in number, but in totality (*unum non numero dici, sed universitate*). Thus, if somebody speaks of one man, or one horse, one is in this case taken as a number ; for there may be another man, and a third, and equally a horse. But where we speak of one in such a way that a second and third can no longer be added, there one is taken not as a number, but in its totality. If, for example, we speak of the one sun, the word 'one' is used in such a sense that no second or third can be added to it. So much the more God, when he is called one, is to be understood not as one in number, but in his totality, one in the sense that there is no other God." (p. 77.)

However touching these words of the father of the church are by their dim striving to raise his conception to a higher level, it is evident that both that father of the church and the author are struggling only with polytheism and want the only God, but fail to understand that the words "one, only" are words expressing number and so cannot be applied to God, in whom we believe. His saying that God is "one or only not in number" is tantamount to saying: "The leaf is green or greenish not in colour." It is evident that here the idea of God as one sun by no means excludes the possibility of another sun. Thus this whole passage brings us only to the conclusion that for him who wants to follow the consequent discussions it is necessary to renounce the idea of God as the beginning of everything, and to lower this idea to the semi-pagan concept of a one and only God as he is conceived in the books of the Old Testament. In the chapter of the proofs from the Old Testament, texts are quoted which reduce the conception of God to the one, exclusive God of the Jews, and there is an exposition of a dispute this time no longer with the heretics, but with modern science. The opinion of modern science that the God of the Jews was conceived by them differently from what God is conceived now by believers and that they did not even know the one God, is called a bold, manifest calumny.

" After that it is a bold, manifest calumny to assert that in the Old Testament there are traces of the teaching of polytheism and that the God of the Jews, according to their Sacred Books, was only one of the gods, a national god, like the gods of the other contemporary nations. In confirmation of the first thought they point to the passages in Holy Scripture where God is given the name of Elohim (gods, from 'Eloah,' god) in the plural number, and where he is made to speak: Let us make man in our image, after our likeness (Gen. i. 1 and 26); we will make him an help meet for him (Gen. ii. 18), and elsewhere. But when that same Moses, in whose books these passages are to be found, so often and so much in detail preaches monotheism as the chief part of the Sinaitic legislation ; when he calls all the pagan gods vanities and idols, and in every way tries to guard the Jews from following them (Lev. xvii. 7 ; Deut. xxxii. 21, and elsewhere), there can be no doubt but that he did not, contrary to his opinion, openly express any belief in polytheism, and so we cannot but agree with the holy fathers of the church that here God is indeed represented in the plural, but that not the idea of the plurality of gods is expressed here, but of the divine persons in one and the same God, that is, that there is here an indication of the mystery of the Holy Trinity." (pp. 79 and 80.)

To any one reading the Old Testament it is clear that the conception of the God of the Old Testament is not at all the idea of a one God, but of a particular God, one only for the Jews. Why prove the contrary, when that is so unnecessary ? What startles us here is not so much the intentional shutting of the eyes against what is manifest, but the unscrupulousness and incomprehensible boldness with which that is denied which is so evident to everybody who reads the Scripture, that which for hundreds of years has been worked out and made clear by all thinking men who busy themselves with these subjects.

It would be useless to quote passages from the Bible, from which it is clear that the Jews recognized their God as one only in comparison with other gods. The

whole Pentateuch is filled with such passages: Joshua
xxiv. 2; Gen. xxxi. 19, 30; Psalm lxxxvi. 8; the
first of Moses' commandments. We wonder for whom
these discussions are written; but what is most remarkable is that all that is said to those who are
seeking for an explanation of the God-revealed truths
about God. In order to reveal to me the truth about
God, which is in the keeping of the church, I am told
unintelligible words, God is one and three, and, instead
of explaining it, they begin to prove to me what I and
every believer know and cannot help knowing, namely,
that God has no number; and, in order to prove that to
me, I am taken down to the sphere of low, savage conceptions about God, and, to fill the cup, they quote in
proof of God's unity from the Old Testament what
obviously proves the opposite to me; and, in order to
confirm these blasphemous speeches about God, they
tell me that the plurality of the expression is a hint
at the Holy Trinity, that is, that the gods, as on
Olympus, sat there, and said: "Let us make!" I
feel like throwing it all away and freeing myself from
this tormenting, blasphemous reading, but the matter
is one of too much importance. It is that doctrine
of the church which the masses believe in and which
gives the meaning of life to them. I must proceed.

There follow confirmations of the unity of God from the
New Testament. Again there is proved what cannot and
ought not to be proved, and again with these proofs there
is a debasing of the idea of God and again unscrupulous
manipulations. In proof of the unity of God the following is quoted:

"The Saviour himself, in reply to the question of a
certain scribe, Which is the first commandment of all?
answered, The first of all the commandments is Hear, O
Israel; The Lord your God is one Lord (Mark xii.
28–29)." (p. 81.)

The author does not see that this is only a repetition of an Old Testament sentence, and that it says, " Your God is one." But more remarkable still is the following :

" In other cases he expressed this truth not less clearly or even more clearly, when, for example, to a man, who called him blessed teacher, he remarked, ' No one is blessed except the one God.' " (p. 81.)

The author does not see that here the word " one " has not even a numerical meaning. Here " one " does not mean " the only God," but " only God." And all this in order to prove what is included in the conception of God, which no one who pronounces the word " God " can doubt. Why this blasphemy ? One is involuntarily led to believe that all that is only in order intentionally to debase the conception of God. It is impossible to imagine any other purpose.

But that is not enough for the author. He considers it necessary to adduce more proofs of the unity (that is, of what cannot be connected with the idea of God) from reason. Here are the proofs of reason :

" The proofs of the unity of God, such as the holy fathers and the teachers of the church have used on the basis of common sense, are almost the same as those which are generally used at the present time for the same purpose. Some of them are borrowed from the testimony of history and the human soul (anthropological), others, from the examination of the universe (cosmological), others again, from the very conception of God (ontological)." (p. 83.)

In the first place, this is not correct, because such proofs have never been used to prove the unity of God. They have been adduced to prove the existence of God, and there they have their place and are analyzed in Kant. In the second place, it is proved that none of them are conclusive to reason. Here are the proofs as offered by the theologian :

"(1) All nations have preserved an idea of the one God."

That is not true. The author himself has just overthrown the polytheists.

"(2) On the agreement of the pagan authors."

This again is not true. It cannot be a proof, because it does not refer to all pagan writers.

"(3) On the innateness of the idea about one God."

This is again not true, because Tertullian's words, which are quoted in confirmation of this position, are said about the innateness of the idea about God, but not about the innateness of the idea about the unity of God.

" Listen," Tertullian says to the pagans, " to the testimony of your soul, which, in spite of the prison of the body, of prejudices, and bad bringing up, of the fury of the passions, of the enslavement to false gods, when it is roused as though from intoxication or from a deep profound sleep, when it feels, so to speak, a spark of health, involuntarily invokes the name of the one true God and cries : ' Great God ! Good God ! Whatever God may give ! ' Thus his name is to be found on the lips of all men. The soul also recognizes him as the Judge in the following words : ' God sees, I hope to God, God will recompense me.' And pronouncing these words, it turns its glances, not to the Capitol, but to heaven, knowing that there is the palace of the living God, that from there and from him it has its origin. On the testimony of the soul according to the Christian nature (*naturaliter Christianœ*)." (p. 84.)

This exhausts the anthropological proofs. Here are the cosmological proofs :

" (1) The universe is one, consequently God is one."

But why there is one universe is not apparent.

" (2) In the life of the world there is order. If there existed several rulers of the universe, many gods, naturally divers among themselves, there could not be such an orderly flow and agreement in Nature ; on the contrary, everything would turn into disorder and become chaos; then each god would govern his own part, or the whole universe, according to his will, and there would be eternal conflicts and strife."

" (3) For the creation and government of the world one almighty, omniscient God is sufficient ; what, then, are other gods for ? It is obvious that they are superfluous."

Those are the cosmological proofs. What is this ? A bad joke ? Ridicule ? No, it is a Theology, the disclosure of God-revealed truths. But that is not all. Here are the ontological proofs :

" (1) By the common consent of all men, God is a being than whom there can be nothing higher or more perfect. But the highest and most perfect of all beings can be only one, for, if there existed others, too, equal to it, then it would cease being the highest and most perfect of all, that is, it would cease being a god."

Here the sophism proves nothing, and only makes us doubt the strictness and exactness of the thoughts of the holy fathers, especially of St. John Damascene.

The first proof that there can be but one most perfect and highest being is the only correct reasoning on the attribute of him whom we call God, but is by no means a proof of the unity of God ; it is only an expression of the fundamental concept of God, which by its very essence excludes the possibility of uniting this idea with the conception of number. For, if God is what is highest and most perfect, then all the previous proofs from the Old Testament and others about God being one only impair that idea. But, again, as in the discussion of comprehensibility and incomprehensibility, the author obviously needs here, not clearness and agreement of thought, but the mechanical connection with the tradition of the church ; this connection is preserved to the detriment of the idea, and at all cost.

After these proofs follow special proofs of the unity of God in opposition to the bitheistic heretics, and these proofs have no connection with the subject. And after all that it is assumed that the first dogma about the unity of God has been disclosed, and the author proceeds with the teaching about the moral application of this first dogma.

The author has the idea that every dogma is necessary for the saving faith. One dogma about the "one God" has been revealed, and so it is necessary to show how this dogma is helpful in the salvation of men. It is like this :

"Three important lessons can we draw for ourselves from the dogma about the unity of God. Lesson the first : in respect to our relation to God. 'I believe in one God,' utters every Christian, beginning the words of the Symbol, — in one, and not in many, or two, or three, as the pagans and certain heretics used to believe : and so him alone shall we serve as God (Deut. vi. 13 ; Matt. iv. 10) ; and love him alone with all our heart, and with all our soul (Deut. vi. 4, 5) ; and put all our confidence in him alone (Psalm cxvii. 8, 9 ; 1 Peter i. 21) ; at the same time we must keep away from all kinds of polytheism and idolatry (Exod. xx. 3–5). The pagans, while believing in one supreme God, at the same time recognized many lower gods, and among this number included incorporeal spirits, good and bad (genii and demons), and deceased persons who had in some way been famous in life. We, too, worship good angels, and we worship holy men who in their lifetime have excelled in faith and piety ; but we must not forget that we have to worship them, according to the teaching of the Orthodox Church, not as inferior gods, but as servants and ministers of God, as intercessors for us before God, and as promoters of our salvation, — we must worship them in such a way that the whole glory should refer mainly to him alone as wonderful among his saints (Matt. x. 40).   The pagans used to make sculptured figures of their gods and builded idols, and in their extreme blindness recognized these idols as gods, offering them divine worship: let not any of the Christians fall into similar idolatry! We, too, use and worship the representations of the true God and of his saints, and bend our knees before them; but we use and worship them only as holy and worshipful representations, and do not deify them, and, in making our obeisances to the holy images, we worship not the wood and paint, but God himself and his saints, such as are represented in the images: such ought to be the true worship of the holy images, and then it will not in the least resemble idolatry." (pp. 89 and 90.)

That is, according to this preceding discussion, we are given a lesson to do precisely as the idolaters are doing, but to remember certain dialectic distinctions, as here expounded.

" It is well known that the pagans personified all human passions and in this shape deified them; we do not personify the passions in order to deify them; we know how to value them, but, unfortunately, Christians frequently serve their passions as though they were gods, though they themselves do not notice that. One is so given to belly service and in general to the sensual pleasures that for him, according to the expression of the apostle, God is his belly (Phil. iii. 19); another is so zealously concerned about acquiring treasure and with such love guards it that his covetousness can, indeed, not be called otherwise than idolatry (Col. iii. 5); a third is so much occupied with his deserts and privileges, real and imaginary, and places them so high that he apparently makes an idol of them and worships them and makes others worship them (Dan. iii.). In short, every passion and attachment for anything, even though it be important and noble, if we abandon ourselves to it with zeal, so as to forget God and act contrary to his will, becomes for us a new god, or idol, whom we serve; and a Christian must remember firmly that such an idolatry can never be coextensive with the service of the one God; according to the words of the Saviour: No man can serve two masters; ye cannot serve God and mammon (Matt. vi. 24)."   (pp. 90 and 91.)

What is this?   Where is this taken from?   What a lot of things have been said and connected with the unity of God! How do they all result from it? There is absolutely no answer to that.

"Second lesson, in respect to our relation to our neighbours.   Believing in the one God, from whom we all have our being, through whom we live and move and are (Acts xvii. 28), and who alone forms the aim of all of us, we are naturally incited toward union among ourselves."

And still more texts and still less connection with the preceding. If there is any connection, it is only a verbal one, like a play of words: "God is one, — we must strive after oneness."

"Finally, the third lesson, in respect to our relation to ourselves.   Believing in God, one in substance, let us see to it that in our own being we may reëstablish the primitive union which has been impaired in us through sin. To-day we feel the cleaving of our being, the disunion of our forces, abilities, strivings; we delight in the law of God after the inward man : but we see another law in our members, warring against the law of our mind, and bringing us into captivity to the law of sin which is in our members (Rom. vii. 22–23), so that in each of us there are, not one, but two men, an inward and an outward, a spiritual and a carnal, man.   Let us see to it that we put off concerning the former conversation the old man, which is corrupt according to the deceitful lusts ; and that we put on the new man, which after God is created in righteousness and true holiness (Ephes. iv. 22–24), and that we thus may again appear just as one in our substance as when we came out of the hands of the Creator."

And so forth. Without the least connection with the dogmas about the unity of God, but with a play on the word "unity," there proceeds a discussion on the moral application of the dogma, but not a word is there for the solution of the question about the unity and trinity. I proceed to the next division of Chapter I.

IV.

I. Of the essence of God.

Of the essence of God? It was said that God is incomprehensible in his essence. Then it was said that he was a trinity. But I receive no reply to my answer, and get a new problem: God, who is incomprehensible in his essence, will be disclosed to me in his essence.

"The question of what God is in his essence (οὐσία, φύσις, essentia, substantia, natura), became, even in the first centuries of Christianity, a subject of especial attention for the teachers of the Church, on the one hand, as a question in itself of great importance and close to the mind and heart of each man, and, on the other hand, because at that time the question was taken up by the heretics, who naturally provoked against themselves the defenders of Orthodoxy."

Again, in order to disclose the truth to me, I am introduced to discussions and to the exposition of the opinion of this man and of that, and all of them are false, and:

"Avoiding all similar finesses, the Orthodox Church has always held only to what it has pleased God to communicate to her about himself in his revelation, and not having at all in mind the determination of the substance of God, which it recognizes to be incomprehensible and, therefore, strictly speaking, indeterminable, but wishing only to teach its children as precise, exact, and accessible an idea about God as is possible, it says about him as follows: 'God is a Spirit, eternal, all-good, omniscient, all-just, almighty, omnipresent, unchangeable, all-sufficing to himself, all-blessed.' Here it points out to us, in the first place, the incomprehensible essence of God (or nature, or substance), as much as it can be comprehended now by our reason, and, in the second place, the essential attributes by which this essence, or more correctly, God himself, is distinguished from other essences." (pp. 94 and 95.)

The essence, nature, substance of God is pointed out to us, and so are the attributes by which God is distinguished from other essences. What are we talking about? About a limited being or about God? How can God be distinguished from others? How can we distinguish in him substance, nature, and attributes? Is he not incomprehensible? Is not he higher and more perfect than anything? Less and less do I understand the sense of what they are trying to tell me, and it is becoming clearer and clearer to me that for some reason they need inevitably, by rejecting sound reason, the laws of logic, conscience, for some secret purposes they need to do what they have been doing until now: to reduce my conception about God and the conception of all believers to a base, semi-pagan conception. Here is what is said about this nature and about the attributes of him who is here called God:

" 17. The conception about the essence of God. God is a spirit. The word 'spirit,' indeed, more comprehensibly than anything else signifies for us the incomprehensible essence or substance of God. We know of only two kinds of substances: material, complex substances, which have no consciousness or reason, and immaterial, simple, spiritual substances, which are more or less endowed with consciousness and reason. We can nowise admit that God has in himself the substance of the first kind, since we see in all his acts, both of creation and of foresight, the traces of the greatest reason. On the other hand, we are of necessity forced to assume the substance of the latter kind in God, through the constant contemplation of these traces." (p. 95.)

In confirmation of these unintelligible, perverse, intricate words there are quoted the words of St. John Damascene, which are almost as unintelligible and perverse.

" By knowing what is ascribed to God and from that ascending to the essence of God, we comprehend not the essence itself, but only what refers to the essence (τὰ περὶ τὴν οὐσίαν,) just as, knowing that the soul is incorporeal, inquantitative, and invisible, we do not yet comprehend its essence ; just so we do not comprehend the essence of a body, if we know that it is white or black, but we comprehend only what refers to its essence.   But the true word teaches us that the Deity is simple and has one action (ἐνεργείαν,) simple and doing good in everything." (p. 96.)

However painfully hard it is to analyze such expressions, in which every word is a blunder or a lie, every connection of a subject and predicate a tautology or a contradiction, every connection of one sentence with another a blunder or an intentional deception, it will have to be done.   It says " spirit signifies substance."

Spirit is only the opposite of substance.   Spirit is, above all, a word which is used only as an opposition to every substance, to everything visible, audible, tangible, perceptible by the senses.   Essence, nature, substance is only a distinction of perceptive, sensual objects.   By their nature, by their substance, by their essence, stones, trees, animals, men are distinguished.

But spirit is that which has not the essence of Nature. What, then, can the words, " Spirit signifies substance," mean ?   Further : " We know only two kinds of substances, complex material and simple spiritual substances." We do not know and cannot know any simple spiritual substances, because " spiritual substance " is a mere contradiction.   The plural number used with simple spiritual substance is another internal contradiction, because what is simple cannot be two or many ; only with what is not simple do we get distinction and plurality. The addition to the word " substances " of " simple, spiritual, more or less endowed with consciousness and reason," introduces another internal contradiction, by suddenly joining to the simple concept that of consciousness and reason, according to the degree of which this something, which is called simple spiritual substances, is divided.

The words, " To admit that God has in himself the substance of the first kind," to be consistent, ought to have been, " To admit that the one God is complex, material substances," which is the merest absurdity, is an admission that the one God is a multiplicity of varied substances, of which it is impossible to speak. The words, " We are of necessity forced to assume the substance of the latter kind in God, through the contemplation of the works of his creation and foresight, in which traces of the highest reason are visible," signify not at all that God is a spirit, but that God is the highest reason. Thus, in examining these words, it turns out that, instead of saying that God is a spirit, they say that God is the highest intelligence, and in confirmation of these words are quoted the words of St. John Damascene, who says a third thing, namely, that the Deity is simple.

What is remarkable is that the conception of God as a spirit, in the sense of opposing it to everything material, is indubitable to me and to every believer, and has clearly been established in the first chapters about the comprehensibility of God, and that cannot be proved. But, for some reason, this proof is attempted, and blasphemous words about the investigation of the essence of God are pronounced, and the argument ends by proving that, instead of being a spirit, God is reason, or that the Deity is simple and has but one action. What is all that proved for ? Why, in order, when the need for it shall arise during an argument, to introduce the conception not of the one, simple spirit, but of spiritual essences, more or less endowed with consciousness and reason (men, demons, angels, who will be required later on), but more especially for that connection with the word "spirit," which later will play an important part in the exposition of the doctrine. We shall soon see for what purpose.

"And if, indeed, the revelation itself represents to us God as a spiritual being, our supposition must pass over to the stage of an indubitable truth. Now revelation teaches us, indeed, that God is purest spirit, not connected with any body, and that, consequently, his nature is entirely insubstantial, not partaking of the slightest complexity, simple." (pp. 95 and 96.)

From the words "purest spirit," not connected with any "body," it appears at once that the word "spirit" is no longer understood in the sense in which it is taken in all languages, not as it is understood in the gospel discourse with Nicodemus, "The spirit bloweth where it listeth," that is, as a complete opposite to everything material, but as something that can be defined, separated from something else. Then Holy Scripture is quoted to prove that God is spirit, but, as always, the texts prove the very opposite.

"Can any hide himself in secret places that I shall not see him? saith the Lord. Do not I fill heaven and earth? saith the Lord (Jer. xxiii. 24; Psalm cxxxix. 7–12); (b) everybody has a definite shape and so can be represented, but God has no sensual form, and so the Old Testament strictly prohibited his being represented: To whom then will you liken God? or what likeness will you compare unto him? (Is. xl. 18, 25); take ye therefore good heed unto yourselves; for ye saw no manner of similitude on the day that the Lord spake unto you in Horeb out of the midst of the fire: lest ye corrupt yourselves, and make you a graven image, the similitude of any figure, the likeness of male or female (Deut. iv. 15–16); (c) for the same reason everybody may be visible, but God is called the invisible God (Col. i. 15; 1 Tim. i. 17; Rom. i. 20), whom no man hath seen at any time (John i. 18 and vi. 46), and in particular, whom no man hath seen, nor can see (1 Tim. vi. 16; cf. Exod. xxx. 18–23); (d) everybody, being composed of parts, is destructible and perishable, but God is the immortal king of the ages (1 Tim. i. 17)." (pp. 96 and 97.)

Is it not clear that God who seeth everywhere, who has spoken from the midst of the fire on Mount Horeb, who has no similitude, that is, no form, who is immortal, is a spirit? It is evident that it is necessary to be able to speak of God as of a definite being, something like a man; but it is also necessary to speak of God as of an entirely simple, inaccessible spirit. It is the old catch; in all the chapters of this book, two different conceptions are purposely united into one, in order, in case of necessity, to exchange one for the other and, making use of that, mechanically to pick out all the texts of Scripture and so mix them up that it shall be possible to blend what is discordant.

After that follows a statement of the teaching of the church and, as always, not the exposition of the dogma, not an explanation, not a discussion, but a controversy. The controversy is against the anthropomorphists and pantheists. It is argued that it is not true that God is clothed in flesh and is in everything like man. If the Scripture speaks of his body, "we must by his eyes, eyelids, and vision understand his all-seeing power, his all-embracing knowledge, because through the sense of vision we obtain a fuller and more correct knowledge. By his ears and hearing we must understand his merciful attention and reception of our prayers; for even we, when we are asked, graciously incline our ear to the supplicants, showing them our favour by means of this sense. By his mouth and speaking we must understand the manifestation of God's will, for we, too, manifest our intimate thoughts by means of our lips and through speech. By his food and drink — our agreement with the will of God, for by means of the sense of taste we satisfy the necessary demands of our being. By smelling — the acceptance of our thoughts as directed toward God, and of our hearty disposition, for by means of the sense of smell do we become aware of perfume. By his face we must understand his manifestation in his works, for our faces also manifest us. By his hands — his active force, for we, too, do everything useful and, especially, everything costly with our own hands. By his right hand — his succour in just works, for we, too, in performing more noble and important deeds, such as demand a greater force, most generally make use of the right hand. By his touch — an exact knowledge and investigation of the smallest and the hidden, because those who are touched by us cannot conceal anything upon their bodies. By his feet and walking — his coming and appearance, in order to aid the needy, or defend them against enemies, or to do some other act, even as we walk with our feet to some destination. By his oath — the inalterableness of his counsel, for between us, too, mutual agreements are confirmed by an oath. By his anger and fury — his loathing and hatred of evil, for we, too, become angry and hate what is contrary to our will. By his forgetfulness, sleep, and dreaming — his slowness in wreaking vengeance on his enemies, and his delaying his succour until the proper time." (pp. 99 and 100.)

These explanations and refutations of the anthropomorphists, independently of the arbitrariness and unintelligibility of the explanations (as, for example, why by food and drink is to be understood our agreement with the will of God), these explanations descend lower and lower into the sphere of petty, often stupid, dialectics, and farther and farther does the hope recede of having the God-revealed truths explained.

After this, in the 2d division, there are adduced the proofs of the fathers of the church that God is an incorporeal, immaterial essence, and the same argument is continued. What is quoted is not the false, but the queer, reasoning of the fathers of the church, which shows that the fathers of the church were far from that conception of God which is common with every believer at the present time. They take pains to prove, for example, that God is not limited by anything, or is not subject to suffering, or not subject to destruction. No matter how worthy the labours of these fathers have been in the time of struggle against the pagans, the statement that God is not subject to suffering has involuntarily the same effect upon us as would have the statement that God does not need any raiment or food, and proves that to a man who argues the indestructibility of God the conception of the Deity is not clear and not settled. It does not explain anything to us and only offends our feeling. But, apparently, the compiler needs it: precisely what offends our feeling is what he needs, namely, the abasement of the idea of God.

In the 3d division the compiler quotes, in the shape of a proof, that invective which the fathers of the church uttered in defence of their opinion:

" In connection with this it is important for us to notice that the ancient pastors, rebuking the errors of the anthropomorphists, called their opinion a senseless, most stupid heresy, and accounted the anthropomorphists, who held this opinion, as heretics."

And as the last argument of the church the following is adduced:

" For this reason we hear, among other things, in the ' order of Orthodoxy,' which the Orthodox Church performs in the first week of the Great Lent, the following words: 'Anathema on those who say that God is not spirit, but flesh!'"

That ends all we know about the substance of God, namely, that he is a spirit. What is the deduction from all that? That God is not an essence, but a spirit: all that results from the conception of God, and all believers cannot help thinking otherwise. This is partly confirmed by this article. But, in addition to that, we have the statement that this spirit is something special, separate, almost incomprehensible. In this verbal blending of the contradictions consists the subject matter of Art. 18. What the purpose is, appears clearly from the following 18th article.

"18. The idea of the essential properties of God, — their number and division. — The essential properties in God (τὰ οὐσιώδη ἰδιώματα, *proprietates essentiales*), or, in one word (ἀξιώματα, δόγματα, ἐπιτηδεύματα, *attributa, perfectiones*), are such as belong to the divine essence alone and distinguish him from all other beings, and so they are properties which are equally applicable to all the persons of the Holy Trinity, who form one in their essence, for which reason they are also called general divine properties (ἰδιώματα κοινά) in contradistinction to special or personal attributes (τὰ προσωπικὰ ἰδιώματα, *proprietates personales*), which belong to each person of the Deity taken separately and thus distinguish them among themselves." (p. 102.)

It turns out that God, a simple spirit, has properties which distinguish him from all other beings. More than that: in addition to the general, divine attributes, there are others, which distinguish the same God in the three persons, though nothing has as yet been said about what the Trinity, and what a person is.

"It is impossible to define the number of essential or common properties of God. Though the church, in giving us a sound idea about God, mentions some of these

('God is a Spirit, eternal, all-good, omniscient, all-just, almighty, omnipresent, unchangeable, all-sufficing to himself, all-blessed'), it at the same time remarks that God's general properties are endless, for everything which is said in revelation about God, one in essence, in a certain sense forms the properties of the divine being.   Consequently we, following the example of the church, shall limit ourselves to the analysis of some of them, the chief ones, such as more than any others characterize the essence of God and embrace or explain the other, less perceptible properties, and such as are more clearly mentioned in the divine revelation." (p. 102.)

The attributes of God are numberless, and so we are going to speak of some of them.   But, if they are numberless, a few of them are an infinitely small part, and so it is unnecessary and impossible to speak of them.   But not so judges the Theology.   Not only of some, but of the chief ones among them!   How can there be a chief one in an endless number?   All are equally infinitely small.

"We shall speak of such as more than any other characterize the Deity."

Characterize how?   God has a character, that is, the distinction of one god from others.   No, it is clear that we are talking about something else and not about God. But let us proceed.

"In order to have distinct ideas about the essential properties of God and to expound the teaching about them in a certain system, the theologians have since antiquity tried to divide them into classes, and of such divisions, especially in the mediæval and modern period, many have been invented, and all of them, though not in the same degree, have their virtues and their defects. The main reason for the latter is quite comprehensible : the attributes of the divine being, like the essence itself, are entirely incomprehensible to us.   Therefore, without making a vain attempt to find any one most perfect division of them, we shall select the one which to us appears most correct and most simple." (pp. 102 and 103.)

The properties of the essence of God, as well as the essence itself, are *quite incomprehensible* to us. Well? Let us not scoff and talk of the incomprehensible! No. " We shall select a division which to us will appear most correct."

" God, according to his essence, is a spirit; but in every spirit we distinguish, in particular, in addition to the spiritual nature proper (the substance), two main forces or faculties: mind and will."

How can there be the division into mind and will in a simple spirit? Where was that said? There was a general statement about the spirit, but there was nothing said about its having mind and will. Mind and will are words with which we, men, and only a few of us, distinguish in ourselves two activities. But why has God that?

" In conformity with this, the essential properties of God may be divided into three classes: (1) into properties of the divine essence in general, that is, into such as belong equally to the spiritual nature (substance) of God and to its two forces, to mind and will, and distinguish God, as a spirit in general, from all other beings; (2) into properties of the divine mind, that is, such as belong only to the divine mind; and finally (3) into properties of the divine will, that is, such as belong only to the divine will."

Had I not better throw it all up? For is that not the delirium of an insane man? No, I said to myself that I would analyze strictly and thoroughly the whole exposition of the Theology.

Then follow 60 pages on the properties of God. Here are the contents of these 60 pages:

" 19. The properties of the divine essence in general. God, as a spirit, is distinguished from all other beings in general, in that they are all limited in their existence and in their forces, consequently more or less imperfect, while he is an unlimited spirit, or limitless, hence all-perfect." (pp. 103 and 104.)

"God is distinguished from all other beings in general." This false conception of God as distinguished from all other beings is apparently needed because before and many times afterward and here it says that God is limitless, and therefore it is impossible to say that the limitless can be distinguished from anything.

"In particular, all other beings: (*a*) are limited in the beginning and during the continuation of their existence; all of them have received their existence through God and are in constant dependence on him, and partly on each other; God does not receive his existence from anybody, and in nothing is he dependent on anybody, — he is self-existing and independent; (*b*) they are limited in the manner or form of their existence, for they are inevitably subject to the conditions of space and time, and so are subject to changes; God is above all conditions of space, — he is immeasurable and omnipresent, — and above all conditions of time, — he is eternal and unchangeable; (*c*) finally they are limited in their strength, both in quality and in quantity; but for God there are no limits even in this respect, — he is all-powerful and almighty. Thus the chief qualities which belong to God in his essence in general are: (1) unlimitedness or all-perfection, (2) self-existence, (3) independence, (4) immeasurableness and omnipresence, (5) eternity, (6) unchangeableness, and (7) almightiness."

Then, God is distinguished from other beings in particular:

"(1) By his unlimitedness or all-perfection." Why unlimitedness is equal to all-perfection remains unexplained, both here and elsewhere.

"(2) By his self-existence and (3) independence." What

difference there is between self-existence and independence again remains unexplained.   Self-existence is explained as follows:

" God is called self-existent because he does not owe his existence to any other being, but has his existence, and everything else which he has, from himself."

His independence is explained on p. 110 as follows:

" Under the name of independence in God we understand a quality by force of which he is in his essence and forces and actions determined only by himself and not by anything external, and he is self-satisfied (αὐτάρκης, ἀνενδεής), self-willed (αὐτεξούσιος), self-ruled (αὐτοκράτης), — this property of God results from the preceding.   If God is a self-existent being and everything he has he has through himself, that means that he is not dependent on anybody, at least not in his existence and powers." (p. 110.)

Thus, in the first attribute of unlimitedness there is attached to it, for some reason, the idea of all-perfection (an unused and badly compounded word), which from its composition has an entirely different meaning from unlimitedness.   But the words " self-existence " and " independence," which, according to the definition of the author himself, express the identical idea, are separated.

(4) Immeasurableness, which is only a synonym of unlimitedness, is suddenly combined into one with omnipresence, which has nothing in common with that idea.   Then:

(5) Eternity and (6) unchangeableness are again separated, though they form one idea, for changeableness takes place only in time, and time is only the consequence of changeableness.

(7) Almightiness, which is defined by the concept of unlimited force, though neither before nor later will there be anything said about force.   But that is far from being all.   We must remember that after the disclosure of the essence of God in himself (Art. 17,

RE CLASSIF NO   *891.733*
                 T588
CUTTER NO
                 v.13

CHECK DUP   SHELF

SEND FOR LC

MARK SPINE

MAKE POCKET

PULL CAT BOOKS

ACCESSION BOOK

ADD ACC NO TO CDS

WHITE

CORRECT CDS

ADD ON   UNIT

OVERSIZE

p. 95), we have had disclosed to us the essential properties of God (Art. 18, p. 102).   Of the essential properties of God there have now been disclosed to us the
essential properties of God in general (Art. 19, p. 103).
We still are to get the disclosure of the properties, at
first, of God's mind (Art. 20, p. 122), and then of the
properties of God's will (Art. 21, p. 129).

"God's mind may be viewed from two sides: from the
theoretical and from the practical side, that is, in itself
and in relation to God's actions.   In the first case we
get the idea of one property of this mind, of omniscience;
in the latter, of another, of the highest all-wisdom."

God knows everything in himself.   What else does
he know if he has all-wisdom ?   On p. 127 it says:

"All-wisdom consists in the completest knowledge of
the best purposes and the best means, and at the same
time in the fullest ability to apply the latter to the first."

The knowledge of the best purposes and means !   But
how can an unlimited, all-satisfied being have any purposes ?   And what concept of means can there be applied
to an almighty being ?   But that is not enough:

"Holy Scripture defines in detail the subjects of the
divine knowledge.   It bears testimony in general to
the fact that God knows everything, and in particular,
that he knows himself and everything outside of himself:
everything possible and actual, everything past, present,
and future." (p. 122.)

Then, in parts, with quotations from Holy Scripture,
the author proves that God knows (*a*) everything, (*b*)
himself, (*c*) everything possible, (*d*) everything existing,
(*e*) the past, (*f*) the present, (*g*) the future.   But God is
outside of time, according to the Theology, above time, —
so what past and future is there for him ?   And God is
outside of space, — he is an unlimited, limitless, omniscient being, — how can there be anything " outside of "
him ?   " Outside of " means beyond the limits, beyond

the borders of something limited. I am not exaggerating, am not on purpose expressing myself in a strange manner, on the contrary, I am using every effort to soften the wildness of the expressions. Read pp. 123–125! What am I saying! Open those two volumes anywhere, and read them! It is all the time the same, and the farther you proceed, the more liberated from all laws of the connection of thoughts and words!

"21. The will of God may be viewed from two sides: in itself and in relation to creatures. In the first case it presents itself to us (a) in the highest degree free according to its essence, and (b) all-holy in its free activity. In the latter it appears, first of all, (a) all-good, — since goodness is the first and chief cause of all divine acts in relation to all creatures, rational and irrational; then, (b) in particular, in relation to rational creatures only, true and correct, for it is revealed to them in the form of a moral law for their wills, and in the form of promises or moral incitements toward the performance of this law; finally (c) all-just, in so far as it watches the moral actions of these creatures and repays them according to their deserts. Thus the chief properties of the will of God, or, more correctly, the chief divine properties according to his will, are (1) highest freedom, (2) completest holiness, (3) infinite goodness, (4) completest truth and correctness, and (5) infinite justice." (pp. 129 and 130.)

So it turns out that the limitless, unlimited God is free, and this is proved by texts. And, as always, the texts show that those who wrote and spoke those words did not understand God and only approached a comprehension of him and spoke of a strong, pagan god, but not of the God we believe in.

"I have made the earth, the man and the beast that are upon the ground, by my great power and by my out-stretched arm, and have given it unto whom it seemed meet unto me (Jer. xxvii. 5). I will have mercy on whom I will have mercy, and I will have compassion on whom I will have compassion (Rom ix. 15; cf. Exod. xxxii. 19). And he doeth according to his will in the army of heaven, and among the inhabitants of the earth: and none can stay his hand, or say unto him, What doest thou? (Dan. iv. 35; cf. Job xxiii. 13). The Most High ruleth in the kingdom of men, and giveth it to whomsoever he will (Dan. iv. 17, 25, 32). The king's heart is in the hand of the Lord, as the rivers of water: he turneth it whithersoever he will (Prov. xxi. 1). Are not two sparrows sold for a farthing? and one of them shall not fall on the ground without your Father; but the very hairs of your head are all numbered (Matt. x. 29, 30). (c) In the redemption of man: Having predestinated us unto the adoption of children by Jesus Christ to himself, according to the good pleasure of his will (Ephes. i. 5). Having made known unto us the mystery of his will, according to his good pleasure which he hath purposed in himself (Ephes. i. 9). And Christ the Saviour gave himself for our sins, that he might deliver us from this present evil world, according to the will of God and our Father: to whom be glory for ever and ever (Gal. i. 4, 5). (d) For our regeneration and purification" (all this is an account of the manifestations of God's freedom): "Of his own will begat he us with the word of truth, that we should be a kind of firstfruits of his creatures (James i. 18). But the manifestation of the Spirit is given to every man to profit withal; for to one is given by the Spirit the word of wisdom; to another, the word of knowledge by the same Spirit. . . . But all these worketh that one and the self-same Spirit, dividing to every man severally as he will (1 Cor. xii. 7, 8, 11).

"The holy fathers and teachers of the church, who in

their writings mentioned the divine freedom in general, frequently expressed their ideas with peculiar clearness, in three cases, (*a*) when they armed themselves against the ancient philosophers, who affirmed that the universe was eternal and had sprung from God not by his will, but of necessity, as the shadow from the body, or the glow from the light, (*b*) when they refuted the errors of the pagans and certain heretics, who asserted that everything in the universe and God himself were subject to fate, and (*c*) when, wishing to define wherein the image of God consisted in us, they assumed it to be in man's free will. In all these cases they pointed out that God was not subject to any necessity and quite freely determined himself toward actions; that he had created in the beginning everything which he had wished and as he had wished, and continued to do everything in the world only by his will, and that he, in general, in his essence, was self-willed.

"Indeed, if God is a most perfect spirit, and an independent and almighty spirit, our reason, too, must be conscious of the fact that God is free in the highest degree according to his essence; freedom is a most essential property of a conscious spirit, and he who is all-powerful and holds everything in his power, himself not dependent on anything, cannot be subject to necessity or compulsion.

"(2) Completest holiness. Calling God holy (ἄγιος, *sanctus*), we profess that he is completely pure from all sin, that he cannot even sin, and in all his acts is entirely true to the moral law, and so he hates the evil and loves only the good in all his creatures." (pp. 130–132.)

The holiness consists in God's not sinning, and in his hating evil. And again a confirmation of this scoffing from Holy Scripture.

"(3) Infinite goodness. Goodness in God is a property by which he is always ready to confer, and actually does confer, as many benefits as each of the creatures is able to receive by its nature and condition."

And here is how this goodness is confirmed:

"Goodness is the chief cause of creation and providence; God has existed and continued in bliss since eternity, without having any need of any one; but only of his infinite goodness he wanted to make other beings the copartners of his bliss, and so he gave them existence, adorned them with various perfections, and did not stop lavishing upon them all benefits which are necessary for existence and bliss." (p. 138.)

From eternity, that is, an endless number of years, God lived in bliss by himself and with all his all-wisdom had not thought before of creating the world. Thus goodness, which is to be taken in the sense that the idea of evil cannot be connected with the idea of God, is mutilated in this conception and debased to the lowest, blasphemous representation.

"(4) Completest truth and verity. We profess God as being true and veracious (ἀληθινός, πιστός, *verax, fidelis*), because whatever he reveals to creatures he reveals correctly and exactly, and in particular, no matter what promises or threats he utters, he always carries out what he says."

True to whom? The idea of threat and punishment, the idea of evil, connected with God! And then texts which confirm the statement that God cannot lie!

"(5) Infinite justice. Under the name of justice, or truth (δικαιοσύνη, *justicia*), we here understand the property in God by which he metes out the due to all moral creatures, namely, he rewards the good and punishes the bad." (p. 140.)

The all-good God metes out eternal punishment to people for a sin committed in the temporal life. And that is confirmed by texts:

"And the unrighteous will hear the heavy doom of the unbiased judge: Depart from me, ye cursed, into everlasting fire, prepared for the devil and his angels (Matt. xxv.

41). Besides, holy Scripture (*b*) bears testimony to the fact that the curse of the Lord is in the house of the wicked (Prov. iii. 33 ; cf. Prov. xv. 25), and he shall bring upon them their own iniquity, and shall cut them off in their own wickedness (Psalm xciv. 23) ; (*c*) calls God a consuming fire : For our God is a consuming fire (Heb. xii. 29 ; Deut. iv. 24), and (*d*) in human fashion ascribes to him anger and vengeance : For the wrath of God is revealed from heaven against all ungodliness and unrighteousness of men, who hold the truth in unrighteousness (Rom. i. 18 ; cf. Exod. xxxii. 10, Num. xi. 10, Psalms ii. 5 and lxxxviii. 5-7, 16, Ezek. vii. 14). Vengeance is mine ; I will repay, saith the Lord (Rom. xii. 19 ; Heb. x. 30 ; Deut. xxxii. 35). Lord God of vengeance, God hath not shewn himself (Psalm xciv. 1)." (p. 142.)

This apparent contradiction did not arrest the author, just as he had not been arrested by the contradictions in each division of the properties of God, but here he stopped, apparently because the contradiction had been observed long ago and there had been objections raised, and the holy fathers, on the basis of whom the whole book is written, had expressed themselves in regard to it. Here is what the holy fathers had said about it :

" The true God must of necessity be both good and just; his goodness is a just goodness, and his truth a just truth ; he remains just even when he forgives us our sins and pardons us ; he remains good when he punishes us for our sins, for he punishes us as a father, not in anger or revenge, but in order to mend us, for our own moral advantage, and so his very punishments are a greater proof of his paternal goodness toward us and his love than of his truth."

The question is how to solve the contradiction between goodness and justice. How can a good God punish with eternal fire for sins ? Either he is not just, or not good.

The question seems to be both simple and legitimate. The author makes it appear that he is answering the question when he quotes the authorities of Irenæus, Tertullian, Clement of Alexandria, Chrysostom, Hilary, Augustine. There are plenty of authorities, but what have they said? They have said: "You ask whether God can be just if there is eternal torment for a temporal sin? And we answer that God must be both just and good. His goodness is just goodness, and his justice is good justice." But that is precisely what I am asking: How is this? How can a good and just God punish with eternal torment for a temporal sin? And you say that he punishes like a father for our moral good, and that his punishments are a proof of his goodness and love. What kind of correction and love is this, to burn for ever in fire for a temporal sin? But the author thinks he has explained everything, and he calmly finishes the chapter:

"Every sound mind must acknowledge the completest justice in God. Every injustice toward others can arise in us only from two causes, — from ignorance or from the error of our mind and from perversity of will. But in God these causes cannot take place: God is an omniscient and most holy being; he knows all the most hidden deeds of moral beings and is able worthily to appreciate them; he loves every good by his own nature, and hates every evil also by his nature. Let us add that God is at the same time an almighty being who, therefore, has all the means at hand in order to recompense others according to their deserts." (pp. 143 and 144.)

I have quoted this merely to show that I do not leave out a thing. That is all which is used to solve the contradiction. The disclosure of the essence of God in himself and in his essential properties is finished. What was there in it? It began by saying that God was incomprehensible, but the statement was added that at the same time he was comprehensible in part. This knowledge in part is disclosed to us in such a way that God is one, and not two or three, that is, to the idea of God there is added an improper concept of number which, by the first definition, is not applicable to him.

Then it is disclosed to us that in the partly comprehensible God we none the less know the distinction between his essence and his properties. The definition of the essence of God consisted in saying that he was a spirit, that is, an immaterial, simple, uncomplicated being, which, therefore, excludes all subdivision. But immediately after that it is disclosed that we know the properties of this simple essence and are able to subdivide it. About the number of these properties it says that it is infinite, but from this infinite number of properties of the simple essence, the spirit, fourteen properties are disclosed to us. After that we are suddenly told that this simple essence, the spirit, differs from all other beings and, besides, has mind and will (nothing is said about what is to be understood by the words " mind " and " will " of a simple essence, the spirit), and on the basis of the fact that the simple essence is composed of mind and will, fourteen properties are divided into three classes : (a) essential properties in general. The essential properties of the divine essence in general (I change nothing and add nothing) are again subdivided (aa) into essential properties of the divine essence in general which distinguish it in general (sic !) from other beings, and (bb) into essential properties of the divine essence in general which distinguish it in particular from other beings, and thus we receive (aaa) unlimitedness, to which for some reason all-perfection is unexpectedly attached by a sign of equality, (bbb) self-existence, (ccc) independence, (ddd) immeasurableness and omnipresence (again unexpectedly patched on to it), (eee) eternity, (fff) unchangeableness, (ggg) almightiness. The properties of the divine mind are (a) omniscience, (b) the highest wisdom ; and the properties of the divine will are (*a*) freedom, (*b*) holiness, (*c*) goodness, (*d*) truth, (*e*) justice.   The method of the exposition is the same as in the previous parts : obscurity of expressions, contradictions, clothed in words which elucidate nothing, an abasement of the subject, its reduction to the lowest sphere, a neglect of the demands of reason, and the eternally repeated tendency to connect in an external, verbal way the most diversified judgments about God, beginning with Abraham and going on to the fathers of the church, and on that tradition alone to base all the arguments.   But in this part, which has so clearly deviated from the path of common sense (from the very first statements about God, where the determination of the divine properties begin), there is a new feature : there is a composition of words which apparently have absolutely no meaning for the author.   Obviously the words have been detached entirely from the thought with which they were connected, and no longer evoke any ideas.   For a long time I made terrible efforts to understand what is understood, for example, by the various spiritual essences, by the distinctions of the properties and by independence, by the divine mind and will, and could not understand it, and convinced myself that all the author wanted was in an external way to connect all the texts, but that even for the author there did not exist a rational connection in his own words.

22.   This article speaks of the same thing that involuntarily presents itself to one when the properties of the incomprehensible God are counted out to him.   Every person who believes in God cannot help feeling the blasphemy of these subdivisions.   And here the words of the fathers of the church express precisely what each believer feels, namely, that God is incomprehensible to reason, and that all those words and epithets which we have applied to God have no clear meaning and blend into one, and that the conception of God as a beginning of everything

and incomprehensible to reason, is simply indivisible, and
that to divide God according to his essence and properties
is the same as destroying the idea of God.

The essence and the essential properties of God are not
distinguished or divided among themselves in reality : on
the contrary, they are one in God. This idea necessarily
results from those passages of Holy Scripture where God
is represented as the purest spirit and from him are removed all materiality, corporeality, and complexity. If
the essential properties in God were indeed separate and
distinct from his essence and from one another, he would
not be simple, but complex, that is, he would be composed
of his essence and of his properties which are distinct
among themselves. Thus reasoned the fathers of the
church : " The Deity is simple and uncompounded," says
St. John Damascene, " for what is composed of many and
various things is composite. If we shall thus take uncre-
atedness, uncommencedness, incorporeality, immortality,
eternity, goodness, creative power, and similar properties
as essential distinctions in God (οὐσιωδειοφόρας ἐπὶ θεοῦ), the
Deity, being composed of so many properties, will not be
simple, but composite ; but it would be extreme infidelity
to affirm that." (p. 145.)

Other extracts are quoted from the holy fathers in
confirmation of this idea, so that one only wonders what
all those former subdivisions and definitions were for.
But these clear, incontestable arguments, which reëcho in
the heart of each believer in God as full of truth, are
preceded by just such an unexpected discussion as was
given in the case of the comprehensibility and incomprehensibility of God, and such as those which precede the
disclosure of each dogma. In the dogma about God
the statement is made and proved that God is incomprehensible, and then there is a pretence at a proof that he
is comprehensible. For the solution of this contradiction
there is invented the doctrine about comprehensibility in

part. Here it says that the essence and the essential
properties of God are not distinguished or divided, and
immediately on p. 147 it says:

" The essence and the essential properties of God, without being distinguished or divided between themselves in
fact, are, none the less, distinguished in our ratiocination,
and not without foundation in God himself, so that the
concept of any one property of his is not at the same time
a concept of his essence, or a concept of any other property."
(p. 147.)

This proposition, in the author's opinion, necessarily
results from Holy Scripture, and there are quoted the
words of Basil the Great that " our distinctions of the divine properties are not merely purely subjective, no, their
foundation is in God himself, in his various manifestations, actions, relations to himself, such as the creation
and providence, though in himself God is one, simple,
uncompounded."   (p. 149.)

Do you imagine that this palpable contradiction of the
holy fathers is accidentally collated ?   Do you think
that it is solved in any way ?   Not in the least.   That is
precisely what the author needs, and in that lies the meaning of this 22d article.   It begins like this :

" This question has been raised in the church since antiquity, but especially during the Middle Ages, both in the
West and the East, and in solving it men have frequently
fallen into extremes.   The first extreme assumes that
between the essence and the essential properties of God,
as well as between the properties themselves, there is a
real difference (τῷ πράγματι, *realis*), so that the properties
form in God something distinct from the essence and from
each other ; the other extreme, on the contrary, affirms
that the essence and all the essential properties of God are
absolutely identical among themselves, and that they
are not separated, either in fact, or even in our ratiocination (ἐπίνοια νοήσει, *cogitatione*)."   (p. 144.)

The Orthodox Church teaches that both propositions are equally remote from truth. Which, then, is nearer to the truth? Nothing is said about that. Two opposite opinions are put forth, and nothing is said for their solution. I carefully searched in all five pages, and there is not a word in them about how it is to be understood. Not a word. The conclusion of the article is as follows:

" Remarkable are also the words of St. Augustine that refer to the present case : ' It is one thing to be God, another to be Father. Though paternity and essence (in God) are one, it is impossible to say that the Father by his paternity is God, by his paternity all-wise. Such has always been the firm conviction of our fathers, and they rejected the Anomœans as having erred far beyond the limits of the faith, because these heretics destroyed all distinction between the essence and the divine properties.' " (p. 150.)

The end of the chapter. But are the Anomœans right, or why are the words of the blessed St. Augustine remarkable ? that makes no difference. But how are we to understand it all ? The words of St. John Damascene are true, as the author himself says. How are they to be made to agree with the contradictory words of St. Augustine ? And are they true or not ? The author does not even regard it as necessary to answer this, and concludes the chapter.

In the preceding article about the essence and the fourteen divine properties I was struck by the trait of the complete disassociation of ideas and the manifest play with mere contradictory or synonymous words in complete darkness ; but here is another feature of an extraordinary neglect, offensive not only to my reason, but also to my feelings, which is shown to me and to the whole congregation which is listening to the teachings of the church.

In this article is directly expressed a contradiction, and it says : " This is white, and this black," and you cannot say that this is white, nor that this is black, for the church teaches you to recognize both, that is, that the black is white, and the white black, so that here is expressed not only a demand that you should believe what the church says, but that you should repeat with your tongue what it says.

After that comes Article 23 : The moral application of the dogma. The moral application of the first dogma, of the dogma of the divine unity, had struck me only by its inconsistency. The moral rules which were taught on the basis of the unity of God were apparently not deduced from it, but were simply patched on the words, " God is one, we must live in oneness," and so forth. But when I met with the second application and, in looking through the whole work for all the moral rules which were inevitably applied to each dogma, recalled what had been said in the Introduction, that the dogmas of faith and the laws of morality (p. 36) had inseparably been revealed by God to men and were inseparably connected, I understood that these applications were not accidental, but very important, as showing the meaning of the dogmas for the saving life, and so I turned my close attention to them. Here is the application of the dogma about the essence and the properties of God :

" (1) God by his essence is a spirit, and, by the chief property of the essence which embraces all the others, he is an unlimited spirit, that is, most perfect, highest, all-glorious. From this (a) we learn, first of all, to honour and love God, for whom shall we honour and whom love, if not the most perfect, when every perfection naturally evokes these feelings in us ? The love of God, united with respect, forms the foundation of all our obligations toward him (Matt. xxii. 37) ; (b) we learn at the same time that our love of God and our honouring of God must be (aa) sincerest, spiritual : God is a Spirit : and they that worship him must worship him in spirit and in truth, says the

Saviour (John iv. 24) ; every external worship can have a
value only when it is an expression of something inward,
otherwise it displeases God (Is. i. 11–15), and the sacrifices of God are a broken spirit, according to the words
of the Prophet (Psalm li. 17) ; (*bb*) highest and fullest,
because in his perfections God infinitely surpasses all other
beings to whom we are able to feel respect and love ; consequently, him above all else must we love with all our
heart, and with all our soul, and with all our mind, and
with all our strength (Mark xii. 30) ; (*cc*) most profoundly reverential : if even the seraphim, who in heaven
surround the throne of God the All-holder, unable to
endure the grandeur of his glory, cover their faces when
they cry unto one another, Holy, holy, holy, is the Lord of
hosts (Is. vi. 3), then with what trepidation of awe ought
we, the lowest and weakest of his spiritual creatures, to
serve him (Psalm ii. 11) ?

"(*c*) Let us learn to glorify God with our heart and our
mouth, with our mind and all our life, remembering the
words of the Psalmist : Give unto the Lord the glory due
unto his name : bring an offering, and come into his
courts (Psalm xcv. 8 ; cxliv. 3), and the words of the Saviour : Let your light so shine before men, that they may
see your good works, and glorify your Father which is in
heaven (Matt. v. 16).

"(*d*) Let us learn, at last, to turn to God as our highest
good, and in him alone look for our fullest consolation,
repeating with David : Whom have I in heaven but thee ?
and there is none upon earth that I desire beside thee.
My flesh and my heart faileth : but God is the strength
of my heart, and my portion for ever (Psalm lxxiii. 25,
26). However profound the thirst of our mind may be in
its search after truth, God is the highest truth ; however
fiery the striving of our will may be toward the good, God
is the most perfect good ; however insatiable the love of
our heart may be for happiness and bliss, God is the

highest and interminable bliss. Where, then, if not in him, shall we be able to find a full gratification for all the high needs of our spirit ?

" (2) Reflecting, in particular, on the separate proper-ties of the divine essence, which distinguish God from his creatures, we can draw from them new lessons for our-selves. And (*a*) if God alone is self-existent, that is, is in no way under any obligations to any one, while all the other beings, consequently we, too, are under obligations to him, we must (*aa*) constantly humble ourselves before him, according to the words of Scripture, What hast thou that thou didst not receive ? now if thou didst receive it, why dost thou glory, as if thou hadst not received it ? (1 Cor. iv. 7) ; and (*bb*) constantly thank him : for in him we live and move and have our being (Acts xvii. 28). (*b*) If he alone is independent and all-satisfied, and so does not demand our goodness (Psalm xvi. 2), but, cn the contrary, gives to all life and breath, and all things (Acts xvii. 25), we must (*aa*) experience within us a feel-ing of the fullest dependence on him and of the most complete submission to him, and (*bb*) in bringing him gifts or sacrifices not imagine that we are obliging the all-satisfied God in this manner, since all which we have is his property. (*c*) The confidence that we are always before the face of the omnipresent God, no matter where we may be, (*aa*) naturally inclines us to act before him with the greatest circumspection and reverence ; (*bb*) can keep us from sins, as it once kept Joseph from sinning (Gen. xxxix. 9) ; (*cc*) can encourage and console us in all perils, as it consoled David, who said about himself : I have set the Lord always before me ; because he is at my right hand, I shall not be moved (Psalm xvi. 8) ; (*dd*) can incite us to invoke, glorify, and thank the Lord in every place (John iv. 21–24).

" (*d*) Keeping in mind that God alone is eternal, while everything else which surrounds us on earth is temporal and vanishing, we learn (*aa*) not to cleave with the soul to perishable possessions, but to seek the one, imperishable possession in God (Matt. vi. 19, 20); (*bb*) not to put our trust in princes, nor in the sons of man, who may die any moment and leave us without a support (Psalm cxlvi. 3–5), but to put our trust in him who alone has immortality (1 Tim. vi. 16) and will never abandon us.

"(*e*) The thought of God's complete unchangeability (*aa*) can still more incite us to put this exclusive trust in God, for men in general are fickle, the favour of the great and mighty of the earth is easily shaken and passes, the very love of our relatives and friends frequently betrays us, whereas God alone is always the same and unchangeable; (*bb*) can at the same time incite us to imitate the unchangeableness of God in a moral sense, that is, to be as firm and constant as possible in all the honourable pursuits of our spirit, and in our unwavering march along the path of virtue and salvation.

"(*f*) The live faith in almighty God teaches us (*aa*) to implore his aid and blessing in all our undertakings: except the Lord keep the city, the watchman waketh but in vain (Psalm cxxvii. 1); (*bb*) not to be afraid of anything and not to lose courage amidst the greatest dangers, so long as we are doing what pleases him and thus attract his good-will: if God be for us, who can be against us? (Rom. viii. 31); but (*cc*) to fear him and tremble before him, if we do what displeases him: he is able to destroy not only our body, but also our soul in hell (Matt. x. 28).

"(3) If we turn our attention to the properties of the divine mind, we shall find even here many edifying things for ourselves. (*a*) God is omniscient: what consolation and encouragement for the righteous man! Let people who do not know his intentions and are not able to appreciate his actions, insult, and even persecute him, he is rewarded by the knowledge that God himself clearly sees his soul with all its thoughts and wishes, knows all

his deeds in the bloody battle with the enemies of salvation, knows his intentional privations and innocent suffering, knows every sigh and every tear of his amidst heavy
temptation! No matter how hypocritical he may be before men, how much he may try to conceal his criminal
intentions, in what darkness he may be committing his
lawlessness, he cannot help confessing that there is a
being from whom it is impossible to conceal himself, before whom everything is naked and open (Heb. iv. 13),
and that it is possible to deceive men, but never God.
(*b*) God is infinitely wise; and thus (*aa*) let not our
mind and soul be dejected if in social life or in Nature we
shall see any phenomena which seem to threaten a universal ruin and destruction, for all that is done or omitted by
the unsearchable fate of the highest wisdom; (*bb*) let us
not be faint of heart or murmur against God if we ourselves have occasion to be in straitened circumstances, but
let us rather give ourselves altogether to his holy will,
believing that he knows better than we what is useful and
what harmful to us; (*cc*) let us learn according to our
strength to imitate his highest wisdom, tending all the
time toward that supreme aim, which he has set for us,
and selecting for ourselves those most reliable means,
which he himself has outlined for us in his revelation.

" (4) Finally, each of the properties of the divine will
either only offers us a model for imitation, or at the same
time also imparts certain other moral lessons.   (*a*) God is
called supremely free, because he always selects only
what is good, and this he does without any external pressure or incitement; it is in this, then, that our true freedom ought to consist! In the possibility and freely
acquired habit of doing only what is good, only because
it is good, and not in the arbitrary will of doing good and
evil, as people generally think, and still less in the arbitrary will of doing only what is bad: for whosoever com-
mitteth sin is the servant of sin, says our Saviour (John

viii. 34), and, committing evil, we every time lose part of our freedom, more and more submitting to our passions and impure strivings, over which we ought to rule. (*b*) God is supremely holy and has commanded to us: ye shall sanctify yourselves, and ye shall be holy; for I am holy, the Lord your God (Lev. xi. 44). Without this condition we can never become worthy of the most blissful union with the Lord: for what communion hath light with darkness? (2 Cor. vi. 14); nor shall we ever be worthy of seeing God: for only the pure in heart shall see God (Matt. v. 8). (*c*) God is infinitely good to all his creatures and to us in particular; this (*aa*) teaches us to thank him for all his benefits, and for his paternal love to repay him with filial love: we love him, because he first loved us (1 John iv. 19)."

Not only is there no sense in all that, but there is not even any connection except what the French call *à propos*. Indeed, what moral application can there be from the fact that God is one and immeasurable, and a spirit, and trine? What is remarkable is not that the exposition of this moral application of the dogma is written disconnectedly and badly, but that an application has been invented for a dogma that can have no applications at all. Involuntarily it occurs to me: why should I know these incomprehensible, most contradictory dogmas, since from their knowledge absolutely nothing can result?

CHAPTER II. Of God trine in persons.

Before proceeding to the disclosure of the dogma itself, I involuntarily stop at the words "in persons," "God's person." I have read and studied the exposition of the dogmas about the essence of God. There was no definition there of the word person, or hypostasis, which was used in the definition of the Trinity. Only in the passage where the anthropomorphists were refuted it said that under the divine person we must understand "the manifestation of God in his works." But that apparently has no reference to the Trinity. Maybe the definition of this word, so necessary for the comprehension of the Trinity, will become clear from the exposition itself. I proceed to read. Here is the introduction :

"The truths about God, one in essence, and about his essential attributes, so far expounded by us, do not embrace the whole Christian teaching about God. In acknowledging God to be one, we have not yet the right to call ourselves Christians : the one God is professed also by the Jews, who did not accept Christ the Saviour as the Messiah, and who reject Christianity ; he is also professed by the Mohammedans and has been admitted by many old and new heretics in the lap of Christianity itself. The full teaching about God, which it is necessary to keep in the heart and profess with the lips, in order worthily to bear the name of Christian, consists in this, that God is one and trine, one in substance, trine in persons." (p. 156.)

What does that mean ? All the attributes of God, as given in the division about the essence of God, such as unlimitedness, immeasurableness, and the others, exclude the concept of person. The fact that God is a spirit is still less in agreement with persons. What, then, does " in persons " mean ? There is no answer to this, and the exposition goes on.

" This doctrine forms the radical, essentially Christian dogma : directly upon it are based, and, consequently, with its refutal are inevitably refuted, the dogmas about our Redeemer the Lord Jesus, about our Sanctifier the All-holy Ghost, and after that, more or less all the dogmas which refer to the house-management of our salvation. And in professing God as one in essence and trine in persons — " (p. 168.)

In essence God is one, and God, it was said in the preceding, is a spirit. In spite of the essence, it was said that God had fourteen attributes. All the attributes exclude the concept of person. What then is " in persons " ? There must, then, be still a third division. First it was (1) according to the essence and (2) according to the attributes. Now a third division is added : according to persons. On what is this division based ? There is no answer, and the exposition goes on :

" By professing in this manner we differ not only from the pagans and certain heretics, who assumed many or two gods, but also from the Jews, and from the Mohammedans, and from all heretics, who have recognized the one God only."

What do I care from whom I differ ? The less I differ from other people, the better it is for me. What is a person ? There is no answer, and the exposition is continued :

" But being the most important of all the Christian dogmas, the dogma about the Most Holy Trinity is at the same time the most incomprehensible."

That is the very reason why I thirst so much, if not for an explanation, at least for an expression which would be comprehensible. If it is entirely incomprehensible, there can be no answer.

"We saw a number of incomprehensible things when we expounded the doctrine about God one in essence and about his essential attributes, especially about his self-existence, eternity, omnipresence." (p. 167.)

There was nothing incomprehensible about that. All those were expressions from various sides of the first concept about the existence of God, — a concept which is familiar to every believer in God. These expressions were for the most part incorrectly used, but there was nothing incomprehensible in them.

"Many incomprehensible things shall we also see later on, in disclosing the dogma of the incarnation and person of our Saviour, about his death on the cross, about the ever-virginity of the Mother of God, about the action of grace upon us, and so on. But the mystery of Christian mysteries is indisputably the dogma about the Most Holy Trinity: just as there are three persons in one God, so the Father is God, and the Son is God, and the Holy Ghost is God, however not three Gods, but one God, — all this surpasses all understanding." (p. 157.)

That is precisely what I want to know. A father of the church says:

"What manner of reasoning, what power and might of the intellect, what vivacity of the mind and perspicacity of imagination will show me — 'How does the Trinity exist?' And in another place: 'However, what it is, is unspeakable; no tongue of the angels, much less of men, can explain it.'" (p. 157.)

The Trinity is God. What is God and how does he exist? that surpasses my imagination. But if the essence of God surpasses my understanding, I can know nothing about the essence of God. But if we know that he is the Trinity, it is necessary to say what we understand by this appellation. What do these words mean in relation to God? So far there have been no explanations of these words, and the exposition is continued:

" So this is the reason why the heretics who have tried to explain the truths of religion with their own intellect have stumbled over the mystery of the Most Holy Trinity more than over any other dogma. So, if at all anywhere, we must here more especially stick closely to the positive doctrine of the church, which has guarded and defended this dogma against all heretical opinions, and which has expounded it for the guidance of the Orthodox with the greatest possible precision." (pp. 157 and 158.)

It is precisely this exposition that I am in search of, that is, I want to know what is meant by God one and three. For, if I say that I believe, without understanding, and if any one else says that he believes that God is one and three, we are lying, for it is impossible to believe what we do not understand. It is possible to repeat with the tongue, but it is not possible to believe words which not merely have no meaning, but directly violate sound reason. Here is the way the Orthodox Church expounds this doctrine with precision:

" (1) In the symbol of St. Gregory Thaumaturgus, the Bishop of Neocæsaria: 'There is one God, Father of the living Word, of wisdom and self-existing force, and of the eternal form: the perfect progenitor of the perfect, Father of the only-begotten Son. There is one God, one from one, God from God, form and expression of the Deity, active word, wisdom, containing the composition of all, and force building the whole creation; true Son of the true Father, the unseen of the unseen, the incorruptible of the incorruptible, the immortal of the immortal, the eternal of the eternal. And there is one Holy Ghost, issuing from God, having appeared through the Son, that. is, to men; life, in which is the cause of the living; holy source; holiness offering sanctification. To him appears God the Father, who is above all and in all, and God the Son, who is through all. Trinity, perfect in glory and eternity, indivisible and inseparable in dominion. And so there is in the Trinity neither created, nor ancillary, nor additive, which has not been before, or which will come later. The Father has never been without the Son, nor the Son without the Holy Ghost; but the Trinity is invariable, unchangeable, and always one and the same.'

" (2) In the Nicæo-Constantinopolitan symbol: 'I believe in one God the Father — and in one Lord Jesus Christ, the Son of God, the only-begotten, born from the Father before all ages, light of light, true God of true God, born, uncreated, of one substance with the Father — and in the Holy Ghost, the life-creating Lord, who proceedeth from the Father; who with the Father and the Son is worshipped and glorified.'

" (3) In the symbol which is known under the name of that of St. Athanasius of Alexandria: 'This is the Catholic creed: Let us worship the one God in the Trinity and the Trinity in the One, neither blending the hypostases, nor separating the essence. For different is the hypostasis of the Father, different that of the Son, and different that of the Holy Ghost. But that of the Father, and of the Son, and of the Holy Ghost is one Deity, an equal glory, a coeval grandeur. As the Father, so is the Son, and so is the Holy Ghost — Thus: God is the Father, God is the Son, and God is the Holy Ghost; and yet not three Gods, but one God — God is not created by any one, nor born. The Son was not created by the Father himself, nor made, nor born, nor issued from him — And in this Trinity nothing is first or last; nothing more or less; but the three hypostases are complete, coeval with each other and equal.' " (pp. 158 and 159.)

That is the exposition with the greatest possible precision! I read farther down:

"Examining more closely this doctrine of the Orthodox Church about the Most Holy Trinity, we cannot help observing that it is composed of three propositions: one general and two particular, which directly result from the general and disclose it through themselves.

"The general proposition is in God, one in substance, three persons or hypostases: the Father, the Son, and the Holy Ghost. The particular propositions: the first, — as it is one in essence, so three persons in God are equal to each other and uni-existent; and the Father is God, and the Son is God, and the Holy Ghost is God, not three gods, but one God. The second: however, as three persons they are different among themselves by their personal attributes: the Father is not born from any one; the Son is born from the Father; the Holy Ghost proceeds from the Father." (p. 159.)

I have not left out anything, hoping all the time to find an explanation, and what? The author not only does not find it necessary to explain what is said here, but, looking attentively at it, he finds here, too, subdivisions, and he proceeds. (p. 161.)

As I get no definition not only of the persons of the Trinity, but even of the word "person," though there is an unnecessarily detailed statement about the essence and the attributes of God, I involuntarily begin to suspect that the author and the church have no definition of this word, and so speak themselves not knowing what. My suspicion is confirmed by the following article. As always, after the exposition of an unintelligible dogma there follows the exposition of the dispute, which has led to this exposition. And here it says:

"That God is one in substance and trine in persons, has unchangeably been professed by the holy church from the very beginning, as is witnessed by its symbols and other incontrovertible proofs."

From what beginning remains unknown. But from common sense, from the historical data, even from the exposition given here and in Art. 28 of the different opposing opinions, it is evident that there was no such beginning, and that the dogma was formed by degrees. Then follows a confirmation of the fact that the dogma was not formed in an indefinite " very beginning," but at a very definite historical period of church history.

" But the manner of expression of this truth in the first centuries was unequal even among the Orthodox teachers of the faith. Some used the words οὐσία, φύσις, *substantia, natura,* in order to signify the essence or substance of God; others, however only few of them and rarely, used these words to designate the divine persons. Similarly, certain words, ὑπόστασις, ὕπαρξις, or τρόπος ὑπάρξεως, designated the persons in God; others, on the contrary, designated by these words the essence of God, and for the designation of the persons used the words πρόσωπος, *persona.* The different use of the word ' hypostasis ' has even led to considerable disputes in the East, especially at Antioch, and for some time created discord between the Eastern and the Western churches, of which the first taught that it was necessary to profess three hypostases in God, fearing a reproach of Sabellianism, while the others affirmed that there was but one hypostasis in God, fearing a reproach of Arianism. To solve the misunderstanding a council was called in Alexandria (in the year 362), where, together with St. Athanasius the Great, there were present bishops from Italy, Arabia, Egypt, and Libya. At the council, the representatives of both parties were heard, and it turned out that both sides believed precisely alike, differing only in words, both the Orthodox and those who said, ' In God there is one essence and three hypostases,' and the others who said, ' In God is one hypostasis and three persons,' for the first used the word 'hypostasis' instead of πρόσωπος, *persona*, while the latter used it instead of οὐσία, *substantia*, essence." (pp. 160 and 161.)

Farther on it says that if at first the words οὐσία and ὑπόστασις were used differently, or rather, indifferently, in the sixth, seventh, and the following centuries the concept appears as generally accepted, that is hypostasis was used in reference to three, οὐσία to one. Thus, if I had the slightest hope of getting an explanation of what is to be understood by the word "person," of that on the basis of which 1=3, I, after reading this exposition about the use of the words by the fathers, came to understand that such a definition (which is inevitably necessary for the comprehension of the Trinity) does not exist and cannot be; the fathers used words without ascribing any meaning to them, and so used them indiscriminately, now in one, and now in a contrary sense, and finally agreed not on the ideas, but on the words. The same is confirmed by what follows:

"But while the Orthodox teachers of the faith differed only in words, invariably professing one God in the Trinity and the Trinity in One, the heretics perverted —" (p. 162.)

That is, now without any farther explanation, One is equal to the Trinity, and the Trinity is equal to One. But the holy fathers professed:

"The heretics perverted the very idea of the dogma, some of them denying the trinity of persons in God, while others admitted three Gods."

Again some say black, and others say white. Both are wrong, but we say, "Black is white, and white is black." Why is it so? Why, because the church said so, that is, the tradition of those men who believe in that tradition. Here is the idea of the heretics who denied the Trinity:

"(*a*) Even during the life of the apostles: Simon the

Magician taught that the Father, the Son, and the Holy Ghost were only manifestations and forms of the selfsame person, and that the one God, in the capacity of Father, had revealed himself to the Samaritans; in the capacity of the Son, as Christ, to the Jews; in the capacity of the Holy Ghost, to the pagans; (*b*) in the second century, Praxeas affirmed that one and the same God, as concealed in himself, was the Father, but as having appeared in the work of creation and later, in the redemption, was the Son Christ; (*c*) in the third century, Noetus, who also recognized the Father and Son as one person, one God, who had become incarnate and had suffered torment and death; Sabellius, who had taught that the Father, the Son, and the Holy Ghost were only three names, three actions (ἐνέργεια) of one and the same person, God, who had been incarnate and had suffered death for us; and Paul of Samosata, according to whose words the Son and the Holy Ghost were in God, as mind and strength were in man; (*d*) in the fourth century, Marcellus of Ancyra and his disciple Photinus: they preached, after Sabellius, that the Father, the Son, and the Holy Ghost were only names of the selfsame person in God, and after Paul of Samosata, that the Son, or the Word, was the mind of God, and the Holy Spirit, the power of God." (pp. 162 and 163.)

Here is the conception of other heretics:

"The common idea of all these was that although the divine persons, the Father, the Son, and the Holy Ghost, were of one substance, they were not one in substance, and that they had one nature, but had it each separately, as, for the example, three persons of the human race, and so were three Gods, and not one God." (p. 163.)

Without having the question answered whether the teaching of the heretics was true or false, I am unable to say that I understand what they have been saying. Similarly, without entering into a discussion as to whether

it is right that God should be one and three, I am unable
to say that I understand what it means, although the
dogma is expounded in all its fulness, as the author avers.
In all its fulness the dogma is expounded as follows:

" ' Let us worship the one God in the Trinity and the
Trinity in the One, neither blending the hypostases,
nor separating the essence.' Neither blending the essence,
that is, recognizing the Father, the Son, and the Holy
Ghost not merely as three names, or forms, or manifestations of the selfsame God, as the heretics have represented
him, nor as three attributes, or forces, or actions, but as
three independent persons of the Deity, since each of
them, the Father, and the Son, and the Holy Ghost, pos-
sessing a divine mind and the other divine attributes, has
his own, personal properties, ' for one is the hypostasis of
the Father, another, of the Son, and still another, of the
Holy Ghost.' Nor separating the essence, that is, affirm-
ing that the Father, the Son, and the Holy Ghost are one
in essence, exist inseparably one in the other, and, differing
from each other only in their personal attributes, have an
identity of mind, will, and all the other divine attributes,
— not at all as there exist three entities of any class of
beings among the creatures, entities that have one nature.
' Among the creatures,' let us speak with the words of St.
John Damascene, ' the common nature of the entities is
perceived only by the mind, for the entities do not exist
one in the other, but each separate and distinct, that is, in
itself, and each has much to distinguish it from the others.
They differ in place and time, in disposition of the will, in
firmness, in external appearance or form, in habits, in tem-
perament, in worth, in the manner of life, and in the other
distinctive properties, but most of all, because they do not
exist one in the other, but each exists separately. For
this reason we say: two, three, many men. But in
the holy, transubstantial, all-surpassing, incomprehensible
Trinity we see something different, Here the universality

and unity are viewed in fact according to the coeternality of the persons, according to the identity of the essentiality, activity, and will, according to the concord of definitions, according to the identity — I do not say similitude, but identity — of power, almightiness, and goodness, and according to the one tendency of motion —   Each of the hypostases has a unity with the other, not less than with itself; that is, the Father, the Son, and the Holy Ghost are one in all respects but ungeneratedness, birth, and derivation, and are divided only in our ratiocination (ἐπίνοια).   For we know only one God, and only in the properties of fatherhood, sonhood, and derivation do we present a difference —   In the unlimited Deity we cannot assume, as in us, spatial distance, because the hypostases exist one in the other, but in such a way that they are not blended, but united, according to the words of the Lord: I am the Father, and the Father in me (John xiv. 11); nor distinction of will, definitions, activities, power, or anything else, which in us produce a real and complete division.   Therefore we recognize the Father, the Son, and the Holy Ghost not as three Gods, but as one God in the Holy Trinity.'   The whole incomprehensibility of the mystery of the Most Holy Trinity consists precisely in this, that the three independent persons of the Deity are one in essence and entirely inseparable; if they existed separately one from the other, like three entities among the creatures, there would be nothing incomprehensible in that.   'The Deity is one and three: oh, most glorious transformation!'   What is united in essence is divided according to the persons: the indivisible is divided, what is one is trebled: that is the Father, the Son, and the living Spirit, preserving all."   (pp. 164 and 165.)

So here it is, all the doctrine, all the God‑revealed truth, revealed to me in all its fulness for the sake of my salvation.   "The Deity is one and three.   Oh, most glorious transformation!"   The exposition and explana‑

tion are ended, and there will be nothing else.   And this
through the mouth of his church says God the Father to
me, his son, who with all my power am looking for truth
and salvation!   To my entreaty and tears of despair he
replies to me: " The indivisible is divided, what is one is
trebled: that is the Father, the Son, and the living Spirit,
preserving all."   And to the demands of my reason, which
has been given me for the comprehension of God, there is
no other answer.   I cannot say, nor can any one else say,
that I have comprehended it, and so I cannot say that I
believe.   With my tongue I can say that I believe that
" what is one is trebled.   Oh, most glorious transformation!"   But when I say that, I am a liar and an atheist,
and it is precisely this that the church demands of me, that
is, those people who assert that they believe in it.   But
that is not true: they do not believe and nobody has ever
believed it.   What a marvellous phenomenon!   Christianity will soon have existed for a thousand years in
Russia.   For a thousand years the pastors have been
teaching their flocks the foundations of the faith.   The
foundation of the faith is the dogma of the Trinity.   Ask
a peasant, a country woman, what the Trinity is.   Out of
ten hardly one will answer you.   It cannot be said that
that is due to ignorance.   Ask them what the teaching of
Christ consists in.   Everybody will tell you.   And yet
the dogma of the Trinity is not complicated or long.
Why, then, does no one know it?   Because it is impossible to know what makes no sense.

Then there follow proofs that these truths, that is, that
God is a Trinity, have been revealed by God to all men.
The proofs are divided into proofs from the Old and the
New Testament.   In the Old Testament, which forms
the teaching of the Jews, of those Jews who regard the
Trinity as the greatest blasphemy, in this Old Testament
do they look for proofs that God has revealed his three-
fold nature to men.   Here are these proofs from the Old

Testament : (1) Because God said, "Let us make," and not "Let me make : " that was so because he spoke with his Son and the Holy Ghost.   (pp. 165, 166.)

(2) Because he said, "Adam, one of us."   By "us" are meant the three : the Father, the Son, and the Holy Ghost.   (3) The Bible says: "Let us confound their language," and not, "Let me confound ; " consequently the three Gods wanted to confound it.   (4) Because three angels came to Abraham, — those were the Father, the Son, and the Holy Ghost, who came to see Abraham. (pp. 169, 170.)

(5) Because in the Book of Numbers it is commanded that the word "Lord" should be repeated three times. (6) Because in David's Psalter it says, "Their whole host." "Their" proves the Trinity.   (7) A proof of the Trinity is found in the fact that Isaiah said three times, "Holy, holy, holy."   (8) Proofs are found in all those passages of the Old Testament where the words "son and spirit" are used (Psalm ii. 7 ; Is. xlviii. 16, xi. 2, lxi. 1 ; Job xxxiii. 4).   "The Lord hath said unto me, Thou art my Son ; this day have I begotten thee.   The Lord God, and his Spirit, hath sent me, and the Spirit of the Lord shall rest upon him," and so forth.   Those are all the proofs from the Old Testament.   I have not omitted a single one.   The author sees himself that the proofs are poor, and that it is possible to find as many or even more proofs in any book you please, and so he thinks it necessary to give explanations.   Later on he says :

"And why they are not entirely clear, why it has pleased God to disclose in the Old Testament the mystery of the Most Holy Trinity only to a certain degree, — that is concealed in the plans of his infinite wisdom.   The godly teachers assumed for this two main causes : (a) one lay in general in the property of human nature, which was limited and impaired, and had to be led to the knowledge of the highest mysteries of revelation only by degrees, in proportion to its unfolding and strengthening, and receptivity. 'It was not without danger,' reasons St. Gregory the Divine, 'before professing the Divinity to preach clearly the Son, and before the Son had been called (I shall express myself rather boldly) to weigh us down with the sermon about the Holy Ghost, and to subject us to danger and make us lose our last strength, as is the case with people who are burdened with food which is not taken in measure, or who direct their feeble vision to the sun's light; it was necessary for the treble light to shine on the illuminated by progressive additions, as David says, by ascensions (Psalm lxxxiv. 5), progressions from glory to glory, and advancements.' (b) Another cause lay in the quality and weaknesses of the Jewish nation, to whom the Old Testament revelation was made: 'God, in his infinite wisdom,' says the blessed Theodoret, 'was not pleased to communicate to the Jews any clear idea of the Holy Trinity, in order that they might not find in this a good cause for worshipping many gods, — since they had been so prone to follow the Egyptian abomination; this is the reason why, after the Babylonian captivity, when the Jews felt such a distinct loathing for polytheism, we meet in their sacred and even profane books many more passages than before in which the divine persons are mentioned.' We must observe, at last, that, in picking out the places from the Old Testament, which contain references to the Most Holy Trinity, we had in view mainly to prove that the teaching about this mystery is by no means so new in the New Testament, as the later Jews say, and that the pious men of the Old Testament believed in the same tri-hypostatic God, in the Father, and the Son, and the Holy Ghost, in whom we believe — But the foundations of this most important of all the Christian dogmas is, beyond doubt, contained in the Books (Art. 27—b) of the New Testament." (pp. 173 and 174.)

Here are the proofs from the New Testament. The first proof the Theology finds in Christ's conversation with his disciples: Believe me that I am in the Father, and the Father in me (John xiv. 11); and whatsoever ye shall ask in my name, that will I do, that the Father may be glorified in the Son (John xiv. 13). From the fact that Jesus Christ calls himself the Son of the Father, God, just as he taught all men to call themselves the sons of God, it is argued that Jesus Christ is a second person of God. The author says: " Here evidently two persons of the Holy Trinity, the Father and the Son, are distinguished." (p. 175).

The second proof is taken from the passage where Jesus Christ says to his disciples, If ye love me, keep my commandments. And I will pray the Father, he shall give you another Comforter, that he may abide with you for ever; even the Spirit of truth; whom the world cannot receive (John xiv. 15–17). The last verse is not written out, but instead of it the continuation is taken from verse 26 of the same chapter: but the Comforter, which is the Holy Ghost, whom the Father will send in my name, he shall teach you all things, and bring all things to your remembrance, whatsoever I have said unto you. (p. 175.)

From this it is concluded:

" Here all three persons of the Most Holy Trinity are distinguished, namely, as persons : the Son, who speaks of himself: I will pray, — the Father: I will pray the Father, — the Holy Ghost, who is called another Comforter, consequently distinct from the Father; and he will be sent to take the place of the Son with the apostles and to teach them everything; consequently, he is just such a person as the Son." (p. 175.)

Because the paraclete, that is, the comforter, whom Christ promises his disciples after his death, is once during that conversation called the Holy Ghost, it is taken as a proof that Christ in this conversation revealed the mystery of the Holy Trinity.   No attention at all is paid to the meaning which this word has in the whole conversation, for even there the comforter is called the spirit of truth, precisely what Christ calls his teaching. I go away, and come again unto you (John xiv. 28); and I in you, and ye in me (*ib*. 20); if a man love me, he will keep my words: and my father will love him, and we will come unto him, and make our abode with him (*ib*. 23); I will not leave you comfortless: I will come to you (*ib*. 18); for he shall receive the Spirit of truth, and shall shew it unto you (John xvi. 14).

These passages, which explain the whole meaning of the conversation, are not quoted, but the word "holy," which is attached as an epithet to the spirit, is taken as a proof that here Christ spoke of the third person of the Trinity.

Third proof: But when the Comforter is come, whom I will send unto you from the Father, even the Spirit of truth, which proceedeth from the Father, he shall testify of me (John xv. 26).   These words, which quite clearly and simply say that when I shall no longer be alive, and you shall be permeated by the spirit of truth, by that truth which I have taught you, and which proceeds from God, you will convince yourself of the truth of my teaching, — these words are taken as a new proof that here are clearly distinguished, as in the previous texts, all three persons of the Holy Trinity, the Father, the Son, and the Holy Ghost, and at the same time they prove the consubstantiality of the Holy Ghost with God: the Spirit of truth which proceedeth from the Father.

Fourth proof: The words of John (xvi. 15), Therefore said I, that the Spirit of truth shall take of mine, and shall shew it unto you, — the words which clearly speak of the spirit of the teaching as given by Jesus Christ serve as a proof that here mention is made of the consubstantiality with the Son.

Fifth: The words, I came out from God, I came forth from the Father (John xvi. 27, 28), which cannot signify anything but the filial relation of any man to God, precisely what Jesus Christ has preached, are taken as a proof that "here with new force is expressed the idea of the consubstantiality of the Son with the Father."

In the second series of proofs from the New Testament there appear first the concluding words of St. Matthew: Go ye therefore and teach all nations, baptizing them in the name of the Father, and of the Son, and of the Holy Ghost (Matt. xxviii. 19), which Jesus Christ said, when he appeared to his disciples after the resurrection.

Without saying anything about the meaning and the especial character in general of the whole Gospel after the resurrection, of which mention will be made later, these words serve only as a proof, — as which even the church understands it, — that in accepting Christianity it was necessary to acknowledge the Father, the Son, and the Holy Ghost, as the foundations of the teaching. But from this does not follow by any means that God consists of three persons, and so the demands that the words "the Father, the Son, and the Holy Ghost" be used can by no means have anything in common with the arguments about the existence of God in three persons.

The Theology itself admits that the customary formula of baptism can by no means be regarded as a proof of the Trinity of God, and so, on pp. 177 and 178, it explains why it is necessary to understand God in three persons by this. The explanations are as follows:

"The Saviour had before explained to the apostles more than once that under the appellation of the Father was to be understood God the Father who had sent him into the world (John vi. 38–40; vii. 16, 18, 28; xi. 42, and elsewhere) and who is another that beareth witness of him (John v. 32); under the name of the Son he understood himself, whom the apostles indeed professed as the Son of

God who came from the Father (Matt. xvi. 16 ; John xvi. 30) ; finally, under the name of the Holy Ghost he understood another Comforter whom he had promised to send to them in his place from the Father (John xiv. 16 ; xv. 26)." (p. 177.)

No proof is needed that Christ understood God by the Father, for that is admitted by everybody, but there is no proof, and there can be none, that under the Son he meant himself, and under the Holy Ghost a new person of the Trinity. As a proof that he is the second person they adduce the passage (Matt. xvi. 16), where Peter says to Christ what Christ has always said about all other people, that is, that they are sons of God ; and John xvi. 30, where his disciples say to him what he teaches all other men. In proof of the separate existence of the third person there are repeated the same verses (John xiv. 14 and xv. 26), which mean something different.

Under the name of the Comforter Jesus Christ understands the spirit of truth, but cannot understand any third person. The clearest proof of it is that in the gospels there are no proofs ; outside of these passages, which prove nothing, it is impossible to find anything else. But the Theology, not at all embarrassed by this, regards its proposition as proved, and says :

" Consequently, since the Saviour did not consider it necessary to add a new explanation of the above mentioned words (Matt. xxviii. 19), he in the present case understood, and the apostles understood with him, nobody else but the three divine persons by the Father, and the Son, and the Holy Ghost."

In the third series there is one last and chief proof from the New Testament ; those are the words of John in his first Epistle, v. 7 : For there are three that bear record in heaven, the Father, the Word, and the Holy Ghost : and these three are one. The Theology says :

" In this passage there is expressed, even more clearly

than before, the Trinity of the persons in God and the
unity of the essence.   The Trinity of the persons : for
the Father, the Word, and the Holy Ghost are called three
witnesses ; consequently they are distinct from each other
and the Word and the Holy Ghost, mentioned as witnesses with the Father, are not merely two of his attributes, or forces, or actions, but just such persons as the
Father.   The unity of the essence : for if the Word or
the Holy Ghost did not have the selfsame divine nature
and substance with the Father, but a lower, created
nature, there would be an endless distance between them
and the Father, and it would not be possible to say : and
these three are one."

But unfortunately, although this passage, no matter how
weak it is, may serve, if not as proof, at least as an incen-
tive to the assertion that God is one and three, unfortunately not all agree with the theologians.   It says :

" Unjust are those who wish to weaken the power of
this passage, by asserting that the three celestial witnesses,
the Father, the Word, and the Holy Ghost, are represented
as one, not in relation to their essence, but only in relation
to their unanimous testimony, just like the three terrestrial witnesses, who are mentioned in the following verse :
There are three that bear witness in earth, the spirit, and
the water, and the blood : and these three agree in one
(1 John v. 8), form unquestionably one, not by their
essence, but only in relation to the testimony.   It must be
remarked that (a) the apostle himself distinguishes the
unity of the celestial and the unity of the terrestrial witnesses ; of the latter, which are indeed different among
themselves or different in their essence, he expresses himself only by saying : and these three agree in one (καὶ οἱ
τρεῖς εἰς τὸ ἕν εἰσιν), that is, in one, in relation to the testimony ; but of the first he says : And these three are one
(καὶ οὗτοι οἱ τρεῖς ἕν εἰσιν), and not, agree in one ; consequently ' are one ' is a great deal more than what the

terrestrial witnesses are, — they are one, not only in relation to the testimony, but also in their essence. This
is the more certain since (b) the holy apostle himself in
the next verse calls the testimony of the celestial witnesses, without any distinction, the witness of God : If
we receive the witness of men, the witness of God is
greater ; consequently he assumes that the three witnesses
of heaven are one, namely in their Divinity, or are three
persons of God. It is the more certain since (c) the
same holy apostle even before, in his Gospel, mentions
each of the three witnesses of heaven, the Father, the
Son or Word, and the Holy Ghost, and mentions them as
three persons of God, consubstantial among themselves,
when expounding the words of the Saviour : Though I
bear record of myself, yet my record is true : for I know
whence I came, and whither I go. I am one that bears
witness of myself, and the Father that sent me beareth
witness of me (John viii. 14, 18 ; cf. John v. 32, 37) ;
but when the Comforter is come, whom I will send unto
you from the Father, even the Spirit of truth, which proceedeth from the Father, he shall testify of me (John xv.
26) ; he shall glorify me : for he shall receive of mine,
and shall show it unto you. All things that the Father
hath are mine : therefore said I, that he shall take of
mine, and shall shew it unto you (John xvi. 14, 15)."
(pp. 179 and 180.)

Still more unfortunate it is that this solitary passage,
which, however weak it is, at least in some way confirms
the words of the three Gods and of one, that this same
passage turns out, according to the testimony of the Theology, to be debatable, and, according to the unanimous
testimony of all learned criticism, spurious :

"Unfair is the attempt which is made to doubt the
authenticity of the passage under discussion, by pointing
out that it does not exist in certain Greek texts of the
New Testament and in certain translations, especially in

the East, and by showing that it was not used by the ancient fathers of the church, such as St. Gregory the Divine, Ambrose, Hilary, nor by the Councils of Nice and Sardis and others, which were against the Arians, though this verse might have served as an important tool against the heretics, and though some of the fathers have made use of verses 6 and 8 of the same chapter, which are much less strong and decisive. All these proofs of the assumed spuriousness of the verse under discussion are quite insufficient for their purpose and, besides, are refuted by positive proofs: (*a*) if in some Greek texts of the New Testament, which have been preserved until the present, this verse does not exist, it has been and still is in many others. Why then, arises the question, should we give preference to the first over the latter and conclude that it was added to the latter, and not omitted in the first ? On the contrary, justice demands that preference be given to the latter." (pp. 180,.181.)

Those are all the proofs from Holy Scripture of the Old and the New Testament. The only passage from the whole Scripture which presents a similitude of that assertion that God is one and three is spurious, and its reality is confirmed by the polemics of the composer of the Theology.

But there are also proofs from Holy Tradition :

"(28) Confirmation of the same truth from Holy Tradition. No matter how clear and numerous the passages are from Holy Scripture, especially from the New Testament, which contain the doctrine of the Trinity of the persons in one God, it is necessary for us here to turn to Holy Tradition which has been preserved in the church from its very beginning. It is necessary to do so because all these passages from Scripture have been subject to all kinds of interpretations and controversies, which cannot be permanently settled, at least not for a believer, but by the voice of the apostolic tradition and the ancient church. It is necessary also in order to defend the church itself against the unjust rebuke of the freethinkers that the church began to offer the doctrine about the three hypostases in God only with the fourth century, or with the First Œcumenical Council, but that before that time it was entirely unknown to the church, or was presented in an entirely different form. Consequently it is sufficient to take the thread of the tradition to the fourth century, or to the First Œcumenical Council, and to show whether and how the ancient Christian church taught about the Holy Trinity in the first three centuries."

So we have learned from the Theology, that there are absolutely no proofs in Scripture in confirmation of the Trinity, except the polemics of the composer of the Theology ; we have also learned that it is not even possible to assert that the church has always adhered to this tradition and that the only foundation of this assertion is left in the polemical art of the composer of the Theology. I have read all the proofs of Art. 28, which show in fifteen pages that the church has always professed the Trinity, but these arguments have not convinced me, not because I have read more exact and convincing proofs against it, but because my feeling revolts and I cannot believe that God, who has revealed himself to me in such a senseless, wild expression as that " I am one and three, and I am the Father and the Son, and I am the Spirit," should not have given me in his Scripture, or in his Tradition, or in my soul, any means to understand what it signifies, but has condemned me, for the solution of the question about God and my salvation, to have recourse to no other means than believing the argument of the Orthodox Theology against the rationalists, and repeating, without comprehension of what I am saying, the words which the Orthodox Theology will dictate to me.

I was on the point of making my last conclusion about

this dogma, when, immediately after the article about the Tradition, there was revealed to me Art. 29, and as the crown of the whole: The relation of the dogma about the Trinity of the persons in one God to common sense, — " we shall now take the liberty to say a few words about its relation to common sense, in order, on the one hand, to overthrow the false opinions in respect to this subject, and, on the other, to point out and elucidate to ourselves the true opinion. Since antiquity there have existed two false opinions in respect to this matter. Some have asserted that the teaching of the triune God is contrary to common sense, because it is contradictory in itself, but they assert so without any foundation: (a) Christianity teaches that God is one and trine not in the selfsame relation, but in different relations, that he is one in essence, but trine in person, and gives us one conception about the divine essence, and another about the divine persons, so that these concepts in no way exclude each other : where then is the contradiction ? "

Christianity gives us one conception about the essence, and another about the divine persons. That is precisely what I have been looking for, namely, what these different conceptions about the persons and the essence are, but that is not to be found anywhere. Not only is it absent, but there can be no answer, because the words οὐσία and ὑπόστασις now mean something different, and now mean one and the same, and are used indiscriminately.

" If Christianity taught that God is one in essence and trine in essence, or that there are in him three persons and one, or again, that person and essence in God are identical, then there would indeed be a contradiction. But, we repeat, Christianity does not teach that, and he who does not intentionally mix the Christian conceptions of the essence and the persons in God will never think of looking for an internal contradiction in the teaching about the Holy Trinity." (p. 204.)

Does not intentionally mix. Have I not strained all the powers of my mind in order to find in the teaching the slightest difference in the conceptions about the essence and the persons, without finding any? And the author knows that there is none.

"(*b*) In order to call a certain idea contradictory to common sense and to itself, it is necessary first of all completely to grasp this idea, to comprehend the meaning of its subject and predicate, and to see their incongruity. But in relation to the mystery of the Holy Trinity no one can boast of that; all we know is what nature or essence or person among creatures is, but we do not fully comprehend the essence, or the persons in God, who infinitely surpasses all his creations. Consequently we are not able to judge whether the idea of God one in essence and trine in persons is congruous or not; we have not the right to assert that the idea that God one in essence and three in persons includes an internal contradiction. Is it sensible to judge of what is not comprehensible?" (p. 204.)

In division *a* it was said that the conception of the essence was one, and of the persons another, and that Christianity taught it, but this teaching did not appear anywhere; but let us suppose that we have not read what precedes, have not studied the whole book, and have not convinced ourselves that such a distinction exists, and that we believe it. How then is it said in division *b:* that we cannot and have not the right to call an idea " contradictory to common sense without having comprehended the meaning of its subject and predicate "? The subject is 1, the predicate 3, — that is comprehensible. But if the subject is one God and the predicate three Gods, the contradiction is by the laws of reason the same. If, according to the Introduction of the concept of God, one may become equal to three, we shall insensibly be talking about what we do not comprehend, before we insensibly judge of what we do not understand. And it is there where it begins. And these senseless words, according to the confession of the Theology, the highest reason and the highest goodness speaks in reply to the entreaties of his children searching after truth.

"(c) On the contrary, common sense cannot help recognizing this idea as completely true and devoid of any contradiction. It does not comprehend its internal meaning; but on the basis of external testimony it knows conclusively that this idea has clearly been communicated by God himself in the Christian revelation: God is the God of truth." (p. 205.)

What is said cannot be understood, but it is so "on the basis of external, conclusive testimony," so that it is possible, without understanding them, to repeat the words which the Theology speaks; but in this case, as we see, there are none of those external proofs, not only no conclusive proofs, but no proofs at all. Nowhere in Holy Scripture does it say that the Spirit of God is a third person. What Moses wrote about God saying to himself, "Let us make," cannot be called a reliable proof. And the fact that in Jesus Christ's conversation in St. John there is once used the word Holy Ghost when speaking of the truth, is not a conclusive evidence. The fact that in baptizing into Christianity the words, "In the name of the Father, and the Son, and the Holy Ghost," are used is also not an evidence. The spurious verse from the Epistle of John not only does not argue in favour of the Trinity, but is a clear proof of there not being, and never having been, any proof, and that those who wanted to prove it felt so themselves.

From the external evidences there is left only the polemic of the author against those who reject the verse from St. John and against the rationalists who assert that the church did not accept the doctrine of the Trinity until the fourth century. Let us assume that I am so little intelligent and so illiterate that I believe the polemic of the author and agree with him that the dogma of the Trinity is recognized by the One, Holy, Catholic, Apostolic, Infallible Church, and that I want to believe in it.   I cannot believe it, because I cannot form any concept about what is meant by the triune God.   Neither I nor any one else can recognize this dogma, if for no other reason, because the words, as they were expressed at first, have remained, after long speeches, quasi-explanations and proofs, nothing but words which can have no meaning whatever for a man with an unimpaired reason.

On the basis of the sacred church tradition you may assert anything you please, and if the tradition is imperturbable, it is impossible not to recognize as true what is transmitted by tradition; in any case, it is necessary to assert something, but here nothing is asserted, — these are words without any inner connection.   Let us assume that it is asserted that God lives on Olympus, that God is made of gold, that there is no god, that there are fourteen gods, that God has children, or a son.   All those are strange, wild assumptions, but with each of them some idea is connected; but no idea is connected with the assertion that God is one and three.   So, no matter what authority may assert it, even if it be all the living and dead patriarchs of Alexandria and Antioch, and no matter what uninterrupted voice from heaven may call out to me, saying, " I am one and three," I shall remain in the same condition, not of unbelief (there is nothing here to believe in), but of perplexity about what these words mean, and in what language and by what law they may receive a meaning.   For me, a man educated in the spirit of the Christian faith, who after all the erring of his life has retained a dim consciousness of what there is true in it; for me, who by the blunders of life and the seduction of reason have reached the negation of life and most terrible despair; for me, who have found salvation in uniting with it the spirit of religion, which I recognized as the only divine force which moved humanity, and who have been in search of the highest expression of this religion, which would be accessible to me ; for me, who above all believe in God my Father, through whose will I exist, suffer, and agonizingly search after his revelation ; for me to admit that these senseless, blasphemous words are the only answer which I can receive from my Father in response to my entreaty as to how to understand and love him, for me this is impossible.

It is impossible to believe that God, my good Father (according to the teaching of the church), knowing that my salvation or perdition depends on my comprehension of him, should have expressed the most essential knowledge about himself in such a way that my reason, which he has given me, should not be able to comprehend his expressions, and (according to the teaching of the church) should have concealed all that truth, so important to men, under indications in the plural number of verbs and, in any case, in an ambiguous, obscure interpretation of words, such as the Spirit and the Son, in Jesus' farewell conversation in St. John, and in the spurious verse in the Epistle, and that my knowledge of God and my salvation and that of billions of men should depend on a greater or lesser verbal glibness of all the Renans and Makáris. I shall believe him who has the best arguments.

No ! If it were so, God would have given me such an intellect that $1=3$ would be as comprehensible as it is impossible now, and such a heart that it would be a joy to admit three gods, whereas now my heart revolts against them, or, at least, he would have given all that to me in a definite and simple manner, and not in debatable and ambiguous words. God cannot have commanded me to believe. The very reason why I do not believe is because I love, worship, and fear God. I am afraid to believe the lie which surrounds us and to lose God. That is impossible, and not only impossible, but it is quite clear that it is not the truth, that I was mistaken in thinking that I could find an answer and a solution of my doubts in the church. I had intended to go to God, and I found my way into a stinking bog, which evokes in me only those feelings of which I am most afraid: disgust, malice, and indignation. God, that incomprehensible, but still existing one, by the will of whom I live! Thou hast implanted in me this striving after the knowledge of thee and of myself. I have erred, I have searched after the truth in the wrong place. I knew that I erred. I have pampered my evil passions, and I knew that they were bad, but I have never forgotten thee; I have always felt thee, even in moments of erring. I came very near perishing, when I lost thee, but thou gavest me thy hand, and I grasped it, and life was illuminated for me. Thou hast saved me, and I am searching after this alone: to come near unto thee, and to understand thee as much as is possible. Help me, teach me! I know that I am good, that I love and want to love all, and want to love truth. Thou art the God of love and truth, take me nearer unto thee, disclose everything to me, so that I may be able to understand about myself and about thee!

And the good God, the God of truth, replies to me through the mouth of the church: " The Deity is one and trine. Oh, most glorious transformation ! "

Go yourselves to your father, the devil, you who have taken the keys of the kingdom of heaven and have not yourselves entered it and have closed it against others ! You are not speaking of God, but of something else.

VI.

Such is the doctrine about the Trinity in the radical Christian dogma, as expounded in fifty pages. On this dogma are based, and with its refutal are refuted, the dogmas about the Redeemer and Sanctifier, and every one of the dogmas which refer to the house-management of our salvation. I reject this dogma. I cannot help rejecting it, because, by accepting it, I should be renouncing the consciousness of my rational soul and the cognition of God. But, while rejecting this dogma, which is so contrary to human reason, and which has no foundation either in Scripture, or in Tradition, I still find inexplicable the cause which has led the church to profess this senseless dogma and so carefully pick out the imaginary proofs to confirm it. That is the more surprising to me since that terrible, blasphemous dogma, as expounded here, can apparently be of no use to any one or in anything, and since it is impossible to deduce any moral rule from it, as indeed is evident from the moral application of the dogma, — a collection of meaningless words, which are not connected in any way. Here is the application of the dogma:

"(1) All the persons of the Most Holy Trinity, except the common attributes, which belong to them according to their essence, have still other, especial attributes, by which they differ from each other, so that the Father is indeed the Father and occupies the first place in the order of divine persons, the Son is the Son and occupies the second place, and the Holy Ghost is the Holy Ghost and occupies the third place, although by their divinity they are entirely equal among themselves. To each of us the Creator has given, in addition to the properties which we all have in common by our human nature, special properties, special talents, by which our special calling and place is defined in the circle of our friends. To know these faculties and talents in ourselves, and to use them for our own benefit and for the benefit of our friends and for the glory of God, so as to justify our calling in this way, is the unquestionable duty of each man. (2) Differing from each other in their personal properties, all the persons of the Most Holy Trinity are, none the less, in a constant mutual communion: the Father is in the Son and in the Holy Ghost; the Son is in the Father and in the Holy Ghost; the Holy Ghost is in the Father and in the Son (John xiv. 10). Even thus we, with all our differences according to our personal qualities, must observe the greatest possible communion and moral union among ourselves, being bound by the unity of essence and the bond of brotherly love. (3) In particular, let the fathers among ourselves keep in mind whose great name they bear, even as the sons, and all those who are begotten from the fathers, — and, keeping this in mind, let them see to it that they sanctify the names of father or son which they bear, through an exact performance of all the obligations imposed upon them by these names — (4) Finally, keeping in mind, to what disastrous results the Eastern Christians have been led through their arbitrary reasoning on the personal essence of God the Holy Ghost, let us learn to cling as fast as possible to the dogmas of faith of the teaching of the word of God and the Orthodox Church, and not to cross the eternal boundaries which our fathers in faith have set."

Thus it remains incomprehensible why this dogma is

confirmed.   Not only is it senseless and not based on Scripture or on Tradition, and nothing comes of it; in reality, according to my immediate observation of the believers, and according to my own personal recollection of the time when I myself was a believer, it turns out that I never believed in the Trinity and never saw a man who believed in the dogma of the Trinity.   Out of a hundred men and women among the people not more than three will be able to name the persons of the Trinity, and not more than thirty will be able to say what the Trinity is, and will not be able to name the persons, but will include among them St. Nicholas the Miracle-worker and the Mother of God.   The others do not even know anything about the Trinity.   Among the masses I have not come across any conception about the Trinity.   Christ is called the God-man, as it were, the eldest of the saints. The Holy Ghost is entirely unknown, and God remains the incomprehensible, almighty God, the beginning of everything.   Nobody ever prays to the Holy Ghost, no one ever invokes him.   In the more cultured circles I have also not found any belief in the Holy Ghost.   I have met very many who very fervently believed in Christ, but never have I heard the Holy Ghost mentioned except for the purpose of theological discussion.   The same was true of me: during all those years when I was an Orthodox believer the idea of the Holy Ghost never entered my mind.   The belief in and definition of the Trinity I have found only in the schools, and thus it turns out that the dogma of the Trinity is not rational, not based on anything, is good for nothing, and no one believes in it, while the church professes it.

In order to comprehend why the church does that, it is necessary to investigate the further exposition of the church, and I proceed to do this.   It would be a useless labour in the consequent investigation to point out all the errors, contradictions, senseless statements, and lies, for

the investigation of the first two chapters about the most
important dogmas has sufficiently demonstrated to the
reader what the methods of reasoning and the expressions
of the author are. I will now give a short exposition of
all the dogmas, in their general interrelation, giving the
pages and pointing out the chief propositions which are
adduced in confirmation of the dogmas. I do this in
order from the general connection of the whole teaching
to elucidate the meaning which may not become evident
from the separate passages.

I repeat what was in the beginning, so as to proceed
consistently.

There is a God, and he is one (Art. 13). He is a spirit
(Art. 17). He has an infinite number of attributes; his
attributes, as revealed to us, are as follows (Art. 19).
His attributes in general: unlimitedness, self-existence,
independence, unchangeableness, omnipresence, eternity,
almightiness. The attributes of his mind (Art. 20): omniscience and all-wisdom. The attributes of his will
(Art. 21): goodness, freedom, holiness, truth, justice. God,
in addition to that, has persons. He is one and three
persons. The persons are independent and inseparable
(proofs from Holy Scripture, Arts. 26, 27, and 28). All
three persons are equal to each other, though some have
thought that one is more important than the others. But
that is not true; they are all equal: the Father is God, the
Son is God and consubstantial with the Father; there
are adduced disputes which prove the opposite, and proofs
from Holy Scripture which prove the opposite, and discussions about one God not being subject to another, but
that both have equal power. The same is true of the
divinity of the Holy Ghost. The Father, the Son, and
the Holy Ghost have personal properties. Art. 32. Many
controversies are cited about the personal attributes, and
finally there is an exposition of the dogma that the personal attribute of the Father consists in this, that he is

not generated, but begets the Son, and produces the Holy
Ghost. (p. 263.)

"(*a*) Entirely in a spiritual manner and consequently
without any suffering, without any sensuous secretion:
because the essence of God is immaterial and simple; (*b*)
he begets and produces since eternity and for eternity:
for there has been no time when the Father has not been
the Father of the Son and the producer of the Holy
Ghost, just as there was no time when he was not God,
and what has never begun cannot be said ever to end; (*c*)
he begets and produces in such a way as only he alone
knows and he who is born from him and proceeds from
him, but of the creatures none can comprehend it; (*d*)
finally, beginninglessness and causelessness are exclusively
appropriated by God the Father only in relation to the
other persons of the Holy Trinity, but by their divinity
the Son and the Spirit are also beginningless and causeless, or, rather, the whole Trinity is co-beginningless and
co-causeless." (pp. 263 and 264.)

"41. The personal attribute of God, the Holy Ghost."
(p. 267.)

A controversy of over fifty pages about the question
from whom the Holy Ghost proceeds, whether from the
Father and the Son, or from the Father alone. The dispute is settled by an analysis of external proofs. The
proofs are as follows:

"Who, putting his hand on his heart, will have the
courage to affirm that we, who believe that the Holy
Ghost proceeds from the Father, have deviated from the
truth? Who will dare, in all conscience, to rebuke us
for observing a heresy? If we are rebuked for an error
or a heresy, it would be just as right to rebuke for it all
the holy fathers and teachers of the church; the same as
to rebuke the Œcumenical Councils, not only locally, but
altogether the whole ancient church; the same as to
rebuke the Word of God itself for error and heresy.

Who, we repeat, will be bold enough to utter such blasphemy ? "

Then follows a moral exposition of the dogma of the Trinity, which was quoted before. One cannot help but come to the conclusion that the simplest, clearest application of all the preceding controversies is that one must not speak any foolishness; above all, one must not teach what nobody can understand, and, more important still, one must not impair the chief foundations of faith, love, and charity to your neighbour.

Then follows " Division II. Of God in his general relation to the world and to man. Chapter I. Of God as the Creator." God has created the world.

Here is the way the church teaches about it :

" Unquestionably God is the creator of all visible and invisible creations. First he produced through thought all the celestial powers, as exalted psalmists of his glory, and created all that mental world which, through the grace given to it, knows God and is always and in everything devoted to his will. After that he created out of nothing this visible and material world. At last God created man, who is composed of the immaterial rational soul and the material body, so that from this one man, thus composed, it might be seen that he is the creator of both the worlds, the immaterial and the material." (p. 351.)

After that, as always, follows a controversy :

" Some assumed that the world was eternal; others admitted its emanation from God; others again taught that the world was created by itself, by accident, from the eternal chaos or from atoms; others taught that God has formed it from coeternal matter; but no one could rise to the concept of the production of the world out of nothing by the almighty power of God." (p. 352.)

All these opinions are refuted in Art. 55 :

" God created the world out of nothing." 56. " God

created the world not from eternity, but in time, or together with time." (p. 360.)

The farther one reads the book, the more one has to marvel. It looks as though the problem and purpose of the book consisted in keeping out rational comprehension, not the comprehension of the divine mysteries, but simply the comprehension of what is being said. I can imagine a man who admits that God created the world. Well, what more do you want? He does not care to inquire any farther into the teaching. No, they demand of him that he should recognize that the world is created not from something, but from nothing, not from eternity, but in time. On this point there is a controversy, and it is proved to him that the world was created in time or, more correctly, with time. " Prescience or predetermination were in God before existence." It says, " At one time the world did not exist," that is, it says, if God's prescience be admitted, that when there was no time, God knew the future. And when it says, " At one time the world did not exist," and time did not exist, it says that there was time (for " at one time " means time) when there was no time. And when it says that " God created time," it says (since the verb is used in the past tense), there was a time when God created time.

57. The world was created by all three persons. This is proved by Holy Scripture, and is expressed thus:

" The Father created the world through the Son in the Holy Ghost;" or "everything is from the Father through the Son in the Holy Ghost;" however, not in the sense that the Son and the Holy Ghost performed some instrumental and slavish service at the creation, but that constructively they performed the Father's will. (p. 365.)

58. The manner of the creation. The world was created (1) through reason, (2) through willing, and (3) through the word:

" God created the world according to his eternal ideas

about it, quite freely, by the mere beck of his will. The plan of the world creation had been predetermined since eternity in his ideas; the free will determined to materialize this plan; the beck of his will actually materialized it."

Particularly fine is here the word "ideas."

59. The incitement toward the creation, and its purpose. God created the world for this reason :

"We must believe that God, being good and all-good, though all-perfect and all-glorious in himself, created the world out of nothing for the purpose that other beings, glorifying him, might partake of his grace." (p. 370.)

The purpose of God is glory. Proofs from Holy Scripture and then :

60. The perfection of the creation and whence evil comes into the world. The question is, Whence comes the evil? and the answer is that there is no evil. And the proof for this is as follows :

"God is a supremely all-wise and omnipotent being, consequently he could not have created the world imperfect, could not have created a single thing in it which would be insufficient for its purpose and would not serve for the perfection of the whole. God is a most holy and all-good being, consequently he could not be the cause of evil, either physical or moral, and if he had created an imperfect world, it would have been so, because he was unable to create a more perfect one, or because he did not want to. But both assumptions are equally incongruous with the true concept of the highest being." End of the article. (p. 376.)

There is no evil, because God is good. But how about our suffering from the evil? What sense was there in asking? How can there be any evil, when there is none ?

61. The moral application of the dogma is that it is necessary to glorify God, and so forth.

62. About the spiritual world. " Angels are incorporeal spirits, endowed with reason, will, and power. They were created before the visible world and before man — ; are divided into nine forms — ; and the evil angels themselves were created by God as good, but became evil by their own will."   (p. 377.)

And again, as always, there comes a controversy with those who spoke differently of the angels and the demons. Then proofs from Holy Scripture that there are angels of various orders.

" 65. By their natures the angels are incorporeal spirits, more perfect than the human soul, but limited."

They were created after the likeness of God, and have mind and will.   Proofs from Holy Scripture.

66. Number and degrees of angels.   The celestial hierarchy.

The number of angels is legion, that is, very large. There are various classes of celestial powers.   (p. 396.)

There follows a controversy with Origen about the orders of the angels, and it is proved that there are nine classes of them.   (p. 397.)

" The angels are divided into nine classes, and these nine into three orders.   In the first order are those who are nearer to God, such as thrones, cherubim, and seraphim ; in the second order are dominions, principalities, and powers ; in the third order are angels, archangels, and beginnings.   This division is based partly (a) on Holy Scripture, at least in this respect that in Holy Scripture we meet with the names of all the orders of the angels, as given here — but mainly (b) on Holy Tradition."   (pp. 198 and 199.)

" Of the private opinions the most noteworthy is this, that the division of the angels into nine orders embraces only the names and orders of those that were revealed in the Word of God, but does not embrace many other names and classes of angels which have not been revealed to us in this life, but will become known to us in the life to come."

67. Various appellations of evil spirits and the authenticity of their existence. In addition to the angels there are the devil and his angels.

"That this devil and his angels are accepted in Holy Scripture as personal and actual beings, and not as imaginary beings, is to be seen (1) from the books of the Old Testament, (2) still more from the books of the New Testament." Then follow proofs.

68. The evil spirits were created good, but they themselves became bad. How the good could have become bad is not explained, but there are many proofs from Scriptures. The devils became bad, some fathers of the church say, immediately before the creation of the world, while others say that the devils remained for a considerable time in the state of grace. (p. 406.) The devils became bad not all at once:

"At first one only fell, the chief of them, then he drew after him all the rest. This chief devil, according to some opinions, had been, previous to his fall, the very first and most perfect of all created spirits, who excelled before all the hosts of the angels; but according to the opinion of others, he belonged to the order of the supreme spirits (ταξιάρχων), to the leadership of which the lower orders of the angels were subject, — indeed he was among the number of those among whom the Lord apportioned the government of the parts of the world. The others, whom the fallen morning star drew after him, were the angels who were subject to him, who therefore could easily be carried away by his example, or suasion, or deception." (pp. 406 and 407.)

What sin caused the devils to fall? Some say, because they mingled with the daughters of man, others say through envy, and others again say through pride.

"There have been various opinions as to what the pride

of the fallen spirit, which formed his first sin, consisted in.   Some, on the basis of the words of Isaiah (xiv. 13, 14), have supposed that the devil took it into his head to be equal with God in essence and to sit on the same throne with him, or even dreamed of being higher than God, for which reason he became God's antagonist who exalted himself above all that is called God, or that is worshipped (2 Thes. ii. 4).   Others supposed that the fallen morning star did not wish to bow before the Son of God, having been envious of his privileges, or because he saw from the revelation that this Son of God would suffer some day, and so doubted his divinity and did not wish to acknowledge him as God."

How deep the devils fell, and whether God gave them time for repentance, is also determined (p. 410); it is declared that previous to the creation of the world the devils had a chance to repent, but after that they could no longer do so.

69. The nature of the evil spirits, their number, and degrees.   The nature of the devils is the same as that of the angels ; the number of the devils is very great, and it is assumed that there are orders among them too.   From this is made (Art. 70) a moral application of the dogma. The application of the dogma is here more startling than in the previous cases, but here for the first time this application has a definite purpose :

" (3) The angels of God are all equal among themselves in their nature, but are distinguished according to their powers and perfections, and, consequently, there are among them higher and lower angels ; there are those who rule, and those who are subject ; there is an invariable hierarchy, established by God.   Even thus it ought to be with us : in all the unity of our natures, we differ from each other, by the will of the Creator, through our different faculties and distinctions ; consequently among us, too, there ought to be higher and lower, rulers and subjects, and in our societies God himself arranges the order and hierarchy, enthrones his anointed ones (Prov. viii. 15), gives all the lower powers (Rom. xiii. 1), and ordains for each man his service and place."   (p. 415.)

For the first time a definite rule is patched on a dogma.

71. Soon after the creation of the angels and the devils, God created the material world in this fashion:

" In the beginning God created from nothing the heaven and the earth.   The earth was without form and void. Then God successively produced: on the first day of the world, light; on the second, the firmament or visible heaven; on the third, the gathering of the waters on the earth, the dry land, and the plants; on the fourth, the sun, moon, and stars; on the fifth, fishes and birds; on the sixth, four-footed animals living on the dry land." (p. 416.)

72. Moses' account of the origin of the material world is history.   A proof is given that history began when there was no time.

73. The meaning of Moses' account of the creation is six days.   It is argued that all of Moses' words have to be taken in their literal sense.

74. A refutal of the objections made against Moses' account.   In refutal of the false opinion of the rationalists that there could not be any day and night when there was no sun, the following is said:

" Nowadays, indeed, there could be no day without the sun, but at that time it was possible.   For that only two conditions were needed: (a) that the earth should turn around its own axis, and (b) that the light-bearing matter, which existed even then, should be brought into a quivering motion.   But it cannot be denied that the earth began to turn around its own axis with the very first day of creation; nor that the Creator could in the first three days by his immediate power bring the light-bearing matter into a quivering motion, just as now, beginning with the fourth day, it is brought into motion by the celestial luminaries, which have received this power from God." (p. 423.)

It is necessary to repeat word for word and quickly to admit that God brings the light-bearing matter into motion by his immediate power, as though his problem did not consist in creating the world, but that the manner of the creation should agree with the Bible, rather than admit any departure from the words of Moses, which might harmonize his account with our concepts and knowledge of zoology, physics, and astronomy. The whole history of the creation in six days has to be understood word for word; thus the church commands. This is a dogma.

75. The moral application of the dogma. This application consists in the necessity of attending mass on Sunday and sanctifying the seventh day.

" 76. The Lord our God, at the end of the creation, produced man, who belongs equally to the spiritual world, by his soul, and to the material world, by his body, and so he is, as it were, an abbreviation of the two worlds and has since antiquity justly been called the little world." (p. 427.)

" God in the Holy Trinity said: Let us make man in our image, and after our likeness (Gen. i. 26). And God made the body of the first man, Adam, from the earth; breathed into his face the breath of life; brought Adam into Paradise; gave him for food, besides the other fruits of Paradise, the fruits of the tree of life; finally he took a rib from Adam during his sleep, and from it created the first woman, Eve — " (p. 427.)

77. The essence and meaning of Moses' account of the origin of the first men, Adam and Eve. This account of Moses is to be taken in the sense of history, and not in the sense of an invention or myth, because Moses and the holy fathers understood it in a historical sense. On

the other hand it says (p. 429) : " It is to be understood in the sense of history, but not in a literal sense."

The question as to what is meant by understanding in a historical but not a literal sense remains unanswered.

78. The origin of Adam and Eve and of the whole human race. According to the established order, there follows a controversy. Here are those with whom the controversy is carried on :

" This truth has two kinds of enemies : in the first place those who affirm that there existed men on earth before Adam (Preadamites), and that, therefore, Adam is not the first ancestor of the human race ; in the second place, those who admit that with Adam there were several progenitors of the human race (Postadamites), and that, consequently, men did not originate from one root."

As in many other passages of the book, it is evident that the point is not in the refutal, for there is no refutal, but only in giving utterance to a dogma. A dogma is only the product of a controversy. Consequently it is necessary to put forward that against which an argument is adduced, in order to be able to say wherein the teaching of the church consists. Here, of course, are victoriously refuted the proofs of the first on the basis of Holy Scripture, and the proofs of the second from physiology, linguistics, and geography, — on the basis of those same sciences which are interpreted to suit its own purposes. These proofs of the unity of the human race are remarkable only for this, that here, almost under our eyes, takes place the formation of what is called a dogma, and what, in reality, is nothing but the expression of one particular opinion in any controversy. Some prove that men could not have had one progenitor, others prove that they could. Neither can adduce anything conclusive in their defence. And this dispute is not interesting and has nothing in common with the question of faith, with the question as to what constitutes the meaning of my life. Not one of the disputants is disputing for the sake of solving the scientific question, but each because a certain solution is needed by him. This confirms their tradition.

The Theology adduces proofs that God could have counted days, when there was no sun, by saying that he shook the matter; but to prove that all men originated in one man, we read on p. 437:

" Nowadays the best linguists, after prolonged labours, have come to the conclusion that all languages and all dialects of man are to be referred to three chief classes, the Indo-European, the Semitic, and the Malay, and come down from one root, which they find in the Hebrew language, while others do not define it." (p. 437.)

The Theology says that it knows all about it in this matter. And these ignorant words pass unnoticed in the world of science; but let us imagine that the composer of the Theology, which is quite possible, will turn out to be a father of the church in three hundred years; then his words will serve as a confirmation of the dogma. In another five hundred years God himself who shakes matter may become a dogma. Only such reflection gives an explanation to those strange, wild utterances, which now are taken as dogmas.

79. The origin of each man and, in particular, the origin of the soul. All men originated from Adam, " still, none the less, God is the Creator of each man. The difference is this, that Adam and Eve he created directly, while all their descendants he creates indirectly, by the power of his blessing, which he gave to our first fathers soon after the creation of the world, saying: Be fruitful, and multiply, and replenish the earth." (p. 439.)

Then follow texts of Holy Scripture, and then a minute determination by the church when the soul of man is created:

" The holy church, believing in the divine Scripture, teaches that the soul is created with the body, but not

together with the seed from which the body is formed
does it receive its existence, but, by the will of the Creator, it appears in the body soon after its formation."
(p. 440.)

When this formation of the body takes place it does
not say. For the purpose of elucidation the following is
said :

" At the time when the body is formed it becomes
capable of receiving the soul."

If that does not explain the matter, what follows
explains whence and from what the soul is created by
God. Here we again have a controversy. Some have
said that the soul originated by itself from the souls of
the parents, while others have said that it came from
nothing, directly from the seed. All are wrong :

" God creates the human souls, just as he creates the
bodies, by force of the same blessing, to be fruitful and
multiply, which he gave to our forefathers in the beginning, — he creates them not out of nothing, but out of the
souls of the parents. For, according to the teaching of
the church, although the souls of men receive their existence through creation, the stigma of the ancestral sin
passes to them from the parents, — and this could not be,
if God created them from nothing." (pp. 441 and 442.)

80. The composition of man. Man consists of two
parts, of the soul and the body, and not of three parts.
As usual, there comes after that a dispute and confirmations from Holy Scripture. The dispute is directed
against those who assert that man consists of three parts,
of body, soul, and spirit. That is not so, — he consists
only of body and soul.

81. The properties of the human soul are the following : " (1) It is an independent essence, separate from the
body, (2) immaterial, simple (spirit), (3) free, and (4)
immortal." (pp. 449–453.)

There follow proofs from Holy Scripture. But what is

this soul of mine ? What connection is there between it and the body ? Where are the limits of the soul and the body ? From the definition of the properties of the soul directly result these questions. But there are no answers for them. What is so provoking in this teaching is that it compels you to put questions to which there can be no answers. As the definition of the attributes of God have abased and destroyed in me the conception of God, even so the definitions of the properties of the soul and its origin abase and lower in me the conception of the soul. God and the soul I know as well as I know infinity, not by means of definitions, but in an entirely different way. The definitions destroy this knowledge in me. Just as I know beyond any doubt that there is an infinity in number, so I know that there is a God and that I have a soul. But this knowledge is unquestionable for me only because I was inevitably brought to it. To the certainty of the infinity in number I was brought by addition. To the certainty of the knowledge of God I was brought by the question, " Whence am I ? " To the certainty of the soul I was brought by the question, " What am I ? " And I know beyond any doubt that there is an infinity in number, and that God exists, and that my soul exists, when I am led to this knowledge by means of the simplest questions.

To two I add one, and still one, and again and again, or I break a stick into two, and again into two, and again and again, and I cannot help recognizing infinity. I was born from my mother, and she from my grandmother, and she from my great-grandmother, and the last from whom ? And I inevitably come to God. My hands are not I ; my feet are not I ; my head — not I, my feelings — not I, even my thoughts — not I ; what, then, am I ? I = I, I = my soul. But when I am told that an infinite number is first or not first, even or odd, I no longer comprehend a thing, and even renounce my conception of infinity. The same do I experience when I am told about God, his essence, his attributes, his person; I no longer understand God. I do not believe in God. The same, when I am told about my soul and its properties. I no longer understand about it, and do not believe in my soul. No matter from what side I may approach God, it will be the same: the beginning of my thought, of my reason, is God; the beginning of my love is he again; the beginning of materiality is he again. But when I am told that God has fourteen attributes, mind and will, persons, or that God is good and just, or that God created the world in six days, I no longer believe in God. The same is true of the conception of the soul. When I turn to my striving after truth, I know that this striving after truth is the immaterial foundation of myself, my soul; when I turn to the feeling of my love of the good, I know that it is my soul which loves. But the moment I am told that this soul was placed in me by God from the souls of my parents, when I was in the womb of my mother, and my body was able to receive it, I do not believe in the soul and ask, as ask the materialists: " Show me that of which you speak! Where is it ?"

VII.

82. THE image and likeness of God in man. The image and likeness of God, the purest spirit. According to the teaching of the church, the Theology says, as it said before, that this purest spirit has mind and will, and so the image and likeness of God means mind and will. But mind and will, as we have seen, were ascribed quite arbitrarily to God. In the whole book there is not the slightest hint why we should assume mind and will in God. So it turns out that in the division about God the division of the pure spirit into mind and will was introduced, not because there were any causes for that in the concept of God itself, but because man, comprehending himself as mind and will, has arbitrarily transferred this division to God.

Now, in the division about man, in explaining the word " he was made in the image and after the likeness of God," it says that since the attributes of God are divided into mind and will, the word image means mind, while likeness means will. But the concepts of mind and will have been transferred to God only because we find them in man ! Let not the reader think that I have anywhere omitted the definition of God's mind and will. It does not exist. It is introduced as something known in the definition of the attributes of God, and now the attributes of man are deduced from it. In this article we have the following exposition :

" To be in the image of God is natural for us according to our creation; but to become after the likeness of God

depends on our will.   This dependence on our will exists
in us only potentially; it is acquired by us in fact only
through our activity.   If God, intending to create us, had
not said beforehand, ' We will make ' and ' after our likeness,' and if he had not given us the power to be after
his likeness, we could not by our own force be after the
likeness of God.   But as it is we received at creation
the power to be like God.   But, having given us this possibility, God has left it to us to be the actors of our own
likeness with God, in order to be worthy of an acceptable
reward for our activity, and that we may not be like soul-
less representations made by artists."   (p. 458.)

83. Man's destination is as follows :

" (1) In relation to God this destination of man consists in this, that he shall unalterably remain true to that
high bond or union with God (religion), to which the All-
good has called him at the very creation, while stamping
upon him his image ; in order that, in consequence of this
calling, he may constantly strive after his Prototype with
all the forces of his rational, free soul, that is, in order that
he may know his Creator, and glorify him, and live in
moral union with him.   (p. 459.)   (2) In man's relation
to himself, his destination is that he, being created in the
image of God with moral powers, shall constantly try to
develop and perfect these powers by exercising them in
good deeds, and, in this manner, shall more and more
become like his Prototype.   For this reason the Lord has
more than once commanded in the Old Testament : Ye
shall be holy ; for I am holy, the Lord your God (Lev. xi.
44 ; xix. 2 ; xx. 7), and now we hear in the New Testament from our Saviour : Be ye therefore perfect, even as
your Father which is in heaven is perfect (Matt. v. 48).
However, this purpose of man is essentially not to be distinguished from the first ; on the contrary, it is included
in it and serves as a necessary condition for its attainment."   (pp. 460 and 461.)

Consequently it is the same.

" (3) Finally, the destination of man, in relation to the whole Nature which surrounds him, is clearly determined in the words of the tri-personal Creator himself : Let us make man in our image and after our likeness : and let him have dominion over the fish of the sea, and over the fowl of the air, and over the beasts, and over the cattle, and over all the earth, and over every creeping thing that creepeth upon the earth."

The third is evidently not a destination, but a convenience ; but here it is included as a destination.   There turns out to be one destination : to remain true to the union with God.

84. The ability of the first-born man for his destination, or perfection.   " In predestining man for such a high purpose, the Lord God created him fully capable of attaining this aim, that is, perfect."

85. The special coöperation of God with the first-born man in the attainment of his destination.

In order to attain this high purpose, the preservation of the union with God, God considered it necessary to coöperate with the man.   The first coöperation consisted in this :

" God himself planted a garden eastward in Eden as a habitation for man ; and there he put the man whom he had formed (Gen. ii. 8).   This was, according to the words of St. John Damascene, as it were, a royal house, where man, living, might have passed a happy and blissful life — it was the abiding-place of all joys and pleasures : for Eden denotes enjoyment.   The air in it was perfectly pure.   It was surrounded by bright air, the thinnest and the purest ; it was adorned with blooming plants, filled with perfume and light, and surpassed every representation of sensual beauty and goodness.   It was truly a divine country, a worthy habitation, created in the image of God."   (p. 467.)

Here it is proved that Paradise is to be understood directly as a garden, as described, and we may only presume that Adam, besides the body, enjoyed also his soul. The second coöperation with Adam was this, that God visited him in Paradise (p. 468). The third coöperation consisted in this, that God gave Adam his grace. What grace is, is not explained here. The fourth coöperation consisted in this, that God planted in the garden the tree of life ; and here we suddenly get the explanation that this tree of life was that very grace. The tree of life was the cause why Adam did not die. The fifth coöperation was this, that for the " exercise and development of the physical forces God commanded Adam to make and keep the Paradise (Gen. ii. 15) ; for the exercise and development of his mental powers and the powers of speech, he himself brought to Adam all the beasts to see what he would call them (Gen. ii. 19) ; for the exercise and strengthening of his moral powers in what was good, he gave a certain command to Adam, not to eat of the fruit of the tree of the knowledge of good and evil. And the Lord God commanded the man, saying, Of every tree of the garden thou mayest freely eat ; but of the tree of the knowledge of good and evil, ye shall not eat of it : for in the day that ye eat thereof, ye shall surely die." (pp. 472 and 473.)

If anybody imagines that anything essential is added or omitted here, or in any way transformed, let him read the book itself ! I am trying to cite the most essential and intelligible passages. The Theology represents the question of Adam's fall in the most remarkable manner and insists that it is not possible and not allowable to understand it in any other way. According to the church teaching God has created man for a certain destination, and has created him quite capable of attaining his destination ; it says that he has created him perfect and has shown him every kind of coöperation for the purpose of

attaining his ends. The command about not eating the
fruit was also a coöperation.

86. The command given by God to the first man, —
its necessity and meaning. Of the command about not
eating from the tree of the knowledge of good and evil the
Theology says (1) that this command was very necessary,
(2) that in this command the whole law is contained, (3)
that the command was an easy one and that it was guarded
by a terrible threat. And, in spite of it all, man fell and
did not reach his destination. One would think that it
would be necessary to clear up this contradiction, and one
involuntarily waits for some interpretation of this whole
remarkable event. But, on the contrary, the Theology
bars the way to all interpretation and carefully preserves
it in all its coarseness. It proves that it is not possible
and not allowable to understand the meaning of the second
chapter of Genesis, about the Paradise and the trees
planted in it, in any explanatory way, but that it is necessary to understand it as Theodoret understood it :

"'The Divine Scripture says,' asserts the blessed
Theodoret, 'that the tree of life and the tree of the
knowledge of good and evil grew out from the ground ;
consequently they are by their natures like any other
plants. Just as the rood is a common tree, but receives
the name of a saving cross on account of the salvation
which we receive through faith in him who was crucified
upon it ; even thus these trees are common plants that
grew out from the ground, but, by God's determination,
one of them is called the tree of life, and the other, — since
it has served as a tool for the knowledge of sin, — the
tree of the knowledge of good and evil. The latter was
proposed to Adam as an opportunity for an exploit, and
the tree of life as a certain reward for the keeping of the
command.' (b) This tree is called the tree of the knowledge of good and evil, not because it had the power of
imparting to our first parents the knowledge of good and

evil, which they did not have before, but because, by their eating from the forbidden tree they were to find out experimentally, and did find out, all the distinction between good and evil, 'between the good,' as the blessed St. Augustine remarks, 'from which they fell, and the evil into which they fell,' a thought which is unanimously taught by all the teachers of the church. (c) This tree, according to the opinion of some of the teachers of the church, was by no means destructive and venomous in its nature; on the contrary, it was good, like all the other divine knowledge, but it was chosen by God only as a tool for trying man, and was forbidden, perhaps, because it was too early yet for the new-born man to eat of its fruits.

" 'The tree of knowledge,' says St. Gregory the Divine, 'was planted in the beginning without any evil purpose and was not forbidden through envy (let not the wrestlers against God open their lips and imitate the serpent!); on the contrary, it was good for those who used it in proper time (for this tree, according to my opinion, was the contemplation to which only those may proceed who are perfected by experience), but it was not good for simple people and for those who were immoderate in their desire, even as perfect food is not useful for feeble people who need milk.'—'The tree is good,' blessed St. Augustine, who understands the forbidden tree in a sensuous sense, says to Adam, in the person of God, 'but do not touch it! Why? Because I am the Lord, and you are a slave: that is the whole reason. If you consider this insufficient, it means that you do not wish to be a slave. What is there more useful for you than to be under the power of the Lord? How will you be under the power of the Lord, if you are not under his command?'"

Thus the church understands it, and thus it commands you to understand it. The fact that the tree is called the tree of the knowledge of good and evil; the fact that the serpent says to the woman: You will know good and evil; the fact that God himself says (Gen. iii. 22), that, having eaten of the fruit of the tree, Adam is become as one of us, to know good and evil, — all that we must forget and we must think about the profound account in the Book of Genesis in a most inexact and absurd manner; and all that, not in order to explain anything in this account, but that there should not be left any sense in it except the most apparent and coarse contradiction that God was doing everything for the purpose of attaining one end, while something different resulted.

87. According to the doctrine of the church, the first man lived in the garden and was blessed.   This is told as follows: Adam and Eve lived in bliss in the garden, "and there is no doubt that this bliss of the first men would not only not have diminished in time, but would have increased more and more in proportion with their greater perfection, if they had kept the command which the Lord had given them in the beginning.   Unfortunately for our progenitors themselves as well as for their descendants, they violated this command and thus destroyed their bliss."

88. The manner and causes of the fall of our first parents.   But the serpent came (the serpent is the devil, — that is proved by Holy Scripture) and Adam was tempted and fell, and lost his bliss.

89. The importance of the sin of our first parents. This sin is important because (*a*) it is disobedience; (*b*) the command is easy; (*c*) God had benefited them and only demanded obedience; (*d*) they had the grace, and needed only to wish; (*e*) in that one sin there were many other sins, and (*f*) the consequences of this sin were very great for Adam and for all posterity.

90. The consequences of the fall of our first parents were in the soul: (1) the disruption of the union with God, the loss of grace, and spiritual death.

All this is proved by Holy Scripture, but nothing is said about what disruption of the union with God is, what grace is, what spiritual death is. It would be particularly desirable to know what is meant by spiritual death, as distinguished from corporeal death, since above it was said that the soul was immortal. Other consequences of the fall: (2) dimming of the intellect, (3) proclivity toward evil rather than toward good. But what difference there was between Adam before and after the fall in relation to the proclivity toward evil it does not say. Before the fall there was also a greater proclivity toward evil than toward good, if Adam, as we are told in Art. 89, comitted an evil act when everything drew him on to the good. (4) The mutilation of the image of God. Mutilation means:

" If a coin, which has upon itself the image of a king, is spoiled, the gold loses its value and the image is of no service: the same happened with Adam."

For the body the consequences were: (1) diseases, (2) bodily death. For Adam it was: (1) expulsion from Paradise, (2) the loss of his dominion over the animals, (3) the curse of the serpent, that is, man had to work to earn his sustenance.

We are all used to this story, which we have briefly learned in our childhood, and are all accustomed not to think of it, not to analyze it, and to connect with it an indistinct, poetical representation, and therefore the detailed repetition of this story with the confirmation of its coarse meaning and seeming proofs of its correctness, as expounded in the Theology, involuntarily strikes us as something new and unexpectedly coarse.

The representation of God and of the garden and of the fruits makes us doubt the truth of the whole, and for him who assumes justice there arises involuntarily the simple childish question as to why the omniscient, almighty, and all-good God did everything in such a way that the man who was created by him should perish, and why all his posterity should perish. And every person who will stop to think of this contradiction, will obviously wish to read the passage in Holy Scripture, on which it is based. And he who will do so will be terribly surprised at that striking unceremoniousness with which the church commentators treat the texts. It is enough to read carefully the first chapters of Genesis and the church exposition of the fall of man, in order to become convinced that two different stories are told by the Bible and by the Theology.

According to the church interpretation it turns out that Adam was permitted to eat from the tree of life and that the first pair was immortal, but not only is this not said in the Bible, but the very opposite is mentioned in verse 22 of Chapter III., where it says : lest Adam put forth his hand, and eat of the tree of life, and live for ever. According to the church interpretation the serpent is the devil, but nothing of the kind is said in the Bible, nor could anything be said, because no idea about the devil is given in the Book of Genesis, but it says there : the serpent was more subtile than any beast. According to the church interpretation it turns out that the eating of the tree of the knowledge of good and evil was a calamity for men ; but according to the Bible it was a benefit for men, and thus the whole history of the fall of Adam is an invention of the theologians and nothing like it is mentioned in the Bible.

From the story of the Bible it does not follow that the men ate from the tree of life and were immortal, but the opposite is said in verse 22, nor does it say there that the evil devil tempted man ; on the contrary, what is said is that the most subtile of beasts taught him that. Thus the two chief foundations of the whole story about the sinful fall, namely, the immortality of Adam in Paradise and the devil, are invented by the theologians in direct opposition to the text.

The only connected sense of the whole story according to the Book of Genesis, which is exactly the opposite of the church account, is this: God made man, but wished to leave him such as the animals were, who do not know the difference between good and evil, and so prohibited them from eating of the tree of the knowledge of good and evil. At the same time, to frighten man, God deceived him, saying that he would die as soon as he ate of it. But man, aided by wisdom (the serpent), discovered the deception of God, found out the good and the evil, and did not die. But God was frightened by it and barred his way from the tree of life, to which, to judge from the same fear of God lest man should eat of that fruit, we must assume, according to the sense of the story, man will find his way, as he has found his way to the knowledge of good and evil.

Whether this story is good or bad is another matter, but thus it is told in the Bible. God, in relation to man in this story, is the same God as Zeus in relation to Prometheus. Prometheus steals the fire, Adam the knowledge of good and evil. The God of these first chapters is not the Christian God, not even the God of the Prophets and of Moses, the God who loves men, but a God who is jealous of his power, a God who is afraid of men. And it is the story about this God that the Theology had to harmonize with the dogma of the redemption, and so a jealous and evil God is combined with God the Father, of whom Christ taught. Only this reflection gives a key to the blasphemy of the chapter. If we do not know what it is all needed for, we cannot understand why it was necessary to misinterpret, contort (directly departing from the text) the simplest, most naïve, and profound story, and to make of it a conglomeration of contradictions and absurdities. But let us suppose that the story is correct as told by the Theology: what follows from it?

VIII.

91. THE descent of the sin of the first parents to the whole human race : prefatory remarks. Adam's fall was the cause of the original sin. The exposition of the original sin is preceded by two different opinions. Some, the rationalists, regard original sin as nonsense and assume that diseases, sorrows, and death are the properties of human nature, and that man is born innocent. " Others, the Reformers, fall into the opposite extreme by exaggerating too much the consequences of the original sin in us : according to this teaching, the sin of our first parents entirely abolished freedom in man, and his divine image, and all his spiritual powers, so that the nature of man became tainted by sin : everything which he may wish, everything which he may do, is a sin ; his very virtues are sins, and he is positively unfit for any good. The first false teaching indicated above, the Orthodox Church rejects by its doctrine of the actuality in us of the original sin with all its consequences (that is, original sin taken in its broad sense) ; the latter it rejects by its doctrine about these consequences."

As always, there is an exposition in the form of a heretical teaching which cannot be understood otherwise by any man in his senses. The fact that all men are by their natures subject to diseases and death, and that babes are innocent, is represented in the form of a heresy, and an extreme heresy at that. Another extreme is the teaching of the Reformers. The church teaches the middle way, and this middle way is supposed to be this, that by

original sin is to be understood "that transgression of
God's command, that departure of human nature from the
law of God, and consequently from its aims, which was
committed by our first parents in Paradise and which
from them passed over to us. 'Original sin,' we read in
the Orthodox profession of the Catholic and Apostolic
Eastern Church, 'is a transgression of the law of God,
given in Paradise to our forefather Adam. This original
sin passed from Adam to the whole human race, for we
then were all in Adam, and thus through the one Adam
the sin has spread to all of us. For this reason we are
begotten and born with this sin.' The only difference is
that in Adam this departure from the law of God, and
consequently from its destination, was free and arbitrary,
but in us it is inherited and necessary : we are born with
a nature which has departed from the law of God; in
Adam it was a personal sin, a sin in the strict sense of the
word, — in us it is not a personal sin, not really a sin,
but only a sinfulness of our nature as derived from our
parents; Adam sinned, that is, he freely violated the law
of God and thus became a sinner, that is, caused his
whole nature to deviate from the law of God, and consequently became personally guilty toward God, — but we
have not sinned personally with Adam, but have become
sinners with him and through him: By one man's disobedience many were made sinners (Rom. v. 19); receiving from him our sinful nature we appear in the world as
children of the wrath of God (Eph. ii. 3).

"Under the consequences of the original sin the church
understands those consequences which the sin of our first
parents produced immediately upon them, and which pass
over from them to us, such as the dimming of the intellect, the abasement of the will, and the proclivity to do
evil, diseases of the body, death, and so forth. (pp. 493
and 494.)

"This distinction of the original sin and of its consequences must be firmly borne in mind, especially in certain cases, in order that the doctrine of the Orthodox Church may be properly understood." (p. 494.)

92. The actuality of the original sin, its universality and manner of dissemination. "The sin of our first parents, the Orthodox Church teaches, with its consequences, spread from Adam and Eve to all their posterity by means of natural birth and, consequently, exists unquestionably." (p. 496.)

All that is proved by Holy Scripture, for example like this: "Who can bring a clean thing out of an unclean? not one, even though he hath lived but one day upon earth (Job xiv. 4, 5). Here, evidently, an unclean thing is meant, from which no man is free, and that, too, from his birth. What is this unclean thing? Since, according to Job's description, it appears as the cause of the calamities of human life (verses 1, 2) and subjects man to the judgment of God (verse 3), we must assume that a moral uncleanness is meant and not a physical one, which is the consequence of the moral uncleanness and cannot in itself make man subject to the judgment before God, — what is meant is the sinfulness of our nature, which passes over to all of us from our first parents. To the passages of the second kind belong: (1) the words of the Saviour in his conversation with Nicodemus: Verily, verily, I say unto thee, Except a man be born of water and of the Spirit, he cannot enter into the kingdom of heaven. That which is born of the flesh is flesh; and that which is born of the Spirit is spirit (John iii. 5, 6)." (p. 498.)

It is also confirmed by Tradition:

"For according to this rule of faith the babes, who have not yet committed any sin, are baptized indeed for the remission of sins, that through the new birth there may be purified in them what they have received from their old birth. Utterances of the individual teachers of the church, who lived before the appearance of the Pelagian heresy, such as (a) Justin: 'It has pleased Christ to be born and to suffer death, not because he himself had any need of it, but on account of the human race, which through Adam (ἀπὸ τοῦ 'Αδάμ) was subject to death and the temptation of the serpent.' (b) Irenæus: 'In the first Adam we offended God, by not fulfilling his command; in the second Adam we made peace with him, becoming submissive even unto death; we were under obligation not to any one else, but to him whose command we had violated from the beginning.' (c) Tertullian: 'Man was from the start seduced by the devil to violate the command of God, and so is subject to death; after that the whole human race was made by him a participant (traducem) in his judgment,'" and so forth. (p. 500.)

"We do not quote similar utterances of many other teachers of the church, who lived at that period, as what we have adduced is sufficient to show the whole senselessness of the Pelagians, both the ancient and the modern, who assert that St. Augustine invented the doctrine of original sin, and, on the other hand, to cause the recognition of the whole justice of the words of the blessed St. Augustine to one of the Pelagians: 'I have not invented original sin, in which the Catholic Church has believed since olden times; but you, who reject this dogma, are no doubt a new heretic.' Finally, of the actuality of original sin, which has come down to us from our first ancestors, we may convince ourselves in the light of sound reason, on the basis of incontestable experience." (p. 502.)

What convinces us of it is the fact "(a) that within us there exists a constant struggle between the spirit and the flesh, between the reason and the passions, between the striving after the good and the attraction of the evil; (b) in this struggle the victory is nearly always on the side of the latter: the flesh vanquishes in us the spirit, the passions rule over our reason, the attractions of evil overpower the striving after the good; we love the good according to our nature, wish for it, and rejoice in it, but find no strength in us to do good; we do not love the evil according to our nature, and yet are irresistibly drawn to it; (c) the habit of what is good and holy is acquired by us after much effort and very slowly; but the habit of doing wrong is acquired without the least effort and exceedingly fast, and vice versa; (d) it is exceedingly difficult for us to discard a vice, to vanquish in us a passion, no matter how insignificant; but in order to change a virtue which we have acquired after many exploits, the smallest temptation is frequently sufficient. The same predominance of evil over good in the human race, that we observe now, has been observed by others at all times."

Evidences from the Old Testament and the Epistles that the world is merged in evil. And farther: "Whence comes this discord in human nature? Whence this unnatural struggle of the forces in it and that striving, that unnatural predominance of the flesh over the spirit, of the passions over reason, that unnatural inclination toward evil, which outweighs the natural inclination toward the good? All the explanations which men have thought of for this are inconclusive, or even irrational; the only explanation which fully satisfies us is the one revelation offers us in its teaching about the original, ancestral sin."

Then follows an analysis of these supposed explanations which men have invented. On the question of the original sin, of the sources of evil in the world, and of those explanations which the church offers, we must dwell at a greater length.

Among the number of the dogmas of the church, which have already been analyzed in the preceding parts and which will be analyzed farther on, we meet with dogmas about the most fundamental questions of humanity, about God, about the beginning of the world, about man, by the side of perfectly useless, perfectly senseless propositions, such as the dogma about the angels and the devils, and so forth, and so we will omit what is useless and will necessarily dwell on the important ones.

The dogma about the original sin, that is, about the beginning of evil, touches a fundamental question, and so we must attentively analyze what the church has to say about it. According to the teaching of the church, the struggle which man feels in himself between the evil and the good, and the proclivity to do evil, which the church asserts as an adjudged case, are explained by the fall of Adam and, we must add, by the fall of the devil, for the devil was the inciter of the crime and, having been created good, must have fallen before. But, in order that Adam's fall may explain our proclivity to do evil, it is necessary to explain the fall of Adam and of the devil who tempted him. If in the story of the fall of the devil and of Adam there should be any explanation of that fundamental contradiction between the consciousness of good and the propensity to do wrong, as the church says, then the recognition of the fact that this contradiction, which I am conscious of, is an inheritance from Adam, would be an explanation for me; but here I am told that Adam had just such freedom as I feel in myself and that, having this freedom, he fell, and so I have the same freedom. What, then, does the story of Adam explain to me?

We are all ourselves occupied with that struggle, and we feel and know by internal experience what, as we are told, took place with the devil and later with Adam. Precisely the same takes place in us each day and each minute that must have taken place in the soul of the devil and in that of Adam. If in the story of the freedom of the devil and of Adam, of how they, the creatures of the Good, created for bliss and glory, fell, there were given the slightest explanation of how they could have become evil, since they had been created good, I should understand that my propensity to do evil is the consequence of their special relation to good and evil; but I am told that in them took place precisely what is taking place in me, with the only difference that in them all that happened with less reason than in me: I have a mass of temptations which did not exist for them, and I am deprived of those special coöperations of God which they enjoyed. Thus the story about them not only explains nothing, but even obscures the whole matter; if it comes to analyzing this question of freedom and to explaining it, would it not have been better to analyze it and explain it in myself, rather than in some fantastic beings, like the devil and Adam, whom I am not even able to imagine? After some quasi-refutals of those who are supposed to say that evil is due to the limitation of Nature, to the flesh, to bad education, the author says:

"The most satisfactory solution of all these questions, as far as reason is concerned, the correctest explanation of the evil which exists in the human race, is offered by the divine revelation, when it says that the first man was actually created good and innocent, but that he sinned before God and thus injured his whole nature, and that thereupon all men, who come from him, are naturally born with the original sin, with an impaired nature, and with a propensity to do evil."

There are many errors and many consequences of these errors in this reflection. The first error is this, that if the first man, who was in such unusually favourable conditions for innocence, impaired his nature and did so only because he was free, there is no need for explaining why I impair my own nature. There cannot even be such a question. Whether I am his descendant or not, I am just such a man and have just such freedom, and just such, or even greater, temptations. What is there here to explain ? To say that my proclivity to do evil is due to the inheritance from Adam, means only to roll the guilt from an ailing head on one that is sound, and to judge by traditions, which, to say the least, are queer, about what I already know through inward experience. Another error it is to assert that the propensity to sin is due to Adam, for that means to transfer the question from the sphere of faith to that of reasoning. A strange *quid pro quo* takes place here. The church, which reveals to us the truths of religion, recedes from the foundation of faith, that recognition of a mysterious, incomprehensible struggle which takes place in the soul of each man, and, instead of giving by the revelation of the divine truths the means for the successful struggle of the good against the evil in the soul of each man, the church takes up a stand on the field of reasoning and of history. It abandons the sphere of religion and tells the story about Paradise, Adam, and the apple, and firmly and stubbornly sticks to the barren Tradition, which does not even explain anything or give anything to those who seek the knowledge of faith. The only result of this transference of the question from the chief foundation of any religion, — from the tendency to know good and evil, which lies in the soul of each man, — to the fantastic sphere of history is above all to deprive the whole religion of that only foundation on which it can stand firmly. The questions of faith have always been and always will be as to what my life is with that eternal struggle between good and evil, which each man experiences. How am I to wage that war ? How shall I live ? But the teaching of the church, in place of the question as to how I should live, presents the question as to why I am bad, and replies to this question by saying that I am bad because I became so through Adam's sin, that I am all in sin, that I am

born in sin, that I always live in sin, and that I cannot
live otherwise than in sin.

93. The consequences of the original sin.   This article
expounds, with proofs from Holy Scripture, that the
original sin is in all men, that all are filled with uncleanness, that the reason of all men is dimmed, and that the
will of all men is more prone to do evil, and that the image
of God is blurred.

How would workmen work if it were known to them
that they are all bad workmen, if they were impressed
with the thought that they cannot work well, that such
is their nature, and that, to accomplish their work, there
are other means than their labour?   It is precisely this
that the church does.   You are all filled with sin and
your bent to do evil is not due to your will, but to your
inheritance.   Man cannot save himself by his own strength.
There is one means: prayer, sacraments, and grace.   Can
a more immoral doctrine be invented?

Then follows the moral application of the dogma.

Only one moral application of this dogma is possible,
and that is, to look for salvation outside the striving after
what is good.   But the author, as always, not feeling
himself bound by any logical train of thoughts, throws
into the article of the moral application everything which
happens to occur to him and which has some verbal, external connection with what precedes.

94. The moral application of the dogma.   There are
ten such applications: (1) to thank God for having made
us to perish; (2) the wife should submit to her husband;
(3) to love our neighbour since we are all related through
Adam; (4) to thank God for creating us in the womb of
our mothers; (5) to praise God because we have a soul
and a body; (6) to care more for our soul; (7) to preserve
in us the image of God; (8) to please God —

" May the high purpose toward which we are obliged
to strive always be before our eyes, and may it, like a

guiding star, illuminate our whole murky path of life!"
(p. 514.)

(9) Not to violate the will of God, because "it is terrible to fall into the hands of the living, just God." (p.
514.) "(10) The original sin, with all its consequences,
has passed over to the whole human race, so that we are
all begotten and born in iniquity, impotent in soul and
body, and guilty toward God. May that serve us as a
living, uninterrupted lesson of humility and in the recognition of our own weaknesses and defects, and may it
teach us —" you expect to hear "to be better," but no:
"may it teach us to ask the Lord God for his succour of
grace, and thankfully to make use of the means for salvation which Christianity offers to us!" (p. 514.)

With the moral application of the dogma of the voluntary fall ends the chapter about God in himself, and the
following chapter of the Theology speaks of God in his
general relation to man and to the world. It is impossible to understand the meaning of this whole chapter, if
we do not keep in mind those controversies which must
have been evoked by the strange doctrine about the fall
of man and the consequent doctrine about grace and the
sacraments. In this chapter the Theology tries to remove
the contradiction in which it has placed itself by the history of Adam and of redemption: a good God created
men for their good, but men are evil and unhappy.

IX

CHAPTER II.   Of God as the Provider.

The Theology says of Adam that God aided him, leading him toward the good, but Adam, endowed with freedom, did not wish that good and so became unhappy. After the fall and after the redemption, God has not ceased coöperating with the good in all creatures; but the creatures, through the freedom which has been given to them, do not want that good, and commit evil.

Why has God created men who commit evil and so are unhappy?   Why, if God coöperates with the good in the creatures, does he coöperate so feebly that men, in spite of this coöperation, become unhappy?   Why does this condition, which leads man to misfortune, persist after the redemption, which was to free him from it, and why do men, in spite of the coöperation of God the Provider, again do evil and perish?   To all these simple questions there is no answer.   The only answer is the word "allow." God allows the evil.   But why does he allow the evil, since he is good and almighty?   To this the Theology does not reply, but carefully prepares in this chapter the way for the teaching about grace, about prayer, and, strange to say, about submission to the worldly powers.

Here is the exposition of the dogma:

" Section I.   Of divine providence in general.

" 96. Under the name of divine providence has since antiquity been understood that care which God has for all the beings of the world, or, as this idea is more circumstantially expressed in the Larger Christian Catechism:

' Divine providence is the constant action of the almightiness, wisdom, and goodness of God, by which he preserves
the being and powers of the creatures, directs them to
good ends, assists all that is good; but the evil that
springs up by departure from good he cuts off, or corrects
and turns to good consequences.'   In this way three particular actions are distinguished in the general concept
of the divine providence : the preservation of the creatures, the coöperation, or assistance, given to them, and
the direction of them.

   " The preservation of the creatures is a divine action by
which the Almighty preserves the being of both the whole
world, and also the separate creatures who are contained
in it, with their powers, laws, and activities.   The coöperation, or assistance, given to the creatures is a divine
action by which the All-good, permitting them to make
use of their own powers and laws, at the same time offers
them his aid and succour during their activities.   This is
especially palpable in relation to the rational and free
creatures, who are all the time in need of the grace of
God in order to progress in the spiritual life.   However,
in relation to the moral beings the actual coöperation of
God takes place only when they freely choose and do the
good ; but in all those cases when they according to their
own will choose and do the evil, there takes place only
the permission, but not the coöperation, of God, for God
cannot do evil, and does not wish to deprive the moral
beings of the freedom which he has granted to them.

   " Finally, the direction of the creatures is a divine
action, by which the infinitely All-wise directs them with
all their lives and activities toward their predestined ends,
correcting and turning, as far as possible, their very worst
deeds toward good results.   From this it can be seen that
all the above mentioned actions of the divine providence
differ among themselves.   The preservation embraces also
the existence of the creatures, and their powers and activi-

ties; the coöperation refers mainly to the powers; the direction, to the powers and actions of the creatures. God preserves all the creatures of the world; he coöperates with the good only, and allows the evil ones to perform their evil activities; he also directs all. Not one of these actions is contained in the other: it is possible to preserve a being, without assisting and without directing it; it is possible to assist a being, without preserving and without directing it; it is possible to direct a being without preserving and without assisting it. But, on the other hand, it must be remarked that all three actions of the divine providence are distinguished and divided only by us, according to their different manifestations in the limited and diversified beings of the world and in consequence of the limitation of our mind, but in themselves they are not separable and form one unlimited action of God, because God, who ' at the same time sees everything together and each in particular,' performs everything by one simple, uncomplicated action. He inseparably preserves all his creations, and assists and directs them.

" Divine providence is generally divided into two kinds: into general providence and into particular providence. General providence is the one which embraces the whole world in general, and also the species and genera of beings; particular providence is the one which is extended over the particular beings of the world and over each of the entities, no matter how small they may appear. The Orthodox Church, believing that God ' from the smallest to the largest knows everything precisely, and in particular provides for each creation,' apparently admits both these kinds of providence.

" The ideas of divine providence, as expounded above, exclude: (a) the false doctrine of the Gnostics, Manicheans, and other heretics, who, submitting everything to fate, or recognizing the world as a product of an evil principle, or recognizing divine providence as superfluous for the world, entirely rejected divine providence with all its actions; (*b*) the false teaching of the Pelagians, who rejected in particular the coöperation with rational and irrational beings, regarding this as incongruous with their perfection and freedom, and also (*c*) the contrary teaching of various sectarians, who, believing in unconditional divine predestination, to such an extent exaggerate the divine coöperation with the rational creatures that they almost destroy their freedom, and regard God as the true cause of all their good and bad actions; finally (*d*) the false teaching of certain sophists, both ancient and modern, who admit only the general providence and reject the particular, considering it unworthy of God." (pp. 515–517.)

97. The actuality of divine providence.

98. The actuality of each of the actions of the divine providence. This actuality is proved by texts from the Book of Job, from the Book of the Wisdom of Solomon, from the Psalms, and from elsewhere. These texts prove nothing except that all men who recognized God recognized his almightiness.

99. The actuality of the two kinds of divine providence. Besides the general providence there is described the particular providence about each being taken separately.

100. The participation of all the persons of the Holy Trinity in the act of providence. All the persons take part in providence. This is proved from Holy Scripture; then, in conclusion, the explanation:

"It is not difficult for a believer to explain why all three persons of the Deity take part in the act of providence. That is due to the fact that the providence of the world is an action of divine omniscience, omnipresence, all-wisdom, almightiness, and goodness, — of such attributes as belong equally to all three persons of the Holy Trinity." (p. 532.)

Then follows what pretends to be a solution of the

question which naturally arises with the assertion of the existence of the providence of a good God: whence comes the moral and physical evil?

101. The relation of divine providence to the freedom of the moral beings and to the evil which exists in the world.

"(1) Divine providence does not impair the freedom of the moral beings. Of this we are assured both by the Word of God and by our own conscience and reason, which also assert that we are all the time under the influence of divine providence (cf. Arts. 81, 93), and that we are all free in our moral actions (Arts. 97, 99). In what manner divine providence, with all its effects in the moral world, does not violate the freedom of the spiritual beings, we are not able fully to explain, but we can to a certain extent approach its comprehension."

This is the way God with all his effects does not violate the freedom:

"(a) God is an unchangeable, omniscient, all-wise being. Being unchangeable, he, having deigned to endow the rational creatures with freedom, cannot change his determination so as to oppress or entirely abolish it. Being omniscient, he knows in advance all the desires, intentions, and actions of the free beings. And being infinitely all-wise, he will always find means to arrange his actions in such a way as — "

What you expect is: "not to impair the action of his providence," but that is far from the mark:

"As to leave inviolable the freedom of the actors." (p. 532.)

In a book which treats of God and of faith in him, suddenly enter the basest tricks!

God is unchangeable, and so he cannot change his determination about the freedom of man. But, in the first place, unchangeableness means something quite different. Unchangeableness means that he remains always one and the same. If in the determination of the attributes of God it is added that he does not change his determinations, this false definition is evidently given in order later to fall back on it. But let us admit the impossible, for we know from the Theology about the changing of his own determinations, that the unchangeableness of God means the unchangeableness of his determinations; still, we have no proof of it, and all that is left is a miserable rascally deal.

Among the number of God's attributes, according to the Theology, there are almightiness, completest freedom, endless goodness. The admission by God of moral evil and the punishment for it, due to the freedom of man, contradicts his goodness; and the necessity in which God is placed to arrange things in such a way as to leave the freedom of the actors inviolable contradicts his freedom and almightiness.

The theologians have themselves tied the knot which it is impossible to untie. An almighty, good God, a Creator and Provider of man, and an unfortunate, evil, and free man, such as the theologians acknowledge him to be, are two concepts which exclude each other.

" (b) Divine providence in respect to the creatures is expressed in this, that God preserves them, coöperates with them or allows them to do as they please, and directs them. When God preserves the moral beings, he preserves their existence and their powers; then he, no doubt, does not embarrass their freedom: that is self-evident. When he coöperates with them in the good, he also does not embarrass them in their freedom, because they are still left as the actors, that is, to choose and perform a certain action, and God only coöperates with them, or assists them. When he allows them to commit an evil act, he still less embarrasses their freedom, and permits this freedom to act without his aid, according to its will. Finally, in directing moral beings, divine providence properly directs them toward the aim for which they are created ; and the regular use of their freedom consists in striving for the last aim of their being." (p. 533.)

What ? Was it not said that he allows them to commit evil acts ? How, then, does he direct them toward their aim for which they are created, when their aim, as was said before, was their good ?

" Consequently the divine direction does not in the least embarrass the moral freedom and only assists it in its striving toward its aim.

" (c) We know from experience that quite frequently we are able with our words and motions, and in various other ways, to turn our neighbours to this or that act and to direct them without embarrassing their freedom ; how much more easily the infinitely All-wise and Almighty is able to find means for directing the moral beings in such a way that their freedom shall not suffer by it ? . . . "

The periods are in the book. This whole chapter is striking in that, apparently without any visible necessity, it raises again the question of Adam's fall, transferring it now from the sphere of history to that of actuality. One would think that the question as to whence the evil, both the moral and the physical, came, was decided in the Theology by the dogma of the fall of man. Adam was given freedom, and he fell into sin, and so all his posterity fell into sin. One would think that all was ended, and that there could be no place left for the question of freedom. But suddenly it turns out that after the fall man remains in the same condition that Adam was in, that is, capable of doing either good or evil, even after the redemption, so that again man, the creation of the good God, who is eternally providing for him, may be bad and unhappy ; as it was with Adam, just so it remains in relation to men after the fall and after their redemption. Apparently the Theology needs this contradiction of the good God and the bad, unhappy and free Adam and man.

Indeed it needs it. The necessity of this contradiction will be made clear in the teaching about grace. After this follows : ·

102. The moral application of the dogma. It consists in (1) singing praises to God, (2) hoping in him, (3) praying, (4) complying with God's providence, and (5) doing good to others, even as God does it. With this properly ends the teaching about divine providence. The next section is only a justification of the coarsest superstitions which are connected with this teaching.

Here is what the Theology deduces from divine providence. About divine providence in relation to the spiritual world.

103. The connection with what precedes.

104. God coöperates with the good angels. Proved by Holy Scripture. The angels serve the all-satisfied, all-perfect God.

105. God directs the good angels : (*a*) their serving God.

106. (*b*) Angels in the service of men : (*aa*) in general " they are given for the preservation of cities, kingdoms, districts, monasteries, churches, and men, both clerical and lay — "

107. (*bb*) Angels as guardians of human societies. There are angels of kingdoms, nations, and churches.

108. (*cc*) Angels as guardians of private individuals.

109. God merely allows the activity of evil angels. God only permits the devils to act.

110. God has limited and still limits the activity of the evil spirits, directing it, withal, toward good results. In this chapter there is an account, confirmed by Scripture, of all kinds of devils, of how to protect oneself against them with the cross and with prayers, and what the devils are good for : they humble us, and so forth.

111. The moral application of the dogma about the angels and devils is this, that it is necessary to worship the angels and fear the devil :

"And if we fall in the struggle, if we sin, let us not be frightened before the evil, let us not give ourselves over to despair: we have an advocate with the Father, Jesus Christ the righteous (1 John ii. 1). Let us call him, with sincere repentance for our fall and with sincere faith, and he will raise us up, and will again clothe us with all the weapons, that we may be able to oppose our eternal foe." (p. 575.)

112, 113, 114 impress upon us, with confirmations from Holy Scripture, the idea that God rules the material world, and that therefore the moral application of the dogma is, to pray God for rain, good weather, and healing, and not to risk our healths too much.

116. God's especial care of men.

117. God provides for kingdoms and nations. The essence of this article, confirmed by Holy Scripture, is as follows:

"The health of kings causes our peace — For God has established the powers for the common good. And would it not be unjust, if they bore arms and waged war that we might live in peace, while we did not send up prayers for those who were subjecting themselves to dangers and waging war? Thus this matter (the prayer for the kings) is not merely a graceful act, but is performed by the law of justice." (p. 585.)

And in another place: "Destroy the places of justice, and you will destroy all order in our life; remove the helmsman from the ship, and you will send it to the bottom; take the leader away from the army, and you will give the soldiers into captivity to the enemy. Thus, if you deprive the cities of their chiefs, we shall act more senselessly than the animals which cannot speak, — we shall bite and devour one another (Gal. v. 15), the rich will devour the poor, the strong the weak, the bold the meek. But now, by the grace of God, nothing of the kind happens. Those who live honestly, naturally have no

need of the correctionary measures by the chiefs: law is
not made for the righteous man (1 Tim. i. 9).   But if
vicious people were not restrained by fear of the chiefs,
they would fill the cities with endless calamities.   Knowing this, Paul said: There is no power but of God: the
powers that be are ordained by God (Rom. xiii. 1).   What
the crossbeams are in the houses, the chiefs are in the
cities.   Destroy them, the walls will fall to pieces and
crumble: thus, if the chiefs and the fear which they
cause were to be taken away from the world, the houses,
and cities, and nations would with great boldness fall
upon each other, for there would not be any one to restrain
and stop them and by the threat of punishment to compel
them to keep the peace."   (pp. 585 and 586.)

118. God provides for individuals.   Proved by Holy
Scripture.

119. God provides mainly for the righteous: solution
of a perplexity.   The perplexity is, why are the righteous
unhappy ?   The answer is, that they receive their rewards
beyond the grave.

120. Manner in which God provides for man, and connection with the next part.   There are two methods of
divine providence: natural and supernatural.

121. The moral application of the dogma:

" Himself ruling the kingdoms of earth, the Highest
himself puts kings over them, by means of a mysterious
anointment imparts power and dominion to his chosen
ones, and crowns them in honour and glory for the good
of the nations.   Hence it is the duty of each son of his
country : (a) to stand in awe before his monarch, as before
the anointed one of God; (b) to love him as the common
father, given by the Highest for the great family of the
nation, and weighted down with cares about the happiness
of one and all ; (c) to obey him as one who is clothed in
power from above, and ruling and guided by God in his
affairs of state; (d) to pray for the king that the Lord

may grant him, for the happiness of his subjects, health and salvation, success in everything, victory over his enemies, and many years of life (1 Tim. ii. 1). Through their kings, as their anointed ones, God sends to the nations all their inferior powers. Consequently it is the duty of every citizen : (*a*) to submit to all authority for the Lord's sake (3 Peter ii. 13), for whosoever resisteth the power, resisteth the ordinance of God ; (*b*) to render to all their dues : tribute to whom tribute is due ; custom to whom custom ; fear to whom fear ; honour to whom honour (Rom. xiii. 7)." (pp. 597 and 598.)

Thus ends the First Part of the Theology. With this moral application of the dogma ends the Simple Theology.

SECOND PART OF THE DOGMATIC THEOLOGY

X.

Of God the Saviour and his special relation to the human race (Θεολογία οἰκονομική).

Thus begins the Second Part.

122. Connection with the preceding, importance of the subject, doctrine of the church about it, and the division of the doctrine. "Heretofore we were, so to speak, in the sanctuary of the Orthodox dogmatic theology; now we enter the sanctum sanctorum." (p. 7.)

This Second Part, which enters the sanctum sanctorum, indeed, sharply contrasts with the First.

In the First are shown the propositions and questions which have always lain in the soul of each man: about the beginning of everything — God, about the beginning of the material and of the spiritual world, about man, about the soul, and about man's struggle between the good and the evil.

In this Second Part there is no longer anything of the kind. None of the dogmas which are disclosed here answer any question of faith, but they are arbitrary propositions, which are not connected with anything human, and which are based only on a certain very coarse interpretation of all kinds of words of Holy Scripture, and so cannot be analyzed or judged on the basis of their relation to reason. There is no connection whatsoever. These dogmas may be viewed only in relation to their correctness and their interpretation of the words of Scripture. The dogmas which are expounded here are : (1) the dogma of the redemption, (2) the dogma of the incarnation, (3) the dogma of the manner of redemption, (4) the dogma of the church, (5) the dogma of grace, (6) the dogma of the mysteries, (7) the dogma of the particular retribution, (8) the dogma of the general judgment and of the end of the world. All these dogmas are answers to questions which a man seeking the path of life has not put and cannot put. These dogmas receive an importance only from the fact that the church asserts that it is necessary to believe in them, and that he who does not believe in them will perish. All these are propositions which are in no way connected with questions of faith, and are independent of them. All of them are based only on the demand of obedience to the church.

Composition of division I. Of God the Saviour.

The central dogma of this part is the dogma of the redemption. On this dogma is based the whole doctrine of this part. It consists in this, that in consequence of the supposed fall of Adam his descendants fell into actual and spiritual death, their reason was dimmed, and they lost the image of God. For the salvation of men from this supposed fall the necessity of redemption is proposed, — paying God for Adam's sin. This pay, according to the teaching of the church, takes place by means of the incarnation of Christ, his descent upon earth, his suffering and death. Christ the God descends on earth and by his death saves men from sin and death. But since this death is only imaginary ; since after the redemption men remain actually the same as was Adam, as they were after Adam, as they were in the time of Christ and after Christ, and as men have always been ; since in reality there remain the same sin, the same propensity to do evil, the same death, the same labour pain, the same necessity of working in order to support oneself, which are all peculiar to man, — the whole teaching of the Second Part is no longer a teaching about faith, but pure myth.   For this reason the teaching of this Second Part has a special character. In this Second Part stand out sharply those incipient departures from common sense which were made in the exposition of the dogmas of the First Part, about God, about man, about evil.   Apparently the teaching of the First Part is based on the faith in the Second Part, and the second does not result from the first, as the Theology is trying to make out; on the contrary, the faith in the mythology of the Second Part serves as the basis of all the departures from common sense, which we find in the First Part.   Here is that teaching:

" 124. The necessity of divine assistance for the rehabilitation of man with the possibility for it on the part of man. (1) Man has committed three great wrongs, by not observing the original command of God : (*a*) with his sin he has offended infinitely his infinitely good, but also infinitely great, infinitely just Creator, and thus has been subjected to an eternal curse (Gen. iii. 17–19); (cf. Gen. xxvii. 26); (*b*) he has infected with sin all his being, which was created good : has dimmed his intellect, has perverted his will, has mutilated in himself the image of God ; (*c*) has by his sin produced disastrous results in his own nature and in external Nature.   Consequently, in order to save man from all these evils, in order to unite him with God and make him once more blessed, it was necessary : (*a*) for the sinner to satisfy the infinite justice of God, which was offended by man's fall, — not because he wanted vengeance, but because no attribute of God can be deprived of its proper action : without the execution of this condition man would for ever remain before the justice of God as the child of wrath (Eph. ii. 3), as the child of curse (Gal. iii. 10), and the reconciliation and union of God with man could not even begin ; (*b*) to destroy sin in the whole being of man, to enlighten his reason, correct his will, and reëstablish in him the image of God: because, if, after the justice of God were satisfied, the being of man still remained sinful and impure, if his reason remained in darkness, and the image of God were mutilated, — the communion between God and man could not take place, any more than between light and darkness (2 Cor. vi. 14); (c) to destroy the disastrous results which man's sin has produced in his nature and in external Nature: because, if even the communion of God with man should have begun and should exist, man could not again become blessed, until he should feel in himself or should experience in himself anew those disastrous consequences. Who could execute all the above mentioned conditions? None but the one God." (pp. 10 and 11.)

125. The means chosen by God for the rehabilitation, or redemption, of man, and the significance of that means. "God found for the rehabilitation of man a means in which his mercy and truth are met together, and righteousness and peace have kissed each other" (Psalm lxxxv. 10), and in which his perfections appeared in their highest form and in full concord. This means consists in the following:

"The second person of the Most Holy Trinity, the only-begotten Son of God, voluntarily wished to become man, to take upon himself all the human sins, to suffer for them everything which the just will of God had determined, and thus to satisfy for us the eternal justice, to wipe out our sins, to destroy their very consequences in us and in external Nature, that is, to recreate the world." (p. 15.)

There follow confirmations from Holy Scripture and from the holy fathers.

126. The participation of all the persons of the Most Holy Trinity in the work of redemption, and why the Son was incarnated for this purpose. "However, although for our redemption was chosen, as the best means, the incar-

nation of the Son of God, the Father and the Holy Ghost also took part in this great work." (p. 19.)

Proofs from Holy Scripture.

127. The motive for the work of redemption, and the purpose of the descent upon earth of the Son of God. " I. Why did it please the tri-hypostatic God to redeem us ? There is one cause for it: his infinite love for us sinners.   II. As to the purpose of the embassy and of the descent into the world of the Son of God, that is clearly indicated by the holy church when it teaches us to profess : ' Who has descended from heaven for the sake of us men, and for the sake of our salvation.' " Proved by Holy Scripture.

128. The eternal predetermination of the redemption, and why the Redeemer did not come earlier upon earth.

The redemption had been predetermined from eternity. God, in spite of his goodness, foresaw the fall of man and all his sufferings.   God did not redeem us at once, (1) in order that men might feel their fall and desire their redemption ; " (2) it was necessary that the infection of the sin, which had deeply penetrated the nature of man, should slowly come to the surface." (p. 28.)

For this purpose it was necessary for billions of people to fall into sin and misfortune.

" (3) It was necessary to prepare people for the arrival upon earth of such an extraordinary Messenger of God as was the Redeemer." (p. 28.)

It was necessary for a period of 5,500 years to prepare humanity for it by signs.

(4) It was necessary that humanity should pass a long series of purifications and sanctifications in the host of the holy men of the Old Testament.   (p. 29.)

129. The preparation by God of the human race for the reception of the Redeemer, and the faith in him at all times.   The preparations of the human race were : (1) the

prophecies, such as that the woman would bruise the serpent's head, and so forth.

" From the time of this protoevangely about the Messiah, which was announced even in Paradise, and of the
establishment of sacrifices, which pointed to his sufferings
and death, the saving faith in the Lord Jesus has existed
uninterruptedly with the human race.   In accordance
with this faith Adam called his wife 'life' (Gen. iii. 20),
although he had heard the judgment of the Judge: Dust
thou art, and unto dust shalt thou return (Gen. iii. 19);
according to this faith Eve called her first-born Cain: I
have gotten a man from the Lord (Gen. iv. 1).   Unquestionably in this faith the hypostatic all-wisdom of God, as
the All-wise witnesses and the church professes, guarded
the first formed father of the world, that was created
alone, and delivered him out of his transgression (Wis. of
Sol. x. 1), for there is none other name under heaven
given among men, whereby we must be saved (Acts.
iv. 12), except the name of Jesus Christ." (pp. 30
and 31.)

Besides the prophecies, there were also signs, such as:
the sacrifice of Isaac, Jonas in the belly of the whale, the
paschal lamb, the brazen serpent, the whole ritual of
Moses, and finally the moral and civil laws.

130. The moral application of the dogma is this, that
(1) we ought to learn humility, (2) ought to love God
and one another, and (3) ought to stand in awe before
the wisdom of God.

The dogma of the redemption will be expounded
further on in detail, and in that place will be analyzed
those proofs on which the church bases it; now I will
speak only of the significance which the dogma may have
to thinking people.   It is useless to refute this dogma.
The dogma negates itself, for it does not affirm anything
about what is mysterious and incomprehensible for us, as
was affirmed in the case of the attributes and persons of

God, but asserts something about ourselves, men, about something which is best known to us, and asserts it obviously contrary to reality.   It was possible to refute with proofs of common sense that God the Spirit has fourteen attributes, and so forth, for the attributes of God are not known to us, but there is no need to refute with proofs of common sense the argument that by the incarnation and death of Jesus Christ the human race was redeemed, that is, is freed from the propensity to commit sin, from the dimming of the intellect, from child labour, from physical and spiritual death, and from the unfruitfulness of the earth.   In this case there is not even any need to show that none of the things asserted exist, for everybody knows that.   All of us know full well that they do not exist, that men are evil, die, and do not know the truth, that women suffer in child labour, and that men earn their bread in the sweat of their brows.   To prove the incorrectness of this teaching would be the same as proving that he is wrong who asserts that I have four legs.   The assertion made by a man that I have four legs can only cause me to look for the cause which may have led a man to assert what is palpably wrong.   The same is true of the dogma of the redemption.   It is obvious to all that after the so-called redemption by Jesus Christ no change took place in the condition of man; what cause has, then, the church to assert the opposite?   That is a question which involuntarily presents itself to one.   The dogma is based on original sin.   But the dogma itself about original sin, as we have seen, is a transference of the question about good and evil from a sphere which is accessible to the inward experience of each man to the sphere of mythology.

The most mysterious foundation of human life, — the internal struggle between good and evil, the consciousness of man's freedom and dependence on God, — is, by the doctrine about the redemption, excluded from the consciousness of man and transferred to mythological history. What is said is: 7,200 years ago God created the free Adam, that is, man, and this man fell on account of his freedom and so God punished him and punished his posterity. The punishment consisted in this, that the men so punished were placed in the same position, in regard to the choice of good and evil, in which man had been before the punishment. Thus this teaching, which explains nothing in the essential question about the freedom of man, slanderously accuses God of injustice, which is so out of keeping with his goodness and justice. This injustice is, that the descendants are punished for somebody else's sin. If the teaching about the fall explained anything to us, we might be able to understand the rational cause which has led to the transference of the question from the inner consciousness to the sphere of myths; but there are no explanations for the question about the freedom of man, and so there must be some other cause for it. This cause we only now find in the dogma of the redemption.

The church asserts that Christ has redeemed men from evil and death. If he has done so, there arises the question: Whence comes evil and death among men? And for this the dogma of the fall of man is invented. Christ the God has saved men from evil and death; but men are creatures of the same good God, so how could evil and death have come to men? To this question the myth of the fall of man gives an answer. Adam, having misused his freedom, did wrong and fell, and with him his posterity fell and lost immortality, the knowledge of God, and life without labour. Christ came and returned to humanity all that it had lost. Humanity became unailing, unworking, doing no evil, and undying. In this imaginary state humanity is already freed from sin, suffering, labour, and death, if only it believes in the redemption. It is this that the church teaches, and in this lies the cause of the invention of the redemption and of the fall of man, which is based upon it.

In connection with this dogma of the redemption and with the preceding dogma of the providence of God, there involuntarily arise considerations which are common to both and to all that has been expounded in the First Part of the Theology: Is he the Trinity, and what are his attributes? Has God redeemed me, or not, and how has he redeemed me? Does God provide both for the world and for me, or not, and how does he provide? What business have I with all that? It is clear to me that I shall not understand the ends and means and thought and essence of God. If he is the Trinity, if he provides for us, if he has redeemed us, so much the better for me. Providence and redemption are his business, while I have concerns of my own. This is precisely what I want to know and do not want to err in: I do not want to think that he is providing for me, where I ought to provide for myself; I do not want to think that he will redeem me, where I ought to redeem myself. Even if I saw that everything which the Theology tells me is rational, clear, and proved, I should still not be interested in it. God is doing his work, which I shall never be able to comprehend, and I have to do my work. What is most important and precious to me is to have my work pointed out to me; but in the Theology I see constantly that my work is being made less and less, and in the dogma of the redemption it is reduced to nothing.

XI.

In this chapter is expounded the teaching about the second person of the Trinity. Chapter II. About our Lord Jesus Christ in particular. Section I. About the person of our Lord Jesus Christ, or about the mystery of the incarnation.

The importance and incomprehensibility of the dogma; a short account of it, the doctrine of the church about it, and the composition of the doctrine.

The redemption was accomplished by God, the second person, the man Jesus Christ. The man Jesus Christ is both a man and God. From everything which has been expounded heretofore, the concepts of man and God are not only quite different, but almost diametrically opposed. God is independence, man is dependence; God is the Creator, man is the created; God is good, man is evil. How is the combination of the two concepts, on which all this is based, to be understood ? There follows an explanation, but this explanation, as always, finds its expression in the form of a controversy with those who do not regard Christ as a God, with those who regard him as all God, all Trinity, and with those who regard him as half-God; then with those who did not recognize a human soul in him, with those who said that Jesus Christ was born simple, like anybody else; then with those who separated the man and God in Christ, with those who blended God with the man in Christ, with those who separated God and the man, but said that in him there was but one will, and with those who asserted

248

" that Christ according to his human substance was not the proper son of God the Father, but a son by grace and adoption — "

" Amidst all these numberless heresies in regard to the person of the Lord Jesus, the Orthodox Church has since the apostolic days constantly defended and disclosed one and the same teaching, which it has with peculiar force expressed at the Fourth Œcumenical Council in the following words: ' Following our Divine Father, we all unanimously teach men to profess the one and selfsame Son our Lord Jesus Christ, perfect in divinity and perfect in manhood, truly God and truly man, composed of soul and body; consubstantial with us according to the manhood; in everything like us, except sin; born before all ages of the Father according to the Divinity, but in the latter days according to the manhood of Mary the Virgin, the Mother of God, for the sake of us and of our salvation; the one and selfsame Christ, the Son, the Lord, the only-begotten, unblendingly, unchangeably, indivisibly, inseparably recognized in two essences (no distinction of the two essences being removed by the union, but the attribute of each essence being preserved, as concurring in one person and one hypostasis); not cut or divided into two persons, but one and the same Son, and the only-begotten God, the Word, our Lord Jesus Christ, as anciently the prophets and our Lord Jesus Christ himself have taught us, and as the symbol of our fathers has transmitted it to us.' From this we see that the whole teaching of the Orthodox Church about the person of our Lord Jesus consists of two chief propositions: I. of this, that in Jesus Christ there are two essences, the divine and the human, and II. of this, that these two essences form in him one hypostasis." (pp. 46 and 47.)

It is impossible not to stop here. The words of this definition are a series of contradictions. The concept of essence, as connected with God, excludes the concept of

God, since an unlimited spirit cannot have any essence. Two essences form one hypostasis. But hypostasis can have no meaning, since hypostasis has no significance in language and has never been defined. There is no rational sense in the dogma, but this dogma, like all the others, is based on the church. The church is holy and infallible, and ever since it has existed, from the very beginning, it has asserted this dogma. It is expressed, the Theology says, in Holy Tradition and in Scripture. Let us see whether it is so.

Though I have decided to pass cursorily all this Second Part, nevertheless, at this spot where it is proved that Christ is God, I feel that it is necessary to stop, since this place, though inserted in the middle, as it were, of the disclosure of further truths, which have been expounded in the beginning, in reality is the foundation of the dogma about the Trinity, which was put forward in the beginning; and if there is a dogma about the Trinity, it results only from recognizing Christ as God. Only later is the third person of the Holy Ghost attached to it. The beginning of the assertion that God is not one, but has persons, is due to the deification of Christ. This is what Art. 133 says: " Our Lord Jesus has a divine essence and is the Son of God." This article has for a purpose the proof that Jesus Christ has the divine essence, but not in the sense in which any man created by God has it, but differently from all other men, — he is the second person of God. The same meaning is ascribed to the words "the Son of God." It is proved that Jesus Christ is not a son of God in the sense in which other men are, but an especial Son of God, the only one, the second person of the Trinity. Here are the proofs from the Old Testament :

" In Psalm ii., which all the holy apostles (Acts iv. 24–28 ; xiii. 32–34 ; Heb. i. 5 ; v. 5) and the ancient Jews themselves refer to the Messiah. The Messiah witnesses about himself : The Lord hath said unto me, Thou art my

Son ; this day have I begotten thee (Psalm ii. 7), that is,
I have begotten or beget eternally.   In Psalm cx., which
by the holy apostles (Acts ii. 34–36 ; Heb. i. 13 ; vii. 21,
24, 25) and by the ancient Jews is also referred to the
Messiah, God himself says to him : From the womb, that
is, from my substance, before the morning, that is before
all time, have I begotten thee (v. 3).   The prophet
Micah, in prophesying that the Messiah would arise from
Bethlehem, added that he had also another origin, an
eternal one : Whose goings forth have been from of old,
from everlasting (Mic. v. 2), and this prophecy has also
been referred to the Messiah by the whole Jewish Church
(Matt. ii. 4–6 ; John vii. 42).

"(2) By the Lord God (Adonai, Elohim), and even
Jehovah, a name which is exclusively applied to the one
God.   Such, for example are : (a) the words of Psalm
xlv. : Thy throne, O God, is for ever and ever : the sceptre
of thy kingdom is a right sceptre.   Thou lovest righteousness, and hatest wickedness : therefore God, thy God, hath
anointed thee with the oil of gladness above thy fellows
(v. 6–7), which the apostle (Heb. i. 7–9) and the ancient
Jews have referred to the Messiah ; (b) the words of
Psalm cx. : The Lord said unto my Lord, Sit thou at my
right hand (v. 1), which Christ himself (Matt. xxii. 41–
46) refers to the Messiah ; (c) the prophecy of Malachi :
Behold, I will send my messenger, and he shall prepare
the way before me : and the Lord, whom ye seek, shall
suddenly come to his temple, even the messenger of the
covenant, whom ye delight in : behold, he shall come,
saith the Lord of hosts (Mal. iii. 1), which the Saviour
himself (Matt. xi. 10, 11) refers to the Messiah ; (d) the
prophecy, twice repeated by Jeremiah : Behold, the days
come, saith the Lord, that I will raise unto David a
righteous Branch, and a King shall reign and prosper, and
shall execute judgment and justice in the earth.   In his
days Judah shall be saved, and Israel shall dwell safely :

and this is his name whereby he shall be called, the Lord (Jehovah) is righteous to us (Jer. xxiii. 5, 6; cf. xxxiii. 15, 16)." (pp. 47 and 48.)

Not one of these places refers to Jesus Christ. The Psalmist is speaking of himself, and not of Christ. If it were necessary to understand Christ by " I, me," he would have said so.

" His goings forth have been from of old, from everlasting," means, that the goings forth, that is, the origin of each man, are from the beginning of everything. There is nothing in common here with the divinity of Christ. The words of Psalm xlv. refer only to God, and not to Christ. The prophecies of Malachi refer to any prophet. The words of Jeremiah refer to a certain king, and there is not a shadow of a reference to Christ.

Those are all the so-called confirmations of the divinity of Christ from the Old Testament. There follow confirmations from the New Testament. (1) Here is the passage from the conversation with Nicodemus, which is adduced in proof of the divinity of Christ:

" 13. And no man hath ascended up to heaven, but he that came down from heaven, even the Son of man which is in heaven. . . . For God so loved the world, that he gave his only-begotten Son, that whosoever believeth in him should not perish, but have everlasting life. . . . He that believeth on him, is not condemned: but he that believeth not, is condemned already, because he hath not believed in the name of the only-begotten Son of God (John iii. 13, 16, 18). Here (a) the Saviour in the first words clearly ascribes to himself omnipresence, a property which does not belong to one of the created beings; (b) then he calls himself the only-begotten Son of God (μονογενής), no doubt in the proper sense, that is, as being born from the essence of God, having a divine essence, for to this Son belongs omnipresence, a divine attribute; (c) finally he bears witness that without faith in him as the only-begotten Son of God, who is omnipresent, no salvation is possible for men." (pp. 48 and 49.)

To Nicodemus's question as to how a man can be reborn in order to enter the kingdom of heaven, Jesus replies that no one can enter heaven and come to God except he who knows God already, who already ascends heaven. No matter how these words may be understood, they cannot be interpreted in such a way as that Jesus is speaking about himself, since he is apparently speaking about all men and directly says that what he is speaking about is the son of man. Independently of the fact that from the meaning of the whole conversation with Nicodemus, which begins with Jesus' saying that no one shall see the kingdom of heaven, if he is not born from above, it is evident that Jesus does not refer it to himself, but to all men ; independently of this obvious meaning, everything which is said, is said now of the son of man and now of the only-begotten, or, more correctly, of the one-begotten son, but it does not say that this son of God is exclusively Christ. Above all, these words cannot have the meaning which the church ascribes to them, because the word "son of man" has the definite meaning of the son of man, that is of men, and the appellation of the son of God is precisely what Christ teaches the men to call themselves, and so Christ, if he had intended to say that he stood in an exclusive relation to God, would have been compelled to choose another expression in order to give it that meaning. I cannot permit myself to believe that Jesus should not have been able or willing to express such an important dogma. If, then, he called himself a son of God, and called other people also sons of God, he wanted to say that, so that the text expresses precisely the opposite of what the author wants to prove.

I am not going to quote here evidences from the gospels which directly deny the divinity of Christ, for I will quote them in their proper place, but I will analyze those which are quoted here in what purports to be a confirmation of the divinity of Christ. (2) Another passage is the parable about the " vineyard, which a certain man planted, and set an hedge about it, and let out to husbandmen (Mark xii. 1) ; understanding by it the heavenly Father, who had planted his church among the Jewish nation and had turned it over to the leaders of the nation, the Saviour said that at first the master of the vineyard, at a certain time, sent his servants, one after another, to the husbandmen, in order to receive of the fruit of the vineyard (v. 2). But when the husbandmen beat one of the messengers, and sent him away shamefully handled, and even killed others (v. 3–5), the master decided to send his son to them : Having yet therefore one son, his well-beloved, he sent him also last unto them, saying, They will reverence my son. But those husbandmen said among themselves, This is the heir ; come, let us kill him, and the inheritance shall be ours. And they took him, and killed him, and cast him out of the vineyard (v. 6–8)." (p. 49.)

In this parable the husbandmen, according to the interpretation of the church, mean the Jews, the fruits are the good deeds, the master means God, then why should the son mean the son only ? According to the spirit of the parable, the son, too, must have and does have a transferred meaning. The whole parable proves that by the son something is to be understood, only not the son.

" (3) When the Saviour cured him that was diseased, and the Jews sought to slay him, because he had done these things on the Sabbath day (John v. 16), he, as though in justification, replied to them : My Father worketh hitherto, and I work (v. 17). This answer, in which the Lord Jesus ascribes to himself an equality with God the Father in right and power — "

Jesus told all to pray to God the Father, and to call and regard God as a father, and so this place can only prove the opposite, namely that Jesus regarded himself as just such a man as everybody else, and defined his relation to God just like the relation of all other men to God.   His words, " I am working as my Father worketh," apparently have the same meaning as the words, " Be as perfect as your Father ! "   Here he refers his words to others, but when he says, " I am working as my Father worketh," and refers these words to himself, he speaks of himself as man, and not as God.

" The Jews understood it in the same way : Therefore the Jews sought the more to kill him, because he not only had broken the Sabbath, but said also that God was his Father, making himself equal with God (v. 18)." (p. 49.)

These words, no matter how one may read them, have no other meaning but that St. John, wishing to clear up the real meaning of Christ's sonhood to God, represents an example of a false comprehension of Christ's words. These words denote only that the Jews, rebuking Christ, fell into the same error into which the church is falling now when it praises him.   These words can have no other meaning.

" At that time Jesus did not remark to the Jews that they comprehended him wrongly, but continued : Verily, verily, I say unto you, The Son can do nothing of himself, but what he seeth the Father do : for what things soever he doeth, these also doeth the Son likewise ! (v. 19)."

These words are said in reply to the reproaches that he and his disciples are breaking the Sabbath.   He says that God and he himself do not stop working, or providing, so why should man stop ?   " For as the Father raiseth up the dead, and quickeneth them ; even so the Son quickeneth whom he will.   For the Father judgeth no man ; but hath committed all judgment unto the Son : That all men should honour the Son, even as they honour the Father. He that honoureth not the Son, honoureth not the Father which hath sent him (John v. 21–23)."

What is said about the healing on the Sabbath, is also said here, namely, that a man may cure on the Sabbath, and may decide for himself what is to be done, so long as he lives in a godly manner and tries to be as perfect as the Father, and that man is the Son of God and ought to be honoured like God.

"For as the Father hath life in himself, so hath he given to the Son to have life in himself (v. 26)." (p. 50.)

This means only what Jesus has been teaching all the time, that the true life is the knowledge of the true God, and that each man has this life in himself. All these passages, without speaking of their significance, have one undeniable meaning, namely, that Jesus Christ acknowledges himself to be precisely such a son of God and of man as all other men, and not only does not equal himself to God, as the Jews slanderously say he did, but constantly opposes himself to God. The words "my beloved Son," even if they are spoken from heaven, mean only that Christ is a son of God, like any other man, but beloved of God.

"(4) To the evidence of the Old Testament writings: Search the Scriptures; for in them ye think ye have eternal life: And they are they which testify of me (John v. 39)." (p. 50.)

The Scriptures speak of the Prophet, of his teaching, but there is not even a hint as to his divinity.

"Another similar incident presented itself soon. When the Saviour once came into a temple at Jerusalem, and the Jews, surrounding him, kept asking persistently: How long dost thou make us to doubt? If thou be the Christ, tell us plainly (John x. 24), he, replying to them, said, among other things: I and my Father are one (v. 30)." (p. 50.)

This is a conscious lie. He did not reply, among other

things, "I and my Father are one," but spoke those words for the following reason: He did not say it "among other things," but spoke as follows: Jesus answered them, I told you, and ye believed not: the works that I do in my Father's name, they bear witness of me. But ye believe not, because ye are not of my sheep, as I said unto you. My sheep hear my voice, and I know them, and they follow me: And I give unto them eternal life; and they shall never perish, neither shall any pluck them out of my hand. My Father, which gave them me, is greater than all; and none is able to pluck them out of my Father's hand. I and my Father are one (John x. 25–30).

He said distinctly that his sheep, that is, those who listen to him, cannot be taken from him, because he leads them by the will of God. And what he teaches them is that in which is the will of God.

Only that do the words, "I and my Father are one," mean. And in confirmation of the statement that these words mean nothing else, and in order to caution people not to give a false interpretation to these words, the Evangelist immediately adds the false, coarse conception of the Jews, showing in this manner how the words were not to be understood.

This passage, which clearly denies the divinity of Christ, is rendered by the Evangelist as follows: the words so irritated those who were asking him, that they "took up stones to stone him, saying, For a good work we stone thee not; but for blasphemy, and because that thou, being a man, makest thyself God (v. 31, 33)." About this passage the Theology says:

"However, even at that particular time the Saviour not only failed to remark to the Jews that he did not at all call himself God, as they thought, but, on the contrary, proceeded to prove that idea, by calling himself directly the Son of God." (p. 50.)

How else was he to have called himself, in order to prove to them that he did not consider himself to be God, but a son of God, which he taught all men to be ? Here is the whole passage : Then the Jews took up stones again to stone him. Jesus answered them, Many good works have I shewed you from my Father ; for which of those works do ye stone me ? The Jews answered him, saying, For a good work we stone thee not; but for blasphemy ; and because that thou, being a man, makest thyself God. Jesus answered them, Is it not written in your law, I said, Ye are gods ? (Psalm lxxxii. 6). If he called them gods, unto whom the word of God came, and the Scripture cannot be broken ; say ye of him, whom the Father hath sanctified, and sent into the world, Thou blasphemest; because I said, I am the Son of God ? If I do not the works of my Father, believe me not. But if I do, though ye believe not me, believe the works : that ye may know, and believe, that the Father is in me, and I in him (John x. 31–38).

How could he have said more plainly that he was not God, but that those were in whom was the word of God, and that he called himself, as all other people, a son of God. But the Theology takes this as a proof that Jesus Christ confessed that he was God, equal to God, and proceeds :

" (5) A third, similar, but still more striking case happened before the death of the Saviour. He was brought bound before Pilate to be judged. Here, after listening to many false witnesses against Jesus, the high priest finally rose and solemnly asked him : I adjure thee by the living God, that thou tell us whether thou be the Christ the Son of God (Matt. xxvi. 63 ; cf. Mark xiv. 61), and Jesus, without any hesitation replied : I am : and ye shall see the Son of man sitting on the right hand of power, and coming in the clouds of heaven (Mark xiv. 62). Then the high priest rent his clothes, saying, He hath

spoken blasphemy; what further need have we of witnesses? behold, now ye have heard his blasphemy.   What
think ye?   They answered and said, He is guilty of death
(Matt. xxvi. 65, 66).   And bringing Jesus before Pilate,
the Jews said to him: We have a law, and by our law he
ought to die, because he made himself the Son of God
(John xix. 7).   Thus the Saviour did not hesitate to
confirm the truth of his divinity by his own death."
(p. 51.)

Christ is again asked in court, not whether he recognizes himself to be God, — there is not even a question
about that, — but whether he is the Son of God, and
Christ replies: "I am," and immediately afterward
speaks of the significance of the Son of man, who, according to his expression, "is sitting on the right hand of
power, in the clouds."   He is condemned for calling himself "the Son of God," and from this is deduced the proof
that he is God.   The Jews are all the time accusing
Christ, who is calling all to acknowledge his sonhood of
God, and who is blasphemous because he makes himself
the equal of God.   Christ keeps replying that not he is
one-born, near to God, the Son of God, but the Son of
man, and he repeats the same in court, and for this he
suffers capital punishment.   And this is taken as a proof
of his acknowledging himself to be God, and, considering
the divinity of Christ proved by himself, the Theology
sees a further confirmation of it in the fact that Christ
ascribes to himself, as the Son of man, the one-born God,
the attribute of a divinity.   In proof of this are adduced
the following verses: And no man hath ascended up to
heaven, but he that came down from heaven, even the
Son of man which is in heaven (John iii. 13).   For
where two or three are gathered together in my name,
there am I in the midst of them (Matt. xviii. 20).
Teaching them to observe all things whatsoever I have
commanded you: and, lo, I am with you alway, even

unto the end of the world. Amen (xxviii. 20). And now, O Father, glorify thou me with thine own self with the glory which I had with thee before the world was (John xvii. 5). As the Father knoweth me, even so know I the Father: and I lay down my life for the sheep (John x. 15). All things are delivered unto me of my Father: and no man knoweth the Son, but the Father; neither knoweth any man the Father, save the Son, and he to whomsoever the Son will reveal him (Matt. xi. 27).

All these verses, according to the Theology, show that Christ ascribed to himself divine attributes, — omnipresence, self-existence, eternity, almightiness, omniscience.

All these verses speak only of the oneness of birth of the Son of man with God, but in no way prove the especial divinity of Christ, as the Theology tries to prove. On the same basis it would be just as correct to ascribe a Godhead to Christ's disciples, to whom he on every side repeated one and the same thought, that they were in him and he was in them, just as the Father was in him. With this end the proofs of the Godhead of Christ as expressed by him. After that follow proofs from the words of the apostles.

" III. As Christ the Saviour taught about himself, even so his disciples taught about him, according to the inspiration of the Holy Ghost. For example : (1) The Evangelist Matthew, representing the miraculous conception of the Saviour, refers to him the prophecy of Isaiah : Behold, a virgin shall be with child, and shall bring forth a son, and they shall call his name Emmanuel, which being interpreted is, God with us (Matt. i. 23 ; Is. vii. 14)." (p. 51.)

I quote everything which is said about it in this Theology, without leaving out a single line. This is regarded as the first proof from the words of the apostles. One reads and wonders how it is possible to explain these words as a proof that Christ is God. Emmanuel is a name which means " God with us." This passage is quoted from the prophet to prove that Jesus was the Messiah. What connection there is between these words and the divinity of Christ is absolutely inexplicable. Second proof :

" (2) The Evangelist Mark begins his Gospel with the words : The beginning of the gospel of Jesus Christ, the Son of God (Mark i. 1), and later, when he tells of the baptism of the Saviour, he says : And straightway coming up out of the water, he saw the heavens opened, and the Spirit like a dove descending upon him : and there came a voice from heaven, saying, Thou art my beloved Son, in whom I am well pleased (Mark i. 10, 11)."

The words of the Gospel, " The Son of God," and, " Thou art my beloved Son, in whom I am well pleased," signify only that the beloved Son of God can by no means be God himself.

" (3) The Evangelist Luke quotes the prophecy of the angel to Zechariah about the coming birth of his son John, the forerunner of the Saviour : And many of the children of Israel shall he turn to the Lord their God. And he shall go before him in the spirit and power of Elias (Luke i. 16, 17)." (p. 52.)

The words of the prophecy of the angel to Zacharias refer to God, and not to Christ. Fourth proof :

" (4) St. John begins his Gospel with the words : In the beginning was the Word, and the Word was with God, and the Word was God. The same was in the beginning with God. All things were made by him ; and without him was not anything made that was made (John i. 1–3), that is, he directly calls the Word God, represents it as existing from the beginning, or from eternity, separate from God, and as having created everything which exists. Farther on he writes : And the Word was made flesh, and dwelt among us (and we beheld his glory, the glory as of the only-begotten of the Father, full of grace and truth — for the law was given by Moses, but grace and truth came

by Jesus Christ (John i. 14, 17), that is, he bears testimony
to the fact that this Word is indeed the only-begotten Son
of God the Father, that it became incarnated, and is none
but Jesus Christ." (p. 52.)

That the Word is none but Jesus Christ, who has created
everything, not only does not appear from anything, but to
any one who will carefully read the whole chapter it will
become clear that the word " Logos " has a general, meta-
physical meaning, which is quite independent of Christ.
No matter how this chapter is understood, it is evident
that its meaning is not that Christ is God. In order to
say that, it was not necessary to speak of the Word, nor
of the Light, nor of the birth of men. The proof which
the church deduces from this chapter about the divinity of
Christ is based on the arbitrary connection of one sentence
of verse 1, where it says, " In the beginning was the
Word," with verse 14, where it says that " the Word was
made flesh," and then with verse 17, where it says that
grace was given by Jesus Christ. The first sentence of
the first verse does not stand alone, but is a connecting
sentence between the first and the last. After that,
mention is made of the light which shines on every man
who comes into the world, of the birth of men, of the
power or possibility for all to become the children of
God, — not of Christ alone who was begotten of God, but
of the many which were born of God. All such ideas, far
from confirming the proposition that the Word is Christ,
show directly that the Word, or the Logos, is the beginning of the true life of all men. Then mention is made
of the fact that the Word was made flesh, and from the
subsequent verses we must assume that the appearance of
Jesus Christ is meant. But here, in the 17th verse,
nothing is said about this Word being Christ himself, but
there is reference to the manner in which this Word found
its expression for men; it found its expression in grace
and truth, and, it seems, excludes every possibility of

acknowledging Christ to be God ; immediately it goes on to say : " No man hath seen God at any time," so that the words, " We beheld his glory," can by no means be referred to Christ the God, whereas this very passage is regarded as the best proof of the divinity of Christ.

" Farther on," says the Theology : " No man hath seen God at any time ; the only-begotten Son, which is in the bosom of the Father, he hath declared (v. 18), that is, he shows that Jesus Christ is the only-begotten Son in the proper sense, as existing in the bosom of the Father." (p. 52.)

If the only-begotten Son of the Father professed the God whom no man can ever see, then it is evident that this Son is not God. But the Theology makes the opposite deduction :

" And concluding his Gospel," says the Theology, " the evangelist remarks that the purpose of his writing was to prove the Godhead of Jesus Christ : But these are written that ye might believe that Jesus is the Christ, the Son of God ; and that believing ye might have life through his name (John xx. 31)."

That is simply untrue.   John's remark does not intend to prove the divinity of Christ, but speaks only of Christ's sonhood to God.

" The same apostle in the beginning of his first Epistle calls Christ the Word of life (1 John i. 1), that eternal life which was with the Father, and was manifested to us (v. 2), and at the end of the Epistle he says : And we know that the Son of God is come, and hath given us an understanding, that we may know him that is true, and we are in him that is true, even in his Son Jesus Christ. This is the true God, and eternal life (1 John v. 20), calling here the true Son of God and true God him whom before he had called the eternal life."   (p. 52.)

This discussion is simply unscrupulous.   The words, " he that is true," can apparently not be referred to Christ,

but refer to God.   Those are all the proofs from the
Gospels.

"Finally in Revelation are frequently quoted the words
of the Saviour who appeared to him: I am Alpha and
Omega, the beginning and the ending, the first and the
last (Rev. i. 8, 11, 17, 18 ; ii. 8 ; xxii. 13), and there it
is said that Christ is the prince of the kings of the earth
(i. 5), and king of kings and lord of lords (xix. 16)."
(pp. 52 and 53.)

As any one may see, even in these passages of Revelation, a book which has no significance for the explanation
of the teachings of Christ, there is not even an indication
of the divinity of Christ.   Then follow proofs from the
apostles.

"(5) St. Jude, the apostle, representing the heretics,
says : For there are certain men crept in unawares, who
were before of old ordained to this condemnation, ungodly
men, turning the grace of our God into lasciviousness,
and denying the only Lord God, and our Lord Jesus Christ
(Jude 4)."   (p. 53.)

The oldest texts of the Epistle of St. Jude read as
follows : "Denying the only lord and master ($\delta\epsilon\sigma\pi\acute{o}\tau\eta\nu$),
Jesus Christ."   In the later, and in our texts, it runs as
follows : "Denying the only Lord God, and our Lord
Jesus Christ."   In the first reading there cannot even be
a question about the Godhead of Christ ; in the second,
one would think, there can be even less any question
about the Godhead of Christ, for here God is called, as
he is always called, "only," and after him Jesus Christ
is mentioned as a prophet or righteous man.   But the
absence of such proofs are regarded as proofs.   Even such
are the proofs from the Epistles of St. Paul.   Here they
are :

"(6) St. Paul calls the Saviour in his Epistles : God
manifest in the flesh (1 Tim. iii. 16), the Lord of glory
(1 Cor. ii. 8), the great God (Tit. ii. 11–13), God blessed

for ever (Rom. ix. 4–5), God's own (ἴδιον) Son (Rom. viii. 32), who, being in the form of God, thought it not robbery to be equal with God (Phil. ii. 6); he ascribes to him divine attributes: eternity (Heb. xiii. 8), unchangeableness (Heb. i. 10–12), almightiness (Heb. i. 3; Phil. iii. 21), and says: For by him were all things created, that are in heaven, and that are in earth, visible and invisible, whether they be thrones, or dominions, or principalities, or powers: all things were created by him, and for him: and he is before all things, and by him all things consist (Col. i. 16, 17).

In these Epistles Christ is in three places called God (Rom. ix. 4–5; Tit. ii. 11–13; 1 Tim. iii. 16). I examine the texts, and I discover that all three indications by St. Paul that Christ is God are based on the addition of words to the old texts, and on the incorrectness of the translations and the punctuation. The passage in Timothy is read in various ways. In the oldest texts the word "God" does not occur at all, but instead of it there is a relative pronoun, now of the masculine, and now of the neuter gender. In any case this whole verse refers to Christ, and not to God, and the substitution in later texts of the word "God" for the pronoun cannot serve as a proof of the divinity of Christ. Then follows the passage Tit. ii. 11–13. The verse stands as follows: "Looking for that blessed hope, and the glorious appearing of the great God and our Saviour Jesus Christ." The conjunction "and" is taken by the Theology to be the same as a colon and an equality, and, instead of understanding the passage, as many similar passages are understood, as speaking of the glory of God and of Jesus Christ, these words are taken as a proof of the divinity of Christ. Finally, the last passage is Rom. ix. 5. This passage is read in such a way that Christ is called a blessed God, only because the punctuation mark which ought to stand after "flesh Christ came," has been changed from a period to a comma.

The whole verse ought to read: " Whose (the Jews') are
the fathers, and whose Christ is according to the flesh."
After that there ought to be a period.   Then follows the
usual praise to God: " Who is over all, God, is blessed
forever" (and not " blessed for ever ").   This intentional
error is regarded as a proof of the divinity of Christ.   In
the whole book Christ is mentioned as a prophet, and the
words " Son of God (υἱὸς τοῦ Θεοῦ) are not even used, but
instead, παῖς τοῦ Θεοῦ, that is, more correctly, servant of
God.   Those are all the proofs.

It is evident that those are not proofs, but juxtaposi-
tions of words which may serve as a confirmation of a
proposition which has no foundation whatever in the
Gospels and the Epistles.   For any man who studies
Holy Scripture in the original, who is acquainted with
the criticism of Scripture and of the history of the church,
it is evident that in the first century of Christianity, when
the Epistles and Gospels were written, there was not even
any mention made of the divinity of Christ.   The best
refutal of the proofs of the church about the Godhead of
Christ is found in the vain endeavours which it makes to
find anything resembling a proof.   Everything which
might have looked as an indication, every such a phrase,
every juxtaposition of words, every blunder, every chance
for an incorrect reading, is taken as a proof, but no real
proof exists or can exist, because that idea was foreign to
Christ and to his disciples.   This is especially apparent
from the reading of the Acts of the Apostles in the original.   Here is described the teaching of the apostles, and
here Christ is mentioned many times, and not only is he
not spoken of as God, but no special meaning above any
saint is ascribed to him ; he is called saint, prophet, messenger of God, and not even υἱός, as John and Paul call
him, but παῖς τοῦ θεοῦ, which can in no way be connected
with the present teaching of the church about Christ the
God.   But in order to have clear and manifest proofs of

the fact that the chief disseminator of the teaching of Christ, Paul, never even so much as thought of the divinity of Christ, it is necessary to read those passages of his Epistles which directly determine the relations of Christ to God.

But to us there is but one God, the Father, of whom are all things, and we in him; and one Lord Jesus Christ, by whom are all things, and we by him (1 Cor. viii. 6). One God and Father of all, and in us all (Eph. iv. 6). That the God of Our Lord Jesus Christ, and so forth (Eph. i. 17). The head of Christ is God (1 Cor. xi. 3). Simplest and most indubitable of all it is in 1 Tim. ii. 5 : For there is one God, and one mediator between God and man, the man Christ Jesus.

Indeed, there appears a man who teaches men of the relation which ought to exist between man and God, and preaches this teaching to all men. His relation and that of all men to God he expresses by the relation of the Son to the Father. That there might be no misunderstanding, he calls himself, and men in general, the son of man, and says that the son of man is the Son of God. In explaining man's relation to God, he says that as the son ought to emulate the father, and have one aim and one will with him (in the parable of the shepherd), even so must man strive to be like God and to do the same that God is doing. And he says of himself that he is the son of God. Indeed, what else could Christ have said, since he taught them the sonhood to God ? If he cannot help saying about himself that he is a son of God, since it is this precisely that he is teaching to all men, there cannot be said of him, what neither the Jews, nor he himself had the least idea about, that he was God and the second person of the Trinity; for, though he never denied his filial relation to God, he never ascribed any special importance to it. He was told: " If you are a simple man, like all, eating and drinking with the publicans, you have nothing to teach us about;

but if you are a Son of God, a Messiah, show us your power, or be executed." He denied both. He said : " I am not a simple man, — I am fulfilling the will of God my Father, and teaching men about it; but I am also not a special son of God, but only one who is doing his Father's will, and this I teach to all men."

It is with this that he struggled all his life, and this they now ascribe to him, and try to prove that he said what he actually denied and what, if he had said it, would have destroyed the whole meaning of his teaching. According to the teaching of the church it turns out that God descended to earth only in order to save men. Their salvation consists in believing that he is God. It would not have been much trouble for him to say outright, " I am God," or, if not outright, at least not by such circumlocution that there is a possibility of understanding him quite differently without any desire to do wrong. Let it even be by circumlocution, if only it would be possible to explain his words as meaning that he was God. Well, even if his words were not exact, at least they should not contradict the statement that he was God. But, as it is, he has spoken in such a way that it is not possible to understand him otherwise than that he asserted to many that he was not God. If he had only revealed this secret to his nearest disciples so that they might have imparted it to other men, but, as it is, the disciples taught only that he was a righteous man, a mediator between man and God, and not a God.

Suddenly it turns out that for our salvation, which comes from him, his words have to be comprehended not as he and his disciples have spoken them, and that we must not rely on our common sense, but must believe the church, which, basing itself on tricks and misinterpretations of certain verses, asserts the opposite of what he has said about himself, and what his disciples have said of him. I have not dwelt on this passage in order to prove that Christ is not God, — it is useless to prove that, — for to him who believes in God, Christ cannot be God. That was already evident in the exposition of the dogma of the Trinity and of the whole consequent inevitable tangle, but I have dwelt on this part as on one in which lies the source of all the preceding monstrosities and absurdities. It is evident to me that after Christ's death, his disciples, who were profoundly affected by his teaching, in speaking and writing of him, of the man who taught that all men were the sons of God and must blend with God in life, and who in his life up to his death carried out this subjection of himself to the will of God and this union with him, — it is evident to me that his disciples called him divine and the beloved Son of God on account of the elevation of his teaching and of his life, which fully realized his teaching ; and it is explicable to me how ignorant people, listening to the teaching of the apostles, did not understand it, but instead understood the mere words and on these ignorantly conceived words built up their own teaching and, with the stubbornness which generally goes with ignorance, stuck to their comprehension, denying every other interpretation, even because they were unable to understand it, and how later such ignorant people confirmed this terrible error at the first and the second Œcumenical Councils.

In the dogma of the original sin I can admit the comprehension of those people who in the story of the fall of man can see nothing but that there was an Adam and that he did not keep God's command not to eat of the forbidden fruit. This comprehension is not wrong, it is crude. Even thus I can admit the comprehension of men who say that Jesus was God and by his death and sufferings saved men. This comprehension is not wrong, it is only crude and imperfect. The conception of man's fall as due to the fact that he did not obey God is correct in so far as it expresses the idea that man's dependence, weakness, death, — all those are the consequences of his carnal passions. Just as correct is the statement that Christ was God in so far — as was actually the fact and as John says — as he made God manifest to us. But the moment men begin to assert that the form in which this thought is expressed is the only truth, I no longer can admit what they say, because their elucidations and assertions explain the meaning of the idea which they enunciate, and this idea excludes the possibility of all oneness of faith and clearly shows that the source of their stubbornness in their assertions is crudity and ignorance. It is precisely this that the church has been doing all the time in the name of its sanctity and infallibility.

After this follows Art. 134. The Lord Jesus has a human nature and is indeed the son of the Virgin Mary. Then Art. 135 proves that Christ was born in human form from the Virgin Mary, and that Mary, having given birth to him, remained a virgin. There are quoted proofs for what cannot be comprehended, and explanations of the fathers of the church.

"Not only did they teach so, but they frequently tried to disclose that such a miraculous manner of the Messiah's birth was possible and exceedingly proper : in proof, or as an explanation of the possibility, they pointed to the almightiness of God and to certain other miraculous cases of the kind, as, for example, to the burning bush which did not burn up, and to the fact that the Saviour, after his resurrection, entered through closed doors into the room where his disciples were." (p. 70.)

136. The Lord Jesus is a sinless man. "(1) The Word of God teaches us, in the first place, that the Lord does not partake of the original sin." (p. 75.)

"(2) In the second place, the Word of God teaches us that our Lord Jesus is quite free from any personal sin.

"(3) In pursuance of so clear a teaching of the Word of God, the church has invariably believed that our Lord

Jesus, consubstantial with us according to his manhood, is like us in all but sin. This sinlessness of Christ the Saviour the church has since antiquity understood not merely in the sense that he is free from the original and all voluntary sin, but also in the sense that he cannot even sin and that he is free from all sensuous desires or propensities to sin, free from all inward temptation. Therefore, when Theodore of Mopsuestia took the liberty to assert, among other things, that our Lord Jesus was not exempt from inward temptations and the struggle of the passions, the fifth Œcumenical Council (in the year 553) condemned this heresy as one of the most important ones." (pp. 77 and 78.)

II. On the unity of the hypostasis in Jesus Christ.

137. The actuality of the union in Christ of two natures in one hypostasis. "In professing two natures, a divine and a human, in Jesus Christ our Lord, we at the same time profess that there is in him but one person and that the two natures are in him combined into one hypostasis of God the Word, for we believe that the Son of God assumed in his own hypostasis the human flesh which was conceived in the womb of the Virgin Mary from the Holy Ghost and became incarnate (Epistle of the Eastern Patriarchs on the Orthodox Faith, section 7), and that, consequently, his humanity has in him no especial personality and does not form a separate hypostasis, but was accepted by his divinity into a union with his divine hypostasis. Or, let us say with the words of St. John Damascene, 'The hypostasis of God the Word became incarnate, having received from the Virgin the beginning of our composition, the flesh animated by a reasoning and rational soul, so that it itself became a hypostasis of flesh. . . . One and the same hypostasis of the Word, having become a hypostasis of two essences, does not permit any one of them to be anhypostatic, nor does it permit them to be variously hypostatic among themselves; nor is it the hypostasis

now of one essence, and now of another, but always remains a hypostasis of both hypotases indivisibly and inseparably. . . . The flesh of God the Word did not assume an independent hypostasis and did not become a hypostasis, different from the hypostasis of God the Word, but having in it received a hypostasis, was rather received into the hypostasis of God the Word than became an independent hypostasis.'" (p. 79.)

It is absolutely impossible to render this into one's own words: it is simply the delirium of an insane man. The Trinity in one person breaks up into two, and these two are again one.

"III. Holy Scripture presents the firmest foundations of this truth. It teaches: (1) that in Christ Jesus, with two essences, a divine and a human, there is one hypostasis, one person, and (2) that this hypostasis of the Word or of the Son of God, having accepted and united with itself the human hypostasis with the divine, abides inseparably as one hypostasis of either essence." (pp. 79 and 80.)

All that is confirmed by Holy Scripture, the fathers of the church, and the decrees of the councils.

Finally common sense, too, is invoked:

"IV. And common sense, on the basis of theological principles, cannot help but notice that the Nestorian heresy, which divided Jesus Christ into two persons, absolutely rejects the mystery of the incarnation and the mystery of the redemption. If the divinity and the humanity in Christ are not united into one hypostasis, but form two separate persons, if the Son of God was united with Christ the man only morally, and not physically, and lived in him, as formerly in Moses and the prophets, — then there was no incarnation at all, and it is impossible to say: The Word was flesh, or, God sent his Son, born of a woman; for it would turn out that the Son of God was not born of a woman and did not take upon himself the human flesh, but only coexternally became consubstantial with Christ who was born of a woman. On the other hand, if for us suffered and died on the cross not the Son of God, with his flesh taken up by him into a union with his hypostasis, but a simple man, Christ, who had only a moral union with the Son of God, — then there could not have taken place our redemption, because man, no matter how holy he may be, on account of his limitations, is not able to bring sufficient satisfaction to the infinite justice of God for the sins of the whole human race.   And, by tearing down the mystery of the incarnation and the mystery of the redemption, the Nestorian heresy tore down the whole structure of the Christian faith." (pp. 85 and 86.)

Thus it turns out that what cannot be comprehended or even expressed, what cannot be thought of otherwise than by learning it by heart and repeating these words, is precisely what the whole structure of the Christian faith is reared on.   In connection with the disclosure of this dogma one involuntarily comes to the conclusion that the dogma of the Trinity and those of the redemption, of grace, of incarnation, — that the more monstrous and senseless they are, the more important they turn out to be in the opinion of the church and the more controversies there have been in regard to them.

Have there been so many controversies because the dogma is monstrous, or has the dogma turned out to be so monstrous because it is the outgrowth of controversy and malice ?   I think both have happened.   A dogma which by its nature is monstrous causes controversy, and the controversy makes the dogma still more monstrous. Another remarkable thing is that the more important a dogma is regarded to be by the church, the more controversies and malice and executions there have been, and the less meaning or possibility of moral application it has. The dogmas of the emanation of the Spirit, of the essence of Christ, of the sacrament of communion, have agitated the church in proportion as they were removed from any possibility of a moral application. After that follows:

138. The manner of the hypostatic union in Christ of the two natures. " In what manner the two essences in Jesus Christ, the divine and the human, in spite of their difference, were united into one hypostasis; how he, being perfect God and perfect man, is only one person, — all that, according to the Word of God, is a great mystery of godliness (1 Tim. iii. 16), and, consequently, inaccessible to our reason. But in so far as this mystery is accessible for our faith, the holy church teaches us, on the basis of the same Word of God, that the two essences have united in our Saviour, (1) on the one hand, without blending (ἀσυγχύτως) and unchangeably, or immovably (ἀτρέπτως), in spite of the heresy of the Monophysites, who blended the two essences in Christ, or who assumed in him the transformation of the divinity into flesh; (2) on the other hand, inseparably (ἀχωρίστως), in spite of the error of the Nestorians, who separated the essences in Christ, and of other heretics, who denied that they had been united constantly and uninterruptedly; cf. the Dogma of the Council of Chalcedon." (p. 86.)

This is proved besides from Scripture:

" (3) Finally, also from considerations of common sense, which, on the basis of its natural principles, cannot in any way admit: (a) that the divine and human essences should have blended or mingled in Christ and formed a new, third essence, having lost their attributes, for the Godhead is unchangeable, and the blending or mingling of two quite simple essences, of the human soul and of the divinity, is impossible, and so much the more physically impossible is the blending of the coarse human flesh with the simplest divinity; (b) nor that the divine essence should have changed into a human, or the human into a divine essence: the first is contrary to the unchangeableness and unlimitedness of God, the latter is contrary to the limitedness of man. On the basis of the principles of the revealed, or Christian, theology, reason must tell us that only in the unblended and untransferred union of the two essences in Jesus Christ, and only with their perfect integrity, could have taken place the great work of our redemption, for the Saviour could have suffered on the cross only with his humanity, and only his divinity could give an infinite value to his sufferings. Consequently, to acknowledge in Christ the blending or transmutation of the two essences into one, means to overthrow the mystery of our redemption." (pp. 89 and 90.)

139. The consequences of the hypostatic union of the two essences in Jesus Christ, (a) in relation to himself. " The consequences of the first kind are: I. The communion in Jesus Christ of the two attributes of his essences. It consists in this, that in the person of Jesus Christ each of his essences transfers its attributes to the other, namely, what is proper to him according to his humanity is appropriated to him as to God, and what is proper to him according to his divinity is appropriated to him as to man. II. The deification of the human essence in Jesus Christ. The deification is not in the sense that the human in Christ is changed into divinity, has lost its limitedness, and has received, in the place of the human attributes, other attributes of God; but that, having been received by the Son of God into a union with his hypostasis, it has been communicated to his divinity, has become one with God the Word, and through incorporation with the divinity has been heightened in its perfections to the highest degree to which humanity can rise, at the same time not ceasing to be humanity." (p. 95.)

" III. To Jesus Christ, as to the one person, to the God-man, it behoves us to give one, undivided divine worship, both according to his Godhead and according to his humanity."

"IV. In Jesus Christ there are two wills and two actions." There follow long controversies about the two wills and the two actions. Refutals and proofs from Scripture and from common sense. The mental morbidity has so increased in this chapter that it is painful to read it, if you read with the desire to understand what the author is talking about. Then, in accordance with the subdivision made in the beginning of the chapter, where it said that the consequences of the hypostatic union of Jesus Christ are of two kinds, in relation: (a) to himself, (b) to the Virgin Mary, and (c) to the Most Holy Trinity.

140. (b) In relation to the Most Holy Virgin, the Mother of our Lord Jesus. The consequences of the hypostatic union in relation to the Virgin Mary are analyzed. Contents: a polemic with the Macedonians and the Nestorians. The subdivision about the consequences in relation to Christ and to the Virgin Mary is made only in order to dispute against Nestorius, who called the Virgin Mary the Mother of Christ.

141. (c) In relation to the Most Holy Trinity. It is proved that, in spite of the incarnation, the Trinity remained a Trinity. This is the way it is to be understood:

"The words of St. John Damascene: 'I do not introduce a fourth person into the Trinity, which it shall not be; but I profess the one person of God the Word and of his flesh. The Trinity remained the Trinity even after the incarnation of the Word. The flesh of God the Word did not receive an independent hypostasis, and did not become a hypostasis different from the hypostasis of God the Word; but in it, having received the hypostasis, it became rather received into the hypostasis of God the Word than an independent hypostasis. For this reason it does not remain anhypostatic and introduce another hypostasis into the Trinity.'" (p. 114.)

142. Moral application of the dogma about the mystery of the incarnation. All these dogmas give us the following lessons: (1) all these blasphemous controversies, in the opinion of the author, "confirm the faith in us;" (2) faith reminds us of hope; (3) kindles in us the love for God; (4) teaches us to glorify not only God, but also "to glorify with all the strength of our being the Most Holy, Most Blessed, Glorious Lady, our Mother of God and Ever Virgin Mary;" (5) "to respect in ourselves the dignity of man," because Christ was God and man; (6) "finally, presents to us in the incarnated Son of God a most perfect example for emulation, in accordance with his own words: 'For I have given you an example, that ye should do as I have done to you' (John xiii. 15)." (p. 115.)

XII.

THE following place, " Section 2," as it is called in the Theology, is especially important, although in the middle of the exposition it is called only the 2d Section from Chapter II., Part 2: About God the Saviour in his especial relation to the human race.

In general, the division of the Theology into parts, divisions, chapters, sections, articles, into (1), (2), (3), (a), (b), (c), and so forth, is to such a degree complicated and arbitrary and based on nothing that there is absolutely no possibility of remembering all the subdivisions, and it is necessary to consult the book every minute or learn everything by heart. This place is especially important because here, in this very spot, we find the key to all contradictions. Here is to be found the radical, internal contradiction from which resulted the tangle of all the other parts. Here, in this place, is made the substitution of its own teaching in place of the teaching of Christ, and it is done in such a way that it is not possible at a first glance to discern this substitution, and that it appears as though to the teaching of Christ, which is clear and manifest to all, there were only attached certain revealed truths, which, far from impairing the teaching of Christ, only enhance the greatness of Christ and of his teaching.

The contradiction, which is here imperceptibly carried into the teaching, and which later will form the subject of elucidation in the division on grace, consists in this, that Christ the God saved men by descending upon earth

278

to them who had entirely fallen; at the same time he gave them a law which, when adhered to, will save them. The contradiction consists in this, that, if men were entirely lost and God had pity on them and sent to them his Son (who is also God) to suffer and die for men and take them out of the condition in which they had been before the redemption, that condition ought to have changed; but at the same time we hear the assertion that God also gave a law to men (a law of faith and works), which if they do not follow, they perish just as much as they perished before the redemption. Thus it turns out that if obedience to the law is a condition of salvation, the salvation of men by the death of Christ is superfluous and quite useless. But, if the salvation by Christ's death is real, obedience to the law is useless and the law itself is superfluous. It is necessary to choose one or the other, and the church teaching in reality chooses the latter, that is, it acknowledges the reality of the redemption, but, in acknowledging it, does not dare make the last necessary deduction that the law is superfluous; it does not dare do so because this law is precious and important to every man, and so it acknowledges the law only in words (and that, too, in a very indefinite manner) and carries on all the discussion in such a way as to prove the reality of the redemption and therefore the uselessness of the law. Christ's law is in this exposition something quite superfluous, something which does not result from the essence of the whole matter, something which is not connected with the whole progress of the discussion, and so falls off by itself. That is apparent even from the manner of the expression in the heading: About the act of salvation performed by the Lord, or about the mystery of the redemption, and from the division of the chapter, in which the moral teaching occupies only a small half of the three species of salvation, and from the number of the pages which are devoted to this subject.

Section 2. About the act of salvation performed by our Lord Jesus Christ, or about the mystery of the redemption.

143. How did our Lord Jesus achieve our salvation? He achieved our salvation as Christ. Christ means the Anointed. The anointed were the prophets, the high priests, and the kings. From this the Theology concludes that Christ was a prophet, a high priest, and a king. And on this foundation the salvation through Christ and his ministration to men are divided into three parts, into the prophetic, the sacerdotal, and the regal; why do they make such a division, which, to say the least, is queer? Why is Christ called by the improper name of king, which not only God Christ, but any moral man, would not wish to accept? To this there is no other answer except that so it was written in former Catechisms. First comes: I. About the prophetic ministration of Jesus Christ.

144. Conception of the prophectic ministration of Jesus Christ and the truth of his ministration. It is proved by Holy Scripture that Christ was a prophet.

145. The way in which the Lord Jesus achieved his prophetic ministration, and the essence of his sermon. The prophetic ministration, according to the Theology, consists of two parts: of the law of faith, and of activity. For the salvation of men Christ gives the law of faith and of activity. The law of faith consists in the belief in God the Trinity, in the fall of Adam, in the incarnation, and in the redemption. The law of activity consists in self-renunciation and loving God and your neighbour.

146. This article speaks of Jesus Christ having taught a new, more perfect law in place of the law of Moses. Here is expounded the difference between the law of Christ and the law of Moses, again mainly in relation to faith. In relation to the activity there is but half a page, in which we are informed that the demands of the Gospel law are higher than the law of Moses, but nothing is said

as to the extent to which the execution of these demands is obligatory for salvation, or what they consist in. But, in considering the demands as put forth here, and their execution in reality, it is evident that the law of evangelical activity is not recognized as obligatory for salvation. We are told that by the law of Christ are demanded the endurance and forgiveness of offences, the love of our enemies, self-renunciation, humility, chastity, not only physical, but also spiritual; it is evident that if those are all the demands of Christ's law of activity for salvation, not only will the human race not be saved, but there has not been, and never will be, saved one in a million. It is evident that that is said only in order not to overlook the moral teaching of Christ, and that this teaching has no place and is not wanted in the Theology.

147. Jesus Christ taught the law to all the people and for all times. That the law was given for all men and for all times is proved by texts from Scripture, that is, not by indicating that there can be no other law, but by confirming from Scripture that this law is for all men and for all times, meaning by this law only the law of faith.

148. Jesus Christ taught the only saving law which, therefore, is necessary for the attainment of eternal life. In this article the proof is given that this law gives eternal life, and that is again not proved by an elucidation of the meaning of the moral law, but by the assertion that it is confirmed by Scripture and by the holy fathers, and again the law of faith alone is meant. That is the end of the teaching about the prophetic ministration of Jesus Christ. Then follows what is most essential to the church: II. About the sacerdotal ministration of Jesus Christ, that is, about the redemption.

149. The connection with the preceding; conception of the sacerdotal ministration of Jesus Christ; truth and superiority of this ministration. Here it says:

" As a prophet, Christ the Saviour only announced to us the salvation, but did not then achieve the salvation itself: he enlightened our intellect with the light of true divine knowledge and bore witness that he was the real Messiah who was come to save that which was lost (Matt. xviii. 11); he also explained how he was going to save us, and how we could make his deserts our own, and pointed out to us the straight road to the eternal life. But with his work he saved us from sin and from all the consequences of sin, — with his work itself he earned the eternal life for us through his sacerdotal ministration." (p. 133.)

" But with his work itself he saved us from sin." There is here expressed what constitutes the whole essence of the teaching about the salvation; the sacerdotal ministration, in which are included the demands of the law of activity, was only the " announcement," but the salvation was in the sacrifice, in his death.

" This ministration of our Saviour consisted in this, that he brought himself as an expiatory sacrifice for the sins of the world and thus reconciled us with God, freed us from sin and its consequences, and acquired eternal benefits for us." (p. 133.)

The salvation takes place from that calculation of the divinity which was achieved independently of us. Farther down is the exposition of how it happens that Christ is the high priest, while the divinity brings the sacrifice and Christ is the victim:

" The truth of the sacerdotal ministration of our Saviour (a) was proclaimed in the Old Testament by God himself through the mouth of the prophet Daniel, speaking to the Messiah : Thou art a priest for ever after the order of Melchisedec (Psalm cx. 4); (b) was testified to by Christ the Saviour, in referring to himself the prophetic Psalm, in which he is called the priest for ever after the order of Melchisedec (Matt. xxii. 44; Mark xii. 36; Luke xx. 42); (c) finally, it was disclosed in detail by St.

Paul in his Epistle to the Hebrews.   Here he: (1) clearly and on several occasions called Jesus Christ priest, high priest, sanctifier.   For example: So also Christ glorified not himself to be made an high priest; but he that said unto him, Thou art my Son, to-day have I begotten thee.   As he saith also in another place, Thou art a priest for ever after the order of Melchisedec (Heb. v. 5, 6); Consider the apostle and high priest of our profession, Christ Jesus (Heb, iii. 1); Seeing then that we have a great high priest, that is passed into the heavens, Jesus the Son of God, let us hold fast our profession (Heb. iv. 14–16); (2) it is explained why he is called the high priest of Melchisedec.   That is due to the fact (*a*) that Melchisedec was not only a priest of the most high God, but also the King of Salem, — a king of righteousness and peace, and by this unusual combination of two high ministrations he predicted the unusual high priest of the king (Heb. vii. 2); (*b*) that Melchisedec (since Holy Scripture does not mention his family, nor the beginning and end of his life, nor his predecessor, nor heir) represents the image of Christ, the Son of God, who abideth a priest continually (v. 3); (*c*) finally, that, having received the tenth of the spoils from Abraham himself, he blessed all who were yet in his loins, the sons of Levi, the priests of the Old Testament, and from them received a tithe, — and since without any contradiction the lesser is blessed by the greater, he represented in himself the priesthood of Christ, which was more perfect than the Levitical priesthood of the Old Testament (v. 4–11)."   (p. 134.)

Do you understand it ?   In this part there is noticeable not so much the indifference of the writer as to whether what he says has any sense, as an apparent desire to collect such words as can have no meaning.   If any sense can be made out of this chapter it is this, that Christ sacrificed himself to God for men, and that the one who wrote the Epistle, in which he wished to express the idea that

Christ was the Redeemer of sins, chose an obscure comparison with Melchisedec, and that the church, who accepted all the Epistles of Paul and those that are ascribed to him as writings of the Holy Ghost, has stuck to the word " high priest," which explains nothing and gets things mixed up. The sense is that Christ brought himself as a sacrifice for men. To elucidate it, there are quoted the words of St. Gregory the Divine, St. Epiphanius, and others.

" (b) St. Gregory the Divine : ' He was the victim and also the high priest ; a priest, but also God ; he presented his blood to God, but purified the whole world; he was raised to the cross, but nailed sin to the cross.' (c) St. Epiphanius : ' He sacrificed himself in order that, by bringing a most perfect and living sacrifice for the whole world, he might make void the sacrifices of the Old Testament; himself the victim, himself the sacrifice, himself the sacrificer, himself the king, himself the high priest, himself the sheep, himself the lamb, who became everything for our sake.' "

150. How did our Lord Jesus perform his sacerdotal ministration ? His sacerdotal ministration consisted in this, that (1) men fell by their pride and disobedience. He was humble and obedient, and (2) since men had become worthy of the wrath of God, Christ took upon himself the whole wrath of God (suffered and died), and became the curse. It is impossible to express what is meant by it, — it is necessary to read the article as it is written.

" Here, as the high priest, he really sacrificed himself on the cross as an expiatory victim to God for the sins of the world, and redeemed us with his precious blood (1 Peter i. 19), so that his incarnation and his whole life on earth served only as a preparation and, as it were, a gradual ascent toward that great sacrifice. Consequently, in the Word of God and in the teaching of the church is represented to us —

" 151. Especially the death of Jesus Christ as a sacrifice of redemption for our sake." (p. 139.)

His death is the chief sacrifice of redemption for our sake. God sacrifices to God and redeems an obligation from the good God. All these are internal contradictions. There is a contradiction in every sentence, and these sentences are contradictorily combined with each other. I repeat what I said about the dogma of the Trinity. It is not exactly that I do not believe, — I do not know what there is to believe. I can believe or not believe that to-morrow a city will appear in heaven or that the grass will grow as high as the sun, but I cannot believe that to-morrow will be to-day, or that three will be one and yet three, or that pain does not pain, or that one God was divided into two and yet is one, or that the good God punishes himself and redeems from himself his own error of creation. I simply see that the one who is talking does not know how to talk or has nothing to say.

There is no rational connection. The only external connection is the references to Scripture. They give at least some kind of an explanation, not of what is being talked about, but why such terrible absurdities may be uttered. As in many preceding places, the quotations from Scripture show that the assertion of these absurdities does not take place voluntarily, but results, as in the history of the tree of the knowledge of good and evil, from a false, for the most part, crude, comprehension of the words of Scripture.

Here, for example, in confirmation of the fact that the death of Christ the God has redeemed the human race, there are quoted the passages from the Gospel. From the discourse with Nicodemus: Even so must the Son of man be lifted up: that whosoever believeth in him should not perish, but have eternal life (John iii. 14, 15).

It says " The Son of man must be lifted up." How can that mean the redemption of the human race by

God? He who will read the whole conversation with Nicodemus, will see clearly that it could not mean anything like that. It means precisely what the words themselves mean: the Son of man (meaning by "son" himself as man, or man in general) must be lifted up like the brazen serpent of Moses. By what manner of reasoning can one come to the conclusion that it means the death on the cross, or, more wonderfully still, the redemption?

The next passage adduced as a proof is the one where John says: Behold the Lamb of God, which taketh the sin of the world (John i. 29). This passage runs in Greek as follows: ἴδε, ὁ ἀμνὸς τοῦ θεοῦ ὁ αἴρων τὴν ἁμαρτίαν τοῦ κόσμου. This cannot be translated otherwise than: The lamb which lifts off, takes away the sin of the world. And this passage is translated by "taketh," to which the new translations add "upon himself." And this interpolation is regarded as a proof. The next proof is this: Even as the Son of man came not to be ministered unto, but to minister, and to give his life a ransom for many (Matt. xx. 28).

How can this verse mean anything but that the man, he himself, or man in general, must give his life for men, for his brothers?

Farther: The good shepherd giveth his life for the sheep. I am the good shepherd. I lay down my life for the sheep (John x. 11, 14, 15).

The shepherd gives his life for his flock, just as I am doing. How does the redemption follow from that? When they ask a sign from him, similar to the manna, he says: I am the living bread which came down from heaven: if any man eat of this bread, he shall live for ever: and the bread that I will give is my flesh, which I will give for the life of the world (John vi. 51). Continuing his comparison, he says that he is the only bread that men ought to eat. And this bread, that is, his example and teaching, he would confirm by giving his flesh for the life of the world. How does the redemption follow from that?

Farther: This is my body which is given for you (Luke xxii. 19). And he took the cup, saying, This is my blood of the New Testament, which is shed for many for the remission of sins (Matt. xxvi. 27–28).

Bidding his disciples farewell, with a cup of wine and bread in his hands, he says to them that he is supping with them for the last time and that he will die soon. " Think of me at your wine and bread; with your wine think of my blood, which will flow for you that ye may live without sin; with the bread think of the body, which I am giving for you." Where is here the redemption? "He will die, will give his blood, will suffer for the people," are the simplest kind of expressions. The peasants always say about martyrs and saints, " They pray, work, and suffer for us." This expression means nothing more than that the saints intercede before God for the unrighteous and the sinful.

But that is not enough: they adduce as proof from the Gospel of John the following reflection of the author of the Gospel on the words of Caiaphas: And this spake he not of himself: but being high priest that year, he prophesied that Jesus should die for that nation; and not for that nation only, but that also he should gather together in one the children of God that were scattered abroad (John xi. 51, 52).

It is evident that there are no indications in the Gospel, not to speak of proofs, about the redemption, if such words are adduced as proofs. Caiaphas predicts the redemption, and immediately afterward has Christ killed. That is all which is adduced from the Gospel in proof of the redemption of the human race by Jesus Christ.

After that follow proofs from Revelation and from the writings of the apostles, that is, from those books which the church collected and corrected when it already professed the dogma of the redemption. But in these books, in the Epistles of the apostles, we do not yet see the confirmation of the dogma, but there occur here and there obscure expressions, with which all the Epistles are filled, and which may rudely be interpreted in the sense of the dogma, as has been done by the consequent so-called fathers of the church, but not by those of the first centuries. It is enough to read the history of the church to be convinced that the first Christians did not have the slightest conception about this dogma. Thus, for example :

"The Apostle Peter commands the Christians : Pass the time of your sojourning here in fear : Forasmuch as ye know that ye were not redeemed with corruptible things, as silver and gold, from your vain conversation received by tradition from your fathers : But with the precious blood of Christ, as of a lamb without blemish and without spot " (1 Peter i. 17–19).

Peter says that it is possible to mend only through faith in the teaching which was branded by the death of him who was as innocent as a lamb. And this is taken as a confirmation of the dogma of the redemption.

"Because Christ also suffered for us, leaving us an example, that we should follow his steps — who his own self bare our sins in his own body on the tree, that we, being dead to sins, should live unto righteousness : by whose stripes ye were healed (1 Peter ii. 21, 24). For Christ also hath once suffered for sins, the just for the unjust, that he might bring us to God " (1. Peter iii. 18).

The cruel death of Christ, who left us an example of life to follow him by, ought to make us heal ourselves from sins and come to God. The expression is concise and metaphorical, just as the masses speak when they say that the martyrs have worked for us. And that is taken as a proof : " For I delivered unto you first of all that which I also received, how that Christ died for our sins according to the Scriptures" (1 Cor. xv. 3). "For" means in consequence of our sins. "Christ also hath loved us, and hath given himself for us an offering and sacrifice to God for a sweet-smelling savour" (Eph. v. 2). Christ's love for us brought him to a shameful death. That, too, is considered a confirmation of the dogma. "Who was delivered for our offences, and was raised again for our justification" (Rom. iv. 25). The resurrection is mentioned as a miracle, and it says that he was delivered on account of our sins. "Whom God hath set forth to be a propitiation through faith in his blood, to declare his righteousness for the remission of sins that are past" (Rom. iii. 25). Again a misty, tangled sentence, like all of Paul's expressions, which denote one and the same thing, namely, that the death of a just man has freed men from their previous errors. And all that is regarded as a proof. But the chief proof is found in the interpretations of the fathers of the church, that is, of those men who have invented the dogma of the redemption.

"(a) St. Barnabas: 'We will believe that the Son of God could not have suffered except for us — for our sins he wished to bring as a sacrifice the vessel of the spirit.' (b) St. Clement of Rome: 'We shall look up to our Lord Jesus Christ, whose blood was given for us — we shall look up attentively to the blood, and shall consider how precious his blood is before God, since, having been spilled for our salvation, it obtained the grace of repentance for the whole world.' (c) Ignatius Theophorus: 'Christ died for you, in order that you, believing in his death, might be saved from death.' (d) St. Policarp: 'He suffered death itself for our sins —; he suffered everything for us, that we might live in him.'" (p. 142.)

Or another place, as a sample of that arbitrariness and blasphemous pettiness, with which the whole book is permeated.

" If one of us should ask, not from love of controversy, but from a desire to know the truth: ' Why did the Lord suffer death on the cross rather than any other ?' let him know that that particular death, and no other, could save us, and the Lord suffered precisely that for our salvation, for, if he came for the purpose of taking upon himself the curse which had been upon us, then how else could he become a participant of the curse, if he did not suffer the death which was under the curse ?   And that is the death on the cross, for it is written : Cursed is every one that hangeth on a tree (Gal. iii. 13).   In the second place, if the death of the Lord is the redemption of all, if by it the middle wall of partition is broken down (Eph. ii. 14) and the calling together of the tongues takes place, then how could he have called us to the Father, if he had not been crucified ?   For it is only on the cross that one can die with extended hands.   And so that is the reason why the Lord had to suffer death on the cross and on the cross to extend his arms, in order with one hand to attract to himself the ancient nation, and with the other the pagans, and thus to unite them in himself.   He predicted that about himself when he wanted to show with what kind of a death he meant to redeem all: If I be lifted up from the earth, I will draw all men unto me (John xii. 32). And again : the enemy of our race, the devil, having fallen from heaven, is wandering here in the aerial sphere and ruling over demons who are like him in disobedience, and by means of them he entices with visions those who fall victims to his deception, or in every way tries to hinder those who are tending upwards; thus speaks of him the Apostle Paul, calling him the prince of the power of the air, the spirit that now worketh in the children of disobedience (Eph. ii. 2).   For this reason the Lord came to depose the devil, to clear the air of him, and to open a new path for us to the heavens, as the apostle has said, through a curtain, that is, through his flesh ; but that he could do only through his death, and what death could it have been other than one that takes place in the air, that is, on the cross? For only he who is crucified dies in the air. And thus the Lord has not without cause suffered death on the cross: having been lifted on the cross, he purified the air from the snares of the devil." (p. 144.)

Redemption, the church says, is a fundamental dogma, on which the whole doctrine is based. Where is it expressed? In the Gospels, that is in the words of Jesus Christ himself, who came to save men, and in the words of the evangelists who wrote down the words of Christ, there is not any mention of this dogma. The church asserts that the dogma is expressed in Christ's words, "The Son of man must be lifted up;" in the spurious words, "The lamb which taketh upon himself the sins of the world;" in the words, "The Son of man has come to minister;" in the words, "I am a good shepherd who will not spare my life for my sheep;" then in the words, when, breaking the bread, he said, "This is my body, for you do I break it," and, at last, in what Caiaphas said. That is, obviously, untrue, but, according to the teaching of the church, all this is expressed more clearly in the Epistles, that is, in the interpretations of Christ's words, and more clearly still in the interpretations of the fathers. But the redemption is the fundamental dogma of our salvation, — how is it then that Christ, who came to save us, did not more clearly express the dogma, but left all this to the interpretation of Epiphanius, to the unknown Epistle to the Hebrews, and to others. If this dogma is not only so important that on the belief in it depends all our salvation, but also is simply necessary to men, and Christ came down upon earth out of love for men, he ought to have expressed it clearly and simply at least once, but as it is he did not even hint at it. And everything which I can find out about this great truth, which is necessary for my salvation, I must draw from the writings about

Christ, composed by various persons, and from the interpretations of some fathers, who apparently did not understand themselves what they were saying.   This is what
it goes on to say, what I must believe in, and what Christ
meant to say to all men, but did not say.

152. Very detailed exposition in the word of God of
our redemption through the death of Jesus Christ.

(1) Christ has purified us; (2) has redeemed us; (3)
has reconciled us to God; (4) has freed us from the
slavery of sin; (5) has established a new covenant with
God; (6) has made us the adopted children of God; (7)
has given us the means for being holy; (8) has obtained
eternal life for us.   It turns out that Christ has given us
eight advantages through his sacrifice, but all these advantages are imaginary, for no one has ever seen them or ever
will see them, as was the case with that sleight-of-hand
performer who reeled the Virgin's endless hairs, which no
one could see.

After Christ all of us became pure, holy, no longer
slaves to sin, eternal, and so forth.   Thus the fathers
assure us, and I am compelled to believe this time what
they tell me, not about something invisible, but about
myself, although I know that all that is untrue.   And
again, as always, what is not and cannot be, is explained
at great length.   About the moral law of Christ there is
just half a page, *en passant* ; but about the essences, about
redemption, there is no end to words, though that has
never been and never can be.   One would think that all
has been said, but no, now we get a discussion about
the —

153. Disclosure of the method itself of our redemption
through the death of Jesus Christ.   " The whole mystery
of our redemption through the death of Jesus Christ consists in this, that he in our place paid the debt with his
blood and fully satisfied the justice of God for our sins,
for which we ourselves had been unable to pay ; in other

words, in our place he achieved and suffered everything which was necessary for the remission of our sins.   The possibility in general of such a substitution of one person for another before the judgment of the justice of God, of such an acquittal of a moral debt by one person in the place of another or of others, must necessarily be admitted by common sense: (*a*) when for this substitution we have the will of God and the consent of the Supreme Lawgiver and Judge; (*b*) when the person who has taken upon himself to pay the debt for other delinquent debtors does not himself stand in the place of debtor before God; (*c*) when he voluntarily determines to execute all the conditions of the debt that the Judge may impose upon him, and (*d*) when, at last, he actually offers the pay which fully satisfies the debt.

"All these conditions, which we have borrowed from the example of our Saviour and have only generalized, have all been fulfilled by him in his great deed for our sake: Our Lord Jesus suffered for us pain and death by the will and with the permission of his Father, our Supreme Judge.   It was precisely for this purpose that he, the Son of God, came down upon earth, in order to do, not his will, not his own will, but the will of him who sent him (John vi. 38), and during his whole life busied himself only with doing the will of his Father." (p. 148.)

I have quoted this as a specimen of that involuntarily blasphemous form of speech which is employed by the author, whenever the subject of his speech is a blasphemy. What kind of debt, and pay, and court is he talking about?   What kind of an expression is this, "God busied himself only"?

And thus, (1) Christ suffered for obeying his Father; (2) he was sinless; (3) he suffered voluntarily; (4) the pay for the debt as offered by Christ surpasses the amount of the debt, and a surplus — some change — is left.   It is even analyzed who gets the pay for the debt. All that is not my invention.

"Who received the pay for this redemption? Some represented that it was brought for the prince of this world, the devil, in whose captivity we all are. But St. Gregory discusses as follows: 'For whom and for what was this blood spilled, which he spilled on account of us, the blood of the great and most glorious God and high priest and victim? We were in the power of the deceiver, sold for our sins, having bought our injury by our lust. And if the price of the ransom is given to no other than the one who has us in his power, I ask: To whom and for what reason was this ransom paid? If to the deceiver, then that is offensive. The robber receives the ransom, and receives not only from God, but God himself; for his oppression he takes such an extortionate price that it was right that we should be spared for it! But if to the Father, then, in the first place, in what manner? We were certainly not in captivity to him. And, in the second place, for what reason is the blood of the Only-begotten One agreeable to the Father, who did not receive even Isaac, who was offered by his father, but exchanged the offering, having given a ram in place of the sacrifice of the promise? But from this we see that the Father received the ransom not because he demanded or needed it, but on account of his house-management, and because man had to be sanctified by the manhood of God, in order that he himself might free us, having overcome the tormentor by force, and might lead us up to him through the Son, who mediates and arranges everything in the honour of the Father, to whom he turns out to be obedient in everything.'"   (p. 154.)

154. The extent of the redemptory actions of Christ's death.

Christ's sacrifice not only redeemed the sin, but a surplus was left. This surplus is (1) for everybody; (2)

extends over all sins, (*a*) redeems the original sin, (*b*) every sin, (*c*) all previous sins, (*d*) all future sins. This truth was unanimously preached by the teachers of the church, for example :

"(*a*) By St. John Chrysostom : ' That the benefits given by Jesus Christ are more numerous than the evils destroyed, and that not only the original sin was destroyed, but also all other sins, that the apostles said in these words : The free gift is of many offences unto justification (Rom. v. 16),' and farther : ' By the grace was destroyed not only the original sin, but also all other sins ; and not only the sins were destroyed, but righteousness was given to us, and Christ set aright not only what was injured by Adam, but reëstablished everything in a greater measure and a higher degree.' " (p. 157.)

"(3) For all times, that is, from the beginning of the fall of man to the end of the world. Therefore, (*a*) Christ is called, on the one hand, a lamb, and, on the other, a high priest. Similarly, (*b*) the redemption achieved by him is called eternal, (*c*) and his priesthood unchangeable, for he ever liveth to make intercession for them (Heb. vii. 24, 25). How to understand this intercession for us by Christ the Saviour in heaven, is explained by St. Gregory the Divine : ' To intercede means here (Heb. vii. 25) to negotiate (πρεσβεύειν) for us in the capacity of a mediator, as is said of the Spirit who maketh intercession for us (Rom. viii. 26). . . . Thus also we have an advocate in Jesus (1 John ii. 1), not in the sense that he humbles himself before the Father and falls down before him as a slave : far be from us such a dreadfully slavish thought, which is unworthy of the Spirit ! It is not proper for the Father to demand it, or for the Son to suffer it, and it is not right to think so of God.' The blessed Theophilactes of Bulgaria : ' Some have understood the expression *to intercede for us* to mean that Jesus Christ had a body (and had not put it off, as the Manicheans speak idly). That is precisely what his intercession before the Father is.   For, looking at it, the Father recalls his love for men, for the sake of which his Son assumed the body, and is inclined to charity and mercy.' "   (p. 158.)

By the way, as one reads similar passages, it becomes evident that the whole mysterious, incomprehensible Trinity represented itself in the imagination of the holy fathers in the form of three distinct, quite well defined anthropomorphic beings.   And finally :

" (4) The redemption extends over the whole world." The world of the angels was separated before, but now men unite with it.   Nature was cursed and did not produce of itself ; now this curse no longer exists, so that the redemption extends over everything, except the devils, because the devils were so infuriated.   Some Christians assume that the devils, too, were redeemed : " The opinion of the ancient Gnostics, Marcionites, and Origenists, who extended the action of the redemption to the fallen angels themselves, was rejected by the teachers of the church and solemnly condemned by the whole church at the Fifth Œcumenical Council."

All that is confirmed by Holy Scripture and forms part of a dogma.

155. The consequence of the deserts of the cross of Jesus Christ in regard to himself : the condition of his glorification.   Christ is glorified as a reward for having come down into the world.

156. The relation of the sacerdotal ministration of Jesus Christ to his prophetic ministration.   " Although the chief aim of the sacerdotal ministration of Jesus Christ, that is, of his whole exhaustion and especially of his death on the cross, was to achieve our redemption, he at the same time subjected himself to this exhaustion also for other purposes."   (p. 162.)

The chief aim is the redemption, but in addition there were also the following purposes: (1) to give us an example by his life; (2) to deprive the Jews of their faith in the coming of the Messiah in glory; (3) to make void the laws of Moses; (4) finally, he died in order to give a clear testimony of the truth that he was God, that is, that which he constantly denied being.

All this chapter is remarkable in that it has not the slightest foundation in the Holy Canonical Scripture, but is all based on the apocryphal account, has not the slightest human meaning, and, what is most important, appears to every fresh man quite superfluous. Only by subjecting the Theology to a close study, can one guess what it is needed for. There is but one purpose which this chapter has, and that is, to solve the contradiction that all men perished before Christ, whereas we recognize the saints of the Old Testament. What is to be done with them! And so the apocryphal account of Christ's descent into hell is taken, and the question is solved, and there appears the royal ministration of Christ. After that follows a chapter on the royal ministration of Christ.

" III. 157. Connection with what precedes, conception of the royal ministration of Christ, and the truth of his ministration. The truth of the royal ministration of our Saviour is quite clearly testified to in the Word of God. (1) He was born a king and vested with power. For unto us a child is born, proclaims the prophet Isaiah, unto us a son is given: and the government shall be upon his shoulder: and his name shall be called Angel of the Great Council, Wonderful, Counsellor, The mighty God, The everlasting Father, the Prince of Peace, the Father of the future life. And great is his government, and of his peace there is no end, upon the throne of David, and upon his kingdom, to order it, and to establish it with judgment and with justice from henceforth even for ever (Is. ix. 6, 7; cf. Luke i. 32, 33; Matt. ii. 2). He was a king and had a royal power in the days of his humiliation, for he himself adopted the name of king, as is seen from the accusation which was brought against him by the Jews (Matt. xxvii. 11–37; Mark xv. 1–32), and as he actually affirmed before Pilate (John xviii. 37). He applied to himself the regal power, as the words of his prayer to God show: Father, the hour is come; glorify thy Son, that thy Son also may glorify thee: as thou hast given him power over all flesh, that he should give eternal life to as many as thou hast given him (John xvii. 1, 2). In his very acts he showed himself a king, when he entered Jerusalem, according to the ancient prophecy: Rejoice greatly, O daughter of Sion; shout, O daughter of Jerusalem: behold, thy King cometh unto thee: he is just, and having salvation; lowly, and riding upon an ass, and upon a colt the foal of an ass (Zech. ix. 9; cf. John xii. 15; Matt. xxi. 5), and when he received the solemn acclamation of the people: Hosanna to the Son of David; blessed is the King of Israel that cometh in the name of the Lord (Matt. xxi. 9; John xii. 13). Finally, in all his glory and power he appeared as a king in the condition of his glorification, when he said to his disciples: All power is given unto me in heaven and in earth (Matt. xxviii. 18), and when God actually set him at his own right hand in the heavenly places, far above all principality, and power, and might, and dominion, and every name that is named, not only in this world, but also in that which is to come: and hath put all things under his feet (Eph. i. 20–22)."

Those are the proofs of the regal order which the church ascribes to him who said that what is great before men is an abomination before God.

158. In what actions was the royal ministration of Jesus Christ expressed? His miracles. His ministration was expressed in miracles. They are all counted out: Cana of Galilee, and Lazarus, and the casting out of the devils. "Even thus in the days of the exhaustion of our Saviour, when he was achieving mainly his pro-

phetic and sacerdotal ministration, his miracles showed that he was at the same time the King of the Universe, the vanquisher of hell and death." (p. 168.)

159. The descent of Jesus Christ into hell and his victory over hell. Another regal action of Christ's descent into hell and his victory over it. " I. The teaching that the Lord Jesus actually went into hell with his soul and divinity, when his body was in the grave, and that he went down there to preach salvation, is an apostolic teaching." There follow proofs. But not all agree upon what Christ did in hell. Some say that he took them all out, while others maintain that he took out only the righteous.

" St. Epiphanius: ' Christ's divinity together with his soul went down into hell in order to lead to salvation those who had died before, namely the holy patriarchs.' St. Cassianus: ' Having penetrated into hell, Christ with the splendour of his glory dispelled the impenetrable darkness of Tartarus, broke the brazen doors, and led the holy prisoners, who were kept in the impenetrable darkness of hell, with him to heaven.' St. Gregory the Great: ' The wrath of God, in relation to the souls of the righteous, passed away with the arrival of our Redeemer, for the intercessor of God and of men freed them from the prisons of hell, when he himself went down there and led them up to the joys of Paradise.'

" It must be added that if some of the ancients expressed the idea that Christ led out of hell not only the just men of the Old Testament, but also many others, or even all the prisoners of hell, they expressed that only in the form of guesses, suppositions, private opinions."

160. Resurrection of Jesus Christ and his victory over death. " As Christ destroyed hell by his descent into hell, though he had even before shown his regal power over the forces of hell, even so he vanquished death by his resurrection from death."

161. The ascension of Jesus Christ into heaven, and the opening of the kingdom of heaven to all who believe in him.

" Before the descent upon earth of the Son of God, heaven was, so to speak, shut against all earth-born men and, though in the house of the Father there are many mansions (John xiv. 2, 3), there were no places in them for the sinful posterity of Adam; the just men of the Old Testament, after their death, themselves descended with their souls to hell (Gen. xxxvii. 35). But, after our Lord appeared in the flesh and reconciled God with men, heaven with earth; after he had freed the just men of the Old Testament from hell, by his descent into it, and had risen from the dead, he, at last, solemnly ascended heaven with the human essence which he had assumed and in this manner opened for all people a free access to the kingdom of God."

A proof of this is the expression of the symbol, which is to be taken in the direct sense : Having ascended heaven (in the body), and sitting (in the body) on the right hand of his Father.

162. Will the royal ministration of Jesus Christ come to an end ? The kingdom of Christ will end when there will be the judgment. All will be resurrected. Then Christ will transfer the kingdom to the Father, say some, " but the Evangelist Luke (i. 33) and Solomon (Wis. iii. 4–8) understood the original power, in which, having an uninterrupted dominion from eternity to eternity, the Son never received his dominion from the Father and never will turn it over to the Father."   (p. 178.)

Thus there appears an explanation of the royal dignity of Christ. The words about the kingdom of heaven give the church an idea about the royal dignity of Christ. The royal dignity is considered by the church as something very good and it attaches it to Christ, to him who proclaimed the blessedness of the poor, who preached to them, and who himself said that the last will be the first.

163. Moral application of the dogma about the mystery of the redemption.   One would think that there could be but one application of the dogma : Christ earned above his calculation, with a surplus.   These deserts saved us from all present, past, and future sins; so one has to believe firmly in that, and one is saved.   Thus says a part of the Reformed Church, and thus live all our Orthodox Churches.   But for decency's sake, it says among the lessons that in order to follow the teaching of Christ it is necessary: (1) to believe and live thus; (2) to walk in the regeneration of life; (3) to esteem the law; (4) to give thanks for the sacrifice ; (5) to make the sign of the cross with the hand, because Christ died on the cross ; (6) to live holily ; (7) not to be afraid of suffering ; (8) to pray to him; (9) not to be afraid of the devil; (10) to hope that we shall be resurrected; (11) to hope for the kingdom of heaven.

Christ appears and brings with him a joyful message of blessedness for men.   His teaching is humility, a submission to the will of God, love.   Christ is tormented and executed.   Up to his death he continues to be true to his teaching.   His death confirms his teaching.   His teaching is adopted by his disciples, and they preach him and say that he is equal to God by his virtues, and that by his death he has proved the truth of his teaching. But his teaching is salutary for people.   The crowd joins the new teaching.   They are told that he is a divine man and that by his death he has given us the law of salvation.   Of all his teaching the crowd understands best that he is divine, consequently a God, and that his death has given us salvation.   The crude conception becomes the possession of the crowd and is mutilated, and the whole teaching recedes, and the first place is taken up by the divinity and the saving quality of his death.

The whole business is to believe in this new God and that he has saved us: it is necessary to believe and pray. That is contrary to the teaching itself, but there are teachers who undertake to reconcile and elucidate and they reconcile and elucidate. It turns out that he is God-man, that he is the second person of the Trinity, that sin and a curse were upon us, and he has redeemed us. And the whole teaching is reduced to the faith in this redemption, and the whole teaching is left out and gives place to faith. It is necessary to believe in Christ the God and in redemption, and in that alone lies the salvation.

Of the teaching of Christ, since it cannot be rejected, there is the merest mention. It says that, among other things, Christ taught self-renunciation and love, and that it does not hurt and is even good to follow him. Why follow? Nothing is said about that, since, in reality, it is not needed for salvation, and salvation is obtained anyway by the sacerdotal and royal ministration of Christ, that is, by the very fact of the redemption. Here we have again the same as in the case of the original sin and the deification of Christ. The doctrine about the redemption is obviously crude; a true idea, verbally comprehended, is reduced to a teaching, and a prohibition is imposed on any other interpretation than the one accepted by the church. With a certain effort, as I recall my childish years and some feeble-minded persons, I can imagine how such a narrow conception of the meaning of Christ may be alone accessible. But why not permit me to think, as I do, that Christ has saved us by having discovered the law which gives salvation to those who follow it, and that he has redeemed us by having sealed the truth of his teaching by his death on the cross? My conception includes that of the church, and not only does not destroy anything, but puts forward as the first important work effort, that effort by which, according to the words of Christ, the kingdom of heaven is now received; it does not exactly reject, but merely ascribes less importance to those reflections about the purposes and means of God, about which I can know nothing, and which I understand less the more I am told about them.   Is it not better for me to believe only that God has certainly done the best for me, and that I, too, must do the best I can?   If I am going to do so, without discussing what the redemption consisted in and what it was, whatever it may have been, it will not get away from me.   And how about it, if I put my reliance in the redemption of Christ and neglect that which I ought to do for my redemption?

XIII.

DIVISION II. About God the Saviour and his special relation to the human race.

Such is the title of this division. All this division, with the exception of the last chapter about retribution, is occupied with the exposition of the teaching about the church and its mysteries.

Chapter I. About God as a sanctifier. 165. Conception of sanctification; participation of all the persons of the Most Holy Trinity in the matter of sanctification, and recital of means or conditions for sanctification. In this article, after the teaching and the proofs of the fact that all three persons take part in our sanctification (the Father is the source, the Son — the cause, the Holy Ghost — the one who achieves the sanctification), it says:

"IV. In order that we might be able to make the deserts of our Saviour our own and really be sanctified, he (1) founded on earth his kingdom of grace, the church, as a living instrument through which our sanctification takes place; (2) communicates to us in the church and through the church the grace of the Holy Ghost, as a force which sanctifies us; and (3) has established sacraments in the church, as means through which the grace of the Holy Ghost is communicated to us." (p. 187.)

Christ has founded the church for our sanctification. The concept of the church I met in the very beginning of the Theology. In the very beginning it said that a dogma was a decree of the church, and later on, in the whole exposition of the dogmas, their correctness was defined by stating that the church taught so in regard to

304

them.   But heretofore there has been no definition of the church, of what is to be understood by the word.   From everything which I knew before, from everything which had been expounded so far, I assumed that the church was a collection of believers, established in such a way that it can express and determine its decrees.   But now begins the teaching about the church as being an instrument for the sanctification of men.   It says that the church is Christ's kingdom of grace, that it communicates to us the grace of the Holy Ghost, and that it has sacraments, but nothing is said about the church on which the dogmas which have been expounded heretofore are based ; on the contrary, the church receives here an entirely different meaning from what I ascribe to it as the foundation of the whole teaching about faith.   Then follows :

166. The different meanings of the word " church." The sense in which the teaching about it will be expounded here, and points of view on the subject.   The various meanings of the word " church " are explained.   All three meanings which are ascribed to the word " church " are such that with them is impossible the conception of that church which has established the dogmas.

The first meaning of the word " church " is, according to the Theology, " a society of all the rational and free beings, that is, of the angels and of the men who believe in Christ the Saviour, and of the men who are united in him as in their one head." (p. 187.)

Such a definition of the church not only does not make clearer the conception of the church which establishes dogmas, but imparts in advance to the forthcoming defini- tion of the church certain symptoms, with which it is still harder to understand how such a church could ever have established any dogmas.   The further elucidations of this first meaning do not clear it up.   All it says is : " that in the dispensation of the fulness of times he might gather together in one all things in Christ, both which are in heaven, and which are on earth; even in him: and set him at his own right hand in the heavenly places, far above all principality, and power, and might, and dominion, and every name that is named, not only in this world, but also in that which is to come: and hath put all things under his feet, and gave him to be the head over all things to the church, which is his body, the fulness of him that filleth all in all (Eph. i. 10, 20–23)." (p. 188.)

This, according to the Theology, forms one meaning of the word "church." Here is the second meaning:

"According to the second, less broad and more accepted meaning, the church of Christ embraces all men who profess and who have professed the faith of Christ, every one of them, no matter at what time they have lived and wherever they may be, whether living upon earth, or already in the country of the dead."

According to this second meaning, the church cannot be what I supposed it to be, and cannot establish dogmas, for an aggregate of all men living and of those who have lived at any time cannot express any dogmas. Then follows an analysis who of the dead belong to this church and who do not (pp. 190, 191), and after dividing the church into militant and triumphant, there is given the third meaning of the word "church."

"Finally, in a still narrower, but most accepted and usual sense, the church of Christ signifies only the militant church of the New Testament, or Christ's kingdom of grace. 'We believe as we have been taught to believe,' say the bishops of the East in their epistle on the Orthodox faith, 'in the so-called and real, the One, Holy, Catholic, Apostolic Church, which embraces all in every place, no matter who they may be, who believe in Christ, who, still existing in their earthly pilgrimage, have not yet taken up their abode in the kingdom of heaven.' In this sense we are going to take the church in the present exposition of the doctrine concerning it." (p. 191.)

According to this meaning, by the word "church" are understood all those who believe or have believed in Christ. This meaning is in general intelligible, but even in this sense the church does not correspond to that activity of the church, the sanctification of men, and still less to that other activity, the establishment of dogmas, of which the Theology has been speaking in all preceding chapters. Such a church cannot serve as an instrument of sanctification, for, if by church are to be understood all the believers in Christ, then all believers will be sanctifying all believers. In order that the church should be able to sanctify all believers, it must of necessity be a special institution among all the believers. Still less can such a church establish any dogmas, for, if all believing Christians believed alike, there would be no dogmas and no teaching of the church in refutal of heretical teachings. The fact that there are believers in Christ who are heretics and who reject some dogmas and put forward others which in their opinion are true, shows that the church must of necessity be understood not as all believers in Christ, but as a certain establishment, which not only does not embrace all the Christians, but even is a special institution among Christians who are not heretics.

If there are dogmas which are expressed in definite, unchangeable words, these words must be expressed and worked out by an assembly of men who have agreed to accept this, and not another expression.

If there is an article of a law, there must of necessity exist lawgivers or a legislative assembly. Although I may be able to express myself by saying that the article of the law is a true expression of the will of the whole nation, I, in order to explain this institution, must show that the legislative assembly which gave the law is a true exponent of the will of the people, and for that I must define the legislative assembly as an institution. Just so the Theology, which has expounded so many dogmas, which has recognized them as the only true ones, and which asserts their truth by saying that the church has accepted them as such, must tell us what the church itself is that has established these dogmas. But the Theology does nothing of the kind: on the contrary, it gives to the church the meaning of a union of angels and men, both living and dead, and the union of all believers in Christ, from which can result neither sanctification, nor the establishment of dogmas. The Theology in this case acts as would act a man, who, trying to assert his right to a legacy, instead of announcing first of all those grounds on which he bases his rights, should speak of the legality in general and of the right of inheritance, should prove the falseness of the pretensions of all the others, and should even explain his own management of the debatable property, but should not say a word about that on which his rights are based. That is precisely what the Theology does in all this division about the teaching of the church. It speaks of the foundation of the church by Christ, of the heretical teachings which do not agree with the church, of the activity of the church, but not a word is said as to what is to be understood by the true church, and the definition of the church as such which corresponds with its activity — the sanctification of men and the establishment of dogmas — is given only at the end, and here again not in the form of a definition, but in the form of a description and subdivision. And thus, without giving a definition of the church which would correspond to reality, the Theology says:

" In order that this exposition may be as detailed as possible, we shall view the church: (1) from the more external side, namely, from the side of its origin, dissemination, and purpose; (2) from a more internal side (' more ' — for it is impossible entirely to separate the internal from the external side of the church), and we shall speak of the composition and internal structure of the church; (3) finally, as a consequence from everything which has been said, we shall give an exact idea about the essence itself of the church and of its essential properties." (p. 191.)

167. Here the Theology speaks of the establishment of the church by our Lord Jesus Christ. It is proved that the church, according to the definition of the Theology, — as men who believe in Christ, — was established by Jesus Christ. In this article it is proved that Jesus Christ wished that men, having accepted the new faith, should not maintain it separated from each other, but should form for this purpose a separate religious society.

"The desire to form one society out of his followers, the Saviour has frequently expressed, for example, (a) after the Apostle Peter, in the name of all the apostles, professed him as the Son of God: Upon this rock, that is, on this confession, our Lord then said to us, will I build my church, and the gates of hell shall not prevail against it (Matt. xvi. 18); (b) in the parable of the good shepherd, in these words: I am the good shepherd, and know my sheep, and am known of mine. And other sheep I have, which are not of this fold: them also I must bring, and they shall hear my voice; and there shall be one fold, and one shepherd (John x. 14, 16); (c) in the prayer to the Heavenly Father: That they all may be one; as thou, Father, art in me, and I in thee, that they also may be one in us (John xvii. 20, 21). With the idea of founding his kingdom of grace upon earth he began his first sermon to men, as the Evangelist Matthew tells us: From that time Jesus began to preach, and to say, Repent: for the kingdom of heaven is at hand (Matt. iv. 17). With the same sermon the Lord sent his disciples out among the Jews: Go, he said to them, to the lost sheep of the house of Israel. And as ye go, preach, saying, The kingdom of heaven is at hand (Matt. x. 6–8). And how often he spoke to men about this kingdom of God, both in parables

and not in parables ! (Matt. xiii. 24, 44–47 ; xxii. 2 ; xxv.
1 ; Luke viii. 10, and elsewhere)."   (p. 192.)

All that so far only tells us that Christ wanted to disseminate his teaching, — the teaching about the kingdom
of heaven.   So far nothing contradicts the meaning which
the Theology ascribes to the church.   All believers in
Christ naturally had to unite in faith in Christ.   But
after that the Theology says :

" (2) What Christ intended to do, that he accomplished.
He himself laid the foundation for his church, when he
chose his twelve disciples, who, believing in him and
being under his power, formed one society under one head
(John xvii. 13) and formed his first church ; when, on the
other hand, he himself arranged everything necessary
in order to form a definite society out of his followers,
namely : (*a*) he established the order of the teachers who
were to disseminate his faith among the nations (Eph. iv.
11, 12) ; (*b*) he established the sacrament of the baptism,
in order to receive into that society all those who believed
in him (Matt. xxviii. 19 ; John iii. 22 ; iv. 1 ; Mark xvi.
16) ; (*c*) the sacrament of the eucharist, for the closer
union of the members of the society among themselves
and with him, as the head (Matt. xxvi. 26–28 ; Mark xiv.
22–24 ; Luke xxii. 19, 20 ; 1 Cor. xii. 23–26) ; (*d*) the
sacrament of repentance, for the reconciliation and new
union with him and with the church of those members
who violate his laws and decrees (Matt. xxviii. 15–18),
as also all other sacraments (Matt. xviii. 18 ; xxviii. 19 ;
xix. 4–6 ; Mark vi. 13, and elsewhere).   For that reason
the Lord spoke in the days of his public service about his
church as already existing (Matt. xviii. 17)."   (p. 193.)

Here with the words "definite society" begins the
obvious departure from the given meaning of the church,
and there is introduced an entirely different idea of the
church than as being a union of believers.   Here the Theology is apparently speaking of the teaching church, of

which nothing has as yet been said. It says that Christ appointed teachers for the dissemination of his faith among the nations, although the idea of the teaching church does not enter into the definition of the church as being a union of believers. Still less do the sacraments enter into that definition: both define the church of the chosen among the believers. But let us suppose that the Theology is not sticking closely to its definition, that it expounds the teaching about that exclusive church which has the power to teach and impart the mysteries. Let us see what it is based upon. It says that Christ himself established the church with its teachers and with the sacraments of the baptism, eucharist, and repentance, and the texts are referred to, but not quoted. Here are the texts:

" And now come I to thee; and these things I speak in the world, that they might have my joy fulfilled in themselves (John xvii. 13)." This is adduced as a proof that Christ established the one society, the church. It is evident that the text has nothing in common with the establishment of the church.

" And he gave some, apostles ; and some, prophets ; and some, evangelists; and some, pastors and teachers ; for the perfecting of the saints, for the work of the ministry, for the edifying of the body of Christ (Eph. iv. 11–12)." These words of Paul, who did not even know Christ, are ascribed to Christ. The other texts have been quoted, but striking is the text which proves that Christ established the sacrament of repentance :

" And Jesus came and spake unto them, saying, All power is given unto me in heaven and in earth (Matt. xxviii. 18)."

On this passage the Theology bases the establishment of the sacraments by Christ, without considering that all that is said here is that (according to an incorrect interpretation of the Theology, which will be examined later)

Christ transfers his power to the apostles.   But it does
not say wherein this power is to consist.   Consequently
any false teaching may with equal right be based upon
these words.   But, having picked out these quasi-confirm-
atory texts, the Theology in the end corrects itself and
admits that in the time of Christ there did not yet exist
a church with sacraments and teachers.   In these discussions the Theology already prepares the reader for that
substitution for the conception of the church as a union
of all believers of the conception of a teaching and sacramental church.

In the following discussion the church is mentioned no
longer in the sense in which it was mentioned before, as
being a union of all believers, but as an exclusive church,
separate in its structure and in its rights from all the
other believers.

"(3) Having received power from above (Luke xxiv.
45), the holy apostles, after receiving the divine message,
went forth, and preached everywhere, the Lord working
with them, and confirming the word with signs following
(Mark xvi. 20), and (a) from the believers in various
places tried to form societies which they called churches
(1 Cor. i. 2; xvi. 19); (b) enjoined these believers to
have gatherings in which to hear the word of God and
send up prayers in common (Acts ii. 42, 46; xx. 7); (c)
exhorted them to keep the unity of the spirit in the bond
of peace, presenting to them that they formed one body of
the Lord Jesus, of whom they were but members in particular, and had one Lord, one faith, one baptism (Eph.
iv. 3, 4; 1 Cor. xii. 27), and were all partakers of the
one bread (1 Cor. x. 17), that is, had everything for
their internal as well as their external union; (d) finally,
they were commanded not to forsake their assemblings,
under the penalty of expulsion from the church and eternal perdition (Heb. x. 24, 25).   Thus, with the will and
coöperation of the Saviour, who himself immediately put

down the foundation of his church, it was then planted in all the corners of the world." (p. 194.)

It says that the church was not one, but that there were many separate churches. It says that they were all one body of Christ, but that at the same time there was one church, from which were expelled those who left the assemblings. What kind of a church it was that expelled members it does not say. Thus, it is evident that the Theology no longer is treating about the church which it defined before, but some other church, of which the definition is not given. In the proper place I will show how incorrectly the Theology makes use of the texts of the Gospel, in order to confirm its statements. In the next article it becomes apparent that there is no longer any mention of the church as a union of all the believers in Christ, but of some other kind of a church.

168. The extension of the church of Christ: who belongs to this church, and who does not belong to it.

In this article the proof is brought that to this still undefined church belong all the Orthodox believers. But it does not say who decides the question of Orthodoxy and un-Orthodoxy. At the same time there is a detailed definition of who these un-Orthodox believers are. That is discussed on ten pages. This discussion about the heretics and dissenters, who are excluded from the Orthodox Church, which is not yet defined, is remarkable:

" In order to judge correctly in respect to the propositions disclosed by us as to the heretics and dissenters, it is necessary to know what heresy and what dissent is, and what kind of heretics are meant here. About heresy and dissent we receive the following ideas from the ancient teachers of the church: (a) From Basil the Great: ' The ancients understood one thing by heresy, another by dissent, and still another thing by arbitrary concourse. They called heretics those who fell off and became estranged from faith; dissenters — those who differed in opinion in regard to certain church subjects and questions which admitted of healing; but arbitrary concourses — meetings formed by disobedient presbyters and bishops and the ignorant people;' (b) from St. Jerome: 'Between heresy and dissent there is, in my opinion, this difference, that heresy consists in the subversion of the dogma, while a dissent similarly expels from the church on account of a disagreement with the bishop (*propter episcopacem dissensionem*). Consequently these two things may in certain relations appear different by their origin; but in reality there is no dissent which has not something common with some heresy in its revolt against the church.'" (p. 202.)

Why not tell the truth? The following words are not merely remarkable, but simply disgusting:

"When we say that the heretics and the dissenters do not belong to the church, we do not mean those who hold the heresy or dissent in secret, trying to appear as belonging to the church and outwardly carrying out its regulations; or those who are carried away by heretical and schismatic errors in their ignorance and without any malice or stubbornness, for it is evident that neither have they absented themselves from the society of the believers, nor have they been excommunicated by the power of the church, although they may already be excommunicated by the judgment of God, though neither they nor we may know it: such people it is best to leave to the judgment of him who knows all the secret thoughts of man, and searches their hearts and entrails. But we mean the declared heretics and dissenters, who have already separated themselves from the church or are excommunicated by it, consequently intentional, stubborn, and therefore in the highest degree guilty heretics and dissenters. Against them were chiefly directed the utterances of the holy fathers and teachers of the church, which we have quoted above." (p. 203.)

That is, lie before God, and we will not excommunicate you; but seek the truth and dare not to agree with us, and we will curse you. The church, in the sense in which the Theology takes it, consists in all the believers in Christ, and this church separates the heretics and excommunicates them.

169. The aim of the church is the sanctification of sinners. " The church is ordained and therefore obliged: (*a*) to preserve the precious pledge of the saving faith (1 Tim. vi. 20; 2 Tim. i. 12–14) and to disseminate the teaching of that faith among the nations; (*b*) to keep and use for the good of men the divine mysteries and sacraments in general; (*c*) to preserve its government as established by God and to make use of it in conformity with the intention of the Lord." (p. 206.)

The church is understood as all those who believe in Christ, and yet it speaks of the church as having to perform sacraments, and govern. It is evident that all the believers are not able to perform the sacraments and rule themselves, and so the Theology by the word " church " understands something different, which it puts in the place of the first definition of the church. Farther on it says:

170. Outside the church there is no salvation, and the proof is given that it is necessary to belong to the church. This is asserted in the following way:

" (1) The faith in Jesus Christ who reconciled us with God: for there is none other name under heaven given among men, whereby we must be saved (Acts iv. 12), and even before that the Saviour said: He that believeth on the Son hath everlasting life; and he that believeth not the Son shall not see life; but the wrath of God abideth on him (John iii. 36). But the true teaching of Christ and about Christ is preserved and preached only in his church and by his church, without which there cannot be a true faith (Rom. x. 17)." (pp. 206 and 207.)

Thus the faith in Christ is no longer merely a definition of the church, but it turns out that in the place of the belief in Christ is put the belief in the church.

" (2) The participation in the holy sacraments, whereby are given unto us all divine powers that pertain unto life and godliness (2 Pet. i. 3)." (p. 207.) And —

" (3) Finally, the last, a good, godly life."

The proofs for all that:

" Outside the church there is no hearing, no comprehension of the Word of God; there is no true divine worship; Christ is not found; the Holy Ghost is not communicated; the death of the Saviour does not furnish salvation; there is not the feast of the body of Christ; there is no fruitful prayer; there can be no works of salvation, nor true martyrdom, nor exalted virginity and purity, nor fasting salutary for the soul, nor the benevolence of God. (2) In the church, on the contrary, there is the benevolence and grace of God; in the church abides the triune God; in the church is the knowledge of truth, the knowledge of God and of Christ, and a superabundance of spiritual benefits; in the church are the true saving dogmas, the true faith as derived from the apostles, true love, and the straight path of life." (pp. 209 and 210.)

Everything has been said about the church that the Theology has to say. It was said that it was founded by Christ; it was determined who belonged to it, and who not; its aims and means have been mentioned; it was said that it is necessary to belong to it in order to obtain salvation, but the church itself has not yet been defined. All that was said was that its meaning is — all the believers in Christ, but with this proviso, that the church is composed by those who believe in Christ precisely as the church teaches them to believe in him, that is, the meaning of the church is now modified to mean: all those who believe in the church. But what this church itself is, which sanctifies men and establishes dogmas, has not yet been determined. Only in the 2d Division, in Art. 171, this mysterious church at last gets, not a definition, but a description, from which, at last, we can deduce its definition, which corresponds to its activity, — the sanctification and the establishment of dogmas.

"171. Having determined the extent of his church, having pointed out to it its aim, and having given it the proper means for the attainment of that aim, the Lord Jesus gave it at the same time a definite structure, by which the attainment of this aim is secured and made easy. The organization of the church consists in this: (*a*) according to its composition, it is divided into two essential parts: the congregation and the divinely established hierarchy, which are placed in a certain relation to each other; (*b*) the hierarchy is subdivided into its three essential degrees, which are distinct from each other and are connected among themselves; (*c*) the congregation and the hierarchy are subject to the supreme judgment of the councils, and (*d*) last, the whole harmonious body of the church, which is formed from so many different and wisely apportioned members, has its only head in the Lord Jesus Christ himself, who vivifies it with his Holy Ghost." (pp. 210 and 211.)

Only now do we at last get a definition of what the church is which has been talked about all the time, the same that is to sanctify men, the same that has uttered all the dogmas which have been expounded heretofore. I do not yet protest against this, that the establishment of the church which has determined all the dogmas is one and holy and has Christ for its head, and that it is not possible to find salvation outside it, but I should like first the subject uttered, and then the predicate; I should like first to know what they are talking about that is holy and one and has Christ for its head, and then only that it is holy, and so forth. But in the exposition of the Theology the reverse order has been observed. All the time it spoke

of the unity, holiness, infallibility of the church and expounded its teaching, and only now it says what it is.
Only now it becomes clear from Art. 171 what that
church is which sanctifies men through sacraments, and
which, amidst false dogmas, establishes those that are
true.   It says that the church is divided into a hierarchy and the congregation.   The hierarchy sanctifies
and teaches, the flock is sanctified, ruled, and taught by
the hierarchy.   It must obey, consequently it is only the
hierarchy that sanctifies and establishes dogmas, and so
the hierarchy alone answers that definition of the church,
from which results its activity of the sanctification and of
the establishment of the dogmas, and so the hierarchy
alone is holy and infallible, and only the hierarchy answers
completely to that which has all the time been mentioned
under the name of the church.   In Art. 173, it says that
the pastors must teach the flock, must perform the sacraments for it, and must govern it, and that the flock must
obey.

  " St. Gregory the Divine says : ' As in the body some
parts govern and, as it were, preside, while the other parts
are under their rule and dominion, even so it is in the
churches.   God has decreed that some, for whom this is
more useful, should by word and deed be directed to the
performance of their duties, should remain herded and
under rule, while others, standing above the rest in virtue
and nearness to God, should be pastors and teachers for
the perfecting of the church, and should have the same
relation to others that the soul has to the body, and the
mind to the soul, so that one and the other, the defective
and the superabundant, being like the members of the
body, united and joined into one composition, bound and
coupled with the Spirit, may represent one body, perfect
and truly worthy of Christ our head.   For that reason the
societies of the Christians, who of their own will departed
from their obedience to the bishop and the presbyters,

were regarded by the ancient teachers of the church as unworthy of the name of the church, and were called heretical, a rabble of apostates, evil-thinking, harmful, and so forth.'" (p. 217.)

The church, the one upon which the whole teaching is based, is the hierarchy. The Theology before that expounded about the one church, the kingdom of grace, the body of Christ, the church of the living and the dead and the angels; then of all those who believed in Christ; then by degrees it added to this first definition another concept; then at last the hierarchy is substituted for that church. The Theology knows very well that according to its conception the church is nothing but the hierarchy, and sometimes it says so, as in the Introduction to the Dogmatic Theology, as in the expressions of the Eastern Patriarchs, as always in the expressions of the Catholic Church; but the Theology has at the same time to confirm its definition that the church is an assembly of all the believers, and so it does not like to say directly that the church is the hierarchy. The Theology knows that the essence of the matter is the infallibility and sacredness of the hierarchy, and so it has to prove first that the hierarchy was established by Christ, and that the Theology is an exposition of the dogmas as confirmed by that same hierarchy. All that is necessary is to prove that the hereditary hierarchy was established by Christ, and that we are the inheritors of this hierarchy, and then, no matter how you may understand it, the church, the essence of the church, as the keeper of truth, will be nothing but hierarchs. For that reason the Theology uses all its efforts to prove the impossible, namely, that Christ established the hierarchy, and a hereditary one at that, and that our hierarchy is the legitimate heir, and such and such a hierarchy, not ours, is illegitimate.

172. The flock and the divinely established hierarchy with their mutual relations. " I. It is not difficult to

show, in spite of the opinion of certain evil-thinking
men, that the division of the church into the two above-
mentioned classes has its origin with the Saviour himself.
Unquestionably the Lord himself founded in his church a
special order of men, who formed the hierarchy, and
empowered those men, and only those, to make use of
those means which he gave to the church for its purposes,
that is, he empowered them to be teachers, ministers of
the sacraments, and spiritual guides, and in no way left it
indiscriminately to all the believers, having, on the contrary, enjoined them to obey the pastors." (p. 211.)

" The Protestants, who do not acknowledge that Christ
established in the church a special priesthood, or hierarchy,
affirm that all the believers, by force of the sacrament of
the baptism, are equally priests of the most high God;
but as it is impossible for all to perform the duties of
priesthood, the believers choose from their own midst
special men as their representatives, whom they clothe
in the rights of priesthood."

In the above quotation it says that a large part of
Christendom, the Protestants, do not recognize the hierarchy. This proof is very important, for the whole
teaching of the church has been reduced to the doctrine
about the hierarchy. It turns out that Christians who
are not worse or more stupid than we directly deny
according to Scripture what we assert, that is, the hierarchy. Here is the way the Theology proves the establishment of the hierarchy by God. I cite the following
places from the Theology, which are supposed to prove
the establishment of the hierarchy by Christ. I quote
every one of them, not in order to refute them, for any
one who reads them will see how useless that is, but in
order to present all the proofs of the church in favour of
the hierarchy.

" (1) As we read the Gospel, which contains in itself
the history of the life and words of our Saviour, we see:

(*a*) that he chose from among his followers twelve disciples whom he called apostles : And when it was day, says St. Luke, he called unto him his disciples : and of them he chose twelve, whom also he named apostles (Luke vi. 13), and so he said to them : Ye have not chosen me, but I have chosen you (John xv. 16)." (p. 211.)

That is the first proof. Christ chose twelve apostles. Apostle means messenger in Greek, and so it says that Christ chose twelve messengers. If he had chosen seventeen, he would have sent seventeen messengers. The Theology adduces that as a proof that the hierarchy was established by Christ. To that are added the words : Ye have not chosen me, but I have chosen you. These words were said in the chapter of the farewell speech, where Christ spoke of his love for his disciples, and have nothing in common with the passages in connection with which they are quoted, and still less with the establishment of the hierarchy.

Second proof : " (*b*) That to them alone he gave the command and the power to teach all the nations, to perform the holy sacraments for them and to direct the believers to salvation (Matt. xxviii. 19 ; xviii. 18 ; Luke xxii. 19)."

The verses are not cited. Here they are : Go ye therefore, and teach all nations, baptizing them in the name of the Father, and of the Son, and of the Holy Ghost (Matt. xxviii. 19). Verily I say unto you, Whatsoever ye shall bind on earth shall be bound in heaven : and whatsoever ye shall loose on earth shall be loosed in heaven (Matt. xviii. 18). And he took bread and gave thanks, and brake it, and gave unto them, saying, This is my body which is given for you : this do in remembrance of me (Luke xxii. 19).

The Theology gives only the number of the verses, but does not quote the passages themselves, knowing that the verses do not confirm the statement that Christ gave to anybody a special right to teach the nations. There is nothing there about the power, and nothing about the sacraments. Something is said about baptizing, but it does not say that the breaking of the bread is a sacrament, or that these actions are left in charge of the hierarchy. One cannot help observing the strange phenomenon that continually exactly the same obscure texts are chosen to prove all kinds of theses: such are the texts Matt. xxviii. 19, Luke xxii. 19, John xx. 23, and several others. These texts are repeated a hundred times. On them is based the Trinity, and the divinity of Christ, and the redemption, and the sacraments, and the hierarchy. That is all about the second proof.

Third proof: "(c) That he transferred the power to the holy apostles just as he received it from the Father: All power is given unto me . . .; go ye therefore, and teach all nations, baptizing them in the name of the Father, and of the Son, and of the Holy Ghost (Matt. xxviii. 18, 19); as my father hath sent me, even so send I you. And when he had said this, he breathed on them, and saith unto them, Receive ye the Holy Ghost: whose soever sins ye remit, they are remitted unto them; and whose soever sins ye retain, they are retained (John xx. 21–23)." (p. 212.)

In order to confirm the power which is supposed to be transferred, the texts are tampered with here. The text is quoted as, "All power is given unto me . . .; go ye," and so forth. The real text runs like this: "All power is given unto me in heaven and in earth. (Period.) Go ye therefore, and teach all nations." Considering the period, it cannot be said that he gave the power; but with the several dots and by omitting "in heaven," which cannot refer to the disciples, it is possible to interpret it as that he gave the power to the disciples. The text from John does not say anything about the hierarchy or about the power; all it says is that Christ gave the

Holy Ghost to his disciples and commanded them to teach men, that is to deliver them from sin, as it is correctly translated; but even if it be translated by "remit the sins," the hierarchy does not in any way result from the remission of the sins.

Fourth proof: "(d) That to these twelve he immediately added seventy definite disciples, whom he sent out on the same great work. (Luke x. 1, *et seq.*)" (p. 212.)

The fact that Christ sent out, at first twelve messengers, and then seventy more men, whom he ordered, like pilgrims, without a supply of clothing, without money, to visit the cities and villages, is regarded as a proof that the ruling hierarchy of the present day derives its origin by heredity from Christ. Those are all the proofs that Christ himself established the hierarchy. Everything that could possibly be adduced, has been adduced. In the opinion of the Theology, the quotations with their tampered texts confirm the establishment of the hierarchy. No other proofs could be found. After that follow proofs that later this power was transferred from the apostles to the fathers of the church, and then to the hierarchy which came after them. This is the way the transmission is proved:

"(e) That transmitting his heavenly message to the twelve disciples, he wanted it to pass from them directly to their successors, and from these, passing from generation to generation, to be kept in the world to the end of the world itself. For, when he said to the apostles, Go ye into all the world, and preach the gospel to every creature (Mark xvi. 15), he immediately added, I am with you alway, even unto the end of the world (Matt. xxviii. 20). Consequently he, in the person of the apostles, sent out for the same work and encouraged by his presence all their future successors, and in the literal sense gave the church not only apostles, prophets, and evangelists, but also pastors and teachers (Eph. iv. 11)." (p. 212.)

Here again the texts are changed in order to bring forward a specious proof. It does not follow from anything that after the words, "Preach the gospel to every creature," he said "immediately" afterward, "I am with you alway, even unto the end of the world." Nor can it in any way be said that one passage follows immediately after the other, since one thing is said by one evangelist, Mark, while the other is said by Matthew. Mark says: "Go into all the world, and preach the gospel," which has no meaning of any transmission; but the words, "I am with you alway, even unto the end of the world, Amen," are the concluding words of the Gospel of Matthew, and therefore can by no means signify that he wanted to transmit the power to them. But even if that meant what the Theology wants it to mean, there is nothing to warrant the assertion that he encouraged with his presence all their future successors. That cannot be argued out of anything.

Here is the second proof of the succession:

"(ƒ) Finally, that, having in this manner clothed his apostles with divine power, he, on the other hand, very clearly and with terrible curses compelled all men and the future Christians to receive the teaching and the sacraments from the future apostles, and to obey their words: He that heareth you, heareth me; and he that despiseth you, despiseth me; and he that despiseth me, despiseth him that sent me (Luke x. 16); Go ye into all the world, and preach the gospel to every creature. He that believeth and is baptized shall be saved; but he that believeth not shall be damned (Mark xvi. 15, 16; cf. Matt. x. 14; xviii. 15–19)." (p. 212.)

I do not leave out a single word. And that is given out as a proof not only of the establishment of the hierarchy, but also of the succession, and it says:

"And that is why, even when the Lord ascended to heaven, Matthias was, by his indication, added to the eleven apostles, in the place of Judas (Acts i. 26); and only by the voice of the Holy Ghost were Barnabas and Saul separated for the work whereunto our Redeemer had called them (Acts xiii. 2; cf. ix. 15)." (p. 212.)

This last proof, the meaning of which I absolutely fail to make out, contains the first part of the proofs as to why the hierarchy is to be considered as founded by Christ.

After that follow proofs from the Acts and the Epistles. One would think that here it would be easier to find texts which might confirm the divine origin of the hierarchy, but again the same takes place. It turns out that in all the texts, quoted and not quoted, there is nowhere a word about those rights (as though it were a legal establishment) which the Theology proclaims from the very first words.

" (2) Still more clearly is this intention of the Lord seen in the actions of the apostles who were guided by his Spirit. These actions are of two kinds and both equally refer to the confirmation of the truth under discussion. The actions of the first kind are the following: (a) the holy apostles constantly asserted their right and carried out the obligations which the Lord had enjoined on them (Acts v. 42; vi. 1–5; 1 Cor. iv. 1; v. 4–5; ix. 16), in spite of all obstacles on the part of the enemies who tried to take that divine power from them (Acts iv. 19; v. 28–29)." (pp. 212 and 213.)

These references to the apostles and especially to the Acts are remarkable. The author does not write them out, because he knows that, if anything at all is to be deduced from them, it is the very opposite of what he is trying to prove. Every passage where Christ's disciples preach his teaching is adduced as a proof that the hierarchy was established; for example, in Acts iv. 19, Peter and John said: "Whether it be right in the sight of God to hearken unto you more than unto God, judge ye."

The other references are of the same kind. Thus it goes on for two pages, from which it is clear, to any one who has read even a short Seminary history of the church, that no one at any time, during the first centuries of Christianity, ascribed any especial rights or power to himself. Elders (presbyters, bishops, overseers) were appointed, and all those appellations meant one and the same thing, and were a human institution, which was diversified according to men and places. All that is evident from the texts which are quoted by the Theology itself.

After that follows the third part of the proofs, in which it says directly in the name of the holy fathers that this power was given to the hierarchy by Christ himself. But here we get the proofs only of the fact that those men who ascribed the power to themselves asserted quite arbitrarily that the power had passed to them from God, that is, what now our, and any other, hierarchy asserts at the present time. Here it says:

"(b) The pastors, who formed that special class, always deduced their power from Jesus Christ himself and called themselves the successors of the apostles and the representatives in the church of the Saviour himself. Here, for example, are the words of Clement of Rome: 'Having received a full foreknowledge, the apostles appointed the above-mentioned men (that is, bishops and deacons) and at the same time handed down the rule that when they deceased other experienced men should take up their ministry.' St. Ignatius Theophorus: 'Bishops are appointed in all the corners of the world, by the will of Jesus Christ.' St. Irenæus: 'We can name those whom the apostles have placed as bishops and their successors over the churches down to our time, but they taught nothing of the kind and knew nothing of what the heretics have invented. For, if the apostles knew the secrets, which they revealed only to the perfect, and to no other, they so much the more certainly revealed them to those to whom they entrusted the churches themselves: for the apostles wished that those whom they left as their successors, transmitting to them their own ministration of the teaching, should be quite perfect and without a blemish in every respect.' St. Cyprian: 'We are the successors of the apostles, ruling the church of God by the same power.' St. Ambrose: ' The bishop represents in his person Jesus Christ and is the vicegerent of the Lord.' St. Jerome: ' With us the place of the apostles is occupied by the bishops.' " (pp. 214 and 215.)

Having armed itself with these proofs, that is, with the barren assertions of those men who appropriated to themselves the divine power, that this power had been transferred to them from God, the Theology now gives the direct definition of the church, a part of which (namely, the words of Gregory the Divine) I have quoted before. After that it says (from p. 217–229) that there are three degrees of the ecclesiastic hierarchy: the episcopal, the presbyteral, and the diaconal; but, it is necessary to remark that there are no more of them. The utterances of the fathers of the church confirm that:

" Clement of Alexandria: 'The degrees of bishops, presbyters, and deacons, which exist in the church, are, in my opinion, the representation of the angelic order.' Origen: ' Paul speaks to the rulers and chiefs of the churches, that is, to those who judge the people who are in the church, namely, to the bishops, presbyters, and deacons.' Eusebius of Cæsaria: ' Three orders: the first of the presiding officers, the second of the presbyters, the third of the deacons.' " (p. 223.)

174. There is a detailed description of the different orders of the spiritual persons among themselves and in relation to their flocks.

" The bishop is the chief overseer in his own particular church (Acts xx. 28 ; cf. Epistle of the Eastern Patriarchs about the Orthodox faith, section 10). First of all he has the power over the hierarchy under his rule and over the clergy. All priests and servants of the church are obliged to obey his injunctions, and without his permission nothing is done in the church; all are subject to his surveillance and judgment (1 Tim. v. 19), in consequence of which he may subject them to various punishments. In addition to the clergy, the whole flock which is entrusted to his care is subject to the spiritual power of the bishop. He is under obligation to watch over the execution in his eparchy of the divine laws and church commandments. He has more especially and preëminently the right to bind and loose, according to the rules of the holy apostles, the holy councils, and according to the unanimous testimony of the ancient teachers of the church. For that reason the apostles so forcibly impressed all the believers with the necessity of obeying the bishops. The presbyters have also power to bind and loose, and in general to feed the flock of God which is entrusted to them (1 Peter v. 1, 2), but this power they receive from their archpastor by means of the sacramental ordination. Some chosen ones are, by the will of the bishop, admitted, in general to bear with him the burden of the church government and even form with him for that purpose a permanent council. But, according to an old expression, they only serve in the place of the bishop's eyes and in themselves, without his consent, can do nothing. But the deacons have not received from the Lord the right to bind and loose, and so in themselves do not have any spiritual power over the believers. But the deacons may be the eye and the ear of the bishops and presbyters, as also the hands of the presiding officers, with their consent, for the purpose of performing ecclesiastic duties.

" After all which has been said, we find quite comprehensible the high names and expressions which are applied to the bishops, such as that they are alone, in the strict sense, the successors of the apostles, that the church is resting firmly on its bishops, as on supports; that a bishop is 'a living image of God on earth, and, by force of the sacramental power of the Holy Ghost, a prolific source of all the sacraments of the church, by means of which he procures salvation; and so he is as necessary for the church as breathing is for man, as the sun is for the world' (Epistle of the Eastern Patriarchs, Section 10); that in the bishops is the centre of the believers who belong to his eparchy; that he is even the particular head of his spiritual realm; that, finally, as Cyprian says, 'the bishop is in the church, and the church (which is subject to him) is in the bishop, and that he who is not in communion with the bishop is not in the church.'" (pp. 227–229.)

The pastors of various degrees, united among themselves, decide, and the people have to obey, and all that which is called the church not merely as an ornament of speech, but in reality, that is, that organ which expresses the faith which men must follow, — that church is the bishops.

175. This article shows that the church is the bishops, and that the higher power above them is an assembly of all the bishops, which is called a council, that is, of several bishops. In this article there is a very detailed account, such as is given in the Statute about the justices of the peace, about the relations of all these persons among themselves:

"From this may be seen, without any new proofs, that the right to sit in councils, both local and œcumenical, and the right to pass on ecclesiastical matters belong exclusively to the bishops as the heads of the separate churches; and the presbyters, who in everything depend on their local archpastors, may be admitted to the councils only by their consent, and then only as counsellors, or assistants, or their plenipotentiaries, and may occupy only the second place. Even so may be admitted the deacons, who must stand before the face of the bishops. For this reason the councils were by the holy fathers of the church generally called assemblies of the bishops. The Second Œcumenical Council called the Symbol of Faith which was composed at the first council, 'the faith of 318 holy fathers' (for that was the number of bishops present at that council); the council in Trullo called the definitions of faith of all the previous œcumenical councils 'profession or faith of the holy fathers, the bishops, according to the number of those who met at these councils.'" (p. 231.)

Then comes Art. 176, in which we have an exposition of Christ's being the head of the church. That is apparent (1) from the fact that Christ before the ascension said, not to the church but to his disciples, " I am with you to the end of the world, Amen." In the Theology, the following words are added to that: " and with all your future successors," and that is taken as a proof that all those who call themselves the interpreters of Christ regard themselves as his successors.

" (2) From this fact in particular that, although he entrusted the power of teaching to the apostles and their successors, he told them to call him only the supreme teacher, who invisibly, through them, taught the believers (Matt. xxiii. 10), and so he said : He that heareth you heareth me ; and he that despiseth you despiseth me (Luke x. 16)." (p. 232.)

This passage with its references is striking. I thought that nothing in the Theology would startle me, but the boldness with which this verse is quoted, and with which an opposite significance is given to it, is staggering. Here is the verse, or, rather, the whole passage : But be not ye called Rabbi : for one is your Master, even Christ ; and all ye are brethren. And call no man your father upon the earth : for one is your Father, which is in heaven.

Neither be ye called masters: for one is your Master, even Christ (Matt. xxiii. 8–10).

This very verse, these words, which are said directly against those who call themselves teachers, fathers, and masters, — this verse is connected with the verse (Luke x. 16), which has absolutely nothing in common with the first, and is adduced as a proof that those very teachers, who call themselves so against the command of Christ, have Christ as their head. After that follow proofs that (Art. 177) the church is One, (179) Holy, (180) Catholic and Universal, and (181) Apostolic.

In Division III., about the Universal Church, it says:

"III. The special privilege of the Catholic, or Universal, Church consists in this, that in matters of faith 'it cannot err in any way, nor deceive, nor be deceived; but, like Divine Scripture, it is infallible and has eternal dignity' (Epistle of the Eastern Patriarchs, Section 12), a privilege of which enough has been said by us in the proper place."

The moral application of this dogma for the first time results directly from the dogma. The application of the dogma consists in obeying the church.

"(1) The Lord Jesus founded his church that it might regenerate men and educate them for eternal life; and so our relation to it has to be that of children to their mother; we are obliged to love the church of Christ as our spiritual mother and to obey it in everything as our spiritual mother. In particular our Lord Jesus: (2) enjoined the church to keep and teach to men its divine doctrine; it is our duty to receive this teaching from the mouth of the God-given church, and to understand it precisely as the church, which is instructed by the Holy Ghost, understands it; (3) he entrusted to the church the performance of mysteries and, in general, sacraments for the sanctification of men; it is our duty in awe to make use of the saving mysteries and all the other sacraments, which it performs over us; (4) he entrusted the church with the guidance of men and with confirming them in their godly lives; it is our duty without murmuring to submit to the inspiration of such a guide and holily to execute all the commands of the church; (5) he himself established the hierarchy and priestly order in the church, pointed out the difference between the flock and the pastors, and showed each a definite place and service; it is the duty of all the members of the church, of the pastors and the flock, to be that which they are called to be, and to keep well in mind that we have gifts differing according to the grace that is given to us (Rom. xii. 6), and that to every one of us is given grace according to the measure of the gift of Christ (Eph. iv. 7)." (p. 246.)

So that is what the church is as an establishment, as a keeper and announcer of truths, of dogmas! That on which the whole Theology is based is a self-constituted hierarchy and, in distinction from all others, a hierarchy which regards itself alone as holy and infallible and as being the only one that has the right to preach the divine revelation. Thus the whole doctrine of the church, as the Theology teaches it, is all based on establishing the conception of the church as the only true keeper of divine truth, in order to substitute for this conception that of a certain, definite hierarchy, that is, to connect a human institution, the outgrowth of pride, malice, and hatred, which utters dogmas and instructs the flock only in that teaching which it alone regards as true, with the conception of the assembly of all believers who have invisibly at their head Christ himself, — the mystical body of Christ. To that the whole teaching of the Theology reduces itself.

This teaching asserts that the only, true church, — the body of Christ, is it alone. The train of thought is as follows: Having collected the disciples, God revealed the truth to them and promised to be with them. That truth is complete and divine.   The truth which we preach is the same truth.   Even leaving out of discussion the fact that for every man who has read Holy Scripture and who has seen the arguments which the Theology adduces in proof, it is evident that Christ never established any hierarchy, any church, in the sense in which the Theology understands it ; leaving out of consideration that for every one who reads history it is evident that many men have imagined themselves to be such churches, while they contended with one another and did one another harm, — there involuntarily rises the question: on what grounds does our hierarchy consider itself to be the true one, and the other hierarchies and assemblies not to be true ? Why is the Nicene symbol an expression of the true, holy church, and why not the Arian symbol, which our hierarchy has been contending against, for were not the bishops, partisans of Arius, as much ordained by succession from the apostles as the partisans of the Nicene symbol ?   And if this ordainment does not save men from error, why is our church the keeper of truth, and not of untruth ?   The Theology does not even make an attempt at answering this, for by its doctrine it cannot give any answer, since subjects that are arbitrarily passed upon cannot be proved, and so the hierarchy says only that it is right because it is holy and infallible, and it is holy and infallible, because it is a follower of the hierarchy which has acknowledged the Nicene symbol.   But why is the hierarchy which has acknowledged the Nicene symbol the true one ?   To that there is, and there can be, no answer, so that the recognition of the hierarchy, which calls itself the true, holy, only, universal and apostolic church, is only an expression of a demand that faith should be put in it, an assertion like the one made by a man who says, " Upon my word, I am right."   But this assertion is particularly weakened by the fact that every assertion of the hierarchy about being holy is always due

to this, that another hierarchy, which on some point dis-
agrees with it, says precisely the opposite and asserts that
it is right and to the words, " It is permitted to us and to
the Holy Ghost," replies that the Holy Ghost lives in it,
— something like what happens when two men swear,
denying each other.

All the theologians, no matter how much they may try
to conceal it, speak and do nothing else.   The church —
the union of all believers, the body of Christ — is only
an adornment of speech, in order to add importance to a
human institution, the hierarchy and its assumed succession, upon which everything is built up.   Remarkable
and instructive in this respect are the attempts of the
modern theologians, of Vinet and his followers, of Khomyakóv and his scions, to find new supports for the teaching about the church, and to build up the definition of the
church not on the hierarchy, but on the whole assembly
of the believers, on the flock.   These new theologians,
without noticing it themselves, in their attempts to make
stable the tree which is planted without roots, make it
fall entirely.   These theologians deny the hierarchy and
prove the falseness of that foundation, and they think that
they are giving it a different foundation.   But, unfortunately, this other foundation is nothing but that sophism
of theology, under which it tries to conceal the crudity of
its doctrine about the church being the hierarchy.   That
sophism the new theologians take for a foundation and
they completely overthrow the doctrine of the church,
while they themselves are left with a most palpable
sophism, but without a foundation.

Their error is like this : The church has received among
believers two main meanings, — one, that the church is a
human, temporal institution, and the other, that the
church is the totality of men living and dead, who are
united by one true faith.   The first is a definite historical
phenomenon : an assemblage of men subject to certain

rules and regulations, and one from which statutes may issue. Whether I speak of the Catholic Church of such and such a year, or of the Roman, or Greek Orthodox Church, I am speaking of certain people, — the Pope, patriarchs, bishops, — who are organized in a certain manner and who in a certain way direct their flocks. The second is an abstract idea, and if I speak of the church in this sense, it is evident that attributes of time and place cannot be its definitions, and under no circumstance can there be definite decrees, expressed in definite words. The only definition of such a church, as the carrier of divine truth, is a correspondence with what is the divine truth.

The equating of these two conceptions to each other, and the substitution of one for the other, has always formed a problem of all Christian confessions of faith. An assemblage of people, wishing to convince others that it possesses the absolute truth, asserts that it is holy and infallible. Its holiness and infallibility it builds on two foundations: on the manifestations of the Holy Ghost, which find their expression in the holiness of the members of that community and then in miracles, and on the legitimate succession of the teachership, which proceeds from Christ.

The first foundation does not stand criticism: holiness cannot be measured or proved; miracles are detected and proved deceptions, and so miracles cannot be adduced as proofs, so there is left but one proof, the correct succession of the hierarchy. That, too, cannot be proved, but equally it cannot be refuted, and so all the churches hold themselves on that foundation; on that argument alone do the churches at the present time hold themselves, and it is the only one on which they can hold themselves. If a Catholic, an Orthodox, an Old Ceremonialist, affirm that they have the truth, they can incontrovertibly base their assertions only on the infallibility of the succession of the keepers of the Tradition. The

Catholic Church recognizes the Pope as the head of the hierarchy, and in its development inevitably had to acknowledge the infallibility of the Pope. The Greek Church could fail to recognize the Pope, but in not recognizing the necessity of that supreme member of the hierarchy, it could not help but recognize the infallibility of the hierarchy itself; even so the Protestant Church, in failing to recognize Catholicism during its decadence, could not help but recognize the infallibility of that hierarchy whose dogmas it recognizes, for without the infallibility of the succession of the keepers of the Tradition it would have no foundation for the assertion of its truth.

All the churches maintain themselves only by recognizing the infallibility of that hierarchy which they accept. You may not agree in saying that such and such a hierarchy is the only correct one, but when a man says that he accepts as true the hierarchy whose dogmas he accepts, you cannot prove to him the incorrectness of his dogmas. That is the only indestructible foundation, and so all the churches cling to it. Now, the new theologians destroy this only foundation, thinking that they are substituting a better one for it. The new theologians say that divine truth is kept, not by the infallibility of the hierarchy, but in the totality of all believers who are united in love, and that only to men who are united in love is divine truth given, and that such a church is defined solely by faith and oneness in love and in concord. This reflection is good in itself, but, unfortunately, from it cannot be deduced a single one of the dogmas which the theologians profess.

The theologians forget that, in order to recognize a certain dogma, it was necessary to recognize Tradition to be holy and definitely expressed in the decrees of the infallible hierarchy. But by rejecting the infallibility of the hierarchy, it is impossible to affirm anything, and there is not a single proposition of the church which could unite all the believers. The affirmation of these theologians that they recognize those decrees which express the faith of all undivided Christians and reject all the arbitrary decrees of the separate Christians is quite incorrect, because there has never existed such a complete oneness of the Christians. Side by side with the Nicene symbol, there was an Arian symbol, and the Nicene symbol was not accepted by all, but only by one part of the hierarchy, and other Christians recognized that symbol only because they recognized the infallibility of the hierarchy which expressed it, saying, " It pleased us and the Holy Ghost." But there has never been a time when all the Christians agreed on anything, and the councils were assembled for the very purpose of getting in some manner away from the controversies about the dogmas, which divided the Christians.

Thus the oneness in love has, in the first place, never existed, and, in the second place, this oneness in love, by its very essence, cannot be expressed or defined in any way. The new theologians affirm that by church they understand the union of all the believers, the body of Christ, and by no means the infallible hierarchy and a human institution; but the moment they touch on matters of the church, it becomes evident that by church they understand, and must of necessity understand, a human institution. The cares of all these theologians, beginning with Luther, about the relation of church and state, prove conclusively that these theologians understand by church a still more debased human institution than is understood by the Catholics or the Orthodox. The church theologians are more consistent in their discussions. The church, according to their doctrine, is the bishops and the Pope; thus they speak, and so it is. The Pope and the bishops must, according to their teaching, stand at the head of all worldly institutions, and there can be no question about the relation of the church to the state. The church is always the head of everything. Among the Protestants there appears, in spite of the apparently high significance which they ascribe to the church, the question about the relations of church and state. They are all busy now separating or freeing the church from the oppression of the state, and all of them complain of the wretched condition of divine truth and of Christ at its head, who is in captivity under Bismarck, Gambetta, and so forth, but they forget that if the state can exert any influence on the church, it is evident that, in speaking of the church, we are speaking not of the divine truth which has Christ at its head, but of a human institution.

Men who believe in the teaching of the church cannot base their faith on anything but the legality, the regularity of the succession of the hierarchy. But the regularity and legality of the succession of the hierarchy cannot be proved in any way. No historical investigations can confirm it. On the contrary, historical investigations not only fail to confirm the regularity of any hierarchy, but show directly that Christ did not establish an infallible hierarchy, that in the first times it did not exist, that that system arose in the time of the decline of the Christian teaching, during the time of hatred and malice on account of some interpretation of dogmas, and that all the most varied Christian teachings have asserted just as positively their rights in the regularity of the succession in their church, and have denied that regularity in others, so that the whole doctrine of the Theology, which in regard to the church is not verified in any respect, comes down for me to the desire of certain persons to advance, in opposition to other teachings (which have just such pretensions and which with just as much right assert that they are in the right), their own teaching as the only one which is true and holy.

So far I have not seen in this teaching anything true

and holy, and not even anything rational and good.   The attempts of these theologians, especially of our Khomya-kóv, to overthrow the foundation of the church, the infallibility of the hierarchy, and to put in its place the mystical conception of all the believers who are united in love, is the last convulsion of this church teaching, a support which brings the whole structure to its fall.   Indeed, a remarkable *quid pro quo* takes place here.   To conceal its crude assertion that the church is the infallible hierarchy, the Theology cloaks itself with false definitions of the church in the sense of an assemblage of all the believers.   The new theologians grasp this external and false definition and, imagining that they are basing their church upon it, destroy the one essential support of the church, the infallibility of the hierarchy.   Indeed, for any one who does not even wish to trouble himself to investigate the arguments of the church about the infallibility of the hierarchy, it is sufficient to read all that which the Protestant literature has worked out in this respect.   The foundation of the infallibility of the hierarchy is destroyed in the name of the foundation of the church as an assemblage of believers united in love.   However, an assemblage of believers united in love can, obviously, not define any dogma, or a Nicene symbol, as Khomyakóv and other theologians believe.

An assemblage of believers united in love is such a general conception that upon it no common creed, or dogma, common to all the Christians, can be based, so that the work of the new theologians, if they are at all consistent, reduces itself to this, that the only foundation of the church, the infallibility of the church, is destroyed, but the new one is left what it was, a mystical conception from which can follow no creed, much less a confession of faith.   The only foundation is the infallibility of the hierarchy, — for those who believe in it.

XIV.

SECTION II. Of divine grace as a force with which the Lord sanctifies us. This whole division expounds the Saviour's special relation to men. Section I. expounded the conception of the church, that instrument by which the human race is saved; now, it would seem, ought to be expounded those means by which men are saved, but that will be expounded in Section III. This 2d section will expound wherein the salvation will actually consist. It is this doctrine that will be expounded in this section. This doctrine is called the doctrine about grace. What is meant by the word "grace"?

Art. 183 begins with various definitions of grace:

"1. Under the name of divine grace is in general understood all that which the Lord gives to all his creatures without any deserts on their parts (Rom. xi. 6; 1 Peter v. 10)."

That is the definition of grace. Then follow subdivisions.

"For that reason divine grace is divided into natural and supernatural. To natural grace belong all natural gifts of God to the creatures, such as, life, health, reason, freedom, external well-being, and so forth. To supernatural grace belong all gifts which are communicated by God to the creatures in a supernatural manner, in addition to the gifts of Nature, when, for example, he himself directly enlightens the mind of rational beings with the light of his truth, and strengthens their will with his power and coöperation in matters of godliness. This supernatural grace is divided into two species: into the grace of God the Creator, which he communicates to his moral creatures that abide in a condition of innocence; he communicated it to man before his fall, and even now imparts it to his good angels; and into the grace of God the Saviour, which he has given more properly to fallen man through Jesus and in Jesus Christ (Tit. iii. 4)." (p. 248.)

This latter subdivision is further subdivided into three parts: grace is divided into (1) the incarnation of Christ and the redemption; (2) extraordinary gifts for the advantage of the church, such as prophecy, miracles, and so forth, and (3) —

" Last, by grace is understood a special force, a special action of God, which is communicated to us on account of the deserts of our Redeemer, and which achieves our sanctification, that is, which, on the one hand, purifies us from sin, renovates, and justifies us before God, and, on the other, confirms us and turns us back to virtue for eternal life. In this latter sense grace forms the proper subject of the dogmatic teaching about it." (p. 249.)

This latter subdivision contains in it three more particular conceptions.

" (1) It is: (a) a special force, a special divine action in man, as is to be seen from the words of the Lord himself to the Apostle Paul: My grace is sufficient for thee: for my strength is made perfect in weakness, and then from the words of St. Paul: Most gladly therefore will I rather glory in my infirmities, that the power of Christ may rest upon me (2 Cor. xii. 9). (b) It is given to us for nothing, on account of the deserts of Jesus Christ, as the same apostle teaches us: For all have sinned, and come short of the glory of God; being justified freely by his grace through the redemption that is in Christ Jesus (Rom. iii. 23, 24). (d) It is given to us for the sake of our sanctification, that is, for our purification and justification, for our success in godliness and salvation. That is confirmed by the following passages in Scripture: Grace and peace be multiplied unto you through the knowledge of God, and of Jesus our Lord, according as his divine power hath given unto us all things that pertain unto life and godliness, through the knowledge of him that hath called us to glory and virtue (1 Peter i. 2, 3), and so forth. This sanctifying grace is, for the greater clearness of its teaching, subdivided into two particular kinds. It is called external in so far as it acts upon man externally, through external means, such as, the Word of God, the preaching of the Gospel, miracles, and so forth; and internal, in so far as it acts directly in man himself, destroying the sins in him, enlightening his reason, exciting and directing his will toward the good. It is called temporary, when it produces special impressions upon a man's soul and coöperates in his special good deeds; and constant, when it abides constantly in man's soul and makes him righteous and pleasing before God. It is called premonitory, when it precedes each good deed and incites man to commit good deeds; and accompanying or coactive, when it accompanies each good deed. It is called sufficient, when it imparts to man sufficient force and convenience to act for his salvation, though it may not be accompanied by the action itself on the part of man; and real, when it is accompanied by the action itself and produces in man saving fruits." (pp. 249 and 250.)

Thus there are in all fourteen different kinds of grace, and all those will be properly disclosed. All the contrary opinions will be refuted, and everything will, according to the usual method, be confirmed by Holy Scripture. In no part of the doctrine, so manifestly as in the doctrine about grace, will the remark be confirmed that the less the doctrine is necessary in order to explain the meaning of life to man and to guide him to union with God, the more has the church been talking about it, the less it is comprehensible, and the more controversies, lies, malicious attacks, wars, and executions have taken place because of it, as we know from history.   Indeed, what can be more remarkable, for uselessness, than this remarkable teaching about grace, about what, according to the definition of the Theology, is given by God to his creatures without the least desert on their part.   One would think that according to this definition grace is the whole of life, everything, for everything is given to us by God without the least desert on our part, and that therefore the relation of man to grace is the relation of man to life.   So it is, but since the Theology understands man's relation to life in the most perverse manner, all the discussions about grace reduce themselves to the attempt to lower the meaning of life to a most monstrous and crude conception.

First it takes the account of the creation of man, in which Holy Scripture expresses in the person of Adam the relation of man's freedom to grace, that is, to the external world.   The whole account is taken by the Theology in the historical sense only.   Adam fell, and the whole human race perished, and before Christ there was no relation of man's freedom to grace, that is to life, there was no life, and men did not do wrong.   Christ came and redeemed the whole human race, and then, speaking strictly, according to the teaching of the Theology, there was again destroyed the relation of man's freedom to grace, to the external world, for according to the church teaching man became all holy and now does only what is good. But, as we know, nothing of the kind has ever happened, and the whole meaning of the Old Testament and Gospel teaching and of all moral and philosophical teachings consists only in finding a solution of the contradictions of good and evil, which are struggling in man.   Although theology asserts that man after his redemption became entirely good, it knows that that is an untruth.   It is not true that all men were bad before the redemption and became all good after that, and so the Theology sees that the question, as it stood before Adam, — whether to eat or not to eat the apple, and as it stands before us, — whether to live or not to live according to the teaching of Christ, is still standing before men, and so it was compelled to invent a doctrine by which the question of what man must do should be supplanted by the question of what he ought to confess and speak. And for that purpose is invented the teaching, at first, of the church, and now, of grace.

But, as we shall later see, this teaching about grace is insufficient, and there is invented another, a new teaching about faith, which is to coöperate in the obfuscation before people of the chief religious and moral question as to how men ought to live. It is impossible connectedly to render this teaching about grace in the manner in which it is expounded. The more you penetrate into it, the less you comprehend it. You read and fail to understand, not only what is being expounded, but even why it is all expounded. Only after reading the whole Theology through, after reading the chapter on the sacraments and on the mysteries, and recalling the contradiction with reality, which is put in the dogma of the redemption, is it possible, at last, to divine the cause which made them invent those strange aberrations, and to explain to ourselves that remarkable doctrine.

The explanation of the doctrine about grace I find to be as follows: the hierarchy (for exactness' sake I will from now on use this word instead of the obscure " church ") teaches us that Christ redeemed the human race, destroyed sin, evil, death, diseases, and the unfruitfulness of the earth. In reality nothing of the kind has been destroyed; everything was left as of old. How, then, justify the unjustified assertion ? In order to justify it, it is necessary to attach to the salvation of the human race by Christ another condition, without which this salvation cannot take place, so as to have the right to say that the redemption took place, but is not active, because men did not observe the condition with which alone it is active. That teaching is grace. The Theology says outright :

" Divine grace is necessary for the sanctification of sinful man in general, that is, in order that the sinner shall be able to come out from his sinful state, become a true Christian, and, in this manner, make his own the deserts of the Redeemer, or else be changed, purified, justified, renovated, and then abide in godliness and attain eternal salvation." (p. 259.)

Thus the redemption became active only on condition that grace be obtained, and so the non-achievement of the redemption is explained by the absence of grace, and the whole aim of the believers is now directed toward obtaining grace, and grace is transmitted through the sacraments. This sanctification by sacraments, that is, the drawing of people toward sacerdotal rites, forms another cause for the teaching about grace. Thus the teaching about grace has two causes, one — logical, an explanation of the statement that the whole world has changed, whereas it has not, and the other — practical, the use of sacraments and mysteries as means for obtaining grace.

The doctrine about grace is, on the one hand, an inevitable result of a false premise that Christ by his redemption has changed the whole world, and, on the other, it is the foundation of those sacerdotal rites, which are necessary for the believers, in order to throw dust in their eyes, and for the hierarchy, in order that it may take advantage of its sacerdotal calling. This teaching about grace is in itself striking by its complexity, entanglement, and absolute barrenness of contents. If previously some parts of the teaching involuntarily reminded one of a man who pretended before a public to measure hundreds of yards of the imaginary hair of the Virgin, this teaching may be compared with the action of this man, who, after measuring the imaginary hairs, should make it appear that the hairs which he has measured out have become tangled and he is trying to unravel them. Besides, this teaching about grace, the purpose of which is to pull the wool over the eyes of the believers because of the non-achievement of the promise of redemption, and to increase the income of the clergy, bears in itself that terrible germ of immorality which has morally corrupted the generations that confess this teaching. If a man is going to believe in the deception that he can be cured from diseases by the grace of the chrism, or that he will be immortal if he receives the grace, or in the concealment of the fact that the earth continues to be unfruitful, — all these deceptions have been comparatively harmless, but the deception about man's being always sinful and impotent and about the uselessness of his striving after good, if he does not acquire grace, — this teaching cuts down to the root everything which is best in human nature. The immorality of this teaching could not help but startle all the best men who have lived amidst this confession, and so against this side of the doctrine — about the relation of man's freedom to grace — have risen the more honest men in the church itself, and so this question has been complicated by endless controversies, which until the present divided the different creeds.

In Art. 184 there is an exposition of these controversies about grace :

"The dogma about grace which sanctifies sinful man has been subject to very many mutilations on the part of the heterodox and heretics. I. Some of these have erred and still err, in a greater or lesser degree, as regards the necessity of grace for man. To these belong the Pelagians, Semi-Pelagians, Socinians, and rationalists. The Pelagians, who appeared in the beginning of the fifth century in the Western church, taught as follows: 'Since Adam by his fall in no way impaired his nature and consequently his descendants are born without any natural corruption or original sin, they may by mere natural forces attain moral perfection and have no need for that purpose of any supernatural divine aid and force.' Against Pelagius and his followers first of all rose St. Augustine, who wrote very many works in refutal of them. There rose also many other pastors of the church, and both in the East and in the West there met in a short time more than twenty councils which unanimously condemned that heresy. The defenders of the truth unanimously maintained: (a) that man, who has fallen and is born in original sin, cannot in himself create any spiritual good without the aid of grace; (b) that by it are to be understood not merely the natural forces of man, the law of Moses, the teaching and example of Jesus Christ, external aids, but the supernatural power of God, which is inwardly communicated to man's soul; (c) that this grace does not consist merely in the remission of former sins, but offers real assistance in keeping man from committing new ones; (d) it not only illuminates reason and imparts to it the knowledge of what is to be done and what avoided, but also gives it the strength to carry out what has been found good, and pours love into the heart; (e) it not only makes easier for us the execution of the divine commands, which we are supposed to perform by ourselves, though inconveniently so, but acts as an assistance, without which we are not able to execute the divine law and to do the good which coöperates in our salvation.

"At the present time the teaching of the Orthodox Church, as directed against the heresy of the Pelagians, may be seen in the three following rules of the Council at Carthage, which is accepted among the number of the nine local councils, and which met to refute Pelagius: 'If any one says that divine grace, by which men are justified in Jesus Christ our Lord, is active only in the remission of sins already committed, but does not in addition to that furnish any assistance, unless new sins be committed : let such a one be anathema. For divine grace not only gives the knowledge of what is proper to do, but also inspires us with love, that we may be able to carry out what we know.' 'If any one says that the same divine grace, which is about Jesus Christ our Lord, aids us only in keeping us from sinning, since by it is revealed and manifested to us the knowledge of sins, so that we may know what to seek and what to avoid, but that by it are not given to us the love and the power of doing that which we have found good to do : let such a one be anathema. For both are the gifts of God, both the knowledge of what is proper to do, and the love of the good which it is proper to do.' 'If any one says that the grace of justification is given to us so that what may be performed by our free will may be more conveniently done through grace, for, without receiving divine grace, we have been able, though inconveniently, to perform the divine commandments : let such a one be anathema. For of the fruits of the com- mandments the Lord has not said : Without me you will do inconveniently, but he has said : Without me ye can do nothing.' "

That, according to the Theology, is the first error. The second error consists in this, that to some God has given grace and has preordained them to the judgment, while to others he has given grace and has preordained them to salvation. This is the way it has to be considered :

" We believe that the all-good God has preordained to glory those whom he has chosen from eternity ; and whom he has rejected he has turned over to the judg- ment, not, however, because he wishes in this manner to justify some, and leave others and judge them without cause : for that is not characteristic of God, who is common to all, and is not a revengeful Father, who will have all men to be saved, and to come unto the knowledge of the truth (1 Tim. ii. 4) ; since he foresaw that some will make good use of their free will, while others will not, he has preordained some to glory, and others he has condemned. Of the use of freedom we judge in the following manner: since divine goodness has given us the divine grace, which, like the light illuminating the path of those who walk in darkness, guides us all, those who wish freely to submit to it (for it assists those who have it, and who do not oppose it) and to fulfil its commands, which are absolutely necessary for salvation, for that reason receive a special grace, which, coöperating with them and strengthening and constantly perfecting them in divine love, that is, in those good works, which God demands of us (and which also the premonitory grace has demanded), justifies them and makes them preordained; but those, on the contrary, who will not obey and follow grace, and who therefore do not fulfil the divine commandments, but, following the instigation of Satan, make ill use of their freedom, which God has given them for the purpose of arbitrarily doing good, are given over to eternal condemnation. But what the blasphemous heretics say of God's preordaining and condemning, without paying any attention to the works of the preordained or the condemned, we regard as madness and ungodliness." (pp. 255 and 256.)

The error cannot be rendered in one's own words; here it is:

"In regard to the nature of the sanctification or justification, as taken in its broad meaning, the Protestants assert that it consists: (a) not in that the divine grace acts inwardly on man and actually, on the one hand, purifies him from all sins, and, on the other, coöperates with the renovated, righteous, holy; (b) but in this, that, by God's will, the sins are pardoned only externally and are not put against the man, though in reality they remain in him, — that Christ's righteousness is put to his account only in an external manner. Such is the teaching of the Lutherans and of the Reformers. The teaching of the Orthodox Church is of an entirely different kind. Speaking of the fruits of the sacrament of baptism, in which properly takes place our justification and sanctification through grace, the church teaches:

"'In the first place, this sacrament destroys all sins: in babes — original sin, and in grown persons both original and arbitrary sin. In the second place, it reëstablishes for him that righteousness which he had in the condition of innocence and sinlessness.' And in another place: 'It cannot be said that the baptism does not free from all former sins, but that they remain indeed, but no longer have any force. It is extreme ungodliness to teach in that manner; it is an overthrowing of faith, and not a confession of it. On the contrary, every sin which exists or has existed before the baptism is destroyed and is regarded as though it did not exist or had never existed. For all the forms under which baptism is represented show its purifying power, and the utterances of Holy Scripture give us to understand that through it we receive complete purification, which is seen from the very name of baptism. If it is a baptism by the Spirit and by fire, it is evident that it offers complete purification, for the Spirit purifies completely. If it is light, every darkness is dispelled by it. If it is regeneration, everything old passes away; and this old thing is nothing but the sins. If the man who is baptized is divested of the old man, he is also divested of sin. If he is invested in Christ, he with the same becomes sinless through baptism (Epistle of the Eastern Patriarchs, Section 16).'" (pp. 256 and 257.)

186. The necessity of grace for the sanctification of man in general. It is proved by Holy Scripture, and this is the way it is determined by the councils:

"If any one asserts that for our purification from sins God waits for our desire, and does not confess that the desire itself to purify ourselves takes place in us through the emanation of the Holy Ghost and his coöperation, he contradicts the Holy Ghost." (p. 262.)

It is not permitted to believe that God is waiting for our desire to purify ourselves, but we must believe that the Holy Ghost, that is, the same God in another person, produces this desire to purify ourselves. If the desire has already taken place and I am myself a creature of God, and the desire is directed toward God, it is evident that this desire must not be acknowledged as anything else but as having emanated from God. All these utterances remain completely unintelligible, if we do not keep in mind the aim toward which they lead. This aim consists in replacing the tendency to do good by the external actions of the sacraments which impart grace. Further:

"If any one asserts that a man may, by the force of his nature, think rightly, or choose something good, which refers to eternal salvation, and agree to receive the saving, that is, the evangelical, sermon without the illumination and instigation of the Holy Ghost, he is seduced by a heretical spirit (Rule VII.)." (p. 262.)

A man cannot wish for anything good without the inspiration of the Holy Ghost; but the inspiration of the Holy Ghost is imparted through grace; grace is communicated through the sacraments; and the sacraments are communicated by the hierarchy.

187. The necessity of grace for faith and for the very beginning of faith, or for a man's conversion to Christianity. "Divine grace, which is necessary in general for man's illumination and salvation, is necessary in particular for his faith and for the very beginning of the faith in the Lord Jesus." (p. 263.)

Proofs from Holy Scripture and decrees of a council:

"If any one says that the increase, as well as the beginning of faith, and the very disposition toward it, by which we believe in the justification of the ungodly and proceed to the regeneration in the sacrament of baptism, are in us not by the gift of grace, that is, by the inspiration of the Holy Ghost, who directs our will from unbelief to belief, from godlessness to godliness, but takes place naturally, — such a one proves himself to be an opponent of the apostolic dogmas (Rule V.)." (p. 267.)

The meaning of the decree is that the believers must acknowledge that the change from godlessness to godliness cannot take place naturally, but is only the result of grace, that is, of some unnatural, external action. But if our will is completely directed by the Holy Ghost, then what free will has the Theology just been speaking about when it said that God wants all men to be saved, but that he foresaw that some would make good use of their free will, while others would not? If he wants to save and everything depends on him, why does he not save?

"188. Being necessary for the very conversion of man to Christianity, for his faith, and for the beginning of faith, divine grace remains necessary for man even after his conversion, so that he may fulfil the evangelical law for a worthy life according to Christ." (p. 271.)

Proofs from Holy Scripture conclude with this:

"Although man may be inclined toward good before his regeneration, and choose and do moral good, nevertheless, in order that he may be able after his regeneration to do spiritual good (for the works of faith, being the cause of salvation and being performed by supernatural grace, are generally called spiritual), it is necessary for grace to premonish and guide, so that he cannot by himself do works that are worthy of a life according to Christ, but can only wish or not wish to act in accordance with grace." (p. 274.)

The meaning of this discussion is still more definite, and its expression is much bolder. Here it says distinctly that, although a man may be able to do good deeds without grace, he loses the possibility of doing good deeds the moment he accepts the teaching of the church, and can only wish for it, by invoking the aid of the hierarchy. But even the desire for grace, as has just been said, is given only by the Holy Ghost, that is, again by grace. The Theology is evidently moving in a magic circle.

"189. If without divine grace man cannot become a believer, or believe in Christ, or do deeds that are worthy of a life according to Christ, it follows naturally that without the coöperation of divine grace man cannot abide in the Christian faith and godliness to the end of his life."

Here it says that the coöperation of this external grace is not exhausted by baptism and faith, but that for the salvation the constant aid of the hierarchy is needed. All that would seem to be clear, but now follows Art. 190, which refutes the heretics. In this and the following articles the whole disconnection of the teaching becomes manifest.

The hierarchy needs a teaching which would reduce the whole teaching about life to a teaching about the sacraments, but that cannot be expressed outright: the immorality of such a teaching is too obvious. Besides, there have been many controversies in regard to this question. Some reflected consistently: if grace saves, the free efforts of man are useless; others said: if the free efforts of man are needed, the whole thing lies in them, and grace is imparted to them; but our Theology refutes both, and itself becomes entangled and persists in that tangle.

"Contrary to the errors of the Calvinists and Jansenists, which are that God gives his grace only to a few men, whom he has unconditionally preordained to righteousness and eternal bliss, and therefore gives an invincible grace, the Orthodox Church teaches: (a) that divine grace extends over all men, and not only on the preordained to righteousness and eternal bliss; (b) that the preordainment of some by God to eternal bliss and of others to eternal damnation is not unconditional, but is based on the foreknowledge whether they will take advantage of the grace, or not; (c) that divine grace does not embarrass man's freedom, does not act invincibly upon it, and (d) that, on the contrary, man takes an active part in what divine grace works in him and through him (Epistle of the Eastern Patriarchs, Section 3)." (pp. 277 and 278.)

The preceding article defines man's salvation in such a way that it obviously no longer results from his efforts, but completely depends on the communication of grace from without. Consequently there had naturally to appear the reflection: if salvation depends not on man, but on God, and God is omniscient, some people are predetermined to salvation, and others to perdition. But the Theology does not agree with the Calvinists.

191. Divine grace extends over all men, and not only over those who are preordained to righteousness and eternal bliss. Proofs are adduced to refute the Calvinists. And here it turns out involuntarily that in refuting the Calvinists the Theology refutes all the decrees of the councils, which determined that man cannot save himself by his own efforts.

"St. John Chrysostom: 'If Christ lighteth every man that cometh into the world (John i. 9), how then do men remain without illumination? He actually illuminates everybody. But if some, voluntarily closing the eyes of their intellect, do not wish to receive the beams of this light, their abiding in darkness does not depend on the nature of the light, but on the ungodliness of those who by their will deprive themselves of that gift. For the grace has poured forth on all, and those who do not wish to make use of such a gift must, in justice, blame themselves for their blindness.' St. Ambrose: 'He rose, like a mysterious sun, for everybody; if some one does not believe in Christ, he deprives himself of the universal benefit.'   St. Augustine: ' God sent not his Son into the world to condemn the world; but that the world through him might be saved (John iii. 17).   And then as to the physician: he came to cure a patient; and he who does not wish to keep the commands of the physician achieves his own ruin.   The Saviour came into the world, — why is he called the Saviour if not because it is his aim to save the world, and not to condemn it?   Do you not wish to be cured by him?   You will be your own judge.'" (p. 280.)

Before this it was said in the councils that he who asserts that for our purification from sins God expects our consent, and that we can choose the good, is not right, but here it suddenly turns out that a man must choose by all means.   Then follows Art. 192, which is to prove that there is a predetermination, and that there is no predetermination.

" 3. St. Paul teaches distinctly that divine predetermination is based on prescience, saying: For whom he did foreknow, he also did predestinate to be conformed to the image of his Son . . . , moreover whom he did predestinate, them he also called; and whom he called, them he also justified (Rom. viii. 29, 30).   He did not simply predestinate, says the apostle, but he predestinated, because he foreknew; whose deserts he foresaw, those he preordained, or, as St. Jerome expresses himself: ' Of whom God knew that they would be conformed to the image to his Son in their lives, those he preordained to be conformed to him in the glory itself.' "

This whole article about predestination bears upon itself the distinctive character partly of the Byzantine but more especially of the Russian theology.   Here is repeated what we find in all debatable passages of the Theology.   Some theologians say that the whole matter is in works, while others say that the whole matter is

in grace. Either may be proved with a certain degree
of consistency, but Russian theology never takes the
trouble to analyze thought and to go consistently from
deduction to deduction. It says: You say it is grace,
then we will generalize it and say: it is both works and
grace, and it does not in the least trouble itself about the
fact that one excludes the other. It strings out a few
unintelligible sentences, quotes the fathers of the church,
and comes to a conclusion, imagining that the question is
solved. Proof from Scripture.

"4. The doctrine about the unconditional predestination of God is contrary to common sense. Common
sense is convinced that God is just and that, consequently,
he cannot without any cause preordain some to eternal
happiness, and others to eternal damnation. It is convinced that God is infinitely good and, consequently, can
not without any cause condemn any one to eternal perdition. It is convinced that God is infinitely all-wise and,
consequently, cannot give man freedom and yet embarrass
it by his unconditional predetermination and take away
the whole moral value of its actions." (p. 286.)

This discussion directly ignores everything which has
been said against it in the previous articles. And with
this obvious contradiction the whole argument is closed.

Art. 193 still more mixes up the matter. Here there
is a contradiction in every word: "Though God worketh in
us to do of his good pleasure (Phil. ii. 14), and we are not
able without his grace to undertake anything, nor accomplish anything truly good: still that divine power, working in us and through us, in no way embarrasses our
freedom and does not draw it invincibly to the good."
(p. 286.)

What does that mean? Translating the sentence into
intelligible language, it turns out that grace does not
embarrass our freedom, but we can do nothing good without it. Where is the freedom? According to this defi-

nition it consists only in doing all kinds of evil. The whole discussion is of the same character, so that in conclusion it says :

" 5. Common sense on its side cannot help but remark that if divine grace embarrasses man's freedom and draws it forcibly to the good, then every merit is taken away from a man's good actions, every incitement to do good, and in general his whole morality is undermined, and the cause of it all is God himself! Can such ideas be admitted ? It is true, reason cannot explain in what way the mighty power of God, acting upon man, leaves his freedom intact, and cannot with certainty define their mutual relations ; but none the less this mystery must be for us above all doubt, since we have so many grounds for belief that man is not only not deprived of liberty under the influence of grace upon him, but also actively takes part in its action, which takes place in him and through him." (p. 288.)

That is, in other words, the Theology confesses that it does not understand anything of what it has said, but that it thinks that it is necessary to believe in that mystery, that is, in something meaningless and contradictory, which it is even impossible to express.

Art. 194 continues the tangle, proving that man takes an active part in what divine grace accomplishes in him and through him.

" St. Theodoret : ' The apostle called it a gift of God not only to believe, but also to suffer gloriously (Phil. i. 29), without rejecting the participation of the free will (of man), but teaching us that the will in itself, deprived of grace, cannot achieve anything good. Both are necessary : our readiness, or desire, to act, and the divine coöperation. And as for those who have not that desire it is not enough to have the grace of the Spirit, even so, on the other hand, the mere desire, not strengthened by grace, cannot gather the riches of the virtues.' " (p. 291.)

Thus the article asserts that a man who cannot do anything good without grace at the same time takes part in the action of grace. Leaving out the absurdity, contradictoriness, and immorality of the whole doctrine, one asks himself involuntarily : For what and for whom is that wanted ? And if any one needs it, what is that tangle for ? All right, a man cannot do anything without grace : then say so. But no, the proof is given that man cannot be saved without grace, and yet he must look for that grace, and coöperate, and through the whole tangle it would seem impossible to answer the question what it is all for. And if we did not know what is going to follow, we should get no answer. But there is a direct answer : grace, as understood by the hierarchy, is not the grace of the Calvinists, a preordained salvation, but the grace of the hierarchy, — its sacraments, and these have to be sought for.

The sacraments are transmitted to the flock by the priests, and the priests get money for them. Consequently it is impossible to be saved without grace, and grace must be looked for in the sacraments. What is bad about it is that with that is not only destroyed the whole moral significance of the teaching of Christ, but every moral teaching is obscured by the search after these sacraments which can be bought for money. But what is to be done ? Without it there would be no hierarchy. Consequently the whole doctrine about grace is very important. That alone can explain to us the wonderful doctrine about grace.

XV.

THE doctrine about grace is now regarded by the Theology as firmly established, and there begins the exposition of the statement that upon it is based the doctrine about sanctification :

"In rejecting the error of the Protestants, who under the name of justification or sanctification of man by grace understand the mere remission of sins, although man in reality perseveres in them, and a mere external imputation of the righteousness of Christ, though in reality man does not become righteous, but as a condition for justification and sanctification recognize only faith on the part of man, the Orthodox Church teaches : (*a*) that the sanctification of man consists in his being actually purified from sin by the grace of God and, with its aid, becoming righteous and holy." (pp. 292 and 293.)

Here by the words "sanctification of man" are meant the sacraments. Thus, after the proofs from Holy Scripture, is quoted the utterance by St. John Chrysostom :

"The Jewish priests had the power to cleanse bodily leprosy, or, more correctly, not to cleanse, but to testify to the cleansing. But these (the Christian priests) have received the power not merely to testify the cleansing, but completely to cleanse (ἀπαλλάτειν παντελῶς), not the bodily leprosy, but the impurity of the soul."

Thus the action of grace, which heretofore was unintelligible, so long as the question was about grace in the abstract, becomes clear at once. Grace is a holiness which is communicated by the priests, and so we now can comprehend what is meant by the statement that grace is necessary for salvation, and that man cannot be saved by good works without the sanctification through sacraments. Without the teaching about the sacraments a man will strive to become better. According to the doctrine of the hierarchy that is not necessary ; what is needed is nothing but grace. To seek grace means to seek the sacraments. To seek the sacraments means to accept the sacraments from the priest. The concluding words of this article are important, because they strikingly confirm the proposition which I have enunciated that the dogma of redemption is one of the foundations of the sacerdotal institution, of the hierarchy :

" The reëstablishment or redemption is nothing but the reduction of man to his original condition, in which he was before the fall. But before the fall man was actually innocent, righteous, and holy. Consequently it is necessary for him through this reëstablishment to return to precisely the same condition. In other words, if those who are reëstablished, or justified, remain as before in sin, without righteousness or holiness, and receive only a remission of sins, and externally cloak themselves in the righteousness of Christ, there is in that case no reëstablishment properly speaking, and it is nothing but a phantasm or a seeming reëstablishment." (p. 297.)

Reëstablishment is man's elevation to the former state of innocence. Redemption, according to the assertion of the hierarchy, has done that. But the hierarchy itself sees that nothing of the kind exists : redemption has done nothing of the kind. In what, then, is this reëstablishment to be assumed ? It is impossible to recognize that the reëstablishment consists in this, that actually good men, having learned the law of Christ, do more good than evil, because in that case only good men would be redeemed, and bad men would be in perdition. Nor is it possible to assume that the bad men are no longer bad,

and that they are reëstablished in innocence, because
Christ has redeemed them ; consequently it becomes
necessary to invent an imaginary innocence and holiness,
and such visible instruments for the communication of
sanctity as will make it possible to assure all men without exception that, no matter how bad they may be, they
are none the less holy.   And it is precisely this that is
invented.

But for the rearing of this artificial building, the imaginary redemption, the teaching about grace is not sufficient :
there is needed a new link in this chain of deception.
And so, in Art. 197, there is an exposition of that very
method of self-deception by means of which men, doing
good deeds, cannot regard their deeds as good, if they do
not observe certain conditions established for the purpose,
and unrighteous and not innocent men may in fulfilling
those conditions regard themselves as reëstablished, holy.
This self-deception is based on the conception of faith,
which is introduced into the book now for the first time,
and which is understood in an intentionally most mixed
up manner.   What is said is that faith is the first condition on the part of man for his sanctification and salvation.   A most tangled definition of faith is given : its
tendency is to substitute for the idea of faith an action
which is in the power of each man, and the conclusion is
drawn that he who believes that he is becoming sanctified
and reëstablished in complete sanctity and innocence,
that he alone is actually reëstablished in complete sanctity
and innocence.   But, if one believes that he is holy, and
there is no other means for ascertaining his sanctity but
the faith in his sanctity, it is impossible to assert that he
is actually holy, though he may unquestionably regard
himself as such.   If an insane man believes that he has
a tower on his nose, there can be no doubt about his
actually imagining that there is a tower on his nose, but
no one will think of asserting that there is really a tower

on his nose. And yet on precisely such a consideration is built the whole doctrine about the sanctification through faith. Here is the discussion:

"197. Divine grace, which achieves our sanctification, indeed extends over all men, but does not act upon them against their will, and in fact sanctifies a sinner, and thereupon saves him, only when certain conditions are observed on his part. The first of these is faith."

This unexpected introduction into the discussion of the idea of faith is particularly remarkable because all those dogmas which have been disclosed to us heretofore, beginning with the concept of God, were nothing but truths of faith. Up till now there has not once been any mention made about faith and there has not been any definition of what is to be understood by the word "faith." Heretofore it was assumed that faith was that correct knowledge of God, as indeed the Eastern Patriarchs say, that correct conception about God, which lies at the foundation of every other knowledge, and that everything else resulted from faith, but there has by no means been given that definition of faith by which it is the action of the human will. Here it turns out to be some kind of an action:

"(1) Under the name of faith in general is understood here the free acceptance and appropriation by man with all the powers of his soul of those truths which it has pleased God to reveal to us in Christ for our salvation. By faith is meant this acceptance and appropriation, because the revealed truths are for the most part incomprehensible to our reason and inaccessible to knowledge, but can be appropriated only through faith." (p. 298.)

Grace does not act against the will. Men must make an effort of will in order to accept it. Faith is a free acceptance, an appropriation of incomprehensible truths. Involuntarily there arises the question: how does the appropriation take place? Through reason, or through the will? Impossibly through reason, since the truths are incomprehensible; consequently through the will. What, then, is meant by "to appropriate by an effort of will"? Speaking plainly, it means "to obey." Thus faith, according to this definition, is reduced to obedience. Precisely in this way the word "faith" is understood in the Theology, though farther down, to obscure the definition, another misty definition is made, in which faith is mixed up with charity and hope. (p. 301.)

"The necessity of faith for our sanctification and salvation is comprehensible also from considerations of reason. Without faith we cannot appropriate to ourselves the truths of the divine revelation; consequently we shall not know what God has done for our salvation, nor what we are obliged to do. In this manner revelation, together with the whole house-management of salvation, will remain foreign to us, and we shall be foreign to revelation and salvation. In believing in Christ the Saviour and in his revealed word, we, so to speak, open our soul for all divine actions of salvation upon us; and in not believing, we shut ourselves up against these actions, and repel the divine assistance. For this reason, although faith is roused in us by premonitory grace and in its origin is a divine gift, it becomes on our part, the moment it is germinated in us, with our free consent, the first instrument for the actual acceptance in our soul of the saving grace, or of the divine powers that pertain unto life and godliness (2 Peter i. 3), the very first condition for our regeneration, sanctification, and salvation through grace." (pp. 303 and 304.)

Heretofore I understood faith as the foundation of man's whole activity, but here faith is spoken of as an activity. Involuntarily the question arises: on what is the activity based, which is seeking the faith and even choosing in advance the faith, which it is seeking? Strangest of all is the fact that nothing has been said about faith so long as the revealed, fundamental truths of faith about God, creation, man, soul (for it is necessary to believe in all that) were expounded; nothing was said about faith, but here, where it behoves the Theology to expound about sanctification and reëstablishment, which do not exist, it suddenly becomes necessary to define faith, and unexpectedly faith is defined, not as the knowledge of God, but as confidence in what the hierarchs say. Indeed, under the word "faith" the Theology understands something quite different from what it is generally understood to mean. This is seen in the clearest and quickest way from the following passage of Filarét's Catechism. There is there a question about which is more necessary, faith or good works. And the answer is: "Faith, because Scripture says, Without faith it is impossible to please God." And immediately after that comes the question: "Why must good works be inseparable from this faith?" And the answer: "Because it says, Faith without works is dead." The second answer to the question as to why good works must be inseparable from faith, because faith without works is dead, destroys the separation of faith from good works. If faith cannot exist without good works, why then separate them, and say: (1) faith, and (2) good works. This logical blunder is not an accidental one.

The same intentional blunder is repeated in the Theology. It is clear that by the word "faith" the Theology does not want to understand what the word actually means, not what Paul and the Eastern Patriarchs understand by it, and what we understand by it. "Faith is the substance of things hoped for, the evidence of things not seen, that is, a trust in the unseen as though it were seen, in what is wished and waited for, as if it were present," says Paul. Paul says nothing about this evidence and hope being communicated by any one. "By faith we mean the correct knowledge of God and of divine subjects," say the Eastern Patriarchs. "Nobody can be saved without faith," they say further on. "Faith is the substance of things hoped for, the evidence of things not seen, and a correct understanding about God." The same it is understood by all men to be. We perish in this life without the knowledge of God, — faith gives us salvation. All the works of salvation are by that very thing good works, and all good works are good only because they are works of salvation, which result from our knowledge of God, that is, from faith. Faith is not exactly inseparable from good works, but is the only cause of good works; but good works are inevitable consequences of faith. Consequently, it would seem impossible to ask which is more important: faith or good works? that is the same as asking which is more important, the sun or its light? And yet precisely such a division has been made in consequence of having given to faith a false, narrow definition, not of faith, but of trust and obedience.

The separation of faith from works, and the comparison between them, show clearly that by faith is understood something different from the definition given by Paul and by the Eastern Patriarchs, and from what the word itself means, but what it signifies here is what the Eastern Patriarchs say in another place: "We believe as we are taught to believe (Section 10)." It is evident that in Filarét, as well as in all the theological works, by faith is meant only an external agreement with what theology preaches, and this mere agreement is regarded as necessary for sanctification and salvation, and so we get here a definition not merely of faith in general, but at the same time of what men ought to believe in, and an explanation that he who believes will get great advantages, and he who does not believe will fare badly. Before this, in the exposition of each dogma, there was an exposition of the dogma, say of God, the Trinity, redemption, the church, and the causes which led us to that faith were adduced, but nowhere was it said that it was necessary to believe and that it was profitable to believe. But here, instead of proofs, instead of the disclosure of truths, we suddenly hear that it is necessary to make a free effort, not to oppose oneself, but to try to believe, and that he who believes will be saved, and he who does not believe will perish.

Before this were disclosed the God-revealed truths, and it was assumed that this disclosure led us to the only aim of the teaching, to faith, that is, to the knowledge of God. Now an opposite method is used: we are told that in order that the truth about sanctification should be disclosed to us, it is necessary first to believe in that sanctification: believe, and then everything will be disclosed to you. But does not the whole purpose of the teaching consist in bringing me to faith? But if you abandon that path of the disclosure of truths which lead me to faith, and tell me that it is necessary to believe what you say, as any man would say it, if he wanted to be believed, I have no longer any right to believe. If it comes all to a question of trust, my trust will depend only on the greater or lesser respect for him who is trying to convince me, and on the comparative probability of the evidence of truth. There is, however, no probability of this evidence in the teaching of the hierarchy, as we have seen heretofore, and so only one thing is left for me to do: to become frightened at the threats which are uttered against me for not believing, and, out of fear, to submit my reason to what is called grace, that is, to what the hierarchy teaches.

This attempt to submit our reason, this non-resistance to grace, we have all tried; it not only becomes inactive, but all the proofs in its favour militate against it, the moment a man seriously searches after truth. You say that I shall for ever ruin my soul if I do not believe you, but I do not believe you for the very reason that I am afraid that I may ruin my soul for ever. Especially now, when, after analyzing this article, it has become clear to me that the Theology, in taking up that which is most precious and important to it, the establishment of the sacraments, has itself declined to ascribe any meaning to that institution, and has been unable to justify it by anything but a naïve assertion that it is necessary to believe that it is so.

By reducing in this manner the conception of faith to trust and obedience, and by dividing the inseparable, the Theology has involuntarily arrived at the question about the relation to each other of these two imaginary, unthinkable conceptions of faith, trust in what you are told, and good works, which are independent of faith. The following Art. 198 analyzes the relation of these two imaginary conceptions.

In order to understand the following article, it is necessary to keep in mind that since the earliest times when the false conception of trust in place of faith was introduced, there has arisen the question as to what saves, whether faith, or good works, and that those who have confessed this teaching have since the earliest times been divided into two hostile camps. Some say that faith saves, and others say that works save. Our Theology, with its customary method and complete freedom from all bonds of logic, affirms that both save. And here is the import of the following 198th article:

"However, no matter how great may be the value of faith, which embraces in its broader sense both hope and charity, and although this faith is the first condition for the appropriation by man of Christ's deserts, — it alone is not sufficient for its aim. By faith alone a man may receive his justification and cleanse himself from sin in the sacrament of baptism, only when he just enters the kingdom of Christ's grace: he may after that receive the gifts of grace through the other sacraments of the church. But, that he may be able, after having entered the kingdom of grace, to preserve the righteousness and purity which he has acquired in baptism; that he may be

able to make use of the gifts of the Holy Ghost, which
he has received through all the other sacraments ; that he
may be able to strengthen himself in his Christian life
and gradually rise in Christian sanctity ; that, finally, he
may be able, after having completed his terrestrial activity,
to appear as justified and sanctified at the terrible judgment of Christ, — for all that, in addition to faith, he
needs good works, that is, those in which faith, hope, and
charity, which abide in the soul of a Christian, are expressed in an external manner, as in their fruits, and
which may serve as a precise execution of the divine
will, which has been imparted to us in the Gospel law."
(p. 305.)

After that are adduced proofs from Holy Scripture,
which directly deny the whole preceding division into
faith and works, and the preëminence of faith over
works :

"(*a*) That faith alone without works is insufficient for
salvation, is testified : (*aa*) by Christ the Saviour himself :
Not every one that saith unto me, Lord, Lord, shall enter
into the kingdom of heaven ; but he that doeth the will of
my Father which is in heaven (Matt. vii. 21 ; cf. xvi. 27) ;
(*bb*) by Apostle James : Ye see then how that by works
a man is justified, and not by faith only (James ii. 24) ;
(*cc*) by Apostle John : He that saith, I know him, and
keepeth not his commandments, is a liar, and the truth is
not in him (1 John ii. 4) ; (*dd*) by Apostle Paul : For not
the hearers of the law are just before God, but the doers
of the law shall be justified (Rom. ii. 13) ; (*b*) that a
Christian is obliged to show his faith, hope, and charity in
good works : Even so faith, if it hath not works, is dead,
being alone . . . shew me thy faith without thy works.
. . . For as the body without the spirit is dead, so faith
without works is dead also (James ii. 17, 18, 26) ; every
man that hath this hope in him (in our Lord Jesus)
purifieth himself, even as he is pure (1 John iii. 3) ; he

that hath my commandments, and keepeth them, he it is that loveth me (John xiv. 21); my little children, let us not love in word, neither in tongue; but in deed and in truth (1 John iii. 18); (c) that men are called to the kingdom of Christ's grace for the very purpose that they may do good works : For we are his workmanship, created in Christ Jesus unto good works, which God hath before ordained that we should walk in them (Eph. ii. 10); For the grace of God that bringeth salvation hath appeared to all men, teaching us that, denying ungodliness and worldly lusts, we should live soberly, righteously, and godly, in this present world; looking for that blessed hope, and the glorious appearing of the great God and our Saviour Jesus Christ; who gave himself for us, that he might redeem us from all iniquity, and purify unto himself a peculiar people, zealous of good works (Tit. ii. 11–14.)"   (pp. 305 and 306.)

All the texts quoted, especially those from the evangelists, show incontestably that faith cannot be separated from good works and that works are the results of faith, and consequently it would seem that this article directly destroys the whole meaning of the preceding article about the first meaning of faith.   But the Theology is not in the least embarrassed by that.   In the first article it contended against all the Christians who recognized salvation in works, and here it contends against those who recognize it in faith, and calmly destroys its own propositions, which does not keep it in the end from declaring triumphantly that the true teaching consists in accepting both, in spite of the fact that one excludes the other.

Indeed, no matter how irregular the separation of faith from works is, if that separation has once taken place in the conception of the believers, it is naturally possible to affirm that either faith alone or works alone can save.   If through faith we become completely purified and holy, good works evidently are superfluous.   They are assumed in themselves, but no longer form an aim. But if we are saved by an effort of our will, as was said in the preceding article, it is obvious that first of all there must be that condition of will, that is, the act, and then only will there be faith and salvation. Both assertions are logical and consistent, but our hierarchy, arming itself with faith in itself, regards any logical consistency as superfluous; it enunciates both the contradictory propositions in the same breath. The concluding words of the article, which are to prove the necessity of good works, prove precisely the opposite.

"We cannot do good works except with the coöperation of divine grace, for which reason they are called the fruits of the Holy Ghost (Gal. v. 22). But since in the performance of good works we need the participation of our free will; since through this free participation in good works we express our faith, charity, and hope in God; since this participation frequently costs us great endeavours and troubles in our struggle with the enemies of our salvation, the world, the flesh, and the devil, — our Lord God has been pleased to take our good works into account, and, in proportion as we succeed in godliness with the aid of grace, he has been pleased to increase in us our spiritual gifts, in order that by its aid we may ascend from power to power, from glory to glory (2 Cor. iii. 18)." (p. 311.)

The whole part quoted is a repetition in different expressions of one and the same contradiction: we cannot do good works except through grace, but for that purpose we need the participation of our free will.

The moral application of this dogma is more ludicrous than ever. Indeed, it is very hard to find any moral application for the most immoral of dogmas, whose aim it is to justify and permit vices and give an income to the hierarchy, but still we find à propos: (1) to pray to God that he may give us grace; (2) to thank God; (3) again to pray ; (4) to follow the inspiration of grace ; (5) man who has become as innocent as Adam ought to try to become innocent ; (6) "let us walk with a true heart in the substance of faith to the throne of grace ! "

XVI.

SECTION III. Of the sacraments of the church, as means through which divine grace is communicated to us. The sacraments are defined as follows:

"(1) A sacrament is a holy action which under a visible form communicates to the soul of the believer the invisible grace of God, an action which was established by our Lord, and by which every one of the believers receives divine grace.

"Consequently the nature of the sacraments the church assumes to consist in this, that there are sacramental actions which actually communicate divine grace to the believer, that they 'are not only signs of divine promises, but instruments which necessarily act through grace upon those who proceed toward them.' As essential qualities of each of the sacraments it regards: (a) the divine establishment of the sacrament, (b) some visible or sensual image, and (c) the communication of invisible grace by the sacrament to the soul of the believer." (p. 313.)

It is necessary to direct the attention to the definition of the nature of the sacraments and to the words "divine establishment of the sacraments," in order that we may later be able so much the more clearly to analyze the deception on which the Theology tries to establish the dogma of the sacraments. Seven sacraments are counted out, and the heresies of all the other Christians, except of our hierarchy, are refuted. Here are the heresies:

"(1) Of the nature of the sacraments. According to

Luther, they are simple signs of divine promises for the sake of rousing our faith in Christ, who remits sins. According to Calvin and Zwingli, they are divine signs, by which the one who is chosen is confirmed in the faith into which he is received and in the divine promises, or, he still more confirms his church in his faith than he confirms himself.   The Socinians and Arminians see in the sacraments mere external rites, by which the Christians differ from the Gentiles.   The Anabaptists regard the sacraments as allegorical signs of spiritual life.   The Swedenborgians regard them as symbols of a mutual union between God and man.   The Quakers and our Dukhobors completely reject the visible side of the sacraments, and recognize them only as internal, spiritual actions of the heavenly light.   All these and other similar conceptions about the sacraments, which are held by various Protestant sects, with all their differences, agree in this, that they equally reject the true conception about the sacraments as external sacramental actions, which actually communicate divine grace to the believers, and through it regenerate, renovate, and sanctify man.   (2) Of the number of sacraments.   As though not satisfied with the mere rejection of the true conception about the nature and efficacy of the sacraments, Protestantism has extended its sacrilegious hand upon this, in that it has diminished the number of sacraments, and, although in the beginning the Protestants showed a great diversity of opinions in this matter, they have finally agreed, of course each sect in its own way, to recognize only two sacraments : baptism and the eucharist.   Of our dissenters, the so-called Popeless sectarians, though not denying that seven sacraments have been established, are satisfied with two only, saying, ' In need two of them are sufficient, baptism and repentance, and the others are not necessary.' (3) Of the conditions for the performance and actuality of sacraments.   According to Luther's doctrine, no lawfully

established priest or bishop is needed for the performance
of the sacraments; the sacraments may be performed by
any clergyman or layman, by either man or woman, and
they preserve their power, no matter how they are performed, even without any intention of performing, and
even with ridicule or mystically. A full half of our dissenters, who form the Popeless sect, permit laymen also
to perform the sacraments; but the other half, under
the name of the Popish sect, leave them to the clergy,
but to clergymen who are either under the ban or even
entirely unfrocked, and who have in any case run away
from the Orthodox Church, and have renounced it for the
sake of joining the dissenting sect. On the other hand,
the ancient Donatists, in the twelfth century, and later
the Waldenses and the Albigenses, and beginning with the
fifteenth century, the Wycliffites, fell into the opposite
extreme, asserting that for the performance and efficacy of
the sacraments not only a legally established priest but
even a virtuous priest was needed, and that the sacraments
which were performed by a tainted servant of the altar
had no significance whatever. Finally the Reformers and
Lutherans invented a doctrine that the efficacy of the sacraments depended not on the worth and inner disposition
of the performer of the sacraments, but on the disposition
and faith of the persons who received the sacraments, so
that the sacrament is a sacrament and has power only
during its acceptance and application together with faith,
and that when it is not used, or when it is not accepted
with faith, it is not a sacrament and remains sterile."
(pp. 314–316.)

The Theology does not refute these heresies, but proceeds to expound its doctrine about the sacraments, each
separately. I will analyze each one of these so-called
sacraments, but first it is necessary to point out the deceit
of the specious proof of the divine establishment of the
sacraments, which alone and in one and the same form

will be applied to all the sacraments. The deception consists in the following : in the definition of the sacrament it was said that it is an external action which communicates actual grace, that is, a special spiritual power, given to him who receives the sacrament as established by Christ, and then it is pointed out that Christ has prescribed to the believers and to his disciples (but only in the case of baptism) a certain external action, and from this the conclusion is drawn that Christ has established the sacraments, that is, such actions as, when they are performed by the hierarchy, communicate to the believers a special spiritual power. The deception consists in this, that the assertion is made that Christ established the sacrament, that is, an external action which communicates internal grace, or, to speak more correctly, that Christ established the dogma of the sacrament, that is, the teaching that the immersion into water or the eating of bread and drinking of wine communicates some especial power to him who is immersed, or who eats bread and drinks wine. In order to prove the establishment of the Christian dogma of the sacraments, it is necessary to show that Christ ascribed to those external actions, to which the hierarchy points, calling them sacraments, those properties which the hierarchy ascribes to them, whereas there is not only no indication, but not even the slightest hint at such an understanding of the sacraments as practised by Christ. In asserting that Christ commanded men to bathe and sup in remembrance of him, the hierarchy has not the slightest foundation for the assertion that Christ established the sacraments of baptism and of the eucharist with all the meaning which the hierarchy ascribes to them, and about which there is, and there can be, no hint in Christ's teaching. Thus Art. 202 proves the divine origin of baptism as a sacrament by pointing out that Christ said to his disciples : " All power is given unto me in heaven and in earth. Go ye therefore and teach all nations, baptizing them in the name of the Father, and of the Son, and of the Holy Ghost; teaching them to observe all things whatsoever I have commanded you : and lo, I am with you alway, even unto the end of the world (Matt. xxviii. 18–20) ; he that believeth and is baptized, shall be saved ; but he that believeth not, shall be damned (Mark xvi. 16)."

In the first place, Mark xvi. 16 is a later addition to the Gospel, like that other tempting addition that believers shall take up serpents and not be hurt by drinking deadly things. Even if the genuineness of this passage be admitted, neither from it, nor from Matt. xxviii. 19, does it follow that baptism communicates any special power to those who are baptized. In Matthew men are to be baptized and taught to observe whatever Christ has commanded ; in Mark it is mentioned that he who believes and is baptized shall be saved. Where is there the establishment of the sacrament such as it is defined to be by the Theology ? All that may be said from these verses in Matthew and in Mark in favour of the rite of bathing is that Christ has selected, or, more correctly, has not rejected, the external sign of bathing, adopted by his predecessor John, for all the believers in his teaching.

But everything which is understood by the hierarchy under the invisible action of baptism has been established by that hierarchy, and by no means by Christ. That may be seen from the subsequent exposition of the article, in which there is a detailed account of the visible and the invisible side of the sacrament, for which no indication can be found in Holy Scripture.

203. The visible side of baptism. There is a detailed exposition of the sacrament about what to bathe in, how many times to immerse, who is to do the bathing, and what is to be said during the act. The proof is given that those who do differently are heretics, and that grace does not operate if there is any deviation from these rules.

204. The invisible actions of the sacrament of baptism and its unrepeatedness. Here it is said that at the same time "that the catechumen is visibly immersed in the waters of baptism, with the words, 'The slave of God is recognized . . . in the name of the Father and the Son and the Holy Ghost,' divine grace invisibly operates on the whole being of the one who is baptized and (1) regenerates or re-creates him ; (2) purifies him from all sin, and justifies and sanctifies him ; (3) makes him a child of God and a member of Christ's body ; (4) saves him from eternal punishment for sins and makes him an inheritor of eternal life." All that has not the slightest foundation in Christ's teaching.

205. The necessity of baptism for all. The baptism of babes. Baptism by blood. The proof is given that it is necessary to baptize infants because they are cursed by the original sin, and if an unbaptized child dies, it goes to hell, whereas if it is baptized it goes to heaven. All that is proved from Holy Scripture.

206. Who may perform baptism, and what is demanded of those who are baptized. It is proved that priests ought to baptize, but deacons may sometimes, and sometimes even simple people may. All that is proved from Holy Scripture. To be baptized, one needs faith, the same that was spoken of in the article about grace and repentance. When infants are baptized, the sponsors must guarantee their faith, that is, pronounce the words of the creed and renounce the devil.

It is evident that all that has been established, not by Christ, but by one of the many diverging hierarchies. After baptism follows unction with chrism.

207. Connection with what precedes ; the place of the sacrament of unction with chrism in the series of the rest ; the conception about this sacrament, and its name. "Through baptism we are born into spiritual life, and pure from all sin, justified, and sanctified do we enter into

Christ's kingdom of grace. But as a natural living man, the moment he is born, has need of air, light, and the other external assistances and powers for the support of his existence, for his gradual strengthening, and for his growth, even so it is in spiritual life: immediately after man's birth from above, he has need of the grace-giving powers of the Holy Ghost, which may serve for him as spiritual air and light, and with the aid of which he may not only support his new life, but also constantly strengthen himself and grow. It is these divine powers which pertain unto life and godliness (2 Peter i. 3) that are given to each who is reborn in baptism, through another sacrament of the church, through the sacrament of unction with chrism." (pp. 345 and 346.)

It is proved that the sacrament of unction with chrism was established by Christ. Here are the proofs:

"(1) Gospel history proves that Christ the Saviour had intended and promised to give the Holy Ghost to those who believed in him. In the last day, that great day of the feast, says St. John the Divine, Jesus stood and cried, saying, If any man thirst, let him come unto me, and drink. He that believeth on me, as the Scripture hath said, out of his belly shall flow rivers of living water. (But this spake he of the Spirit, which they that believe on him should receive: for the Holy Ghost was not yet given; because that Jesus was not yet glorified) (John vii. 37–39). Here, evidently, mention is made of gifts of the Holy Ghost, which are offered to and consequently are necessary for all believers in our Lord Jesus, and not of extraordinary gifts, which are communicated only to a few believers for special purposes (1 Cor. xii. 29, and so forth), though it does not say by what visible mediation the necessary gifts of the Holy Ghost are to be transmitted to all believers. (2) The Book of the Apostolic Acts tells us that after Jesus Christ was glorified, the apostles actually gave the Holy Ghost to those

who believed in him, and that they did by the laying on
of hands. Such, for example, is the following case: Now
when the apostles which were at Jerusalem heard that
Samaria had received the word of God, they sent unto
them Peter and John: who, when they were come down,
prayed for them, that they might receive the Holy Ghost:
(for as yet he was fallen upon none of them: only they
were baptized in the name of the Lord Jesus). Then
laid they their hands on them, and they received the
Holy Ghost (Acts viii. 14–17). From this it is quite
clear: (*a*) that the Holy Ghost was communicated by
the apostles, not through baptism (in which the believers
are only regenerated or re-created by the Holy Ghost suddenly, without receiving him for ever), but by the laying
on of hands on the one who is baptized; (*b*) that by this
laying on of hands the apostles communicated to the
believers the gifts of the Holy Ghost, which are necessary
for all who have received baptism, but not extraordinary
gifts, which are communicated only to the few; (*c*) that
this laying on of hands, united with a prayer to God
about sending the Holy Ghost down on those who are
baptized, should form a special sacrament, distinct from
baptism, and (*d*) finally, that this sacrament, distinct
from baptism, has a divine origin, because the apostles in
all their words and acts, in spreading the Gospel teaching,
were inspired by the Holy Ghost, who taught them every
truth, and brought to their remembrance all the things
which the Lord Jesus had commanded them (John xiv.
26 ; xvi. 13)." (pp. 347 and 348.)

The deception which the hierarchy has appropriated to
itself for the purpose of assuring the flock that Christ
has established the sacraments consists, as we have seen,
in taking the slightest hint given by Christ or the apostles in regard to some external action and ascribing to it
the improper meaning of a sacrament, and of asserting
that Christ has established that sacrament. But this de-

ception has some plausibility only in the case of baptism; in the other cases there is not even any cause for deception, and the hierarchy has to invent the cause itself, as it has done in the present case. Because Christ has said, " He that believeth on me, as the scripture hath said, out of his belly shall flow rivers of living water," it follows that all have to be anointed with oil, and that Christ promises a special advantage from it. Then follows the exposition of the dogma.

209. The visible side of the sacrament of unction with chrism. The visible side consists in this, that the anointing is done in the form of a cross and certain words are pronounced. Proofs from Holy Scripture.

210. The invisible side of unction with chrism, and its unrepeatedness. The invisible action consists in this, that the Holy Ghost enters into him who is being anointed, and there enters grace, (1) which enlightens in the truth of faith, (2) confirms in godliness. Mention is made that in former days they began to prophesy and speak in various tongues after it, but now that does not happen, — the Holy Ghost merely enters.

211. To whom the sacrament of unction with chrism belongs, and when it is to be performed. A priest, and not the bishop only, may anoint with chrism, and so the Catholics are wrong, and that is proved at great length.

212. Connection with the preceding. Conception of the sacrament of the eucharist. Its superiority and different appellations.

" Through the sacrament of baptism we enter Christ's kingdom of grace pure, justified, regenerated for spiritual life. In the sacrament of unction with chrism we receive in ourselves the powers of grace, which are necessary for our strengthening and growth in the spiritual life. Finally, in the sacrament of the eucharist we are made worthy for the same high purpose of partaking of the food and drink which gives salvation, — the pure flesh and blood of our Lord Jesus, and most sincerely unite with the very fountain of life (Psalm xxxvi. 9)." (pp. 366 and 367.)

This sacrament, in which we most sincerely unite with God, surpasses all the others:

"(1) By its superabundance of mysteriousness and incomprehensibility. In all the other sacraments the incomprehensibility consists in this, that under a certain visible form divine grace is invisibly operating upon man, but the substance of the sacraments itself, for example, in baptism, the water, in unction with chrism, the chrism, remain unchangeable. Here, on the contrary, the substance itself changes: the bread and the wine, which keep their form, are miraculously changed into the true body and blood of our Lord, and only then, when they have been received by the believers, do they invisibly produce in them their actions of grace. (2) By the superabundance of the Lord's love for us, and by the extraordinary grandeur of the gift, which is communicated to us in this sacrament. In the other sacraments the Lord Jesus communicates to those who believe in him such or such particular gifts of saving grace, in conformity with the substance of each sacrament, — gifts which he acquired for men by his death on the cross. But here he offers as food for his believers his own self, his own body and blood, and the believers, directly uniting with their Lord and Saviour, are in this manner united with the very fountain of saving grace. (3) Finally, by this, that all the other sacraments are only sacraments which act savingly upon man, but the eucharist is not only the most incomprehensible and the most saving of the sacraments, but at the same time is a sacrifice to God, a sacrifice which is brought to him for all the living and all the dead, and gains his favour." (pp. 367 and 368.)

The doctrine about this sacrament indeed differs from all the others. It differs first of all in that it completely departs from the former definition of the sacrament. This sacrament, according to the Theology : (1) not only gives power to him who receives it, but also represents a constantly repeated miracle; (2) gives us God to be eaten up; (3) is a sacrifice which God himself brings for himself, — all kinds of phenomena which do not enter into the first definition. According to the definition of this sacrament, it not only communicates grace to those who receive it, but is also a transmutation of a substance, a conversion of God into food for men, and a sacrifice of God, brought by God himself. But that does not disturb the Theology. It goes on to prove that this especial sacrament was established by Christ.

213. The divine promise of the sacrament of the eucharist, and its very establishment. To prove that this sacrament was established by Christ, there is adduced from the Gospel the sixth chapter of John, the words from the holy supper, and the Epistle to the Corinthians. In looking through the chapter of John, it is easy to see that, avoiding all interpretation and sticking to the literal meaning, he, his flesh and blood, is the bread of life, that he gives that bread of life to men, and that he who will not eat that bread will not have life. Christ promises to give to men the bread of life, which he calls his flesh and blood and, without saying what is to be understood by his flesh and blood, commands men to eat that bread. The only conclusion which can be drawn from that is that men must eat the bread which Christ has called his flesh and blood, that this bread exists and must exist, and that therefore men must seek that bread, as he told them to do, but in no way is it possible to draw the conclusion which the church draws, namely, that that bread is the baked leavened bread and grape wine, not every kind of bread and every wine, but that of which we shall be told that Christ has commanded us to partake of.

The other place on which is based the sacrament of

the eucharist is the passage from the Gospel and from
the Epistle to the Corinthians, where it says that Christ,
bidding his disciples farewell, said to them : " Here I
break bread and give you wine. This is my blood and
my body, which is given to save you from sin. Eat
and drink all of you ! " Christ before his death said to
his disciples, as he broke bread and handed them the
cup: " This wine and this bread are my flesh and my
blood. Drink now and then do it in remembrance of
me ! "   From these words it may be concluded that
Christ, bidding his disciples farewell, told them that he
was dying for men and that he commanded them to do
likewise, that is, like him to give their body and blood for
men ; it is possible to conclude that as he broke bread and
gave them the wine he commanded them to think of him ;
it is possible to stick to the most literal meaning about
the flesh and blood and conclude that he did a miracle
before his disciples and gave them, in the form of bread
and wine, his own body to eat and his blood to drink ; it
is even possible to conclude that he commanded his disciples to perform the same miracle, that is, out of bread
and wine to make the body and blood of each particular
disciple ; if you wish, it is possible even to conclude the
most far-fetched proposition, that he commanded them to
perform a miracle, which was, to make Christ's blood and
flesh out of bread and wine, — but under no consideration
is it possible to conclude what the church concludes from
it, namely, that not only the disciples, whom he addressed,
but certain men at a certain time and under certain conditions must produce something similar to that miracle,
and must believe and assure others that the bread and
wine which they offer is the very body and blood of
Christ ; that, in receiving this bread and wine with the
assurance that they are Christ's body and blood, men are
saved. This conclusion, which our hierarchy makes, is
absolutely impossible, the more so since the hierarchy

asserts that many perform this miracle irregularly. It is impossible to tell when this miracle is performed and when not, for there are no other signs of that miracle but faith in the fact that it is being performed. However, it is superfluous to prove the irrationalness and arbitrariness of this sacrament; it is sufficient to follow out the conclusions to which the Theology leads in this matter, having accepted that conception of it, in order that the absurdity of this sacrament and its blasphemy may become manifest.

214. The visible side of the sacrament of the eucharist. The visible side of the sacrament consists : (1) of the substance employed; (2) of the sacramental action, and (3) of words pronounced. The bread used in it must be of wheat, pure and leavened. There are five pages of proof that the bread must be leavened. The wine must be made from grapes. There are described all the manipulations which the priest must perform during it : the offertory, the liturgy, and the words which are to be pronounced. It also mentions which words are the most important of all.

215. The invisible essence of the sacrament of the eucharist; the actuality of the presence of Jesus Christ in that sacrament. The invisible action consists in this, that not symbolically (τυπικῶς), as some say, not with a superabundance of grace, as others say, not essentially (ὑποστατικῶς), not through the penetration of the bread (κατ'ἐναρτισμόν), " but truly and actually, so that after the sanctification of the bread and wine, the bread is transformed, transubstantiated, transmuted into the true body of Christ, which was born in Bethlehem of the Ever-virgin, was baptized in the Jordan, suffered, was buried, was raised from the dead, ascended to heaven, sits on the right of God the Father, is to appear in the clouds of heaven."

Precisely thus must we believe.

There follows a controversy. All are wrong, but:

" The doctrine of the Orthodox Church about the actuality of the presence of Jesus Christ in the sacrament of the eucharist has imperturbable foundations in Holy Scripture, as well as in Holy Tradition." (p. 386.)

Here is a sample of the proofs why this action is to be understood as the church understands it: " In establishing the eucharist, the Lord established the greatest sacrament of the New Testament, which he commanded to be performed at all times (Luke xxii. 19, 20). But the importance of the sacrament necessary for our salvation, and the nature of the promise, and the nature of the commandment demanded alike that the clearest and most definite language be used, so that it might not lead to any misunderstandings in so important a matter."

216. The manner and consequences of the presence of Jesus Christ in the sacrament of the eucharist. " (1) If this presence consists, as we have seen, in this, that after the sanctification of the holy gifts, there are present in the eucharist and are communicated to the believers not the bread and wine, but the real body and the real blood of the Lord, — that does not mean that he is present in the sacrament, that he, as it were, penetrates (according to the Lutheran heresy) the bread and wine, which remain intact, and only coexists with them (*in, cum, sub pane*) with his body and blood, but that the bread and wine are transformed, transubstantiated, transmuted into the very body and blood of the Lord. (2) Although the bread and wine in the sacrament of the eucharist are transformed properly into the body and blood of the Lord, he is present in this sacrament, not with his body and blood alone, but with his whole soul, which is inseparably connected with this body, and with his very divinity, which is hypostatically and inseparably connected with his humanity. (3) Although the Lord's body and blood are broken in the sacrament of the communion and are

divided up, that happens only with the forms of the bread
and wine, in which Christ's body and blood may be seen
and felt ; in themselves they are completely integral and
indivisible. (4) Similarly, although the sacrament of the
eucharist is performed in endless places of the world,
Christ's body is always and everywhere one, and Christ's
blood is always and everywhere one, and everywhere one
and the same Christ, complete God and complete man,
integrally takes part in it. (5) If the bread and wine
through the sacramental sanctification is transubstantiated into the real body and blood of Christ the Saviour,
that means that from the time of the sanctification of the
holy gifts he is constantly present in the sacrament, that
is, he is present not only in the application and reception
of the sacrament by the believers, as the Lutherans assert,
but even before the reception, for the bread and wine,
having been transubstantiated into Christ's body and
blood, no longer change back into their former substances, but remain the body and blood of the Lord
for ever, independently of whether they will be used by
the believers or not. (6) If the bread and wine in the
holy, life-giving sacraments are the real body and the real
blood of our Lord Jesus, then these sacraments ought to
receive the same honour and divine worship which we owe
to our Lord Jesus himself." (pp. 396–402.)

217. Who may perform the sacraments of the eucharist.
Who may receive the communion, and wherein the preparation for it is to consist.

The power to perform this sacrament belongs to the
bishop. The bishops transfer the power to the presbyters,
but deacons may not perform it ; nor can laymen. But
all, even babes, may receive the communion. There is a
controversy about that.

218. The necessity of the communion of the eucharist,
by all means under two kinds, and the fruits of the
sacrament.

All must receive the communion. Proofs. Men must be communed over bread and wine, and not over bread alone. Again controversy and proofs. For this controversy Hus was burnt and his followers were tortured. I mention only in words the controversy and the proofs. But, O Lord, what a terrible book would be that history of theology, which should tell about all the violence, deceptions, tortures, murders, which have taken place because of each of these controversies! As one now reads about these controversies, all that seems so unimportant and ludicrous, but how much wrong they have done in the world!

219. The eucharist as a sacrifice: (*a*) the verity or actuality of this sacrifice. "In believing and confessing that the most holy eucharist is a true sacrament, the Orthodox Church believes also and confesses, in spite of the aberrations of the Protestants, that the eucharist is at the same time a true and real sacrifice, that is, that in the eucharist is the body and blood of our Saviour, which on the one hand are offered as food to men, and on the other are brought as a sacrifice to God." (p. 414.)

220. (*b*) Relation of this sacrifice to the sacrifice on the cross, and its properties. "The sacrifice which is brought by God in the sacrament of the eucharist is precisely the same as the sacrifice on the cross."

Further on it says that this sacrifice has the property of propitiating God, and so it is necessary immediately after it, and as soon as possible to remember men. That will cause God to help men.

"Since a bloodless sacrifice has the power of propitiating and inclining God toward us, it naturally has the power to gain for us various benefits from God, and, being propitiatory, it is at the same time precatory and intercessory. For this reason the holy church, in bringing a bloodless offering, not only prays God to remit sins and save the living and the dead, but also asks God for all kinds of gifts, spiritual and bodily, which are necessary for human life."

That ends the exposition of the sacrament of the eucharist. It took up eighty pages. Everything which has been expounded here, the whole blasphemous delirium, all that was founded by Christ. The fall is taking place with terrible celerity, the fall from the height of questions into the bog of most incomprehensible superstitions. The first fall happened when it was asserted that God redeemed us in a visible manner, and now the last, when there are described the actions of that grace. There is no place to go any lower. What is the difference between a Chuvash, who smears his God with cream, and an Orthodox, who eats a small piece of his God, or who is hastening to offer five kopeks, that his name may be mentioned in a certain place and at a certain time? Then follows the sacrament of repentance.

221. Connection with the preceding; conception of the sacrament of repentance and its various appellations. "In the three saving sacraments of the church, heretofore discussed by us, there is imparted to man the whole abundance of spiritual gifts, which are necessary for him to become a Christian and, having become one, to abide in Christian godliness and attain everlasting happiness. Baptism purifies sinful man from all of his sins, both the original and the voluntary, and introduces him into Christ's kingdom of grace. Unction with chrism communicates to him divine powers for his strengthening and growth in the life of grace. The eucharist furnishes him with divine food and unites him with the fountain of life and of grace. But since, having become completely cleansed from all sin in the bath of baptism, man is not freed from the consequences of original sin and inherited corruption, such as, in the soul, the propensity to do evil, and in the body, diseases and death (Arts. 91–93), since even after baptism, being a Christian, he may sin,

and even very often (1 John i. 8, 10), and be subject to
diseases, sometimes very serious ones, which bring him
to the grave, — it has pleased the all-good God to establish in his church two other sacraments, as two saving
remedies for his ailing members: the sacrament of repentance, which remedies our spiritual ailments, and the
sacrament of unction with oil, which extends its saving
action over the bodily ailments."

But why only over the ailments? Did we not hear
before that the redemption freed men from diseases and
death, and that this redemption becomes operative through
the sacrament of unction with oil? Consequently unction
with oil destroys diseases and death. But laws are not
written for the Theology. Unction with oil, as will be
seen later, operates against diseases and death, but only a
tiny little bit.

" Repentance, taken in the sense of a sacrament, is a
sacramental action in which the pastor of the church, by
strength of the Holy Ghost, absolves the repentant Christian from all sins committed by him after his baptism, so
that the Christian again becomes innocent and sanctified,
such as he came out of the waters of baptism." (pp. 425
and 426.)

From the standpoint of the church, what is important
in this sacrament is not the humility with which the
repentant man approaches it, not that verification of himself, but only that purification from sin which the hierarchy dispenses by force of an imaginary power. I even
wonder why the church does not entirely abolish this
sacrament, substituting for it that remissory prayer, which
it has introduced and which is said over the dead: " I,
unworthy man, by force of the power given to me, remit
your sins." The church sees only this external imaginary
purification and cares only for it, that is, it sees only the
external action to which it ascribes a curative significance.
What is taking place in the soul of the repentant sinner

is of no consequence to it. Though there are added certain reflections about how the repentant sinner is to
approach the sacrament, they are given only *en passant*
and are no important condition under which the imaginary
purification takes place. The whole matter is in the imaginary purification over which the hierarchy has the
power. The proof is given, as in the case of all the other
sacraments, that it was established by Christ, but, as in
all sacraments, there is not the slightest proof that Christ
uttered the words which he spoke, no matter how we may
understand them, having the sacraments in view.

222. The divine establishment and the efficacy of the
sacrament of repentance. To prove this imaginary power,
there are adduced the words of Matthew (xviii. 17, 18),
which are explained in this sense, that the pastors have
always enjoyed the divinely given right to bind and
loose. The hierarchy understands these words to mean
that it has the right to remit sins, and everything is based
on that conversation: And if he shall neglect to hear
them, tell it unto the church: but if he neglect to hear
the church, let him be unto thee as an heathen man and
a publican. Verily I say unto you, Whatsoever ye shall
bind on earth, shall be bound in heaven: and whatsoever
ye shall loose on earth, shall be loosed in heaven (Matt.
xviii. 17, 18).

Here is the whole passage: " If thy brother shall tres-
pass against thee (these words the hierarchy omits in order
to introduce its own interpretation), go and tell him his
fault between thee and him alone: if he shall hear thee,
thou hast gained a brother. But if he will not hear
thee, then take with thee one or two more, that in the
mouth of two or three witnesses every word may be
established. And if he shall neglect to hear them, tell it
unto the church: but if he neglect to hear the church, let
him be unto thee as an heathen man and a publican.
Verily I say unto you, Whatsoever ye shall bind on

earth, shall be bound in heaven : and whatsoever ye shall loose on earth, shall be loosed in heaven (Matt. xviii. 15–18)."

This clear place, which is given as an instruction for all men, is expounded topsyturvy only because here is used the word ἐκκλησία, assembly, which later has received a different meaning, and is represented as a confirmation of an imaginary power of the hierarchy, which is that of remitting sins.

But, let us assume, contrary to the text and to common sense, that these words were addressed by Christ not to all men, but exclusively to his disciples ; let us assume that he gave them the power to remit sins, — in what way does from that result the sacrament of repentance, which makes each who receives it an innocent man ? Again there is the old trick : a sacrament, which was established after Christ, and of which no one in his time could have had any conception, is ascribed to Christ. Then follows the exposition of the rules of that sacrament.

223. Who may perform the sacrament of repentance, and who receives it.   This sacrament, that is, the remission of sins, may be performed only by the priests.

224. What is demanded of those who approach the sacrament of repentance ?   Approaching repentance it is necessary to have : (1) contrition for sins.   There is even a description of the character of that contrition : " As regards the nature of the contrition respecting the sins, it is necessary to see to it that it does not result merely from the fear of punishment for the sins, not from the conceptions in general of the deleterious consequences for us arising from them in the present and in the future life, but mainly from love for God, whose will we have violated, and from a living consciousness that with our sins we have offended our greatest benefactor and Father, have appeared ungrateful before him, and have become unworthy of him ;" (2) an intention of not sinning again ;

(3) an oral confession of our sins, and then the priest says: " Our Lord and God Jesus Christ, with the grace and gifts of his philanthropy, may forgive thee, my child, all thy trespasses, and I, unworthy priest, by the power given me forgive and loose thee from all thy sins, in the name of the Father and the Holy Ghost. Amen." (p. 437.)

And then the man is purified. It is very useful and necessary that the guiltiness of the sins should be loosed by the priest's prayer before the last day. But it does not say what will happen if there is not that contrition which is demanded, when there is not the firm and determined intention not to sin again, while the priest gives the remission of sins; but we know that there never is that contrition which is demanded, nor that intention not to sin and to believe. Thus from the whole description of this sacrament of the church, which considers all its essence to consist in the power of remitting sins through its hierarchy, we get a kind of a toy, something ridiculous, or, at least, a senseless action.

225. The visible side of the sacrament of repentance; its invisible actions, and its extent.

Here it is proved that there is no sin that could not be forgiven by the hierarchy, except the sin of not believing in what the hierarchy teaches.

226. Penances, their origin and use in the church. " Under the name of penances (ἐπιτιμία) are meant prohibitions or punishments (2 Cor. ii. 6), which, according to the church rules, the minister of the church, as a spiritual physician, determines in the case of certain penitent Christians for the sake of curing their moral ailments."

This power the hierarchy has received from God.

227. The significance of the penances.

228. The incorrectness of the doctrine of the Catholic Church about the indulgences. For twenty-two pages we

get an extended controversy with the Catholics about penances and indulgences. Penances are correctionary punishments, and not punishments of revenge. All that is proved by Holy Scripture against the Catholics, who prove the opposite from the same Holy Scripture. In regard to the indulgences, the question stands as follows : Christ has redeemed the whole world with a profit, — a surplus is left; besides, the priests by their good lives have increased this surplus so that there is now a big pile of goodness. All these profits are at the service of the church. With these profits, which are hard to dispose of, the church, all the time guided by the Holy Ghost, pays God for the sins of its members, and the members pay to it not with something mysterious, but simply with cash. Now this doctrine is not so much objected to, as it is corrected. Our hierarchy agrees to the fact that the church has complete charge of this capital and with this capital pays for the sins of men, remitting the sins to these men in the sacrament of repentance ; but the controversy is as to whether the church or its head may arbitrarily forgive these sins without the penitence of the sinner himself. The Catholics say that it can, our men say that it cannot. Of course, there is no sense in either assertion, just as there is no human sense in the question itself ; but in this case, as in many other controversies with the Catholics and Protestants, our hierarchy, if it has any distinguishing feature at all, is characterized by stupidity and by an absolute inability to express itself in conformity with the laws of logic. Precisely the same happens in this controversy. The Catholics are logically more correct. If the church can remit sins by dint of its power, and the church is always holy, why should it not pardon robbers, as indeed all the churches do? After that follows the sacrament of unction with oil.

229. Connection with the preceding ; conception of unction with oil, and its appellations. "The sacrament of

repentance, as a healing of grace, is intended for all Christians, but only for curing their spiritual ailments. The sacrament of unction with oil is another healing of salvation, which is intended for Christians who are infirm of body, and has for its purpose the healing of not only their spiritual, but also their bodily infirmities." (p. 464.)

Here is precisely a case which confirms what I have more than once said about the characteristic feature of our church, — its stupidity. It was said before that repentance heals the soul of sins, and that unction with oil heals the body of diseases and death. It would, therefore, be necessary to explain why unction with oil cures neither diseases nor death. It cannot be concealed that there is no such cure. About the soul it is possible to say what you please, but here that cannot be done : the matter is too obvious ; it is necessary either not to say anything about its ability to cure death, or to invent something. The Catholics are bound by logic, and so they have decided that this sacrament is imparted as a farewell ceremony over such patients as are sick unto death, and call it the extreme unction. But our church does not refute its power to cure, and has not invented anything to conceal the matter, but, as always, gets out of the difficulty by saying : " It does cure, but only in part, a tiny little bit, and at certain times." Then follow proofs of the divine origin of the sacrament.

230. The divine origin of the sacrament of unction with oil and its efficacy. There is not even a single hint in the Gospels as to the establishment of this sacrament by Jesus Christ, but that does not keep the Theology from asserting that it has been established by God :

" Of the sacrament of unction with oil distinct mention is made in Holy Scripture by Apostle James, when he instructs the Christians : Is any among you afflicted ? let him pray. Is any merry ? let him sing psalms, and immediately adds: Is any sick among you? let him call for the elders of the church; and let them pray over him, anointing him with oil in the name of the Lord; and the prayer of faith shall save the sick, and the Lord shall raise him up; and if he have committed sins, they shall be forgiven him (James v. 14, 15). From these words there are disclosed to us at once the divine origin and its efficacy, as a sacrament. (1) The divine origin: for on the one hand it is evident from the context that the apostle does not speak of unction with oil, as of something new, which the Christians did not know before, but points out to them this means of healing, as something which has existed before and which was universally known to them, and which he commands them to use in case of sickness. On the other hand, it is evident that the apostles never preached anything of themselves (Gal. i. 11, 12), but taught only what they had been commanded by our Lord Jesus (Matt. xxviii. 20), and what the Divine Spirit inspired them with (John xvi. 13); and it is known that they called themselves the servants of Christ, and stewards, and not establishers, of divine sacraments (1 Cor. iv. 1). Consequently unction with oil, which is commanded to the Christians by St. James, as a sacramental healing of diseases, both bodily and spiritual, was commanded by our Lord Jesus Christ himself and by the Divine Spirit. We do not find any statement in Scripture at what particular time our Lord established this sacrament, for many things which he taught and did on earth are not transmitted in writing (John xxi. 25). But it is most natural to think that this sacrament, like two others (baptism and repentance), through which remission of sins is granted, was established by our Lord after his resurrection, when all power was given unto him in heaven and in earth (Matt. xxviii. 18), and when he showed himself to the apostles for forty days and spoke to them of the things pertaining to the kingdom of God (Acts i. 3), that is, of the establishment of his church, an essential part of which is formed by the sacraments." (pp. 465, 466.)

There are no other proofs. What is striking is that not only are there no foundations for any sacrament, but there is not even the slightest cause for this particular sacrament; none the less it is proved that this, too, was founded by God.

231. To whom and by whom the sacrament of unction with oil may be communicated. We are told that all the sick, and not merely the dying, as with the Catholics, may be anointed, and that the anointing may be done by priests, still better, by bishops. Best of all it is if seven priests do the anointing, but even three, or one, may do it.

232. The visible side of the sacrament of unction with oil, and its invisible actions of salvation.

The visible side consists in anointing and saying prayers, and the invisible side; — what do you suppose it is? The invisible side is the healing of bodily infirmities.

" The sacrament of unction with oil is established more particularly for those who are sick in body : consequently the healing of bodily ailments forms the very first saving fruit of this sacrament." (p. 472.)

The healing is classed with the invisible side, because, of course, unction with oil does not produce it. The Theology is not embarrassed, but says outright that there is a cure, but it is invisible.

" This action does not always follow on unction with oil. That is true. But: (a) at times it actually takes place and the patient slowly gets well and rises from his sick-bed. More frequently, (b) the dangerously sick man receives, at least, temporary relief from disease or is strengthened or aroused to bear it, and that is also one of the aims of unction with oil, for the verb ἐγείρω signifies not only ' raise up,' but also ' to rouse, to encourage, to strengthen.' At times, however, (c) those who receive the sacrament of unction with oil do not receive from it

a healing of ailments, perhaps for the same reason that those who receive the sacrament of the eucharist, instead of saving fruits, only eat and drink damnation for themselves (1 Cor. xi. 29), that is, on account of their unworthiness, on account of an absence of a living faith in our Lord Jesus, or on account of hard-heartedness. Finally, (d) to wish or to demand that each time when a man is receiving unction with oil he should be cured of his diseases would be the same thing as demanding that he should never die; but that is contrary to the very plan of our regeneration, according to which it is necessary for us to depose this sinful, mortal body, in order to clothe ourselves in proper time, beyond the grave, in an immortal body. For this reason every man who approaches the sacrament of unction with oil, every sick person, ought entirely to abandon himself to the will of God, who knows better than we, to whom it is more useful to send down a cure and prolong his life, and whose life is to be cut short before its time." (pp. 472 and 473.)

What use was there then of talking about the cure of diseases and of death? And so the first invisible action is the non-existing cure of diseases; the second is the cure of spiritual infirmities.

After that there is a refutal of the doctrine of the Catholics, which ascribed at least some meaning to the sacrament; what is refuted is that this sacrament is meant as a farewell action before death. Then follows the sixth sacrament, established by God.

233. Connection with what precedes. Marriage as a divine institution, and its aim; the conception of marriage as a sacrament, and its appellations. " Three sacraments of the Orthodox Church, baptism, unction with chrism, communion, are intended for all men, so that all may become Christians and then abide in Christian godliness and obtain everlasting salvation. Two other sacraments, repentance and unction with oil, are intended for all

Christians as two saving remedies, one, in case of spiritual infirmities, and the other, in case of bodily and, at the same time, spiritual ailments. But there are two more sacraments, established by God, which, even though they are not predetermined and necessary for all men and though they are not necessary directly for each of the members of the church, are necessary for the purposes of the church in general, for its existence and flourishing condition. Those are: (a) the sacrament of marriage, which communicates to certain persons grace for the natural procreation of children, the future members of the church, and (b) the sacrament of priesthood, which communicates to special persons the grace for the supernatural procreation of the children of the church and for their education for the eternal life." (pp. 475 and 476.)

But, according to its definition, a sacrament is a holy action which under a visible form communicates to the soul of the believer the invisible grace of God. But the procreation of children is not an invisible grace. Besides, in defining a sacrament, it was said: " For the performance of a sacrament three things are needed: a proper substance, such as water is in baptism, bread and wine in the eucharist, oil, and other substances according to the sacrament." (p. 314.)

Here no substance is needed. Marriage apparently does not fit in with the definition of a sacrament, and in general differs from all the other sacraments by this essential feature, that in all the other sacraments (including priesthood) by sacrament are understood external actions, which are performed over something which is supposed to take place, which is not connected with anything real, and which is entirely useless, whereas here by sacrament are meant certain external actions, which are performed over something real, and one of the most important acts in human life. The Theology says:

" Marriage may be considered from two sides: as a law

of Nature, or as a divine institution, and as a sacrament of the New Testament church, which now, after the fall of man, sanctifies this law." (p. 476.)

The sanctifying sacrament consists in this: "In order to sanctify, uplift, and strengthen the law of matrimony, which is holy and pure in itself as to its origin from God and as to its purposes, but which because of the disturbance of human nature has fallen under the harmful influence of sin and has in many ways been distorted by men who have abandoned themselves to sensuality, our Lord Jesus has been pleased to establish in his church a special sacrament, that of marriage. Under the name of this sacrament is understood a sacred action in which to the contracting parties, who before the church make a promise of mutual conjugal fidelity, there is communicated from above, through the blessing of the servant of the church, divine grace, which sanctifies their conjugal union, elevates it to an image of Christ's spiritual union with the church, and then coöperates with them in the blessed acquisition of all the purposes of marriage." (pp. 478 and 479.)

That is, in connection with the law of marriage, which in itself is holy, the hierarchy finds it necessary to sanctify again.

234. A divine origin of the sacrament of marriage, as a sacrament, apparently does not, and cannot, exist in the Gospels, nor is there anything in them to hitch on to, and so the place is chosen in the Gospel where the word "marriage" is used. That place about the marriage in Cana of Galilee, which has nothing in common with the establishment of marriage, not even with its blessing and approval, is taken as a basis. The Theology itself feels, as in the case of the unction with oil, that there is nothing to hitch on to, and so it says:

"Of when and how the Lord established the sacrament of marriage, whether when he was present at the marriage

in Cana of Galilee (John ii. 1–11), or when, in consequence of the well-known question of the Pharisees, he
disclosed the true conception about marriage, and said,
What God hath joined together, let no man put asunder
(Matt. xix. 3–12), or after his resurrection, when for forty
days he appeared to his disciples, and spoke to them of
the things pertaining to the kingdom of heaven, that is,
of what had reference to the establishment of his church
(Acts i. 3), the Gospel does not say anything: for there
are many other things, which Jesus did, which are not
written in these books (John xx. 30; xxi. 25))." (p. 479.)

But that is the very reason why it is considered
proved.

235. The visible side of marriage, and invisible actions.
The visible side of marriage is this, that groom and bride
promise to be husband and wife, and the priest pronounces
certain words. The invisible side: (1) grace sanctifies
the union, as of Christ with the church; (2) strengthens,
as Christ with the church; (3) coöperates in the per-
formances of the obligations, as Christ with the church.
Suddenly there is for some reason introduced the comparison of Christ and the church with husband and wife,
and in that the invisible side of the sacrament is supposed
to lie.

236. Who may perform the sacrament of marriage, and
what is demanded of those who proceed to this sacrament.
Popes may unite in marriage; the Orthodox (or at least
one of the contracting parties an Orthodox) may marry.
All others do not marry, but only cohabit.

237. The properties of Christian marriage, sanctified
by the sacrament. One may marry only one woman, and
divorce is granted only in the case of adultery. All that
is regarded as a sacrament founded by God himself.

Of the sacrament of priesthood.

238. Connection with the preceding; the priesthood,
as a special divinely established ministration in the church

(hierarchy), and its three degrees; conception about priesthood as a sacrament.

"In expounding the doctrine of the sacraments, we have heretofore remarked in the case of each of them that it may be performed and communicated to the believers only by the pastors of the church, by bishops and presbyters. But in order that men may become pastors of Christ's church and receive the power to perform the sacraments, the Lord has established a special sacrament, the sacrament of priesthood." (p. 490.)

Indeed, leaving out of consideration the fact that of all the sacraments not one has been established by Christ as a sacrament, and that in reference to four of them, to unction with chrism, repentance, unction with oil, and marriage, not even the slightest reference has been discovered, — all the sacraments, even according to the definition of the church, become sacraments only when they are performed by pastors of the church, that is, by true pastors, and so all the preceding sacraments are based on this sacrament of priesthood. If this is not a sacrament, and its origin cannot be proved, all the other sacraments fall of themselves, even though their efficacy may be proved. Farther on it says:

"Priesthood is understood in two senses, as a special class of men, a special ministration in the church, known under the name of hierarchy, and as special sacerdotal action, by which men are consecrated and ordained for this ministration. In the first case, we have already discussed the priesthood, and we have seen that the Lord himself established the hierarchy, or the order of pastors, whom alone he has empowered to be teachers in the church, performers of sacraments, and spiritual stewards, and that he has by no means permitted all the believers to assume all that." (p. 490.)

The sacraments may be performed only by priests, but, in order to be a priest, it is necessary that the sacrament of priesthood be performed on him. In the preceding articles it was said that every sacrament is inefficacious, if it is not performed by real priests. In the explanations much was said about the heretical teachings which have a false priesthood. Consequently the whole strength, not only of this sacrament of priesthood, but of all other as well, lies in the clear proofs that the priesthood was established by Christ, that the transmission of this priesthood was established by him, and that among the many existing usurpating priesthoods the one under discussion is the only true one. And so we get:

239. The divine establishment and efficacy of the sacrament of priesthood. The proof is given that this sacrament is from God. Not only are there no proofs of the establishment of this sacrament, but, as in the case of the sacraments of unction with chrism and with oil, there is not the slightest reference to this sacrament in the Gospels. Here are the proofs:

" The divine establishment of the sacrament of priesthood is to be seen from the actions of the holy apostles, who themselves, by the instruction from the Holy Ghost who reminded them of everything which the Lord Jesus commanded them (John xiv. 26), performed this sacrament, and by the laying on of hands raised to the three degrees of the hierarchy." (p. 491.)

Then follow the proofs of the fathers and of the councils, so that it is even more obvious than in the case of the previous sacraments, that this sacrament was invented by the hierarchy independently of the teaching of Christ. Then follows an exposition of the sacrament.

240. The visible side of the sacrament; its invisible action and unrepeatedness. The visible side of the sacrament consists in the laying on of hands on the head, and in the saying certain words.

" The invisible action of the sacrament of priesthood consists in this, that by it, after the prayer, there is actually imparted to him who is being ordained divine grace to correspond to his future ministration, — the grace of priesthood." (p. 495.)

The importance of the sacrament is as follows :

" If any one will reflect how important it is for a man, while he is still burdened with flesh and blood, to be present near the blessed and immortal essence, he will see clearly what honour the grace of the Spirit has bestowed on the priests. By them the sacrifices are offered and all the other high ministrations are performed, which have reference to our dignity and salvation. They still live and move about upon earth, and they have received the power which God has granted neither to the angels, nor to the archangels." (p. 495.) " The grace of priesthood, which is imparted through the laying on of hands, though in various degrees, upon deacons, presbyters, and bishops, and which vests them with a certain measure of spiritual power, abides in the soul of each of them unchangeably, for which reason neither a bishop, nor a presbyter, nor a deacon is a second time ordained for the same dignity, and the sacrament of priesthood is regarded as being unrepeatable." (p. 496.) Controversies about it.

241. Who may perform the sacrament of priesthood, and what is demanded of those who receive it.

" According to the teaching of the Orthodox Church, the power to lay on hands for an order of priesthood belongs only to the immediate successors of the apostles, the bishops."

Then follow long controversies about when this laying on of hands is efficacious, and when not. Priests must be : " (1) Orthodox Christians ; (2) men experienced in the word of faith and in life, according to the righteous word ; (3) if they are chosen to the dignity of bishop, they must be free from the bonds of marriage ; but if they are chosen to the rank of presbyter or deacon, they may, if they so wish, live in a condition of matrimony." (p. 500.)

Then there comes a controversy about celibacy, but the question as to how it is proved that our hierarchy is the true successor of the apostles, and not one of the other hierarchies, which regard themselves as such, is not even mooted, so that of all the sacraments the one on which all the others are based not only fails to be proved or determined, but is also introduced quite arbitrarily and without the least sign by which it may be distinguished from anything resembling it.   After that follows a division which is called Division VIII.   General remarks on the sacraments.   In these general remarks we find an exposition :

243. Of the nature of the sacraments.   " The sacraments are not only signs of divine promises for the purpose of rousing faith in men, not merely simple rites, which distinguish Christians from Gentiles, not only symbols of spiritual life and so forth, as the heretics wrongly think (Art. 200), but sacramental actions, which under some visible form really impart to the believers an invisible grace of God ; they are instruments which of necessity operate as grace on those who approach unto them." (p. 505.)

244. On the septenary number of the sacraments.   It is proved that there are precisely seven sacraments.   From these proofs the very opposite is clearly demonstrated.

" After that we must not be misled by the fact that some ancient teachers, as the need arose, or in conformity with the purpose chosen by them, or for some other reasons, speak in their writings now of two, now of three, and now of four sacraments, without mentioning the rest.   It is quite wrong to conclude from that, as the Protestants have concluded, that the ancient church recognized only two sacraments (why not three or four ?), baptism and the eucharist, for it is known that other teachers of the church at the same time or even earlier mentioned also all the rest ; for it is known that the same teachers, mentioning baptism and the eucharist by name, at times point also to

other similar sacraments and in various passages of their
writings clearly speak separately of each of the seven
sacraments." (pp. 511 and 512.)

Any one who has read church history knows that
there were seven sacraments, precisely seven, because
there are seven gifts of the Holy Ghost, seven candela-
bra, seven seals, and so forth.

245. On the conditions for the performance and efficacy of the sacraments. For the performance of the
sacraments, that is, for the communication of grace to
the believers, are needed: " (1) A legally ordained presbyter or bishop; (2) a legal (that is, according to the
divine ordainment) sacramental action of the sacraments." (pp. 513 and 514.)

" But, on the other hand, many heretics have wrongly
thought: (a) that for the performance and efficacy of
the sacraments is needed not only a legally ordained minister of the church, but also a pious servant, so that the
sacraments performed by tainted servants of the altar
have no significance, or (b) that the actuality and efficacy of each sacrament depends on the faith of the persons receiving it, so that it is a sacrament and has its full
power only during the time of its reception or use with
faith, and that when not used, or in case of acceptance
without faith, it is not a sacrament and remains sterile
(Art. 200). (1) The first is wrong, for the power of
grace of the sacraments depends really on the deserts
and the will of Christ the Saviour, who himself performs
them invisibly, and the pastors of the church are only
his servants and visible instruments, through whom he
imparts the sacraments to men. (2) Wrong is also the
second opinion, which assumes that the power and actuality of the sacraments is in complete dependence on the
faith and disposition of the persons who receive the sacraments." (pp. 514–517.)

That is clear. The sacraments are purely external actions, like incantations against the toothache which act upon people, and there is no sense of speaking or thinking of any spiritual side either on the part of the one who pronounces the incantation, or on the part of those who are being cured. It is necessary to make certain motions with the hands and feet, and grace will come down.

246. Moral application of the dogma. The application of the dogma concludes the section about the sacraments. The only obvious application is to have recourse to the hierarchy for sanctification by means of sacraments. The whole doctrine about the sacraments, after it has been analyzed, is reduced to the following: among the number of senseless, discordant followers of Christ there are some who consider themselves to be ordained by those men who themselves have been ordained by the laying on of hands, who, finally, were ordained by the apostles. These people give no signs of their right of succession, but they assert that the grace of the Holy Ghost has come down to them, and that, in consequence of it, they know seven actions through which the grace of the Holy Ghost descends upon people, and this grace, though it is not determined by anything visible, they are able to bring down on people. The communication of this invisible grace by these men is in reality the doctrine about the sacraments.

XVII

CHAPTER II. Of God as the Judge and Retributer.

Here the didactic part of the Theology is really ended. The doctrine about the sacraments is the aim and crown of all. It is necessary to prove to people that their salvation does not lie in them, but depends on the hierarchy, which can sanctify and save them. All men have to do is to obey and seek salvation; paying the clergy for it in honours and money. The next chapter is really not a teaching, but a threat, which will incite the flock to have recourse to the hierarchy. There is a short recapitulation of the doctrine from the beginning.

247. Connection with the preceding; conception of God as the Judge and Retributer, and the composition of the church doctrine about it.

" For the full rehabilitation and salvation of fallen man it was necessary to perform three great acts: (*a*) to reconcile the sinner with God, whom he has infinitely offended by his fall; (*b*) to cleanse the sinner from sins and make him righteous and holy; (*c*) to free the sinner from the punishments themselves for his sins, and to present to him the benefits which he has earned in accordance with his sanctity (Art. 124). The first act the Lord God achieved himself without our participation, when he sent down upon earth his only-begotten Son, who, having become incarnate and having taken upon himself the sins of the whole human race, has by his death brought full satisfaction to eternal justice, and in this manner has not only redeemed us from sins and from

punishments for sins, but has also made us partake of
the gifts of the Holy Ghost and of eternal happiness
(Art. 153).   The second act the Lord God achieves with
our coöperation.   He has founded on earth his holy
church as a living and constant instrument for our purification from sin and for our sanctification; he sends
down to us in the church and through the church the
grace of the Holy Ghost, as an actual force, which purifies us from sins and sanctifies us; he has established
various sacraments in the church for communicating to
us the various gifts of this saving grace, in conformity
with all the needs of our spiritual life, and it lies with us
whether we shall make use, or not, of the means of sanctification, which God offers to us." (pp. 520 and 521.)

God took pity on men who were perishing from their
evil will, and redeemed them.   But the condition of men
after the redemption remained the same that it had been
in the time of Adam and the patriarchs.   Just as they
who were before the redemption had to look for salvation, so we must do, who come after the redemption.
The difference between the condition of the Old Testament and that of grace is this, that then there did not
exist the mechanical means of the sacraments, but now
it exists.   The difference is this, that Jacob and Abraham
could save themselves by their good lives, by the fulfil-
ment of God's will in life, and now we can be saved
through sacraments.

All that would be very nice, but with this teaching, it
would seem, it would be impossible to recognize retribution, because retribution results from the absolutely free
activity of man, while with salvation through the sacraments man is not free.   Salvation through good works
differs from any other in that it is absolutely free.   A
man is for moral good as free on the cross as at home;
but the salvation through sacraments does not fully, and
sometimes does not at all, depend on the will of man, so

that, in spite of the whole desire to be baptized, anointed, communed, man may not have the chance to be so. Consequently retribution appears as unjust, when grace is taken into consideration. Adam could be punished for the apple; he could have eaten, or not eaten it; but a punishment because a man had no chance or possibility to be baptized or to commune, such a punishment destroys the idea of God's justice, and that is precisely what results from church grace. According to the Old Testament, God is represented as crude and cruel, but none the less just; according to the new grace, as the hierarchy teaches it, he is represented as an unjust judge, as one gone mad, who punishes men for what is beyond their will.

Evidently one cannot get away from the laws of reason. The first error, or lie, of the redemption led up to the greater lie of grace, and grace led to a still greater lie, to the faith of obedience, and this again to the mechanical actions of the sacraments. The necessity of an incitement for the performance of the sacraments led up to retribution, and that teaching has found its expression in a horrifying monstrosity.

God, to save all men, gave his Son up to execution, and from this it follows that if a pope is too late with his sacrament when I am dying, I shall go, if not directly to hell, somewhere where I shall be much worse off than he who has stolen a lot of money and has hired a pope or several popes to be always about him. That is not a misuse, but a direct conclusion. But that does not embarrass the Theology. It says: "The first thing is that God has saved us; the second thing is that he has given us sacraments; the third thing the Lord God achieves after the performance of the second, which he achieves with our help: he then appears as the judge of men, who justly weighs our deserts, whether we have made proper use, or not, of the means of purification from sins and of sanctification, which he has given us on earth, and whether we are worthy, or not, to be freed from punishments for sins and to receive happiness; he appears thereupon as a just Retributer, who determines the due part for each man according to his deserts." (p. 521.)

The means against it are the sacraments. Then follows the usual exposition. In the retribution all three persons of the Trinity take part.

248. The circumstance which prepares the private judgment. Man's death. Death is spoken of as something new and unknown to anybody. The cause of death is the fall of the first man, and from the first man we took that habit. All that is proved.

249. The actuality of the private judgment. It is proved that after death there takes place a private judgment of man in distinction from the general judgment. The judgment, that is, a certain process of investigation and the retribution which follows from it, is ascribed to omniscient and all-good God.

250. Representation of the private judgment: teaching about the torments. "Holy Scripture does not tell us how a private judgment takes place. But an objective representation of this judgment, based mainly on Holy Tradition and in agreement with Holy Scripture, we find in the teaching about the torments (τελωνία), which has existed since antiquity in the Orthodox Church." (p. 528.)

The torments are described and confirmed by Holy Scripture on ten pages. We are told that "at the parting of our soul from our body there will arise before us, on the one hand, a host of the heavenly powers, and on the other, the powers of darkness, the evil keepers of the world, the aerial chiefs of torments, the inquisitors and arraigners of our deeds. Upon seeing them, the soul will be excited, and will be convulsed and tremble, and in confusion and terror will seek for defence among the angels of God; but even when it will be accepted by the holy angels, and under their protection will flit through the aerial spaces and rise to the height, it will encounter various torments, as it were barriers or toll-gates where taxes are collected, which will bar its way to the kingdom and will stop and arrest its striving toward it.   At each of these torments an account of some special sins will be demanded : at the first torment, of the sins committed by means of the lips and mouth ; at the second torment, of the sins of vision ; at the third, of the sins of hearing ; at the fourth, of the sins of smell ; at the fifth, of all lawlessness and abominable deeds done by means of the hands.   To the other torments belong the other sins, such as anger, hatred, envy, vanity, and pride. . . .   In short, every passion, every passion of the soul, every sin will similarly have its tormentors and inquisitors."   (p. 529.)

252. Retribution to the righteous : (a) their glorification in heaven, in the church triumphant.

" Retribution for the righteous, by the will of the heavenly Judge, also has two forms : (a) their glorification, though not yet complete, in heaven, in the church triumphant, and (b) their glorification upon earth, in the church militant."   (p. 534.)

It is hard to understand how the word " glorification " occupies such an important place in the teaching of the church, especially when one thinks of Christ's teaching, which is constantly directed against glory, and one feels with his heart that the love of glory, of glorification, is one of the most petty of human feelings.   I can understand as a reward the contemplation of God, peace, Paradise, Eden, even Mohammed's Paradise, Nirvana ; but in order to understand the reward in glorification, I have to imagine myself in the place of the crudest of men or when I was only fifteen years old.   But the Theology regards glorification as a great reward.   This glorification is represented to consist in this, that wreaths will be put on them and that they will be in honour and glory. That is proved from Holy Scripture.

253. The glorification of the righteous upon earth, in the church militant : (*aa*) the worship of the saints. " At the same time that the righteous Judge and Retributer honours the righteous, after their decease, with a glorification, anticipatory though it be, in heaven, in the church triumphant, he honours them also with a glorification upon earth, in the church militant." (p. 546.)

This glory is again represented in the form of wreaths, gold, precious stones, obeisances, censers, singing, masses, and so forth. Then follow controversies with those who do not consider it necessary to worship the saints in such a way. All that is proved from Scripture.

254. (*bb*) Invocation of the saints. " Respecting the saints, as true servants, favourites, and friends of God, the holy church at the same time invokes them in its prayers, not as some gods, who might help us by their own power, but as our intercessors before God, the only sources and distributers of all the gifts and favours to the creatures (James i. 17), as our representatives and intercessors, who have the power of mediation from Christ, who alone is in the proper sense the independent mediator between God and men, who gave himself a ransom for all (1 Tim. ii. 5, 6). Holy Scripture teaches us that dogma." (pp. 553 and 554.)

It is a dogma. The dogma consists in this, that : (*a*) it is necessary to pray to the saints, (*b*) that the saints hear us, (*c*) that they pray for us.

All that is proved by Holy Scripture, and the proof is concluded by an excerpt from a decree of a council :

" If any one does not confess that all the saints, who have been since eternity and who have pleased God, as before the law so also under the law and under grace, are worthy before him of honour in their souls and bodies, or if he does not invoke the prayers of the saints, as having the permission to mediate for the world, according to the church tradition: anathema."

That is, obviously, a sufficient proof.

255. (cc) The worship of holy relics and of other re-mainders of those who have pleased God.   Besides, it is necessary also to glorify the relics and other remainders of the saints.   That is proved:

" (a) Because when a dead man barely touched the body of Prophet Elisha, he revived, and stood up on his feet (2 Kings xiii. 21); (c) because the mantle of Elijah, which was left by him to Elisha, with its touch opened the waters of the Jordan for the passage of the latter prophet (2 Kings ii. 14); that even the handkerchiefs and aprons of St. Paul, which in his absence were put on those who suffered from diseases or were possessed by devils, cured the diseases and drove out the devils (Acts xix. 12). (2) In the history of the church we find an endless number of similar miracles, which the Lord has performed through the relics and other remainders of the saints for all those who had recourse to them with faith.

" (3) The most startling miracle, with which the Lord has glorified the bodies of many saints, is their incorrup-tibility.   This incorruptibility of the holy relics, this exemption of theirs through the miraculous divine action from the universal law of corruption, serving, as it were, as a living lesson of their future resurrection and as strong incitement to us to worship the very bodies of the saints who are glorified by God and to emulate their faith, is not subject to the slightest doubt.   In Kíev and Nóv-gorod, in Moscow and Vológda, and in many other places of our divinely guarded country openly rest many incor-ruptible relics of saints, and by the incessant miracles, which are wrought on those who have recourse to them in faith, they loudly testify to the truth of their incorrup-tibility."   (pp. 563–567.)

All of us know about the Duke Decroix, of hundreds

and hundreds of incorruptible bodies, due to physical conditions; we know that accidentally a certain Siberian
bishop did not decompose and now is lying in Kíev in a
cellar, waiting for the opening of the relics; we know of
those relics that are kept under a bushel, about the scare-
crows, with which pennies are gathered in for the hierarchy, and whose garments are clandestinely changed by
the members of the hierarchy; we know about the oil
which is poured into the fragrance-spreading heads. Not
a single student of a seminary nor a peasant believes in
all that, so what sense is there in expounding it in the
Theology as a dogma? Even if there were in the Theology
anything resembling a disclosure of the truths of faith,
even if everything were sensible and correct in it, such an
assertion about the relics would invalidate the whole
thing.

The proof is given that the relics and all kinds of handkerchiefs and pantaloons have to be honoured and kissed,
and that pennies are to be put on them, and the whole
concludes with a decree of the Seventh Œcumenical
Council:

"And thus, those who dared to reject the relics of the
martyrs, which they knew to be genuine and true: if they
are bishops or clergymen, let them be deposed; if they
are monks or laymen, let them be deprived of communion." (p. 570.)

But all that is not enough. It is not enough to substitute saints, their fingers and pantaloons, in the place of
God. We need still the images.

256. (*dd*) The worship of the holy images. The
church commands us: (*a*) to use images in churches,
houses, and streets; (*b*) to honour them with the burning
and offering of tapers; and it condemns: (*a*) the ancient
iconoclasts, (*b*) the modern Protestants, (*c*) those who
worship them as though they were gods. There begin
proofs and controversies. Those controversies have cost

much malice, many executions, much blood. Only by an absolute departure from the questions of faith can we explain those controversies and those assertions and proofs, which are adduced in the book.

" III. The endless signs and miracles which the Lord has been pleased to perform through the images for the believers serve as a new incitement for the worship of the holy images. With accounts of these miracles are filled the chronicles, of the church in general, as also of our church in particular. Several images of Christ the Saviour, of his immaculate Mother, of St. Nicholas, and of other saints have, on account of the abundance of miracles wrought by them, since antiquity been known under the name of miracle-working images, and, being found in various places of the Orthodox Church, by the will of God our benefactor, have not yet ceased to be as it were channels or guides of his miraculous power, which gives us salvation." (p. 580.)

It is for these channels of his miraculous power that controversies have existed and differences of opinions still exist: the question is whether they are channels or not. If the Lord has deigned to work miracles through those images, then not only a rude peasant, but even the greatest philosopher cannot help but pray to the image. If a case is decided through a secretary, the secretary has to be invoked, and there is no way out of it. We have long ago descended upon earth from the sphere of questions about religion. The discussion was about sacraments which mechanically impart grace, independently of the spiritual condition of the pastor and believer, only when there are no causes for cassation; and now the subject under discussion is the images, which are channels of miraculous power, which therefore have to be prayed to, though they are not gods.

About the history of these channels we learn from the Theology, that during the first three centuries " the pagans at times rebukingly asked the Christians why they had no certain representations," because "one of the councils in Spain, the one at Elvira, which took place in the year 305, in its 36th rule directly forbade the use of images in temples. But: (*a*) first of all this rule incontestably proves that images were then in use in the churches; (*b*) this rule forbade men to represent upon the walls of the temples that which the Christians worshipped (*quod colitur et adoratur*), that is, as is assumed, to represent God in his substance, which is invisible and unrepresentable; (*c*) not improbable is another guess, which is, that the rule was enunciated in conformity with the conditions of place and time: in Spain just then raged the Diocletian persecution, and the Pagans, who frequently broke into the temples, desecrated the holy representations of the Lord and his saints, and so, in order to avoid that, this rule was adopted for a certain time." (p. 584.)

257. Retribution to sinners: (*a*) their punishment in hell. "The sinners, suddenly after death and the private judgment, depart with their souls to a place of sorrow and grief." (p. 584.)

Proofs from Holy Scripture. The place to which they depart is called the extreme darkness, a fiery furnace. Not all agree where that Gehenna is, but there are several subdivisions in hell: "It may be assumed that hell has its separate abodes, lockups, and dungeons of the souls, its separate divisions, of which one is properly called Hell, another Gehenna, a third Tartarus, a fourth a Fiery Lake, and so forth. At least there is in Revelation a passage where hell and the lake of fire are distinguished (Rev. xx. 13, 14). These unequal torments of the sinners in hell after the private judgment are not full and complete, but only anticipatory."

Proofs from Holy Scripture.

258. (*b*) The possibility which some sinners have of receiving alleviation, and even immunity from the pun-

ishments of hell, because of the prayers of the church. "However, while the Orthodox Church teaches that all sinners, after their death and the private judgment over them, all alike depart to hell, a place of sorrow and of grief, it at the same time confesses that for those who have repented before their departure from the present life, but have not had time to bring the fruits which are worthy of repentance (such as prayer, contrition, the consolation of the poor, and the expression in acts of love for God and for their neighbours), there is still left a chance of getting alleviation in sufferings and even of being completely freed from the bonds of hell.   Such an alleviation and immunity the sinners may obtain, not through any of their own deserts or through repentance (for after death and the private judgment there is no place either for repentance or for deserts), but only through the infinite grace of God, through the prayers of the church, and through the benefactions done by the living for the dead, and especially through the power of the bloodless sacrifice, which in particular the servants of the church bring for every Christian and for the deceased, and which the Catholic and Apostolic Church in general brings every day for all."   (p. 589.)

That is proved. That natural consideration how, if God is just (as a man is just), as the hierarchy understands it, he can forgive a sinner for somebody else's prayers is decided in the following way:

"St. Augustine: 'There is no cause for the slightest doubt that they (prayers of the holy church, saving sacrifices, and alms) are beneficial to the dead, but only to those who before their death have lived in such a way that they can be beneficial to them.   For in behalf of those who have departed without faith, which is accompanied by charity, and without the communion in the sacraments, their friends will in vain perform the works of that godliness, an earnest of which they did not have in themselves, when they were here, and when they did not receive or vainly received divine grace, and treasured up for themselves not mercy, but wrath. Thus, no new deserts are obtained for the dead, when their friends do something good in their behalf, but the consequences are extracted from the foundations which they have laid before.'" (p. 599.)

What good is there, then, in prayers? Is it possible God will not make out the foundations which they have laid before, without the mediation of advocates? What use is there, then, in the prayers and sacrifices of the church? However disagreeable it is to say so, there is no other cause for them except that of collecting pennies. Indeed, this natural heartfelt sentiment of every praying person, in addressing God, to remember the souls of friends, — this holy, this good sentiment, the hierarchy, by its touch, has managed to change into something stupid, base, and degrading.

Then follow reflections about the prayers of the church: (1) the deceased are divided into those for whom it is necessary to pray, and into those for whom it is not necessary to pray (the unrepenting and the stubborn); (2) there is a refutal of the opinions of those who assert that there is no need of praying for those who have passed away having received the last sacrament, on the ground that they are holy as it is; (3) it is proved that it is necessary to pray for them; (4) prayers have an effect only on the private judgment; the same reflection by St. Augustine as quoted above, that prayer is a kind of re-membrance; (6) that there are some who can no longer be saved by prayers, while others may be saved; (7) the church prays "on the third day for the sake of him who on the third day rose from the dead; on the ninth day in commemoration of the living and of the dead; on the fortieth, because for that length of time the people lamented Moses;" (8) in case we pray for those who are already " in heaven or among the number of the rejected," the prayers, " though no longer useful to them, can do them no harm;" (9) " if the church prays for all who have died in repentance, and its prayers are very strong before God and beneficial to them, then all will be saved, and no one shall be deprived of bliss? To that we shall say, 'Let it be so, and oh, if it were so!'" (p. 606.)

259. (c) Remarks about purgatory. Controversy with the Catholics about purgatory, and proofs that they are in the wrong.

260. The moral application of the dogma about the private judgment and retribution naturally is : to be afraid of the judgment and have recourse to the relics and images and pay money to the hierarchy that it may pray for the departed.

Section II. On the general judgment. 261. Connection with what precedes; the day of the general judgment; the uncertainty of that day, and signs of its approach, especially the appearance of the antichrist.

" The private judgment, to which every man is subjected after his death, is not the complete and final judgment, and so naturally makes us wait for another, the full and decisive judgment. At the private judgment the soul receives its award without any participation of the body, although the body has shared with it its good and bad works. After the private judgment, the righteous in heaven and the sinners in hell have opened unto them only an anticipation of that happiness or torment, which they have deserved. Finally, after the private judgment a few sinners still have a chance to alleviate their fate and even to free themselves from the bonds of hell, if not through their own deserts, at least through the prayers of the church. But the day, the last day, will certainly come for the whole human race (John vi. 39–40)." (p. 613.)

The day will come when the body will receive according to its deserts. Then are defined the symptoms of the coming of that day:

" (1) On the one hand extraordinary successes of good upon earth, — the dissemination of Christ's Gospel in the whole world: (2) on the other hand, extraordinary successes of evil and the appearance of the antichrist upon earth."

This is who the antichrist is going to be:

" (a) It will be a definite person, by all means a man, but only a lawless man under the special operation of Satan; (b) he will in his character be distinguished by extraordinary pride and will give himself out as a God; (c) for the purpose of attaining his end he will preach a false doctrine, which is contrary to the saving faith of Christ, an enticing teaching, with which he will draw after him many weak and unworthy people; (d) in confirmation of his teaching and for the greater seduction of men, he will perform false signs and miracles; (e) finally he will perish from the actions of Jesus Christ the Saviour, when he comes to judge the living and the dead. We shall further remark: (a) he will come from the tribe of Dan; (b) he will be a powerful lord, who will usurp the power by force, and will extend his dominion over all the nations; (c) he will cause a terrible persecution of the Christians, will demand divine worship of himself, will draw many after him, and those who will not follow him he will put to death; (d) for the counteraction to the antichrist, God will send from heaven two witnesses, who, as is said in Revelation, shall prophesy the truth and work miracles, and when they shall have finished their testimony, they shall be killed by a dragon, and after three days and a half they shall rise from the dead and ascend to heaven; (e) the dominion of the antichrist will last only three years and a half." (pp. 616–618.)

All that is proved by Holy Scripture.

" It will not be superfluous to remark that the predictions about the antichrist have more than once been applied to various persons. Some, according to the testimony of St. Augustine, saw the antichrist in Nero; others saw him in the Gnostics; others again in the pontiff at Rome and in general in popery : an idea which arose and was quite common in the Middle Ages in the West among many sectarians, but which became especially strengthened with the appearance of Protestant communities, and which has penetrated into their theological systems and has many times been discussed in special works, and so forth." (p. 619.)

The author does not mention that the greater part of the Russian people regards our hierarchy as the hierarchy of the antichrist.

262. Events which are to take place on the day of the general judgment, and their order. " The actions of the antichrist on earth will last to the very judgment day." (p. 619.)

263. The premonitory circumstances of the general judgment: (a) the arrival of the Lord Judge over the living and the dead. On that day the Lord Jesus Christ will come down upon earth. Everything is proved by Holy Scripture.

264. (b) The resurrection of the dead, and the transformation of the living. " On that last day (John vi. 40–44) and just at the time that the glorious descent of the Lord upon earth, surrounded by those who live in heaven, will take place, he shall send before him with a great sound of a trumpet (Matt. xxiv. 31), and the dead shall hear the voice of the Son of God (John v. 25); for the Lord himself shall descend from heaven with a shout, with the voice of the archangel, and with the trump of God : and the dead in Christ shall rise first : then we which are alive shall be changed (1 Thes. iv. 16, 17; 1 Cor. xv. 52)." (pp. 622 and 623.)

That is, in Russian : first all the dead shall arise, and

then the living shall be changed. It is proved by Holy Scripture that there shall certainly be a resurrection of the dead, and that the possibility of the resurrection of the dead cannot be subject to doubt. This is the way it is proved:

" In the world nothing is destroyed or annihilated, but everything remains whole in the power and in the right hand of the Almighty; our bodies lose their existence through death only for us, but not for God, who knows full well all the smallest particles of each dead body, though they may be scattered everywhere and may be united with other bodies, and is always able to reunite these particles into the former organism." (p. 625.)

When it comes to talking about particles, the question is not about replacing the particles, but about the fact that there will not be enough particles to go around. The body of my great-grandfather is rotten : parts of his body have gone into the grass ; a cow has eaten the grass ; a peasant boy has drunk those parts in his milk, and these particles have become his body, and his body has rotted. There will not be enough particles to go around, so that it is absolutely impossible for God to do that by means of the particles. It would be better to prove that in the old way like this :

" (a) In reply to the objection that the resurrection of the dead is incomprehensible to us, men have pointed to other, not less incomprehensible things, such as : the birth of each man, the original formation of the human body out of the dust, the creation of the world out of nothing, and so forth."

That proves the possibility of the resurrection in the body, and the necessity of it is proved like this :

" By the very nature of Christianity it is necessary that, as in Adam all die, even so in Christ shall all be made alive (1 Cor. xv. 22), and that not only our first enemy, the devil, but also our last enemy, death, shall be des-

troyed (1 Cor. xv. 26). Otherwise the purpose of Christ's descent upon earth, the purpose of the whole Christianity, will not be fully realized: man will not be all saved, his enemies will not be all vanquished, and in Christ we shall receive less than we have lost in Adam. (p. 628.) According to their qualities, the resurrected bodies: (1) will be essentially the same that they have been in connection with certain souls during their life upon earth; (2) but, on the other hand, they will also be distinct from the present bodies: because they will arise in a transformed state in resemblance to the resurrected body of Christ the Saviour. They will be: (*a*) incorruptible and immortal; (*b*) glorious or light-bearing; (*c*) strong and sound; (*d*) spiritual. (p. 629.) We shall all of us have eternal bodies, but not all alike. If one is righteous he will receive a heavenly body in which he will be able properly to have relations with the angels; but if one is sinful, he will receive an eternal body, which is to suffer torments for sins, in order to burn for ever in fire and not to be destroyed. (pp. 631 and 632.) Some have thought that after the resurrection of the bodies the distinction of sexes will be abolished; others, on the contrary, have assumed that the distinction will remain; others again, that all the dead will rise as males, an opinion against which St. Augustine had armed himself. Some have divined that all the dead, old men, middle-aged men, youths, and children will rise as being of one age, unto the measure of the stature of the fulness of Christ (Eph. iv. 13); others have said that they will not be of the same age, though they have not admitted that babes and youths would rise in their respective ages, but have thought that they would rise at a maturer age." (p. 632.)

Besides the resurrection of the dead, there is disclosed also the mystery in regard to those whom the judgment will find still living, and who will be transformed in a very short time.

265. The general judgment itself: its actuality, manner, and properties. " Soon after the appearance upon earth of the Judge of the living and the dead in all his glory, when with his voice there shall arise the dead and the living shall be changed, the judgment over them, the general judgment, will begin." (p. 633.) The representation of the general judgment, as sketched to us in the Word of God, shows to us: (1) the Judge sitting on the throne of glory; (2) the executors of his will, the angels; (3) the defendants: (*a*) all the living and the dead people; (*b*) the righteous and the bad; (*c*) the devils. (4) As subjects for the judgment will serve: (*a*) not only the works of men, (*b*) but also their words.

Nothing is said about the devils.

When the judgment is over, the righteous will be separated from the bad. Some will be placed on the right, the others on the left. Then will take place the proclamation of the sentence by the Judge to either division:

" Then shall the King say unto them on the right hand, Come, ye blessed of my Father, inherit the kingdom prepared for you from the foundation of the world (Matt. xxv. 34). Then shall he say also unto them on the left hand, Depart from me, ye cursed, into everlasting fire, prepared for the devil and his angels (*ib.* 41). The holy fathers and the teachers of the church have recognized this representation of the general judgment as unquestionably correct, and have written their interpretations of it."

Here are the interpretations:

" We must not think that the coming of the Lord will be local and carnal, but we must expect him in the glory of the Father suddenly throughout the whole world. . . . But we must assume that much time will be lost before each will see himself and his works; and the mind will in a twinkling of time represent to itself the Judge and the consequences of the divine judgment with unspeakable power; all that the mind will vividly sketch before itself, and in the mightiness of his soul, as in a mirror, will see the pictures of what he has done." (p. 637.)

The Theology says that the judgment is not to be understood as local and carnal, but how is it to be understood? for it says that the judgment will be:

"(1) General. . . . The King comes down from his place in order to judge over the earth; his hosts accompany him in great terror and trepidation.   These mortal members come to be witnesses of the terrible judgment; and all men, no matter how many there have been and are upon earth, come into the presence of the King.   No matter how many have been born or will be born will all come to this spectacle, to see the judgment." (p. 637.)

"(2) Solemn and open. . . . And he will call heaven and earth to be with him at the judgment; and those who are above and far away will appear with terror and trepidation.   And the celestial hosts and the legions of hell will tremble before the Judge who knows no favours, and who will come accompanied by terror and by death."

That is the way Christ will come!

"(3) Stern and terrible: because it will be done according to the whole divine righteousness, and according to nothing but righteousness; it will be a day of wrath and revelation of the righteous judgment of God (Rom. ii. 5.)

"(4) Decisive and the last: because it will unchangeably determine for eternity the fate of each of the defendants."

That is, it will condemn the sinners to torments. Nothing can be added to that.   The only feeling which I experienced in quoting these passages was that of terror and horror before that blasphemy which I was committing in copying and repeating them.

266. Concomitant circumstances of the general judgment: (a) the end of the world. "During that last day, in which the last judgment of God will take place over the whole world, there will also ensue the end of the

world." (p. 638.) "The end of the world will not consist in its being completely destroyed and annihilated, but in its being changed and renovated by fire.—The matter of the reëstablishment of men will come to an end with the general judgment, where will take place the revelation of the sons of God. Consequently, the creatures themselves must be freed from labour and corruption, into the freedom of the glory of the children of God; the whole material world must be purified from the deleterious consequences of human sin and be renovated. This renovation of the world will take place on the last day by means of fire, so that in the new heaven and the new earth nothing sinful will be left, but righteousness alone will abide (2 Peter iii. 13)." (p. 639.)

So here is clearly expressed the idea that the renovation of the world was not achieved by the redemption, that that was spoken of only as an adornment of speech, and that the present renovation will be produced by Christ, not at his first, but at his second coming.

Proofs from Holy Scripture of the correctness of this end and the renovation of the world by fire.

267. (b) The end of Christ's kingdom of grace and the beginning of the kingdom of glory; remarks about the chiliasm, or millennium, of Christ. That is confirmed. The kingdom of grace will come to an end and the kingdom of glory will begin, that is, the real liberation from sin and death, that is, what heretofore has been asserted of the kingdom of grace. Proofs of that from Holy Scripture, and a controversy with those who said that one thousand years before the end Christ would come upon earth, would raise the righteous from the dead and would reign with them for a thousand years. That is not true.

268. Connection with the preceding, and nature of this retribution. After the judgment, Christ will pronounce the sentence. "This retribution after the general judgment will be full, complete, decisive. Full, that is, not

only for the soul of man, as after the private judgment, but both for the soul and the body, — for the full man. Complete: for it will not consist merely in an anticipation of happiness for the righteous and of torment for the sinners, as after the private judgment, but in complete happiness and torment, in accordance with the deserts of each. Decisive: for it will persist unchangeable for ever, and not for one of the sinners will it be possible ever to free himself from hell, though such a chance is open to some of the sinners after the private judgment." (p. 649.)

269. Retribution for the sinners. (a) In what will the everlasting torments consist? The eternal torments of the sinners will consist: (1) in the separation from God and in the curse; (2) in the deprivation of the benefits of the kingdom of God; (3) they will be in hell with the devils, who will torture them; (4) they will experience internal torments; (5) they will experience external torments, of the undying worm and the unextinguished fire.

" When you hear of the fire, do not imagine that the fire of that place is like what it is upon earth: our fire will burn whatever it gets hold of, and changes it into something else; but that other fire will eternally burn the one it gets hold of, and will never stop, — and so it is called inextinguishable. For the sinners, too, have to be vested in immortality, not for their honour, but as an eternal requisite for the torment in hell. No mind is able to imagine how terrible it is, unless from the experience of small calamities one may get a small conception of those great, great torments: if you are ever in a bath-house which is heated more than is proper, you may imagine the fire of Gehenna; and if you ever burn in a high fever, you may mentally transfer yourself to that flame, and then you will be able properly to understand that distinction. For, if the bath-house and the fever torment and worry you so, what are you going to feel when you fall into that river of fire which will be flowing before the terrible judgment?"

(*a*) They will eternally weep and gnash their teeth.

"What will be," says another holy father, "the condition of the body which is subjected to these unending and unbearable torments where there is the inextinguishable fire, the immortally tormenting worm, the dark and terrible pit of hell, bitter sobbing, unusual groans, weeping and gnashing of teeth, and where there is no end to sufferings? From all that there is no liberation after death, and there are no means and no chance to be freed from those terrible torments." (p. 654.)

Such is the condition of the sinner; but what will be the condition of the good God who will eternally look upon it?

270. (*b*) Degrees of the torments of hell. "However, although all sinners will be subjected to torments in hell, they will not be in the same degree, but each in conformity with his sins." (p. 654.)

All that is proved by Holy Scripture.

271. The eternity of the torments of hell. "But differing from each other in degree, the torments of the sinners in hell will by no means differ in respect to duration, for they will be equally eternal and unending for all." (p. 656.)

All that is confirmed by Holy Scripture, and there is a refutal of the opinion that the teaching about the eternity of torments is contrary to common sense (not to common sense, but to some low conception of God).

According to the teaching of the Theology torments that are not eternal are contrary to sound reason.

272. Retribution for the righteous: (*a*) wherein will their happiness consist? "As much as, on the one hand, the Word of God depicts in gloomy colours the fate of the sinners after the general judgment, so, on the other, it depicts in bright and joyous colours the fate of the

righteous. (1) They inherit the kingdom which is prepared for them from the foundation of the world ; (2) in this kingdom, city, house of God, the first source of the happiness of these righteous people will be their constant coexistence and cohabitation with God himself and with the Lord Jesus Christ, and the constant participation in the divine glory, as much as that is possible for a creature ; (3) living all the time with the Lord in the kingdom of heaven, the righteous will be permitted to behold the Tri-hypostatic One face to face."

That is, that terrible God who, having created men out of love, torments them for ever.

273. (*b*) Degrees of the happiness of the righteous :

" The happiness of the righteous in heaven, which is common for all of them, has its degrees, in accordance with the moral dignity of each." That is proved by Holy Scripture.

274. (*c*) The eternity of the happiness of the righteous. The happiness of the righteous is eternal.

275. The moral application of the dogma about the general judgment and retribution. " Oh, if we only thought often and attentively of that great day (Acts ii. 20), the day of wrath and revelation of the righteous judgment of God (Rom. ii. 5), with which some day the whole house-management of our salvation will end ! If we only presented to ourselves vividly and in detail those endless benefits which are prepared for the righteous in heaven, and those eternal torments which await the sinners in hell ! How many incitements we should find for ourselves to abstain from sins and to abide in godliness ! So give us all, O Lord, and for ever, the living and undying remembrance of thy future glorious coming, of thy last terrible judgment over us, of thy most just and everlasting retribution for the righteous and for the sinners, — that in its light and in the light of thy grace and aid we may live soberly, righteously, and godly, in this present

world (Tit. ii. 12), and in that manner finally attain the eternal, blissful life in heaven, so as to glorify thee with all our being, thee, with thy beginningless Father and most holy and good and life-giving Spirit, for ever and ever."

CONCLUSION

So there it is, the whole disclosure of the divinely revealed truths. They have all been disclosed. There is nothing else left. And it is not permitted to understand them in any other way. He who understands them differently: anathema.

A man asks what this world is in which he finds himself. He asks what the meaning of his existence is and what he is to be guided by in that freedom which he feels within himself. He asks all that, and God through the lips of the church established by him replies to him:

Do you want to know what this world is? Here it is:

There is a God, one, omniscient, all-good, almighty. This God is a simple spirit, but he has will and reason. This God is one and yet three. The Father begot the Son, and the Son sits in the flesh at the right of his Father.

The Spirit emanates from the Father. All three of them are Gods, and they are all different and all one. This trine God has existed eternally one in three, and suddenly it occurred to him to create the world and to create it from nothing with his thought, will, and word. At first he created the spiritual world, the angels. The angels were created good, and God created them solely for their own good, but, being created good, these beings suddenly of their own will became bad. Some angels remained good, while others became bad and were turned into devils. God created a very large number of angels and divided them into nine orders and three classes: angels, archangels, cherubim, seraphim, powers, dominions,

431

beginnings, principalities, and thrones. Devils are also divided into categories, but the names of these categories are not precisely known.

Then much time passed and God began to create anew and made the material world. He made it in six days. By day is to be understood the turning of the earth about its axis. And there was morning and evening the very first day. If during those first days there was no sun, God himself shook the illuminating matter, so that there might be morning and evening. God made six days; on the sixth day he made Adam, the first man, out of earth, and blew the soul into him; then he made woman. Man is made out of soul and body. The destination of man is to remain true to the power of God. Man was created good and absolutely perfect. His whole duty lay in this, that he should not eat the forbidden apple, and God not only had created him perfect, but also aided him in every way possible, teaching, amusing, and visiting him in the garden.

But Adam none the less ate the forbidden apple, and for that the good God wreaked revenge on Adam and drove him out of the garden, cursing him, the whole earth, and all the descendants of Adam.

All that is not to be understood in any transferred, but in a direct sense, as having actually occurred. After that, God, that same God in three persons, the omniscient, all-good, almighty God, who had created Adam and cursed him and all his posterity, still continued to provide, that is, to care for their good, for Adam, for his descendants, and for all the creatures which he had made. He preserves the creatures, coöperates with them, and rules over them all and over each in particular.

God rules over the bad and good angels, and over the bad and good men. The angels help God to rule the world. There are angels who are attached to kingdoms, to nations, and to men, and omniscient, almighty, and all-good God, who has created them all, cast down for ever legions of evil angels, and all men after Adam, but has not ceased caring for them in a natural and even in a supernatural manner. This supernatural manner of his care consists in this, that when five thousand years had passed, he found a means for paying himself for Adam's sin, whom he himself had made such as he was. This means consisted in this, that among the persons of the Trinity one is the Son. He, that person, has always been the Son. So this Son issued from a virgin, without impairing her virginity; he entered into the Virgin Mary as her husband, the Holy Ghost, and came out as a Son, Jesus Christ, and this Son was called Jesus, and he was God, and man, and a person of the Trinity.

This God-man has saved men. This is the way he saved them. He was a prophet, a high priest, and a king. As a prophet, he gave a new law; as a high priest he sacrificed himself by dying on the cross, and as a king he performed miracles and went down into hell, let out from it all the righteous, and destroyed sin, and the curse and death in men.

But this means, however strong it was, did not save all men. Legions of legions of devils remained devils, and men must know how to take advantage of that salvation.

In order to take advantage of this means, a man must become sanctified, but only the church may sanctify, and the church is all those people who say about themselves that certain men have laid their hands on them, men upon whom other men have laid hands, and so forth, upon whom hands were laid by the disciples of the God Jesus himself, upon whom hands were laid by God the Son, the Saviour, himself. When God himself laid his hands upon them, he blew, and with that blowing he gave to them, and to those to whom they would transmit it, the power to sanctify men, and that very sanctification is necessary in order to be saved. What sanctifies man and saves him is grace, that means, the divine power which in a certain form is transmitted by the church. In order that this grace should be efficacious, it is necessary for the man who wishes to be sanctified to believe that he is being sanctified. He may even not believe entirely : he must obey the church and, above all, not contradict, and then grace will pass into him. In his life a man who is sanctified by grace must not believe as he has believed before, he must believe that if he does good, he does so because grace is operating in him, and so the only care he must have is that the grace shall be in him. This grace is transmitted by the church by various manipulations and by the pronunciation of certain words, which are called sacraments. There are seven such manipulations :

1. Baptism. When the hierarch of the church has bathed a person in the proper way, that person becomes cleansed from sin, above all, from Adam's original sin, so that if an unbathed infant dies, it will perish as being filled with sin.

2. If he anoints that person with oil, the Holy Ghost enters into him.

3. If the person eats bread and wine under certain conditions and with the conviction that he is eating the body and blood of God, he becomes pure from sin and receives everlasting life.

(In general there is a lot of grace about this sacrament and, as soon and as quickly as possible after it has been performed, a person must pray, and then the prayer will be heard according to the grace.)

4. When the priest has listened to that person's sins, he will say certain words, and the sins are gone.

5. When seven popes anoint a person with oil, his bodily and spiritual diseases will be cured.

6. When the wreaths are put on the bridal pair, the gift of the Holy Ghost will enter them.

7. When the hands are laid on, the Holy Ghost will enter.

Baptism, unction with chrism, repentance, communion sanctify man and sanctify him for ever, independently of the spiritual condition of the priest and of him who receives the sacrament; if only everything is in proper order, and there is no cause for cassation.

In these manipulations lies that means for salvation which God has invented. He who believes that he is sanctified and purified, and will receive eternal life, is actually sanctified and purified and will receive eternal life. All those who believe in that will receive their retribution, at first a private retribution, soon after death, and later a general one, after the end of the world. The private retribution will consist in this, that they will be glorified in heaven and on earth. On earth their relics and images will be honoured with incense and tapers, and in heaven they will be with Christ in glory. But before attaining that, they will pass through aerial spaces, where they will be stopped and questioned by angels and devils, who will contend with each other on their account, and those for whom the defence of the angels shall be stronger than the accusation of the devils will go to Paradise, and those whom the devils shall win will go to eternal torment, into hell.

The righteous, those who will go to Paradise, will there settle in various places, and those who shall be nearer to the Trinity may there, in heaven, pray for us to God, and so we must here worship their relics, their garments, and their images. These objects do miracles, and it is necessary to pray to God near these objects, and then the saints will intercede for us before God. The sinners, all the heretics, the unbaptized, the unbelievers, those who have not received their communion, will go to hell, but they will be there in different places, according to the degree of their guilt, and there they will be to the end of the world.

The prayers of the priests, especially such as will be said immediately after the eucharist, may alleviate their condition in hell.

But there will be an end of the world and a general judgment. The end of the world will be like this: one person of the Trinity, God Jesus, who sits in the flesh in heaven on the right side of his Father, will come down upon earth in a cloud, in the form of a man, such as he had when he was upon earth. Angels will blow trumpets, and all the dead will rise in their very bodies, but the bodies will be a little changed. Then all the angels, all the devils, and all men will assemble, and Christ will judge and will separate the righteous to the right: they will go to heaven with the angels; and the sinners he will put on the left: they will go with the devils to hell, and there they will be tormented with greater torments than burning. These torments will be everlasting. But all the righteous will eternally glorify the good God.

To my question as to what sense my life will have in this life, the answer will be as follows:

God, by his arbitrary will, created a strange world; a wild God, half-man, half-monster, created the world as he wanted it, and he kept saying that it was good, that everything was good, and that man was good. But it all turned out bad. Man fell under a curse, and his whole posterity was cursed, but God continued to make men in the wombs of their mothers, though he knew that all of them, or many, would perish. After he had invented a means for saving them, everything was as of old, and even worse, because while, as the church says, men like Abraham and Jacob could save themselves by their good lives, I am now certainly going to perish, if I was born a Jew, or a Buddhist, and accidentally do not come in contact with the sanctifying action of the church, and I shall be eternally tormented by the devils; more than that, —

if I am among the number of the fortunate, but have the misfortune to regard the demands of my reason as legitimate and do not renounce them, in order to believe the church, I perish just the same. More than that, — even if I believe everything, but have not had time to receive the last sacrament and my relatives absent-mindedly forget to pray for me, I shall just as much go to hell and remain there.

According to this teaching the meaning of my life is an absolute absurdity, much worse than what presented itself to me by the light of my reason. Then I saw that I was living and was enjoying life so long as I was living, and that when I died I should not feel anything. Then I was frightened by the meaninglessness of my own life and by the insolubility of the question: What are my strivings, my life, for, since all that will end ?

But now it is much worse: all that will not end, but that absurdity, somebody's arbitrary will, lasts for ever. To the question as to how I should live, the answer of this teaching directly denies everything which my moral feeling demands, and demands that which has always appeared as the most immoral thing to me, — hypocrisy.

From all the moral applications of the dogmas there results but this: Save yourself by faith ; you cannot understand what you are commanded to believe, — say that you believe, crush out with all the powers of your soul the necessity of light and truth, say that you believe, and do what results from faith. The matter is clear. In spite of all the statements that good works are for some reason necessary, and that it is necessary to follow the teaching of Christ about love, humility, and self-renunciation, it is evident that those works are not needed, and the practice of life of all the believers confirms that. Logic is inexorable. What is the use of works, when I am redeemed by God's death, when even all my future sins are redeemed, and when it is necessary only to believe. And how can I struggle and strive after the good, in which alone I formerly understood good works to consist, when the main dogma of faith is this, that man cannot do anything by himself, and everything is given gratis by grace. All that is necessary is to look for grace; but grace is not obtained by me alone; it is imparted to me by others. Even if I do not succeed in sanctifying myself with grace during my lifetime, there are means for making use of it even after my death: I can leave money for the church, and they will pray for me. All that is asked of me is that I should try to find grace. Grace is given by sacraments and by the prayers of the church, consequently I must have recourse to them and put myself in such a state that I may never be deprived of them; I must have popes around me or live near a monastery, and leave as much money as possible for memorial masses. More than that. Having thus secured my future life, I may calmly enjoy this life, and for this life make use of the instruments given to me by the church, praying to God the Provider to aid me in my earthly works, for I am told in what manner these prayers will be most efficacious. It is most efficacious to pray near images and relics, during the liturgy.

And the answer to the question of what I should do results directly from the teaching; this answer is too familiar to everybody, and too coarsely contradicts conscience, but it is inevitable.

I remember, when I did not yet doubt the teaching of the church, I read the words of the Gospel, Blasphemy against the Son of man shall be forgiven you, but blasphemy against the Holy Ghost shall not be forgiven you, neither in this world, neither in the world to come, and I could not understand those words.

But now those words are only too terribly apparent to me. Here is that blasphemy against the Holy Ghost, which will not be forgiven, either in this world, or in that to come.

That blasphemy is the terrible teaching of the church, the foundation of which is the teaching about the church.

(Just as this volume was going through the press, there appeared in England a second edition of the Russian original. It comes in time to be utilized for the correction of a number of inaccuracies and for the insertion of the following conclusion, which is absent in the first edition. What has to be omitted is a number of unessential quotations from Makári's Theology. — *Translator's Note.*)

THE Orthodox Church!

With this word I no longer can connect any other conception than that of a few hirsute men, extremely self-confident, deluded, and ignorant, in silk and velvet, with diamond panagias, called bishops and metropolitans, and thousands of other hirsute men, who are in a state of the grossest, most servile servility to those dozens of men, who, under the guise of performing certain sacraments, are busy cheating and fleecing the people.

How can I believe in this church, which to man's profoundest questions about his soul answers with petty deceptions and insipidities, and affirms that no one must dare to answer these questions in any other way, and that in everything which is most precious in my life I should not be guided by anything but what it points out to me? I may choose the colour of my pantaloons, I may choose my wife according to my liking, but in everything else — precisely that in which I feel myself to be a man — I must be guided by them, those idle, cheating, and ignorant people.

In my life, in the holiness of my soul, I have for a guide and pastor the parish priest, a dull, illiterate lad who has been let out of the seminary, or a hard-drinking old man whose only care it is to take in as many eggs

and kopeks as possible. They command the deacon to
yell half the time, " Many years for the Orthodox, godly "
harlot Catherine II. or " for the most godly Peter," the
robber, the murderer, who blasphemed over the Gospel,
and I am compelled to pray for them. They command
me to curse, burn, and hang my brothers, and I must cry
after them " anathema."   These people command me to
regard my brothers as cursed, and have to cry " anathema."
They command me to drink wine out of a spoon and swear
that it is not wine, but the body and blood, and I must do so.

But this is terrible !

It would be terrible, if it were possible ; but in reality
it is not so, not because they have weakened in their demands, — they still shout " anathema," or " many years,"
if they are commanded to do so, — but because in reality
no one listens to them.

We, the experienced and cultured people (I recall my
thirty years outside the church), do not even despise
them : we simply pay no attention to them and do not
even have the curiosity to know what they are doing,
writing, and saying. A pope has come, — very well, give
him half a rouble. A church has been built for vanity's
sake, — very well, dedicate it, send for a shaggy-maned
bishop, and give a hundred roubles.

The masses pay still less attention to them. During
Butter week we must eat pancakes, and during Passion week we must prepare ourselves for communion ; and
if there arises a spiritual question for one of our kind,
we go to clever, learned thinkers, to their books, or to the
writings of the saints, but not to the popes ; and the people from the masses turn dissenters, Stundists, Milkers,
the moment the religious sentiment is awakened in them.
Thus the popes have for a long time been serving only
themselves, and the weak-minded and rascals and women.
It is to be assumed that very soon they will be instruct-
ing themselves only.

That is so, but what does this mean, that there still are wise men who share this delusion ? What does the church mean, which has led them into such impassable forests of stupidity ? The church, according to the definition of the hierarchs, is an assembly of the believers, of infallible and holy priests.

All of them have asserted with one accord that the pastors of the church are the true successors of the apostles, and that they alone have through the succession received the legitimate power and duty of being the guardians and interpreters of the divine revelation, while all the lay people are to listen to the voice of their pastors, and have no right to teach.

" It is not proper for a layman," says the 64th rule of the Œcumenical Council, " to utter words, or to teach and take upon himself the teacher's dignity, but to obey the orders established by God, to open his ear to those who have received the grace of the teacher's words, and by them to be instructed in the divine Word. For in the one church God created various orders, according to the words of the apostle (1 Cor. xii. 27, 28), which Gregory the Divine explains, showing clearly the orders contained in them, when he says, ' This order, O brothers, let us respect and guard : let one be the ear, and the other the mouth, one the hand, and the other something else ; let one teach, and the other be taught.' And after a few words he proceeds : ' Let him who learns be in obedience, and him who gives give with pleasure, and him who serves serve with zeal. Let us not all be the tongue, though this be nearest to all, nor all apostles, nor all prophets, nor all commentators.' And after a few words he says again : ' Wherefore hast thou made thyself a shepherd, being a sheep ; wherefore dost thou make thyself a head, being a foot ; wherefore dost thou pretend to lead the armies, since thou art placed in the rank of the soldiers ? ' And in another place he enjoins wisdom :

' Be not rash with thy mouth (Eccl. v. 2); being poor, labour not to be rich (Prov. xxiii. 4); try not to be wiser than the wise. And if one be found guilty violating the present rule, let him be removed from the communion with the church for the period of forty days.' "

After this it is obvious in what sense the word " church " is to be taken, when reference is made to its infallibility in matters of teaching. Infallible, without doubt, is the whole church of Christ in general, which consists of pastors and the flock. But, since the class of pastors are more particularly enjoined to watch, preach, and interpret to people the divine revelation (636); since the flock is compelled in this holy matter unflinchingly to follow the voice of their God-given instructors (Ephes. iv. 11–15; Acts xx. 28; Heb. iv. 13–17), — it is evident that in disclosing the teaching of the infallibility of the church it is necessary above all to have in view the teaching church (637), which, however, is inseparably connected with the instructed church (638).

From this it is clear what the church means by church : it means nothing but the exclusive right for it to teach. In explanation of this right it says that it is infallible. And it is infallible, it says, because it derives its teaching from the source of truth, — from Christ.

But the moment there are two teachings, which equally deduce their teachings from Christ, this foundation, the proofs, and everything reared upon it fall to pieces, and nothing is left but incitements for such an absurd teaching. The impelling causes are as obvious now, at the sight of the palaces and carriages of the bishops, as they were in the sixth century, if we look at the luxury of the patriarchs, and as they were in the first apostolic times, if we take into consideration the desire of each teacher to confirm the truth of his teaching. The church affirms that its teaching is based on the divine teaching. Proofs are incorrectly adduced in this case from the Acts and the epistles, because the apostles were the first people who put forth the principle of the church, the truth of which has to be proved, and so their doctrine can as little as the later doctrine assert that it is based on Christ's teaching. No matter how near in time they may be to Christ, they are, according to the church doctrine, men, while he is God. Everything which he said is true; everything which they said is subject to proof and rejection. The churches felt this, and so hastened to put on the apostolic teaching the seal of the infallibility of the Holy Ghost. But if we brush aside this snare and take up Christ's teaching itself, we cannot help but be struck by that bold impudence with which the teachers of the church wish to base their doctrine on the teaching of Jesus Christ, who denied all that which they want to affirm.

The word ἐκκλησία, which has no other meaning than that of assembly, is used but twice in the Gospels, and that, too, only in Matthew: On thee, on my faithful disciple, as on a rock, I shall establish my union of men, and the other time in this sense, that if thy brother will not hear thee, tell it in an assembly of men, because what ye shall loose here (meaning "your anger, your annoyance") will be loosed in heaven, that is, in God. Now, what have the priests made of it?

Having appeared upon earth, in order to accomplish the great work of our redemption, the Saviour at first claimed only for himself the right to instruct people in the true faith, which he had received from the Father. The Spirit of the Lord is upon me, because he hath anointed me to preach the gospel to the poor; he hath sent me to heal the broken-hearted, to preach deliverance to the captives, and recovering of sight to the blind, to set at liberty them that are bruised, to preach the acceptable year of the Lord (Luke iv. 18, 19); and passing through the cities and villages, preaching the Gospel, he added, To this end was I born, and for this cause came into the world (John xviii. 37), for therefore am I sent (Luke iv. 43); enjoining at the same time the people and the disciples, But be ye not called Rabbi: for one is your master, even Christ (Matt. xxiii. 1, 8, 10).   Then he transferred his divine right of the teachership to his disciples, to the twelve and the seventy, whom he purposely chose for this great ministration from the midst of his hearers (Luke vi. 13 ; cf. x. 1, and the following): at first he transferred it only temporarily during the days of his earthly existence, when he sent them to preach the Gospel of the kingdom only to the lost sheep of the house of Israel (Matt. x. 5–16, and elsewhere), and later for all time, after his resurrection, when, having himself accomplished all his work upon earth and going up to heaven, he said to them, As my Father hath sent me, even so send I you (John xx. 21); go ye therefore, and teach all nations, baptizing them in the name of the Father, and of the Son, and of the Holy Ghost (Matt. xxviii. 19); and on the other hand he very clearly and with terrible threats enjoined all men and future Christians to receive the teaching of the apostles and to obey them: He that heareth you heareth me ; and he that despiseth you despiseth me ; and he that despiseth me despiseth him that sent me (Luke x. 16; cf. Matt. x. 14; xviii. 15, 19; Mark xvi. 16).

Finally, at the same time that the Lord transferred his divine right of the teachership to the apostles, he expressed the wish that from the apostles this right might pass directly to their successors, and from the latter, passing from generation to generation, might be preserved in the world to its very end.   For he said to his disciples, And he said unto them, Go ye into all the world, and preach the gospel to every creature.   Go ye therefore, and teach all nations, baptizing them in the name of the Father, and of the Son, and of the Holy Ghost: Teaching them to observe all things whatsoever I have commanded you:

and lo, I am with you alway, even unto the end of the world (Mark xvi. 15 ; Matt. xxviii. 18–20).

" But these disciples evidently could not live to the end of the world, and if they were able to preach the Gospel to all the nations which were contemporaneous with them, they certainly could not preach it to the nations of the subsequent times. Consequently, in the person of his apostles the Saviour sent out all their future successors to the work of the universal preaching, and also encouraged them with his presence. This is not a simple divination of the mind, but the positive doctrine of one of the apostles themselves, who said that Christ himself gave his church not only apostles, prophets, evangelists, but also pastors and teachers (Ephes. iv. 11)."

Even if we accept that incomprehensible, obviously interpolated passage about baptizing in the name of the Father, the Son, and the Holy Ghost, there is not a word to point to the church. On the contrary, there is a direct indication that no one should call himself a teacher.

What can more clearly be said against the church, according to the ideas of the church ? And this very place, as though in ridicule of its exact meaning, they quote ! And against the teachership ? Not two or three passages speak against the teachers, but the whole meaning of the Gospel (We have taught in thy name ; go into eternal fire, ye who are working iniquity) : all the speeches to the Pharisees and concerning the external worship, — that the blind should not lead the blind, for they would fall down together, — but mainly the whole meaning of Jesus' teaching in John and in the other gospels. He comes to announce the good to those who are lowly in spirit, and he calls them blessed. He repeats several times that his teaching is accessible and intelligible to babes and to the imprudent, in contradistinction to the wise and the learned. He chooses the foolish, the imprudent, the downtrodden, and they understand him ; he says that he came, not to teach, but to fulfil; and he fulfils with his whole life. He repeats again and again that he who will fulfil will find out whether it is from God, and that blessed is he who fulfils, and not he who teaches: that he who fulfils is great, and not he who teaches. He is angry only with those who teach. He says, Do not judge others. He says that he alone opened the door for the sheep, and that he knows the sheep, and the sheep know him. And there the uncalled pastors — the wolves in sheep's clothing — came in the garments of harlots, stood up before him, and said — they, the doers of iniquity — that not he, but they, were the door for the sheep.

The impelling causes are comprehensible, especially during the first times, when the first Paul spoke of the church, of the infallibility. It is comprehensible how an excitable man, who is carried away by the true faith, may have failed fully to understand the spirit of the teacher, and so departed from his teaching. It is comprehensible for that nearest time, as well as later, under the pressure on Constantine's power, how they could have been carried away by the desire as quickly as possible to establish their external faith; we can understand all the wars which were waged in the name of this departure from the spirit of the teaching. But the time has come for separating the sheep from the goats, for they have already separated themselves in such a way that the true teaching can no longer be met with in the churches. And it is clear that the teachership of the church, though it arose from a small departure, is now the worst enemy of Christianity, and that its pastors serve what they please, except the teaching of Jesus, because they reject it.

The doctrine about the teaching church is now a doctrine which is purely inimical to Christianity. Having departed from the spirit of the teaching, it has corrupted it to such an extent that it has reached a point where it rejects it with the whole life: instead of humility there is grandeur; instead of poverty, luxury; instead of not judging our neighbours, the most cruel condemnation of all; instead of forgiving offences, hatred and wars; instead of endurance of evil, punishments. And all men deny one another, but not themselves.

The name of Christ's kingdom cannot save it, but in its definition there is, in addition to the definition as a church of pastors, also another obscure definition as a church of the pastured, who must obey. What is understood by the first is clear, but what is to be understood by the second is completely obscure.

An assembly of believers?

If believers have come together, believing in one and the same thing, they constitute an assembly of believers. There is such an assembly of believers in Wagner's music, an assembly of believers in the social theory.

To them the word "church" is not applicable, with the concept of infallibility, which is attached to it, and that is all there is to it. It is an assembly of believers and nothing else, and it is impossible to see the limits of this church, because faith is not a carnal matter. The religion of our popes can indeed be felt in the vestments, the panagias, and all the remaining nonsense, but the faith of the believers, that one thing which is the life and the light in men, cannot be felt, and it cannot be said where it is and how much there is of it. Consequently, this is said only for the purpose that the pastors may have some one to herd, and there is no other meaning to it. The church, all this word, is the name of a deception by means of which one set of men wants to rule another. There is no other church, and there can be none. Only in this deception, which is based on the true teaching and is carried on by all the churches, have there appeared all those monstrous dogmas which distort and conceal the whole teaching of the church, — such as the divinity of Jesus and of the Holy Ghost, and the Trinity,

and the Virgin Mary, and all the savage customs called
sacraments; it is evident that they have no sense and are
of no use to any one, except the dogma of the sacrament
of orders, which is needed for the purpose of enabling men
to collect eggs.

But who would have preserved the Holy Scripture?
What would people have believed in and who would have
taught, if there had not been the church?

Not those have preserved the Holy Scripture who have
disputed, but those who have believed and done. The
Holy Scripture is a tradition of days and life. The only
teaching that is needed is the one which teaches through
life, so that their light may shine before men. People
have always believed in works only. If ye believe not
me, believe my works. Neither I, nor any one else, is
called to judge others, and the past. I see that works
alone are capable of adoption, and teach me and the people,
and only the doctrine and the controversies corrupt the
people and deprive them of faith. Indeed, all these theological controversies were carried on in reference to matters which are of no use to any one, which are not the
subject of faith. It has come to such a pass that as
a subject of faith there presents itself the question as to
the infallibility of the popes and of Mary, who bore a
child in a strange manner, and so forth.

Life has never been a subject of faith: it could not
be the subject of a controversy, — for how will you show
faith, while I show works?

" But where is the true church of the true believers?
How can we find out who is in the right, and who not? will
those ask who do not comprehend the teaching of Jesus.
Where is the church, that is, where are its limits? If
you are in the church, you cannot see its limits. But
if you are a believer, you will say: " How can I be saved?
What do I care about judging others?"

To him who has comprehended the teaching of Jesus,

the teaching consists in this, that to me, to my light, the power is given to go to the light, to me my life is given. Outside of it and beyond it there is nothing but the source of all life, — God.

The whole teaching of humility, the renunciation of wealth, the love of my neighbour, has only this meaning, that I can make this life infinite in itself. Every relation of mine to another life is only an exaltation of my own, a communion and oneness with it in peace and in God. Through myself only can I comprehend the truth, and my works are the consequences of the exaltation of my life.

I can express this truth in myself. What question can there be for me, who understand life thus (I cannot understand it otherwise), as to what others think, how they live ? As I love them, I cannot help but wish to communicate my happiness to them, but the one tool which is given me is the consciousness of my life and its works. I cannot wish, think, believe for another. I exalt my life, and this alone can exalt the life of another ; and is not another myself ? So, if I exalt myself, I exalt all.

I am in them, and they in me.

The whole teaching of Jesus consists only in what the common people repeat with simple words : — to save one's soul, — but only one's own, because it is everything. Suffer, endure evil, do not judge, — all this tells the same. At every contact with the affairs of the world Jesus teaches us by his example of complete indifference, if not contempt, how we must bear ourselves toward worldly matters, — toward raiment, toward tribute for the church and for Cæsar, toward litigations about inheritance, toward the punishment of the sinning woman, toward the spilling of the costly ointment. Everything which is not thy soul is not thy concern. Seek the kingdom of God and his righteousness in your soul, and everything will be well. Indeed, my soul is given into my power, even as it is given to another. Souls other than mine I not only cannot rule over, but am not even able to comprehend; how, then, can I mend and teach them? And how can I waste my strength on what is not in my power, and overlook that which is in my power? Outside the teaching, Jesus showed by his life the falseness of the structure of this world, in which all pretend to be busy with the good of others, whereas their aim is nothing but a pampering of their lust, a love of darkness. Look at any evil whatsoever, and you will see that every man gives out as his pretext the good of his neighbour. When you see that a man is taking hold of another, and insulting him, saying that he is doing so for the good of humanity, try to find out what it is that the man wants, and you will see that he is doing it for his own sake.

Failing to comprehend all this, the false faith has enticed people into the vicious desire to teach others and has given birth to the church with all its horrors and monstrosities. What will happen, if there shall be no church? There will be what now is, what Jesus has said. He spoke, not because he wanted to, but because it is so. He said, Do good deeds that men, seeing them, may glorify God. And it is only this one teaching which will be and has been ever since the world has existed. In works there is no diversity, but if in the confession, in the comprehension, in the external worship, there is and shall be any diversity of opinion, it does not touch the faith and the works, and is in nobody's way. The church wanted to unite these confessions and external worships, and itself broke up in innumerable sects, one denying the other, and has thus shown that neither the confession nor the worship is a matter of faith. The business of faith is only the life in the faith. Life alone is higher than anything, and cannot be subjected to anything but God, who is cognized through life alone.

THE END.